# ROMANTICISM AND THE USES OF GENRE

# Romanticism and the Uses of Genre

DAVID DUFF

OXFORD
UNIVERSITY PRESS

2009

# OXFORD
#### UNIVERSITY PRESS

Great Clarendon Street, Oxford ox2 6dp

Oxford University Press is a department of the University of Oxford.
It furthers the University's objective of excellence in research, scholarship,
and education by publishing worldwide in

Oxford  New York

Auckland  Cape Town  Dar es Salaam  Hong Kong  Karachi
Kuala Lumpur  Madrid  Melbourne  Mexico City  Nairobi
New Delhi  Shanghai  Taipei  Toronto

With offices in

Argentina  Austria  Brazil  Chile  Czech Republic  France  Greece
Guatemala  Hungary  Italy  Japan  Poland  Portugal  Singapore
South Korea  Switzerland  Thailand  Turkey  Ukraine  Vietnam

Oxford is a registered trade mark of Oxford University Press
in the UK and in certain other countries

Published in the United States
by Oxford University Press Inc., New York

© David Duff 2009

The moral rights of the author have been asserted
Database right Oxford University Press (maker)

First published 2009

British Library Cataloguing in Publication Data
Data available

Library of Congress Cataloging in Publication Data
Data available

Typeset by SPI Publisher Services, Pondicherry, India
Printed in Great Britain
on acid-free paper by the
MPG Books Group, Bodmin and King's Lynn

ISBN 978–0–19–957274–8

3 5 7 9 10 8 6 4 2

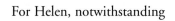For Helen, notwithstanding

# *Preface*

This book explores the place of genre, and genre theory, in British Romanticism. My primary concern is not the fate of individual genres—though this forms part of the argument—but the concept of genre itself, and the role it played in the literary culture of the Romantic era. By genre theory, I mean not only the explicit theories of genre articulated by Romantic writers and critics, but also the assumptions about and attitudes to genre implicit in actual works of literature. My field of inquiry ranges from paratextual minutiae such as titles, subtitles, and prefaces (all of which may reveal, or strategically conceal, a text's generic affiliations) to the historical and cultural force fields that shape the long-term destinies of genres; and from questions of form and structure—the internal architecture or 'morphology' of genre—to issues of generic function and status, the institutional and ideological dimensions of genre. The emphasis of the book is on poetry, but a wider spectrum of genres is considered, a recurrent theme being the relationship—hierarchical, competitive, combinatory—*between* genres. To address this large and complex subject, I examine many types of evidence and employ a variety of analytical techniques, including structural critique, reception history, bibliographic inquiry, and close 'generic' reading of individual texts. But the chapters that follow share a single overriding aim, which is to understand the distinctive genre-consciousness of the Romantic period, from the perspective not only of authors, but also of editors, publishers, booksellers, reviewers, and ordinary readers, all of whom had investments in and uses for the notion of genre. The book is thus intended both as a study of Romanticism and as a contribution to the history of poetics. By explaining the generic codes, written and unwritten, that underpin the literary practices of Romanticism, I hope also to chart a poorly understood phase in one of literary theory's most enduring but problematic concepts—that of genre.

Genre theory is a disputatious field, and Romantic studies no less so. Bringing the two together has entailed a degree of risk. In writing this book, I have sometimes been drawn into generalizations that may strike the reader as reckless, and at other times dwelt on minuscule details to a degree that might seem obsessive. The project has brought home to me, sometimes uncomfortably, the force of the structuralist claim that the task of poetics is not to interpret the individual work but to discover the conditions of possibility of such works; or to treat individual works not for their own sakes but as manifestations of larger trends. When not charting broad cultural trends and conditions, much of my attention has been devoted to what Gérard Genette terms the 'thresholds' (*seuils*) of texts:[1] interpreting the significance of titles, subtitles, prefaces, and footnotes. Metalanguage, horizons of expectation, and critical theory are accorded as much space as actual literary performance.

---

[1] Gérard Genette, *Seuils* (Paris: Éditions du Seuil, 1987); trans. Jane E. Lewin as *Paratexts: Thresholds of Interpretation* (Cambridge: Cambridge University Press, 1997).

It may therefore seem that I have underplayed what Friedrich Schlegel calls that 'beautiful and indeed necessary' part of the reading experience when we 'give ourselves entirely' to a poetic work, and 'let the writer do with us what he will'.[2] This impression is misleading in so far as what has ultimately driven this inquiry is a fascination with the reading experience, and with the power of art to (in another Schlegelian phrase) 'cast its enchantment upon us'.[3] The resources of genre are, I believe, part of that power. For the artist, the encounter with genre is a moment of differentiation as well as assimilation. Generic codes are both invoked and modified in the act of writing, and it is through contact with the generic that individual identity is established. That is to say, the poet works against as well as within genre; more often than not, within and against several genres simultaneously. This is part of the dialectic of archaism and innovation referred to in one of my chapter titles, a title I borrow not from Schlegel but from a later genre theorist in the Romantic tradition, the Russian Formalist Yuri Tynianov.[4] His thesis, taken up by Mikhail Bakhtin and others, is that literary genres are both static and dynamic entities, retrogressive and progressive at the same time. In the hands of the best creative artists, genre is at once an archive and a drawing board, a storehouse of tradition and a spur to originality.

This fact, true of all epochs, has, I argue, a special relevance for the Romantic period. It was at this historical moment that archaism and innovation—on the face of it, antithetical impulses—became, for the first time, fully conscious and theoretically explicit literary trends. The tension between the drive to 'make it old' and 'make it new' generated one of the most dynamic phases in the history of literature, and produced an attitude to genre that was revolutionary in two senses: iconoclastic and transformative but also atavistic (revolving, returning to origins). The attendant complications are played out in the brilliant theoretical writing of the period as well as in its rich creative literature. Romantic genre-consciousness is thus, among other things, a special kind of *self*-consciousness about genre. As the market for literature expanded, and the traditional categories and protocols of the neoclassical genre-system became increasingly obsolete, the forms and functions of genres altered, and generic contracts had to be negotiated afresh. The self-descriptive, self-justificatory character of Romantic literature—its ineluctable critical dimension, as Paul de Man called it[5]—was part of that negotiation. The paratextual, preludial (Wordsworth's term is 'preparatory'[6]) quality of much Romantic writing was another manifestation of the same impulse. Many writers, it seems, could no longer 'perform' genres in a straightforward way: they had to problematize, ironize, theorize their relationship to genre. A paradigmatic Romantic genre (or, as I argue in Chapter 4, a

[2] Friedrich Schlegel, 'On Goethe's *Meister*' (1798), in Kathleen Wheeler (ed.), *German Aesthetic and Literary Criticism: The Romantic Ironists and Goethe* (Cambridge: Cambridge University Press, 1984), 62.
[3] Ibid. 63 ('his' replaced with 'its').
[4] Yuri Tynianov, *Arkhaisty i novatory* ('Archaists and Innovators'; Leningrad, 1929).
[5] Paul de Man, *Blindness and Insight: Essays in the Rhetoric of Contemporary Criticism*, 2nd edn (London: Routledge, 1983), 80, summarizing Friedrich Schlegel's *Athenaeum* fragment no. 238.
[6] Wordsworth's description of *The Prelude*, as yet untitled and unpublished, in the Preface to *The Excursion* (1814).

paradigmatic mode of affiliation to genre) was the fragment or sketch; another was the generically mixed work or *Mischgedicht*, a focal point of Romantic theory and practice in Britain as well as Germany.

Yet this was the same period that witnessed the birth of the unashamedly 'generic' literature we now call 'genre fiction' (the gothic novel is arguably the first example), that saw an enthusiastic revival of previously outmoded literary forms, and that brought into being many new genres of poetry, prose, and drama, some of which still thrive two centuries later. It is the coexistence of these contradictory tendencies—towards the dissolution and transcendence of genres, and towards their consolidation and exploitation—that this book seeks to document and explain. The book is therefore organized not into studies of discrete genres, but into interlinked essays that move between individual case studies and broader issues. Each chapter addresses a particular aspect of Romantic genre-consciousness that reveals itself at different levels and in a variety of contexts: in the literary theory of the period, in its creative practice, and in the larger workings of the literary economy. The chapters presuppose one another and contribute to a cumulative argument, but they can be read separately or out of sequence—though the Introduction should probably come first.

During the ten or more years it has taken me to research and write this book, I have picked many brains, plundered many libraries, and tapped many budgets. A full inventory of my debts would overstretch my memory and exceed the limits of a preface, but certain individuals and institutions have been of particular service, and it gives me pleasure to record my appreciation. Among friends and colleagues, past and present, at Aberdeen, I am especially grateful to Paul Coates, Gordon Graham, David Hewitt, Hazel Hutchison, Clark Lawlor, Ali Lumsden, Liam McIlvanney, Tom Nichols, Gert Ronberg, George Rousseau, Paul Schlicke, Michael Syrotinski, Jan Todd, the late Robin Gilmour and George Watson, and members of my Romanticism and Genre postgraduate seminar. Catherine Jones, Adam Potkay, and Dana van Kooy shared ideas and read parts of the manuscript, offering valuable comment. Paul Hamilton gave expert guidance on the German dimension of my topic, enabling me to clarify key strands in my argument. Susan Manning provided incisive feedback on some eighteenth-century material. Ainsley McIntosh compiled the index. I also thank John Birtwhistle, Marilyn Butler, Jack Donovan, John Frow, and Fiona Stafford for their support of my work at different stages; and especially Tim Webb, who was an inspirational presence throughout. Graham Allen, Pam Clemit, Greg Dart, Marilyn Gaull, Tom Heacox, and Judith Thompson have been stimulating interlocutors, as has my brother Alistair, a labourer in a neighbouring academic vineyard. Other members of my family also deserve thanks: Richmond and Claire generously hosted my many research trips to London; Virginia and Victor welcomed me in fine style to the Lake District; and my mother, Christine, provided a comfortable retreat in the Cotswolds (at the price of countless games of Scrabble). Above all, I thank Helen Lynch, whose acute insight and irreverent scrutiny of my ideas and writing have helped to shape and sustain this project. In this, she has been assisted by our formidable daughters, Konstancja and Miriam, who gave no quarter to academic mannerism and paternal folly.

Part of Chapter 3 has previously been published in *Eighteenth-Century Life*, and a section of Chapter 2 appeared in *The Wordsworth Circle* and *La questione Romantica*.

My Conclusion incorporates material published in a *Festschrift* for my former Gdansk colleague Andrzej Zgorzelski. In each case, the original versions have been heavily revised, sometimes beyond recognition. My thanks to the respective editors and publishers for permission to reprint. I also thank the organizers of, and audiences at, the many conferences and seminars where draft material from the book was presented: these dialogues were indispensable. For supplying material and other services, I am indebted to the staff of Aberdeen University Library (Gilian Dawson, Iain Beavan, and the Historic Collections team in particular), the Bodleian Library, the British Library, the British Museum, Cambridge University Library, the Houghton Library at Harvard College, the National Art Library at the Victorian and Albert Museum, the National Library of Scotland, the Wordsworth Trust at Grasmere, and the Library of Congress in Washington DC. The British Academy and the Carnegie Trust funded a number of research trips, and the Arts and Humanities Research Council a vital period of research leave. The University of Aberdeen gave additional financial support and study leave.

My final debt is to the editorial and production staff at Oxford University Press, especially Andrew McNeillie, Jacqueline Baker, Keira Dickinson, Ariane Petit, and my copy-editor, Laurien Berkeley; and to the Press's anonymous readers, who gave exceptionally helpful advice.

                                                                        D.D.

# Contents

# List of Illustrations

# Introduction

Ideas about genre are inseparable from Romanticism. The very word 'Romantic' derives from the name of a literary genre, and one of the earliest and commonest definitions of Romanticism consists simply of the tautological claim that it was a 'revival of romance'. Other definitions have linked it to the ascendancy of lyric, the birth of the 'historical novel' and 'national tale', the rise of autobiography, or the emergence of some other literary form that is held to epitomize the artistic temper of the movement. Such definitions have, however, coexisted with a virtually opposite claim which, until recently, exerted an even stronger interpretative hold. This is what I call the anti-generic hypothesis, the belief that Romanticism was fundamentally hostile to genre, or interested in genres only for the purposes of dissolving or transcending them. This argument has taken many forms, the most radical of which, dating from the period itself, equated Romanticism with an outright rejection of received literary categories, as in Victor Hugo's denunciation of the 'pseudo-Aristotelian code', that 'worm-eaten beam' from 'the old shack of scholasticism',[1] or Friedrich Schlegel's dismissal of traditional theories of genre for being 'as primitive and childish as the old pre-Copernican ideas of astronomy'.[2] A more subtle version, developed by twentieth-century critics, maintains that Romantic ideas of originality, spontaneity, and self-expression, and the associated doctrine of 'organic form', were incompatible with the concept of genre, which was grounded in notions of convention and imitation; an erosion of generic distinctions and dismantling of genre theory were thus inevitable consequences of the shift from a mimetic to an expressive poetics.[3] Seen in this light, the Romantic literary revolution involved not so much a reordering of the generic hierarchy—the ascendancy of some favoured genre, new or old—as the emergence of a new mode of literary consciousness that recognized few, if any, formal conventions, and, in one critic's words, 'brought about a virtual extinction of all the traditional genres'.[4]

---

[1] Victor Hugo, Preface to *Cromwell* (1827), in Lilian R. Furst (ed.), *European Romanticism: Self-Definition* (London: Methuen, 1980), 123–4.

[2] *Athenaeum Fragments* (1798), no. 434, in Friedrich Schlegel, *Philosophical Fragments*, trans. Peter Firchow (Minneapolis: University of Minnesota Press, 1991), 90.

[3] M. H. Abrams, *The Mirror and the Lamp: Romantic Theory and the Critical Tradition* (New York: Oxford University Press, 1953), ch. 1.

[4] P. W. K. Stone, *The Art of Poetry 1750–1820: Theories of Poetic Composition and Style in the Late Neo-Classic and Early Romantic Periods* (London: Routledge and Kegan Paul, 1967), 147. Cf. Robert Langbaum, *The Poetry of Experience: The Dramatic Monologue in Modern Literary Tradition* (New York: Norton, 1957), 232–3; and Morse Peckham, 'Toward a Theory of Romanticism', *Publications of the Modern Language Association of America*, 66/2 (1951), 5–23: 11.

Recent scholarship has challenged the anti-generic hypothesis, and argued, too, against the practice of equating Romanticism with a single dominant genre. Stuart Curran's seminal *Poetic Form and British Romanticism* (1986) assembled a wealth of evidence to show that Romantic poets were proficient across a wide spectrum of genres, including some—the sonnet, epic, and romance, for example—which they were reviving after long periods of neglect or decline. For Curran, the notion of a 'generic breakdown in British poetry' was a myth promulgated by post-Romantic critics like John Stuart Mill and John Keble, who mistook the 'remarkable freedom' with which Romantic poets manipulated traditional genres for a 'total liberation from them'.[5] Where previous criticism had associated Romanticism with a narrowing of the genre-spectrum—a blurring of generic boundaries or a subsuming of other poetic forms into lyric—Curran demonstrated that, on the contrary, the Romantics effected a major expansion of the generic repertoire, inspired in part by their rediscovery of the generic diversity of the Renaissance. Other scholars have supplemented Curran's findings, charting Romantic deployments of other poetic forms— elegy, georgic, and satire, for example—and the development of new genres, or quasi-genres, such as the 'conversation poem', 'sketch', and 'fragment'.[6] Notwithstanding the rhetoric of resistance to genre that was sometimes part of Romanticism's self-descriptions, the evidence of the poetry suggests that Romantic writers were in practice fascinated with poetic form and 'formal agency' (Susan Wolfson's phrase), and that 'the politicizing of form . . . is more crucial to Romantic poetics than the anti-formalism with which its practices were retrospectively tagged'.[7]

Similar conclusions have been drawn in recent work on Romantic prose and drama. In contrast to earlier critics who saw the Romantic period as artistically dominated by poetry, literary historians now recognize that this was a crucial phase too in the rise of the novel, a development measurable both quantitatively—in terms of sales figures, earnings, and numbers of authors and readers—and qualitatively, in terms of technical complexity and intellectual ambition. The proliferation of genre variants, once regarded as a symptom of artistic decline, is now interpreted as a sign of strength, the list of novelistic subgenres from the period including, among others, gothic and sentimental novels, historical romances, national tales, Menippean satires, 'silver fork novels', and the two ideologically opposed (but formally similar) types of political fiction that critics have dubbed the 'Jacobin' and 'anti-Jacobin novel'.[8] All of these forms found a place in the lucrative fiction market, and the novel's critical status

[5] Stuart Curran, *Poetic Form and British Romanticism* (New York: Oxford University Press, 1986), 207–8.

[6] See e.g. the section 'Romanic Forms' in Nicholas Roe (ed.), *Romanticism: An Oxford Guide* (Oxford: Oxford University Press, 2005); and genre chapters in Duncan Wu (ed.), *A Companion to Romanticism* (Oxford: Blackwell, 1998), and Charles Mahoney (ed.), *The Blackwell Companion to Romantic Poetry* (Oxford: Blackwell, 2010).

[7] Susan J. Wolfson, *Formal Charges: The Shaping of Poetry in British Romanticism* (Stanford, Calif.: Stanford University Press, 1997), 20–1, 27. Cf. Alan Rawes (ed.), *Romanticism and Form* (Basingstoke: Palgrave Macmillan, 2007).

[8] For these and other subtypes, see Gary Kelly, *English Fiction of the Romantic Period, 1789–1830* (London: Longman, 1989); and Richard Maxwell and Katie Trumpener (eds), *The Cambridge Companion to Fiction in the Romantic Period* (Cambridge: Cambridge University Press, 2008).

also improved, the genre becoming (in some quarters at least) an accepted part of the generic canon.[9] Biography and its new offshoot, 'autobiography' (a term coined around 1800), enjoyed similar success, one manifestation being the flourishing of the so-called 'familiar essay', a genre whose trajectory interestingly mirrors that of lyric.[10] The period is notable, too, for the growth of travel writing, educational writing, scientific writing, and many other types of discursive prose, disseminated in part through the vastly expanded periodical press. Like the novel, many of these genres underwent significant formal transformation, and the experimentalism characteristic of Romantic poetry is also evident in many spheres of prose. Indeed, the development of poetry and prose in the period were inextricably connected, the two feeding off one another even as they competed for supremacy.

Commercial success in the sphere of drama, if we exclude repertory theatre, was confined mainly to popular genres, in particular melodrama and variants such as pantomime, harlequinade, and burletta.[11] Ideological subtlety is alien to melodrama, and 'formal agency' in this context often meant simply the moral and political propagandism (radical or conservative) for which the genre is notorious. But the period also generated, partly in reaction to melodrama, more sophisticated kinds of political and philosophical drama, often consciously modelled on earlier dramatic forms such as ancient Greek or Elizabethan tragedy, medieval miracle plays, or Caroline masque.[12] These include some of the most formally innovative dramas of the period, among them Joanna Baillie's *Plays on the Passions* (1798), Leigh Hunt's allegorical masque *The Descent of Liberty* (1815), Byron's 'dramatic poems' and 'mysteries', and Thomas Lovell Beddoes's 'Dithyrambic in the florid Gothic style', *Death's Jest Book* (1829). Even in melodrama, scholars have identified previously unsuspected levels of formal inventiveness, and a taste for generic experimentation—shared by contemporary audiences, though rarely approved by reviewers—that went beyond the conjunction of music and drama that gives melodrama its name. Dance, acrobatic displays, sound effects, and many kinds of visual spectacle became an integral part of melodrama, a generic hybridity resulting in part from the legal restriction preventing 'illegitimate' (unlicensed) theatres from presenting the spoken

---

[9] Homer Obed Brown, *The Institutions of the English Novel* (Philadelphia: University of Pennsylvania Press, 1997).

[10] For links between the essay form and lyric, see Thomas McFarland, *Romantic Cruxes: The English Essayists and the Spirit of the Age* (Oxford: Clarendon Press, 1987). Recent work on Romantic biography includes Annette Cafarelli, *Prose in the Age of Poets: Romanticism and Biographical Narrative from Johnson to De Quincey* (Philadelphia: University of Pennsylvania Press, 1990); Arthur Bradley and Alan Rawes (eds), *Romantic Biography* (Aldershot: Ashgate, 2003); and James Treadwell, *Autobiographical Writing and British Literature, 1783–1834* (Oxford: Oxford University Press, 2005).

[11] Michael Hays and Anastasia Nikolopoulos (eds), *Melodrama: The Cultural Emergence of a Genre* (Basingstoke: Macmillan, 1999); David Mayer, *Harlequin in his Element: The English Pantomime, 1806–1836* (Cambridge, Mass.: Harvard University Press, 1969); for burletta, David Worrall, *The Politics of Romantic Theatricality, 1787–1832: The Road to the Stage* (Basingstoke: Palgrave Macmillan, 2007).

[12] For an overview, see Daniel O'Quinn and Jane Moody (eds), *The Cambridge Companion to British Theatre, 1730–1830* (Cambridge: Cambridge University Press, 2007).

word.[13] While disabling in certain respects, this restriction was also clearly a spur to artistic creativity, and helps to account for what Jeffrey Cox and Michael Gamer call the 'restless eclecticism' for which the period's drama is notable.[14]

A similar dynamic underpins the rise of visual caricature and print satire, quasi-literary genres which are eclectic by definition, relying as they do on topical allusion and on parodic techniques which target not just the content but also the form and publishing formats of other publications. While the Romantic period has long been acknowledged as a golden age of both visual caricature and textual parody, recent scholarship has emphasized the symbiotic relation between these two media, and pinpointed the ways in which visual and textual elements combine. Literary satires such as Shelley's broadside ballad *The Devil's Walk* (1812) or his parodic 'tragedy' on the Queen Caroline affair, *Swellfoot the Tyrant* (1820), or even a comic epic poem like Byron's *Don Juan* (1819–24), would be inconceivable without the period's vibrant journalistic subculture, which promoted a continuous interchange between the textual and the visual, highbrow and lowbrow, the literary and the political. Increasingly, that subculture is studied for its own aesthetic interest, not just as a context for canonical works. As Marcus Wood observes, the 'formal richness' of the works of William Hone and George Cruikshank, for example, rivals that of the major Romantic poets, and to 'read' such artists 'demands the breaking-down of genre distinctions and notions of high and low art'.[15] The fact that satire is a didactic, propagandistic medium makes it no less artistic and no less Romantic, though its prominence in the period may require us to revise our ideas about the supposedly anti-didactic quality of Romantic art (an issue I take up in Chapter 3). Just how theoretically and historically self-conscious such deployments could be is suggested by Hone's projected *History of Parody*, an unfinished *magnum opus* which originated in his successful use of historical precedents to defend himself in his trial for blasphemous and seditious libel in 1817[16]—an interesting demonstration of the legal uses of genre (defence not *of* but *by* genre). John Strachan's analysis of the culture of advertising uncovers yet another 'department of literature' which has important interconnections with more familiar Romantic genres, as well as being a site of artistic innovation in its own right.[17]

Part of the stimulus for recent work on Romantic genres has been the revaluation of the concept of genre in modern literary theory, and the realization that many critical methodologies in use today have their origins in Romantic genre theory.[18] To invoke Bakhtin's theory of 'novelization', for example, to explain generic developments in the Romantic period is no mere anachronism, since the theory substantially derives from

---

[13] Jane Moody, *Illegitimate Theatre in London 1770–1840* (Cambridge: Cambridge University Press, 2000).

[14] Jeffrey N. Cox and Michael Gamer (eds), *The Broadview Anthology of Romantic Drama* (Peterborough, Ont.: Broadview, 2003), introd., p. xvii.

[15] Marcus Wood, *Radical Satire and Print Culture 1790–1822* (Oxford: Clarendon Press, 1994), 269.

[16] Ibid. 12.

[17] John Strachan, *Advertising and Satirical Culture in the Romantic Period* (Cambridge: Cambridge University Press, 2007).

[18] See my introduction to *Modern Genre Theory* (Harlow: Longman, 2000).

Goethe and Schiller's essay 'Epic and Dramatic Poetry' (1797) and Friedrich Schlegel's ideas on generic dominance and the evolution of the *Roman*.[19] Equally, New Historicist theories of genre, for all their impatience with 'Romantic ideology', have much in common with eighteenth- and early nineteenth-century sociologies of genre such as Herder's, Shelley's, and Hegel's, not least in their attempt to link the dominant cultural forms of an epoch to its social and economic structure or *Zeitgeist*.[20] Even modern 'cognitive' approaches to genre, still at an early stage of theoretical elaboration,[21] have analogies with Enlightenment and Romantic genre theory, an important strand of which involved a shift from formal to psychological conceptions of genre. Schiller's redefinition of poetic genres in terms of 'modes of feeling' (*Empfindungsweise*) in his essay *On Naïve and Sentimental Poetry* (1795–6) is the clearest articulation of this shift,[22] but the pattern is more widespread, and is visible in British as well as European theory (Goldsmith's phrase 'ballad-thinking', taken up by Wordsworth, is a small but telling example, implying that there is a distinctive balladic mode of cognition that can exist beyond the ballad itself[23]). In this book, I highlight connections between Romantic and modern genre theory, and show how awareness of them can enhance our understanding of both the genre-consciousness of the Romantics and our own conceptual investments in these various paradigms.

Romantic genre studies, once predominantly formalist, are now, for the most part, historically based. The idea that the startling changes in the literary genre-system were linked to the turbulent history of the Romantic period, in particular the social and political upheavals associated with French Revolution, was first put forward by contemporary observers like Francis Jeffrey, William Hazlitt, and Leigh Hunt, who spoke of a 'revolution in literature' analogous to the political one in France.[24] Revived by M. H. Abrams in his influential essay 'English Romanticism: The Spirit of the Age' (1963), this analogy continues to shape interpretation of the period. The 1790s is still regarded as the formative decade, when Britain experienced a politicizing of literary forms on a scale not seen since the 1640s and 1650s, and when the political dynamic of transformation—rapid, fundamental change—became also a dominant *aesthetic* principle, making this an era of unparalleled formal experimentation in both the 'low' and 'high' cultural spheres. The convergence of aesthetic and ideological imperatives—a heightened sense both of the autonomy of art and of its instrumental power—is what gives the literature of the 1790s its distinctive charge,

---

[19] See Ch. 5 below, p. 164 n. 30.

[20] James Chandler, *England in 1819: The Politics of Literary Culture and the Case of Romantic Historicism* (Chicago: University of Chicago Press, 1998).

[21] See Peter Stockwell, *Cognitive Poetics: An Introduction* (London: Routledge, 2002).

[22] See Ch. 2 below, p. 93.

[23] Oliver Goldsmith, *Beauties of English Poesy*, 2 vols (London, 1767), ii. 84, observes of Thomas Tickell that 'there is a strain of ballad-thinking' through all his poetry, a claim reiterated by Wordsworth in his letter to Alexander Dyce, 10 May 1830, in *The Letters of William and Dorothy Wordsworth: The Later Years, 1821–53*, ed. Ernest de Selincourt, 2nd edn, rev. Alan G. Hill, 4 vols (Oxford: Clarendon Press, 1978–88), ii. 260.

[24] For references, see M. H. Abrams, 'English Romanticism: The Spirit of the Age' (1963), in Harold Bloom (ed.), *Romanticism and Consciousness: Essays in Criticism* (New York: Norton, 1970); further examples are cited in my 'From Revolution to Romanticism: The Historical Context to 1800', in Wu (ed.), *Companion to Romanticism*.

and explains what Judith Thompson calls the 'complex and highly political process of negotiation, appropriation, and subversion' through which writers mobilized their chosen genres.[25] One important conclusion from such studies is that the transformations of *form* which are a hallmark of Romantic literature are often linked to changes of *function*, much of the technical experimentation of the period being attributable to ideologically driven genre-reform programmes.

The search for historical explanations of generic transformations that had previously been seen as evidence of a Romantic aspiration to 'transcend' genre has not confined itself to the political sphere. Equally important, scholars have shown, were social, economic, and cultural factors, including the expansion of literacy, professionalization, and the growth of the leisure industry. Changes in the book trade, especially from the 1770s, were particularly salient. These included the decline of patronage, changes in copyright law, the growth of subscription publishing, new marketing techniques (catalogue sales, remaindering, newspaper advertising), the rise of the circulating library, and the introduction of new print technology (stereotyping, machine-made paper, the steam press) facilitating inexpensive mass production. Cumulatively, these developments had profound effects on the way literature was written, published, sold, and read; and the willingness of literary historians to investigate these effects has led to a radically new understanding of the generic economy of the Romantic period. Whatever may be said about the attitudes to genre among the poets who form the core of the Romantic canon, the picture that emerges from recent work on, say, the gothic novel, or from studies of the day-to-day workings of the publishing industry, is of a dynamic print culture in which genres were more often being exploited than transcended, and in which generic terminology played a key role in both the marketing process and the broader organization of knowledge.[26] The more we learn about the material conditions of writing and reading, the mechanisms of publication, distribution, and review, and the vast hinterland of popular literature that surrounds the golden city of the Romantic canon, the less tenable is the hypothesis that this was a literary culture that had moved 'beyond genre'.[27] Indeed, it could be argued that the Romantic period, in so far as it witnessed the formation of a mass reading public and a modern literary market, experienced not so much a dissolution of genres as a consolidation and commodification of them—in some areas of the market, at least. Even trends such as 'novelization' and genre-mixing may ultimately have an economic explanation, since,

---

[25] Judith Thompson, ' "A Voice in the Representation": John Thelwall and the Enfranchisement of Literature', in Tilottama Rajan and Julia M. Wright (eds), *Romanticism, History, and the Possibilities of Genre: Re-forming Literature 1789–1837* (Cambridge: Cambridge University Press, 1998), 123.

[26] See e.g. Lee Erickson, *The Economy of Literary Form: English Literature and the Industrialization of Publishing, 1800–1850* (Baltimore: Johns Hopkins University Press, 1996); Michael Gamer, *Romanticism and the Gothic: Genre, Reception, and Canon Formation* (Cambridge: Cambridge University Press, 2000); and William St Clair, *The Reading Nation in the Romantic Period* (Cambridge: Cambridge University Press, 2004).

[27] Paul Hernadi, *Beyond Genre: New Directions in Literary Classification* (Ithaca, N.Y.: Cornell University Press, 1972).

as Clifford Siskin has shown, reconfigurations of the genre-system were connected with long-term shifts in the division of labour.[28]

Whether focused on authors, readers, publishers, or genres, the scholarship of the last few decades has profoundly altered our perception of the relationship between Romanticism and genre. Critics today no longer rely on disabling assumptions about the essentially restrictive and reactionary nature of genre, nor do they regard the Romantics' own views on genre as necessarily a reliable guide to their practice. Where an early twentieth-century theorist like Benedetto Croce could speak of the concept of genre as a classical 'superstition', inimical to the true idea of the aesthetic,[29] most critics today would concur with Thomas Beebee's statement that genres are a 'precondition for the creation and reading of texts',[30] a reversal of attitude summed up by the title of Adena Rosmarin's book *The Power of Genre* (1986). For Rosmarin, the power in question is interpretative—she defines genre as a 'hermeneutic tool' employed by readers and critics[31]—but one could equally argue that genres confer *expressive* power, serving the needs of writers; and that, in more tangible ways, genres also have commercial and ideological power. This is the premiss of Tilottama Rajan and Julia Wright's collection *Romanticism, History, and the Possibilities of Genre* (1998), which demonstrates through an impressive range of examples how the Romantics, far from rejecting the power of genre, were actively discovering and harnessing it.

Recognition of this cultural fact has restored a missing dimension to our understanding of Romanticism. Particularly welcome has been the attention paid to the rhetorical and ideological functions of genre, not just at the level of content, but also in the more hidden politics of form and style. As recent studies by Susan Wolfson, Richard Cronin, William Keach, and others have shown, metre and stanza form can be as 'political' as any other aspect of genre, and the manipulation of formal and linguistic conventions was as integral to Romantic efforts at genre-reform as its revision of traditional subject matter.[32] Equally illuminating is the emphasis placed by critics like Neil Fraistat and Paul Magnuson on the relationship between genre and 'location' (the publishing context), and on the paratextual devices (title, preface, notes) which advertise or explicate a text's generic affiliations, or which—to use an important Wordsworthian term—define the metrical 'contract' between writer and reader.[33] In these areas too, Romantic writers, together with their

---

[28] Clifford Siskin, *The Work of Writing: Literature and Social Change in Britain, 1700–1830* (Baltimore: Johns Hopkins University Press, 1998).

[29] Benedetto Croce, *Aesthetic as Science of Expression and General Linguistic*, ed. Douglas Ainslie, 2nd edn (London: Peter Owen, 1953), 449.

[30] Thomas O. Beebee, *The Ideology of Genre: A Comparative Study of Generic Instability* (University Park: Pennsylvania State University Press, 1994), 250; for a comprehensive development of this idea, see John Frow, *Genre* (London: Routledge, 2006).

[31] Adena Rosmarin, *The Power of Genre* (Minneapolis: University of Minnesota Press, 1985), 49–50.

[32] Wolfson, *Formal Charges*; Richard Cronin, *The Politics of Romantic Poetry: In Search of the Pure Commonwealth* (Basingstoke: Macmillan, 2000); William Keach, *Arbitrary Power: Romanticism, Language, Politics* (Princeton: Princeton University Press, 2004).

[33] Neil Fraistat, *The Poem and the Book: Interpreting Collections of Romantic Poetry* (Chapel Hill: University of North Carolina Press, 1985); Paul Magnuson, *Reading Public Romanticism* (Princeton: Princeton University Press, 1998); John Hollander, 'Romantic Verse Form and the Metrical Contract', in Bloom (ed.), *Romanticism and Consciousness*.

publishers and readers, are now seen to be deeply and inescapably engaged in the workings of genre.

Fruitful though such methodological departures have proved, there are, nevertheless, certain problems with these revisionist approaches. To regard Romantic anti-formalism—or anti-genericism—as merely a retrospective critical myth is to underestimate the pronounced strain in Romantic theory and practice that does indeed seek to reject, downgrade, or otherwise problematize inherited notions of genre. When Coleridge, echoing German theorists, drew his famous distinction between 'organic' and 'mechanical form' ('Form as proceeding' and 'Shape as superinduced'),[34] or when Barry Cornwall said that it makes no difference whether a poem 'be called an epic or a romance, an epistle or a dirge, an epitaph, an ode, an elegy, a sonnet, or otherwise' as long as it is 'full of the *material* of poetry',[35] they were not simply concealing their artistic methods and mystifying the nature of the aesthetic, as in Jerome McGann's 'Romantic ideology' argument.[36] Rather, they were voicing a widely held belief that artistic values had altered, and that literary merit could no longer be measured by the putative status of an author's chosen genre, or by a text's conformity to preconceived generic rules. Though the Romantics were adept at recognizing and exploiting the resources of genre, they were also alert to artistic possibilities that appeared to lie beyond them, and they cultivated a notion of literariness that often sought to elude or transcend traditional conceptions of genre. For every instance of generic utterance, in the critical or creative sphere, there were others that put the premiss of genre in question.

What is at stake, then, is not simply a contradiction between Romantic theory and practice, but contradictions *within* the theory and practice. The theoretical tensions can be seen most clearly in German Romanticism, where genre is the subject of relentless theoretical dispute, the disputants often holding flatly contradictory views. To take one example, the negative tenor of Friedrich Schlegel's remark already quoted about the 'childishness' of traditional genre concepts is in marked contrast to the ecstatic tone of Athenaeum Fragment 116, with its famous call for a 'progressive universal poetry' that would 'reunite all the separate genres of poetry', dissolve the distinction between poetry and prose, and absorb all other forms of knowledge.[37] These antithetical statements represent only two strands in a complex web of definitions and speculations about genre that fills Schlegel's published and unpublished writings. Other strands include theorization of the triad of lyric, epic, and dramatic poetry; conjectural histories of the cultural origins and evolution of genres; comparisons of ancient and modern versions of genres; discussion of the dominant genre in different epochs; and the radical proposition that 'each poem is a genre in

---

[34] *The Collected Works of Samuel Taylor Coleridge*, v: *Lectures 1808–1819 On Literature*, ed. R. A. Foakes, 2 vols (London: Routledge and Kegan Paul, 1987), i. 495, ii. 224. See Ch. 2 below, p. 83.

[35] 'On English Poetry' (1825), in Barry Cornwall [Bryan Procter], *Essays and Tales in Prose*, 2 vols (Boston, 1853), ii. 147.

[36] Jerome McGann, *The Romantic Ideology: A Critical Investigation* (Chicago: University of Chicago Press, 1983).

[37] *Philosophical Fragments*, 31–2. See Ch. 5 below, pp. 171–6.

itself' (*Jedes Gedicht eine Gattung für sich*).[38] Friedrich's brother August Wilhelm Schlegel shared his fascination with genre, as did the latter's wife, Caroline, and other illustrious contemporaries such as Goethe, Schiller, Novalis, Jean Paul, Hölderlin, Tieck, Schelling, and Humboldt, all of whom developed distinctive positions ranging from outright hostility to genre, to the almost mystical belief in it voiced in the pages of *The Athenaeum* and elsewhere. It was left to Hegel in his *Aesthetics* (delivered as lectures in the 1820s and published posthumously in 1835) to try to synthesize these various lines of inquiry and offer a comprehensive account of the place of genre in a modern theory of the arts, but a more revealing text for my purposes—as will be seen in Chapter 2—is Friedrich Schlegel's *Dialogue on Poetry* (1800), a philosophical symposium on the subject of genre that skilfully dramatizes the conflicting views of the Jena school. In the German context, then, what defines the 'Romantic' attitude to genre is not one position or another but rather the coexistence of opposed theories, and the heightened consciousness of this issue to which the whole debate bears witness.

The argument of this book is that British Romanticism displays a similar hyperconsciousness about genre, and a comparable clash of attitudes. In the British context, however, the period's preoccupation with genre takes different forms, reflects local conditions, and often finds more indirect expression. Compared with Germany, British literary criticism was generally of an empirical rather than speculative bent, and the 'species of criticism' that James Harris in his essay *Upon the Rise and Progress of Criticism* (1752) had termed 'philosophical' (the kind which involves 'a deep and philosophical Search into the primary Laws and Elements of good Writing'[39]) had, by the end of the eighteenth century, been largely displaced by 'corrective' (editorial) and 'historical' criticism, and by periodical reviewing. Partly because of the distrust of theory awakened by the French Revolution,[40] Britain developed something of an aversion to speculative thought just as Germany was experiencing its philosophical and critical boom. Even when the political threat receded, the formidable power of review journalism, with its ethos of instant judgement, complicated the relationship between poetry and philosophical criticism, and between the writer and the reading public. There is thus no real equivalent in Britain to the philosophical genre theory of German Romanticism. No single British work of the period can compare with Schlegel's *Dialogue on Poetry*, Schelling's *Philosophy of Art* (1801–4), or Hegel's *Aesthetics* as a sustained theoretical reflection on the problem of genre. The words 'critical' and 'criticism' lack the magical charge they carried in Germany in this period, in the wake of the three great *Critiques* of Kant.[41]

---

[38] Friedrich Schlegel, *Literary Notebooks, 1797–1801*, ed. Hans Eichner (Toronto: University of Toronto Press, 1957), 116 (no. 1090), quoted by Peter Szondi, 'Friedrich Schlegel's Theory of Poetical Genres: A Reconstruction from the Posthumous Fragments', in his *On Textual Understanding and Other Essays*, trans. Harvey Mendelsohn (Manchester: Manchester University Press, 1986), 93.

[39] [James Harris], *Upon the Rise and Progress of Criticism* ([London?], 1752), 4–5.

[40] David Simpson, *Romanticism, Nationalism, and the Revolt against Theory* (Chicago: University of Chicago Press, 1993).

[41] Walter Benjamin, 'The Concept of Criticism in German Romanticism' (1920), in his *Selected Writings*, i: *1913–1926*, ed. Marcus Bullock and Michael W. Jennings (Cambridge, Mass.: Belknap Press, 1996).

Yet theory is crucial to British Romanticism. The 'revolution in literature' described by Jeffrey, Hazlitt, and others was also a revolution in literary theory. The same year that Schlegel published his *Dialogue on Poetry* in *The Athenaeum*, Wordsworth published his Preface to *Lyrical Ballads*, another epoch-making dialogue on poetry, albeit one with his principal interlocutor (Coleridge) erased. The theories Wordsworth put forward in the Preface were as innovative as the poems, and the combination of the two proved explosive. From that moment onwards, Romantic theory and practice went hand in hand, enriching and complicating one another, and contributing to a view of the new poetics as a composite theory and practice, and a theory-in-practice. In this sense, *Lyrical Ballads* served a similar function in Britain to Goethe's *Wilhelm Meister's Apprenticeship* (1795–6) in Germany, as the iconic, self-theorizing, generically hybrid text which became the focal point of critical efforts to understand the literary spirit of the age (whoever can interpret Goethe's *Meister* properly, said Friedrich Schlegel, 'could, so far as literary criticism is concerned, retire forever'[42]). The 'internalization' of genre which Harold Bloom defines as a hallmark of Romanticism[43] was thus, in part, a *theoretical* self-consciousness about genre. To write poetry in this period was also, of necessity, to write *about* poetry: its form, its purpose, its value, its destiny. Every significant body of work by a British Romantic poet includes a significant body of theoretical writing, published or unpublished; and a central ambition of writers in both countries was to create a type of art that would synthesize poetry and philosophy—the genre-to-end-all-genres that Friedrich Schlegel called 'transcendental poetry', Coleridge and Wordsworth the 'philosophical poem'.[44]

Britain thus experienced its own version of what Henry Crabb Robinson, echoing Friedrich Schlegel, called the German 'aesthetic revolution'.[45] Genre theory is central to this. Albeit often at a lower plane of abstraction, and without the framework of transcendental idealism that underpins German critical discourse of this period, problems of genre figure prominently, even obsessively, in British critical writing, not least in Romantic writers' reflections on their own art. To hear the full discussion, we need to range widely and listen carefully. Formal theoretical essays like Shelley's *Defence of Poetry* (written in 1821) are only one source. Theoretical reflection on genre can be found too in prefaces, advertisements, epigraphs, footnotes, letters, notebooks, marginalia, and table talk, paratextual forms which are themselves the

[42] *Critical Fragments*, no. 120, in *Philosophical Fragments*, 15. For German responses to *Meister*, see Ernst Behler, *German Romantic Literary Theory* (Cambridge: Cambridge University Press, 1993), 165–80. British critical reaction was, by contrast, generally hostile, as the reviews of Carlyle's 1824 translation indicate: even the Germanophile De Quincey, reviewing for the *London Magazine*, saw little to admire, while Jeffrey, in the *Edinburgh Review*, found the 'German idolatry' of *Meister* incomprehensible; *Jeffrey's Criticism: A Selection*, ed. Peter F. Morgan (Edinburgh: Scottish Academic Press, 1983), 159–60.

[43] Harold Bloom, 'The Internalization of Quest Romance', in Bloom (ed.), *Romanticism and Consciousness*.

[44] Schlegel, *Athenaeum Fragments*, no. 238, in *Philosophical Fragments*, 51–2; for the British 'philosophical poem', see Ch. 3 below, pp. 113–15.

[45] Diane I. Behler, 'Henry Crabb Robinson as a Mediator of Early Romanticism to England', *Arcadia*, 12 (1977), 117–55: 119. For Friedrich Schlegel's use of this phrase, see Ernst Behler, *German Romantic Literary Theory*, 55.

subject of theorization in this period.[46] Titles and subtitles are especially indicative, as places where generic affiliations and aspirations are directly revealed or strategically concealed.[47] Contemporary reviews are another vital site: generic conventions and traditions are a major reference point in Romantic-era reviewing, and discussion of individual works often opens into larger discussions of genre. Most important of all, literary works themselves reveal theoretical assumptions about genre, a type of applied theory which is an essential but often neglected part of the corpus of Romantic genre theory. The range of views expressed and attitudes revealed cannot be easily summarized, but they include many kinds of both attraction and resistance to genre, and a desire to rethink traditional assumptions and categories that was as strong, if not always as explicit, as in Germany.

Like their German counterparts, too, British writers and critics show a marked tendency to hold conflicting views simultaneously. A good example is Robert Southey, a poet whom Coleridge credited with having attempted 'almost every species of composition known' as well as introducing several new ones,[48] and who also became an equally versatile prose writer. This practical mastery of the generic repertoire is complemented by a broad expertise in the critical exposition of genres, demonstrated in letters, prefaces, footnotes, reviews, edited collections like his *Specimens of the Later English Poets* (1807) and *Select Works of the British Poets* (1831), and his pioneering essay 'On the Lives and Works of our Uneducated Poets' (1831).[49] Southey's mode of commentary on matters of genre ranges from purely formal definitions in the neoclassical manner to nuanced sociological histories of genre, and also includes such playful speculations as his wildly original idea for a new taxonomy in which novels are arranged 'according to the botanical system of Linnaeus', with 'Monandria Monogynia' as 'the usual class, most novels having one hero and heroine',[50] or his equally fanciful classification of poets according to linguistic mood, 'amiable' poets being 'in the sentimental or indicative mood', 'didactic poets . . . in the imperative', 'satirists in the potential', and 'amourists in the optative'.[51] Yet this indefatigable practitioner and analyst of genre also denounced, on occasion, virtually all of the genres he utilized. The ode, the poetic form in which he made his reputation, he derided in 1797 as 'the most worthless species of composition as well as the most difficult', and vowed to abandon[52] (a vow he broke when he took up the post of Poet Laureate in 1813). Of pastoral, he wrote: 'No kind of poetry can boast of more illustrious names or is more

---

[46] Notably by Isaac D'Israeli, whose *Literary Curiosities*, discussed in Ch. 2, inaugurated a tradition of paratextual genre theory that continues today in studies such as Gérard Genette, *Paratexts: Thresholds of Interpretation* (1987), trans. Jane E. Lewin (Cambridge: Cambridge University Press, 1997); Anthony Grafton, *The Footnote: A Curious History* (London: Faber, 1997); and Kevin Jackson, *Invisible Forms: A Guide to Literary Curiosities* (London: Picador, 1999).

[47] Genette, *Paratexts*, ch. 4; Anne Ferry, *The Title to the Poem* (Stanford, Calif.: Stanford University Press, 1996).

[48] *The Collected Works of Samuel Taylor Coleridge*, vii: *Biographia Literaria*, ed. James Engell and W. Jackson Bate, 2 vols (London: Routledge and Kegan Paul, 1983), i. 64.

[49] First published as a prefatory essay to John Jones, *Attempts in Verse* (London, 1831).

[50] Robert Southey and Samuel Taylor Coleridge, *Omniana, or, Horae Otiosiores* (1812), ed. Robert Gittings (Fontwell: Centaur Press, 1969), 70 (no. 58: 'Classification of Novels').

[51] Ibid. 62 (no. 48: 'Poetical Moods and Tenses').

[52] Robert Southey, *Poems* (Bristol, 1797), untitled prefatory note.

distinguished by the servile dullness of imitation nonsense',[53] a generic paralysis he tried to heal with his own iconoclastic variant, the 'English Eclogue'. He made similar accusations about epic, ridiculing the 'multitude of obscure epic writers' who 'copy with the most gross servility their ancient models', and even threatening to write a whole book devoted to 'Analysis of Obscure Epic Poems',[54] but managing nonetheless to write half a dozen quasi-epic poems to his own commercially successful formula.

Professional critics were no more consistent. Hazlitt has been seen as the archetypal Romantic critic in his adoption of psychological criteria, his focus on the literary producer rather than the product, and his use of impressionistic concepts like 'gusto' and 'intensity'. Like other Romantics, he derided the 'French school' of criticism—what we now call neoclassicism—with its 'dry and meagre mode of dissecting the skeleton of works, instead of transfusing the living principles',[55] and celebrated what he saw as the dismantling of generic hierarchies and conventions by iconoclastic poets like Wordsworth. His critical instincts are resolutely anti-authoritarian, and his reading practices eclectic and cross-generic. Yet in practice Hazlitt often uses genre as both an evaluative yardstick and an interpretative tool, praising writers who have fulfilled or extended the possibilities of a genre (for instance, Milton in his political sonnets[56]) and condemning those who have misunderstood the expressive logic of their chosen form, or concocted inept generic mixtures. Inspired by a reading of A. W. Schlegel's *Lectures on Dramatic Art and Literature* (in Black's 1815 translation), he takes Aeschylus to task for the 'imperfect dramatic form' of *Seven before Thebes*, refers to Aristophanes' comedies as 'monstrous allegorical pantomimes', and describes French attempts at tragic drama as 'tragedy in masquerade'.[57] He passes a similar verdict on Southey's attempt at courtly panegyric in *A Vision of Judgment* (1821), accusing him of having so far infringed generic convention as to have utterly compromised his sycophantic tribute to the late king (the implication is that Southey remains an aesthetic radical though now politically conservative).[58] Elsewhere he excoriates modern German tragedy for 'setting at naught all the received rules of composition', and declares it a 'violation of decorum' from beginning to end, as well as 'an insult and defiance to Aristotle's definition of tragedy'.[59] His many discussions of his own preferred medium, the 'familiar' essay, reveal deep insight into the relationship between language, thought, and form, and his account of the essay as an 'experimental' rather than a 'dogmatical' mode of

---

[53] Robert Southey, *Poems*, 2nd edn (London, 1800), prefatory note to 'English Eclogues'.

[54] Unpub. letter from Robert to Thomas Southey, 1 Mar. 1799, cited by Lynda Pratt, 'Patriot Poetics and the Romantic National Epic: Placing and Displacing Southey's *Joan of Arc*', in Peter J. Kitson (ed.), *Placing and Displacing Romanticism* (Aldershot: Ashgate, 2001), 103 n. 25.

[55] 'On Criticism', *Table Talk* (1822), in *The Complete Works of William Hazlitt*, ed. P. P. Howe, 21 vols (London: Dent, 1930–4), viii. 217.

[56] 'On Milton's Sonnets', *Table Talk*, in *Complete Works*, viii. 174–81.

[57] '[A. W.] Schlegel on the Drama', *Edinburgh Review*, 26 (Feb. 1816), in *Complete Works*, xvi. 73, 79, 90.

[58] 'Mr. Southey', *The Spirit of the Age* (1825), in *Complete Works*, xi. 81.

[59] 'On the Spirit of Ancient and Modern Literature—On the German Drama, Contrasted with that of the Age of Elizabeth', *Lectures on the Dramatic Literature of the Age of Elizabeth* (1820), in *Complete Works*, vi. 360.

writing is a vital contribution to the then largely unformulated poetics of that genre.[60] Throughout his work, an interest in literary aesthetics is counterbalanced by an acute sense of the ideology of genres, his arguments often hingeing on Schilleresque distinctions between ancient and modern versions of a given genre, and on hard-headed analysis of the power politics which he shows to be an inescapable feature of imaginative activity.

These conflicting impulses can be seen even more sharply in the poet–critic Leigh Hunt, a pivotal figure in second-generation Romanticism and a significant literary presence until well into the nineteenth century. Widely read, and gifted with brilliant journalistic antennae, Hunt offers fascinating insight into the shifting literary and critical currents during his long professional life. In his early career especially, Hunt displayed a passionate interest in genre, experimenting with a wide range of lyrical, narrative, and satirical poetic forms as well as various types of drama and virtually every kind of discursive prose. His knowledge of earlier literary traditions, especially of the Italian Renaissance, made him an important contributor to the revivalist movement, and he was personally responsible for reintroducing a number of previously obsolete genres, including the Jonsonian masque and the 'sessions of the poets' genre from the seventeenth century (his *Feast of the Poets* of 1811 is a modern re-creation). Like Hazlitt, Hunt was acutely alert to the politics of genre, and sought in his poetry to liberalize and democratize ideologically suspect genres, often provoking controversy in the process.[61] His habit of prefacing his literary productions with extended critical histories of their genre, as in the forty-page essay on masques appended to *The Descent of Liberty* (1815) or the essay on pastoral drama attached to his translation of Tasso's *Amyntas* (1820), is another example of theoretical self-consciousness, and of what Coleridge and Wordsworth saw as the need of an author (especially an experimental author) to create the taste by which he is to be enjoyed— or, put differently, to establish the generic 'contract' by which he is to be understood. Hunt's fascination with the history of genres is characteristic of his time, as are the conclusions he draws about the cultural variability of genres and the need to adapt traditional genres to modern conditions.

As with other Romantic writers, though, when Hunt turns to the more general question of what poetry actually is, this interest in generic form and function tends to yield to affective, psychological concerns. His typology of poetic kinds in the Preface to his collected *Poetical Works* (1832) begins as a discussion of the varieties of narrative verse but quickly becomes a list of such nebulous categories as 'the poetry of thought and passion' (Shakespeare and Chaucer), of 'poetical abstraction and enjoyment' (Spenser), of 'scholarship and rapt ambition' (Milton), and of 'heartiness' (Burns).[62] Similarly, when he came, many years later, to assemble an anthology of *Selections from the English Poets* (1844), he organized it not by genre or historical

---

[60] 'On the Periodical Essayists', *Lectures on the English Comic Writers* (1819), in *Complete Works*, vi. 91; 'On Familiar Style', *Table Talk*, in *Complete Works*, viii. 242–8.

[61] For examples, see Jeffrey N. Cox, *Poetry and Politics in the Cockney School: Keats, Shelley, Hunt and their Circle* (Cambridge: Cambridge University Press, 1998), chs 2 and 4.

[62] Preface to *The Poetical Works of Leigh Hunt* (1832), in Leigh Hunt, *Selected Writings*, 6 vols (London: Pickering and Chatto, 2003), vi: *Poetical Works, 1822–59*, ed. John Strachan, 77.

period, but around the aesthetic principles of Imagination and Fancy, words he placed in the title of the collection.[63] In the introductory essay, 'An Answer to the Question: "What is Poetry?"', he breaks down the art of poetry not into its constituent genres, with their familiar rankings, but into 'different kinds and degrees of imagination, some of them necessary to the formation of every true poet, and all of them possessed by the greatest'.[64] There is no better illustration of the paradigm shift from mimetic to expressive criteria posited by Abrams: the hierarchy of forms has been replaced by a hierarchy of mental faculties. Yet the theoretical tensions in Hunt's poetics are there from the start.

The contradictions multiply if we examine how different Romantic writers responded to the same genre. Take the sonnet, a poetic form whose improbable but spectacular revival in the late eighteenth century, and continued popularity in the nineteenth, underline the familiar idea of Romanticism as a 'renaissance of the Renaissance'. All the major Romantic poets, including Blake, made repeated use of the form, as did countless other writers, the scale of production fully justifying Curran's reference to a 'burgeoning sonnet industry'.[65] Like other genres in the ascendant, the sonnet spawned multiple subtypes—the 'elegiac sonnet', the 'descriptive sonnet', the 'pastoral sonnet', the 'political sonnet'—and was the focus of frequent technical innovation, including Keats's reworking of sonnet rhyme schemes, experiments with sonnets of more than fourteen lines by Bowles, Smith, Dermody, Coleridge, and others, the embedding of sonnets within novels (a trend started by Goethe in *The Sorrows of Young Werther*), and Shelley's fusion of sonnet form with Dantean *terza rima* and the strophic patterning of the Pindaric ode in his 'Ode to the West Wind'. New theories of the sonnet also abounded, among them the psychological definition Coleridge appended to his unpublished anthology of sonnets (1796),[66] Thelwall's iconoclastic 'Essay on the English Sonnet' in the *Universal Magazine* (1792),[67] and Mary Robinson's Preface to her sonnet cycle *Sappho and Phaon: In a Series of Legitimate Sonnets* (1796), which takes a conservative stance but injects new arguments for preferring the ancient Italian form to modern variants.[68] The impact of the sonnet craze is evident, too, in the invention of new words like

---

[63] Hunt's *Imagination and Fancy, or, Selections from the English Poets, illustrative of those First Requisites of their Art; with Markings of the Best Passages, Critical Notices of the Writers, and an Essay in Answer to the Question 'What is Poetry?'* (London, 1844) was one of a projected sequence of anthologies, others of which were to treat Action and Passion, Contemplation, and Wit and Humour. Of these, only the last was completed (in 1846). Hunt's editorial matter from these volumes is included in vol. iv of the *Selected Writings*.

[64] *Selected Writings*, iv: *Later Literary Essays*, ed. Charles Mahoney, 8.

[65] Curran, *Poetic Form and British Romanticism*, 38.

[66] See Ch. 2 below, p. 87 n. 115.

[67] Reprinted as an appendix to Judith Thompson's edition of Thelwall's *The Peripatetic* (Detroit: Wayne State University Press, 2001). In the brief section 'The Sonnet' in *The Peripatetic* itself, Thelwall restates his preference for Charlotte Smith over Milton, defending the supposed illegitimacy of Smith's sonnets in quasi-political terms: 'they owe much of their beauty to the glorious crime—if such it be to burst the fetters of arbitrary authority, and exert the free-born energies of the soul' (pp. 130–1).

[68] Mary Robinson, *Sappho and Phaon: In a Series of Legitimate Sonnets* (London, 1796), preface, in Duncan Wu (ed.), *Romantic Women Poets: An Anthology* (Oxford: Blackwell, 1997), 184–7.

'sonnetize' and 'sonneteering', both coined in the 1790s. Half a century later, Romantic fascination with the theory and practice of the genre found a fitting monument in a lavishly produced anthology entitled *The Book of the Sonnet* (1867), containing a long theoretical essay by Leigh Hunt, 'On the Cultivation, History, and Varieties of the Species of Poem Called the Sonnet'.[69]

The Romantic sonnet revival has been exhaustively documented and perceptively analysed.[70] What is not fully appreciated, however, is the scale of the critical controversy it provoked, or the level of ambivalence towards the genre shown by most of its practitioners. Throughout the period, the sonnet attracted as much negative commentary as positive. Many reviewers objected to the relentless production of sonnets and the willingness of writers like Charlotte Smith to pander to a lazy readership and greedy publishing industry by issuing an expanded edition of her *Elegiac Sonnets* year after year. The contempt for the sonnet shown by Dr Johnson, who had dismissed it as an insignificant genre 'not very suitable to the English language',[71] was echoed and amplified in the Romantic period by critics who resented the genre's ability to absorb the most dubious tendencies in modern literature—sentimentality, egotism, the cult of simplicity, the gothic. Others regarded the genre as simply past its sell-by date, a quaint anachronism. The fact that it had been revived mainly by women poets gave further grounds for objection, though some reviewers welcomed this, seeing the genre as a safely marginal outlet for female literary aspirations (at a later stage, the sonnet was reclaimed by male poets, a proprietorial manoeuvre typical of the fraught genre–gender politics that marked the period[72]). Much was made, too, of the acrimonious quarrel between two of the early revivalists, Anna Seward and Charlotte Smith, over the 'legitimate' form of the sonnet and the acceptability or otherwise of deviations from that norm, of which there were many.[73] This quarrel set the tone for subsequent critical debate on the

---

[69] *Selected Writings*, iv. 291–320. Hunt's essay was completed by 1857, two years before his death.

[70] See e.g. Curran, *Poetic Form and British Romanticism*, ch. 3; Jennifer Ann Wagner, *A Moment's Monument: Revisionary Poetics and the Nineteenth-Century English Sonnet* (Madison: Fairleigh Dickinson University Press, 1996); Joseph Phelan, *The Nineteenth-Century Sonnet* (Basingstoke: Palgrave Macmillan, 2005); Paula R. Backscheider, *Eighteenth-Century Women Poets and their Poetry: Inventing Agency, Inventing Genre* (Baltimore: Johns Hopkins University Press, 2005), ch. 2; *European Romantic Review*, 13/4 (2002), special issue on the sonnet, ed. Daniel Robinson; and the annotated anthology by Paula R. Feldman and Daniel Robinson (eds), *A Century of Sonnets: The Romantic-Era Revival, 1750–1850* (New York: Oxford University Press, 1999).

[71] *Dictionary* (1755), quoted in entry for 'Sonnet' in Joseph Epes Brown (ed.), *The Critical Opinions of Samuel Johnson* (1926; New York: Russell and Russell, 1961), 236.

[72] Daniel Robinson, 'Reviving the Sonnet: Women Romantic Poets and the Sonnet Claim', *European Romantic Review*, 6/1 (1995), 98–127; Philip Cox, *Gender, Genre and the Romantic Poets* (Manchester: Manchester University Press, 1996), 42–50. For further examples of the 'gendering' of genre in this period, see Lilla Crisafulli and Cecilia Pietropoli (eds), *Romantic Women Poets: Genre and Gender* (Amsterdam: Rodopi, 2007); Irene Tayler and Gina Luria, 'Gender and Genre: Women in British Romantic Poetry', in Marlene Springer (ed.), *What Manner of Woman: Essays on English and American Life and Literature* (Oxford: Blackwell, 1977); and Marlon Ross's path-breaking study, *The Contours of Masculine Desire: Romanticism and the Rise of Women's Poetry* (New York: Oxford University Press, 1989).

[73] Curran, *Poetic Form and British Romanticism*, 31 and 225 n. 7.

sonnet, and, like other disputes over 'legitimate' and 'illegitimate' versions of genres, could be seen as a touchstone in the shift from a prescriptive (neoclassical) to a descriptive (Romantic) poetics—though in this case there was no clear outcome.

What is most revealing, though, is the contradictory attitude of the major poets. Coleridge, who produced numerous sonnets of both a traditional and an experimental kind, also wrote a sequence of sonnet parodies, reprinted in *Biographia Literaria* (1817), that deride the very techniques he had sought so assiduously to master.[74] Southey did likewise, his parodic sonnets appearing as 'The Amatory Poems of Abel Shufflebottom' alongside serious sonnets in his collected *Minor Poems* (1815). He had already voiced his dissatisfaction with the genre in a prefatory note to his *Poems* (1797), saying of his youthful sonnets that, given a second chance, 'I would have adopted a different title, and avoided the shackle of rhyme and the confinement of fourteen lines.' Wordsworth, who turned to the genre in earnest in 1802, and by the end of his life had produced over five hundred examples, confessed to Walter Savage Landor in 1822 that he had once thought the genre 'egregiously absurd', and that, had he not fallen into the habit of writing sonnets, he 'might easily have been better employed'.[75] John Clare, arguably the finest of all Romantic sonneteers, remarked on 'the short winded peevishness that hovers round this 14 line article in poetry'.[76] Byron, meanwhile, marked his completion of two Petrarchan sonnets by vowing in his journal never to write another (a vow he soon broke). 'They are', he wrote, 'the most puling, petrifying, stupidly platonic compositions.'[77] Almost wherever it is used by the Romantics, the sonnet provokes some kind of backlash or apologia from its user, an ambivalence also manifest in the many 'sonnets upon sonnets' written in the period, by Burns, Wordsworth, Keats, and others.

In certain respects, the sonnet may be a special case, in so far as the genre is founded on a paradox: its expressive possibilities are inseparable from its formal constraints, a point forcibly made in Wordsworth's 'Nuns fret not' sonnet. This invites ambivalence and makes the genre peculiarly vulnerable to criticism. But the controversy surrounding the sonnet recurs with other genres, including epic, supposedly the most prestigious and critically secure of genres. Curran cites a letter to the *Edinburgh Review* in 1808 in which a correspondent tells of a 'tea-drinking in the west of England, at which there assisted no fewer than six epic poets', an anecdote that encapsulates what Southey dubbed the 'epomania' of the time.[78] The Romantic

[74] Nehemiah Higgenbottom (*pseud.*), 'Sonnets Attempted in the Manner of Contemporary Writers', first pub. in *Monthly Magazine* (Nov. 1797).

[75] To Walter Savage Landor, 20 Apr. 1822, in *Letters of William and Dorothy Wordsworth: Later Years*, i. 125–6.

[76] Quoted by Ian Jack, *English Literature, 1815–1832* (Oxford: Clarendon Press, 1963), 137.

[77] Lord Byron, *Letters and Journals*, ed. Leslie A. Marchand, 12 vols (London: Murray, 1973–82), iii. 240 (journal entry for 17–18 Dec. 1813).

[78] Robert Southey, *Life and Correspondence*, ed. C. C. Southey, 6 vols (London, 1849–50), ii. 121, quoted by Curran, *Poetic Form and British Romanticism*, 158. On Romantic 'epomania', see also Brian Wilkie, *Romantic Poets and Epic Tradition* (Madison: University of Wisconsin Press, 1965), ch. 2; Herbert F. Tucker, *Epic: Britain's Heroic Muse 1790–1910* (Oxford: Oxford University Press, 2008), chs 2–3; and, for female contributions, Adeline Johns-Putra, *Heroes and Housewives: Women's Epic Poetry and Domestic Ideology in the Romantic Age (1770–1835)* (New York: Lang, 2001).

epic revival is indeed, as Curran remarks, an 'amazing phenomenon', all the more so in that this was a genre that many considered obsolete prior to its revival.[79] But the trend did not please everyone. The proliferation of epics that some considered proof of the revitalization of British poetry after a century of decline, others saw as a mark of further decline. The quantity may have been impressive but the quality was not, and many believed that the fashion for hastily produced and easily consumed epics was confirmation that this once noble genre had become a meaningless commodity. Although himself an instigator of the craze, Southey came to the conclusion that the title of epic had been 'degraded' by this overproduction, and dropped the label from the second edition (1798) of his *Joan of Arc*, while continuing to write epics by another name.[80] This hypocrisy annoyed Byron, who lacerated Southey in a footnote, pointing out that if other recent epics were 'degraded', Southey's reconstructions of the genre were even worse: 'Joan of Arc was marvellous enough, but Thalaba was one of those poems "which, in the words of Porson, will be read when Homer and Virgil are forgotten, but—*not till then*".'[81]

Yet Byron, too, was ambivalent about epic, upholding the traditional status of the genre in *English Bards and Scotch Reviewers* (1809) but then subjecting it to a *reductio ad absurdum* in *Don Juan*, a poem which knowingly breaks every generic rule and brings to an ironic conclusion the epic revival that had begun thirty years earlier. The irony derives in part from Byron's sense of the sheer improbability of a modern epic, a feeling intermittently shared by Keats, who confessed to Benjamin Haydon that 'one day he was full of an epic poem; the next day epic poems were splendid impositions on the world'.[82] The two versions of 'Hyperion' are symptomatic of that ambivalence, fragmentary wannabe epics perfectly attuned to an age with large generic ambitions and a short attention span (as Jeffrey remarked, 'the greater part of polite readers would now no more think of sitting down to a whole Epic, than to a whole ox'[83]). Notwithstanding the temporary fashion for long narrative poems, many believed that the epic had been superseded by the novel, and that the modern age required 'something less protracted and monotonous than the sober pomp and deliberate stateliness of the Epic'.[84] The critique could also be retrospective. Romantic

---

[79] Curran, *Poetic Form and British Romanticism*, 158. For perceptions of epic decline, see Dustin Griffin, *Regaining Paradise: Milton and the Eighteenth Century* (Cambridge: Cambridge University Press, 1986).

[80] Southey refers to 'the degraded title of Epic' in his Preface to *Madoc* (London, 1805). Alternative terms he applies to his long narrative poems include 'metrical romance' (*Thalaba*, 1st edn, 1801), 'rhythmical romance' (*Thalaba*, 2nd edn, 1809), 'metrical tale' (*Metrical Tales and Other Poems*, 1805), or simply 'poem' (*Thalaba*, 3rd edn, 1814; *Madoc*, 1805; *The Curse of Kehama*, 1811).

[81] *English Bards and Scotch Reviewers*, note to line 211, in Lord Byron, *The Complete Poetical Works*, ed. Jerome J. McGann, 7 vols (Oxford: Clarendon Press, 1980–93), i. 403. The objection to Southey's comment about Epic appears in Byron's note to line 225.

[82] Quoted by William Michael Rossetti, *Life of John Keats* (London: Walter Scott, 1887), 162.

[83] Review of Byron's *The Giaour*, *Edinburgh Review*, 21 (July 1813), in Donald H. Reiman (ed.), *The Romantics Reviewed: Contemporary Reviews of British Romantic Writers*, facs. repr., 9 vols (New York: Garland, 1972), B ii. 842.

[84] [Francis Jeffrey], review of Joel Barlow's *Columbiad*, *Edinburgh Review*, 15 (1809), 40, quoted by Donald M. Foerster, *The Fortunes of Epic Poetry: A Study in English and American Criticism 1750–1950* (Washington: Catholic University of America Press, 1962), 37.

veneration for Milton was boundless, but the period also harboured opinions such as Horace Walpole's, who defined epic poetry as 'the art of being as long as possible in telling an uninteresting story', and said of Milton that he had 'produced a monster' by writing *Paradise Lost*.[85] Reactions to Spenser were similarly mixed: *The Faerie Queene* was both a model for Romantic visionary epic and byword for tedious allegory.[86]

There was little agreement, either, about the time and effort required to produce an epic. Coleridge declared that he would need to set aside twenty years to write an epic;[87] Wordsworth set aside fifty, and still never finished; Southey could manage one in less than six months; and John Thelwall claimed to have written one 'on the spur of the moment'.[88] To regard an 'epic effusion' such as Thelwall's *The Trident of Albion* (1805) as belonging to the same genre as *Don Juan* or *Jerusalem* is to stretch the definition of epic, but no more so than some contemporary critics were willing to do. The loosening of the category of epic, and the extension of it to include irregular, hybrid, or fragmentary poems such as Thelwall's or Keats's, are as much a part of the epomania as the many 'legitimate' epics that the period produced.[89] The epic resurfaced not only in the traditional form of the twelve-book verse narrative in heroic couplets or Miltonic blank verse, but in four-, six-, eight-, ten-, eighteen-, and twenty-four book variants;[90] in Spenserian stanza, *ottava rima*, heptameter, and unrhymed lyrical metre;[91] as 'sublime allegory', 'epic effusion', 'epic satire', and 'vision'; in varying degrees of fragmentariness; with 'characters & mechanism of a kind yet unattempted' (Shelley's *Prometheus Unbound*[92]) or with no machinery at all; combined with drama and/or lyric; and transposed into the prose form of the novel. These morphological developments far exceed the limited revisions proposed by William Hayley in his *Essay on Epic Poetry* (1782), or the range of variants recognized in standard literary histories of the period. As with other genres, what characterizes the Romantic history of epic is the coexistence of radically different forms of it and starkly contrasting attitudes to it, a complicated situation which both

[85]  Letter to William Mason, 25 June 1782, in *Horace Walpole's Correspondence*, ed. W. S. Lewis, xxix/2 (New Haven: Yale University Press, 1955), 256.

[86]  David Hall Radcliffe, *Edmund Spenser: A Reception History* (Columbia, S.C.: Camden House, 1996).

[87]  Letter to Joseph Cottle, Apr. 1797, in *Collected Letters of Samuel Taylor Coleridge*, ed. Earl Leslie Griggs, 6 vols (Oxford: Clarendon Press, 1956–71), i. 320–1.

[88]  John Thelwall, *The Trident of Albion: An Epic Effusion* (Liverpool, 1805), p. v, quoted by Curran, *Poetic Form and British Romanticism*, 245 n. 6.

[89]  See Ch. 4 below, pp. 152–3.

[90]  John Trumbull, *M'Fingal: A Modern Epic Poem, in Four Cantos* (Hartford, 1782); Henry James Pye, *Alfred: An Epic Poem in Six Books* (London, 1801); Henry Murphy, *The Conquest of Quebec: An Epic Poem. In Eight Books* (Dublin, 1790); Robert Southey, *Joan of Arc: An Epic Poem* (10 books; Bristol, 1796); James Burges, *Richard the First: A Poem in Eighteen Books* (London, 1801); Joseph Cottle, *Alfred: An Epic Poem in Twenty-Four Books* (London, 1800).

[91]  In, respectively, Shelley's *Laon and Cythna, or, The Revolution of the Golden City: A Vision of the Nineteenth Century in the Stanza of Spenser* (London, 1817); Blake's *Jerusalem: The Emanation of the Giant Albion* (London, 1804–20); Byron's *Don Juan*; and Southey's *Thalaba*.

[92]  As described in his letter to Thomas Love Peacock, 6 Apr. 1819, in *Letters of Percy Bysshe Shelley*, ed. F. L. Jones, 2 vols (Oxford: Clarendon Press, 1964), i. 94.

the anti-generic approach and the revisionist position fail to capture, if pursued separately.

In their extreme form, the self-consciousness and ambivalence about genre are an aspect of what Paul Hamilton has called 'metaromanticism', the important strain in Romantic discourse which makes self-critique a form of self-transcendence, and produces the peculiarly reflexive kind of writing that Friedrich Schlegel termed 'the poetry of poetry'.[93] I follow Hamilton in seeing this as a key feature of British as well as German Romanticism, and in appealing to the German parallel, with its fuller theoretical articulation, to help interpret the British situation. Like German writing of the period, the texts of British Romanticism tend to be either over- or underdetermined generically. Typically, they overstate, overperform, or protest too much about their generic affiliations, often by fusing genres and multiplying their generic identity in the manner of a Schlegelian *Mischgedicht*.[94] Or, alternatively, they subvert, ironize, or conceal their generic provenance, aspiring to transcend their chosen genre or delivering only a partial or marginal performance of it—a 'sketch' or 'fragment' of a generic whole no longer available or not yet in existence. At one extreme are ostentatiously heterogeneous works like Blake's *The Marriage of Heaven and Hell* (1790–3) and Thelwall's *The Peripatetic* (1793), which proclaim their generic complexity and promiscuous intertextuality through multiple subheadings, references, and footnotes. At another is Coleridge's 'Reflections on Entering into Active Life: A Poem which Affects Not to be Poetry' (1795), whose teasingly paradoxical subtitle illustrates what might be called the 'metageneric' element of metaromanticism—a writer's wrestle with the premises of his own genre. In the same way, such seemingly different poems as Wordsworth's 'Extempore Effusion upon the Death of James Hogg' (1835) and Shelley's fragmentary 'Satire upon Satire' (1820) are actually part of the same dialectic, the studied spontaneity of the one and the hypergeneric, self-cancelling irony of the other (accentuated by the literal cancellations in Shelley's manuscript[95]) both testifying to an aesthetic self-consciousness which foregrounds genre even as it attempts to dissolve it. In many cases, generic and anti-generic tendencies— the urge to form and to formlessness—coexist within the same text, another reason why Romantic works prove susceptible to such contradictory readings.

Such examples bring home the point—a key feature of the methodology used in this book—that genres cannot be studied in isolation. There are several reasons for this. The first is that genres grow out of one another, a new genre being always a reworking of old ones, and complex genres being built up out of simple ones. In Goethe's words, 'The study of forms is the study of transformations' (*Gestaltenlehre ist Verwandlungslehre*), an axiom that encapsulated the new science Goethe named 'morphology', but one that could also serve—and has done—as a motto for modern

---

[93] Paul Hamilton, *Metaromanticism: Aesthetics, Literature, Theory* (Chicago: University of Chicago Press, 2003), 2; Schlegel, *Athenaeum Fragments*, no. 238, in *Philosophical Fragments*, 51. For the 'metatheoretical' element in Romanticism, see also Leon Chai, *Romantic Theory: Forms of Reflexivity in the Revolutionary Era* (Baltimore: Johns Hopkins University Press, 2006).

[94] See Ch. 5 below.

[95] Steven E. Jones, 'Shelley's "Satire upon Satire": A Complete Transcription of the Text with Commentary', *Keats–Shelley Journal*, 37 (1988), 136–63.

genre criticism.[96] A second reason is that, as Ralph Cohen reminds us, 'a genre does not exist independently; it arises to compete or to contrast with other genres'.[97] The study of forms is thus also the study of counter-forms: Bakhtin's theory of the novel as poetry's dialogic 'Other' is a case in point,[98] and there are many other examples of what Claudio Guillén calls 'counter-genres', genres defined by their opposition to other genres (anti-pastoral, mock-epic, the anti-Petrarchan sonnet).[99] Thirdly, many—perhaps most—texts do not belong to a single genre: they inhabit several simultaneously, a point emphasized by structuralists and poststructuralists alike (this is the premiss of, for example, both Genette and Derrida in their otherwise antithetical approaches to genre[100]). These three basic axioms, now widely accepted by genre critics, have, I suggest, a particular relevance to the Romantic period, not only because this was the epoch that first articulated them. The very idea of Romanticism—an 'ism' deriving from 'romantic' deriving from 'romance'—is an embodiment of these principles, implying as it does a conception of genre that is morphological and 'transcendental'. To understand the transformational dynamic, the dialectic of archaism and innovation, and other genre-shaping forces in Romantic literary culture, we must therefore analyse the interaction of genres rather than constructing separate generic histories, and attempt to see the genre-system as a whole instead of confining attention to isolated parts of it.

It is also important to understand the history of the genre-system itself, particularly in the prior phase we now call 'neoclassicism'. Traditional literary histories posit a straightforward antithesis between neoclassical and Romantic values, and echo the Romantics' own polemics in interpreting Romanticism as a reaction against the rule-bound poetics of neoclassicism. That there were tensions between the mimetic theory of literature governing neoclassicism and the expressive theory underpinning Romanticism is undeniable, and ideas of spontaneity, originality, and organicism did indeed pose a radical challenge to the conceptual premises of neoclassical thought. Yet there were expressive theories of genre as well as mimetic ones, 'organic' models of genre as well as 'mechanical' ones, and accounts of genre that saw incremental change and variation, rather than standardization and stasis, as the constitutive principle of genre. Many of these originated in the eighteenth century, through the influence of critical trends such as primitivism, the theory of the sublime, and the new rhetoric of the Scottish Enlightenment. In my first chapter, I analyse some of these developments, showing how the original premises and categories of neoclassicism were modified in the light of the aesthetic theories of the Enlightenment, to produce the eclectic mixture of ancient and modern ideas found in works such as Hugh Blair's

---

[96] See Ch. 2 below, p. 78.

[97] Ralph Cohen, 'History and Genre', *Neohelicon*, 13/2 (1986), 87–105: 92.

[98] 'Discourse in the Novel' (1934–5), in *The Dialogic Imagination: Four Essays by M. M. Bakhtin*, ed. Michael Holquist, trans. Caryl Emerson and Michael Holquist (Austin: University of Texas Press, 1981).

[99] 'Genre and Countergenre: The Discovery of the Picaresque', in Claudio Guillén, *Literature as System: Essays Toward the Theory of Literary History* (Princeton: Princeton University Press, 1971). For other counter-genres, see Alastair Fowler, *Kinds of Literature: An Introduction to the Theory of Genres and Modes* (Oxford: Clarendon Press, 1982), 174–9.

[100] Genette, *The Architext: An Introduction* (1979), trans. Jane E. Lewin (Berkeley: University of California Press, 1992); Jacques Derrida, 'The Law of Genre' (1980), trans. Avital Ronell, in his *Acts of Literature*, ed. Derek Attridge (London: Routledge, 1992).

*Lectures on Rhetoric and Belles Lettres* (1783). It is this body of knowledge, rather the narrower doctrines of earlier neoclassical critics, which confronted Romantic writers when they turned to the subject of genre, and their polemics conceal significant continuities with these earlier positions.

My second chapter investigates genre theory of the 'high' Romantic period, exploring parallels between Britain and Germany, and taking Schlegel's *Dialogue on Poetry* as a paradigm of the wide-ranging debate on genre that took place in both countries. German influence on British thought is particularly evident in theories of organic form and in philosophical approaches to genre, but German ideas are themselves influenced by eighteenth-century British aesthetics, so a reciprocal comparativism is necessary here. One distinctive feature of the British Romantic debate on genre is the emphasis on political and sociological factors. A legacy in part of the Scottish Enlightenment, this interest in literary sociology was also shaped by the French Revolution controversy, one effect of which was to stimulate a profound rethinking of the functions and powers of literary forms. I trace the contours of this debate, taking the Preface to *Lyrical Ballads* as a focal point but exploring a range of other, less familiar texts, including writings by Joanna Baillie, John Thelwall, John Wolcot (Peter Pindar), and Isaac D'Israeli, all of whom made distinctive contributions to genre theory, either through criticism or through actual literary performance. Later parts of the chapter address the concept of form, connecting German theories of organic form with an earlier British 'language of forms' developed by Shaftesbury and others. My focus here is Coleridge, the leading British theoretician of poetic form, whose development of the organic paradigm produced not only the dazzling insights of the Shakespeare lectures, but also the neo-Kantian aesthetic system of the 'Essays on the Principles of Genial Criticism' (1814) and fresh accounts of many individual genres. I conclude with a discussion of Wordsworth's Preface to *Poems* (1815), a text which, together with other features of the 1815 edition, demonstrates in a peculiarly vivid way the opposing currents that characterize Romantic genre theory.

Subsequent chapters focus on particular areas of development and controversy. Traditional accounts of Romanticism posit a shift in the hierarchy of genres involving a devaluation of didactic poetry and a revaluation of lyric. The rejection of didacticism, typified by Keats's condemnation of poetry that 'has a palpable design on us',[101] is often held to be a defining feature of Romantic literature, and, at a theoretical level, to mark the hegemony of the newly formulated concept of the aesthetic. In Chapter 3, I question this argument, tracing the origins of the anti-didactic principle in eighteenth-century aesthetics but also revealing how Romantic writers make stronger claims than ever for the moral and political utility of literature, and for the role of the author as teacher, legislator, prophet, or healer. Notwithstanding the critical onslaught against the 'French school' of Dryden and Pope, the Romantic period witnessed its own fashion for what Joseph Warton called 'moralizing in verse',[102] and didactic genres such as the georgic and 'philosophical poem'

---

[101] To J. H. Reynolds, 3 Feb. 1818, in *The Letters of John Keats*, ed. Hyder E. Rollins, 2 vols (Cambridge, Mass.: Harvard University Press, 1958), i. 224.
[102] Joseph Warton, *Odes on Various Subjects* (London, 1746), advertisement.

enjoyed an unexpected and paradoxical revival. Analysing these trends, I show that didactic tendencies were also manifest in other genres, and that, when Romantic authors denounced didactic writing, they were not simply engaging in a quarrel with neoclassicism, but responding to tendencies within their own literary culture and, more often than not, within themselves. Again, there are significant parallels with Germany, where notions of disinterestedness and aesthetic autonomy are enriched and complicated by new ideas about 'aesthetic education'.

In Foucault's influential archaeology of knowledge, the advent of historicist thinking in the eighteenth century spelt the end of the classical *episteme* and the beginning of modernity.[103] Many have seen the demise of genre theory as part of this transformation—an abandonment of static classification and generality in favour of historical specificity and evolutionary change. Far from destroying the concept of genre, however, historicism made possible its further elaboration. There is no more typical product of Enlightenment thought than its grand critical narratives about the socio-historical 'progress' of literary genres, and its analogies between the evolution of 'species of composition' and of organic species (the overlap of terminology is not coincidental). History and classification, in other words, are not incompatible: a true theory of genre, as Marcus declares in Schlegel's *Dialogue on Poetry*, would consist of both.[104] In their adoption and elaboration of such theoretical or 'conjectural' histories of genre, the Romantics, both German and British, are direct heirs of the Enlightenment. Chapter 4 explores this legacy, taking the neoclassical 'Ancients and Moderns' dispute as a starting point, and tracing the emergence and eventual dominance of a historical and genealogical understanding of genre. I chart the shifting meaning of 'ancientness', and show how a new perception of the mutability and relativism of cultural forms revealed itself not only in literary criticism and editorial practice, but also in the way literary genres were actually deployed. Using Percy's *Reliques of Ancient English Poetry* (1765) as a touchstone of the ambivalent attitudes of the antiquarian movement, I analyse the tension between a desire to modernize genres and to convey (sometimes fraudulently) a sense of their antiquity. High Romanticism, with its politically inflected cult of innovation, represents a sharpening of this ambivalence, as the antiquarian desire to 'make it old' competes with a fresh aesthetic imperative to 'make it new'. The last part of the chapter discusses some of the strategies by which Romantic writers sought to meet these conflicting demands, and examines the dialectic of archaism and innovation that marks Romanticism's distinctive brand of generic revivalism.

My fifth and final chapter explores the phenomenon of genre-mixing, a pivotal concept in Romantic aesthetics and a recurrent feature of Romantic literary practice. As in other parts of the book, I take a broad view of this complex topic, recalling earlier phases in the history of genre-mixing, and moving between German and British sources. Despite resistance from neoclassical purists, critical tolerance of

---

[103] Michel Foucault, *The Order of Things: An Archaeology of the Human Sciences* (1966; New York: Vintage, 1973).

[104] Friedrich Schlegel, *Dialogue on Poetry and Literary Aphorisms*, trans. Ernst Behler and Roman Struc (University Park: Pennsylvania State University Press, 1968), 76.

genre-mixing dates back at least as far as Shaftesbury, and the Schlegelian idea of the *Mischgedicht*, or generically mixed work, is in part an elaboration of the Enlightenment concept of 'universal poetry', an idea also echoed in Shelley's theory of the 'great poem'. I explain what is distinctive about Romantic as opposed to earlier kinds of genre-mixing, and why 'the combinatorial method', as Friedrich Schlegel called it, acquired such importance in the Romantic period. Challenging previous accounts that focus exclusively on 'organic' models of combination, the chapter discusses two broad types of genre-mixing: what I call 'rough-mixing', where artistic effects are achieved by the clash of juxtaposed forms, and 'smooth-mixing', where forms and languages are seamlessly fused together. In Romantic-era criticism, the latter is often described in organic terms, whereas the former is captured by the metaphor of chemical combination, a metaphor as pervasive in Romantic discourse as the more familiar biological analogies. The chapter concludes with a discussion of how theory and practice combine in the work of Shelley, by setting the combinatorial poetics of *A Defence of Poetry* against his most audacious experiment in generic mixture, *Prometheus Unbound*.

As these introductory remarks suggest, the primary aim of this book is not to study the development of individual genres but to investigate broader patterns in the genre theory and practice of the Romantic period. By way of conclusion, however, I end with a brief case study of the ode, whose remarkable development in this period focuses many of the concerns I have raised. One of the oldest and most conventionalized of genres, the ode also became the site of frenzied innovation and experiment, pressing at one moment towards internalization and self-reflexivity, at another towards an enhancement of its public, ideological function. More paradoxically still, this period witnessed the genre's greatest flowering but also its incipient demise—the ode being at once the beneficiary and the victim of a series of transformations that radically altered the landscape of poetry in general. Attending to these paradoxes will return us, in the final pages of the book, to the question of the dissolution of genres, and to the anti-generic strain in Romanticism. My interest here, though, is in the afterlife of genre: the continued presence of a genre in diminished or displaced forms, including the displaced form of genre theory itself. While exceptional in certain respects, the ode, I argue, is typical in others, and its complicated trajectory in this period is a paradigm of the generic currents and counter-currents that are the subject of this book.

# 1

# The Old Imperial Code

In this age of enlightened reason and discovery, when it is grown a kind of literary pastime to attack every establishment, and when the old fabrics of reason and experience are often exposed to the wanton assaults of genius.—It is but natural, that the old imperial code of criticism should begin to lose some of its authority.

(Henry Boyd, 'A Comparative View of the Inferno', 1785)

## THE DISORDER OF THINGS

In 1789 the London publisher John Bell issued the first ten volumes of an elegant anthology entitled *Bell's Classical Arrangement of Fugitive Poetry*. Projected to run to twenty-five volumes, each costing three shillings, the series was intended to repeat the success of Bell's earlier collections, *The Poets of Great Britain* (109 volumes, 1777–82) and *Bell's British Theatre* (21 volumes, 1776–8), both of which had sold in large numbers and established Bell as a major force in the flourishing anthology market opened up by the ending of perpetual copyright in 1774.[1] Bell had advertised his *Poets of Great Britain* as 'an edition superior in beauty, purity, and convenience, to all preceding publications',[2] and he employs a similar formula for the new collection: a standard format and layout, a modern typeface, good-quality paper, attractive illustrations (an optional extra, for sixpence a volume), and simple but effective branding techniques such as the use of his own name in the title. The royal patent that Bell had acquired in 1788 is also put to good use, the title page of each volume displaying both the name of his bookshop, the impressive-sounding 'British Library, Strand', and his new appointment: 'Bookseller to his Royal Highness the Prince of Wales'.

Unlike his *Poets of Great Britain*, which had begun with Chaucer and ended with Churchill, the new collection consisted almost exclusively of eighteenth-century verse, and placed comparatively unknown authors alongside canonical ones. As an advertisement which appeared the following year in another Bell publication

---

[1] For the dramatic effects of the 1774 decision on the reprint trade, see William St Clair, *The Reading Nation in the Romantic Period* (Cambridge: Cambridge University Press, 2004), 111–39; and Thomas F. Bonnell, *The Most Disreputable Trade: Publishing the Classics of English Poetry 1765–1810* (Oxford: Oxford University Press, 2008), ch. 4.

[2] Quoted by John Brewer, *The Pleasures of the Imagination: English Culture in the Eighteenth Century* (New York: Farrar Strauss Giroux, 1997), 483.

acknowledges (Figure 1.1), many of the poems in the *Classical Arrangement of Fugitive Poetry* are reprinted from previous compilations such as those of Robert Dodsley, George Pearch, and John Almon. 'Fugitive' in this context means uncollected or ephemeral, the purpose of such anthologies, the vogue for which had been established by Dodsley in the 1740s,[3] being to rescue from oblivion poems that had originally appeared in periodicals, circulated in manuscript, or otherwise eluded regular publication—hence the title of Almon's anthology *An Asylum for Fugitive Pieces* (1785), a follow-up to his popular *The New Foundling Hospital for Wit* (1768–73). Where previous miscellanies, though, had emphasized the heterogeneity of their contents by printing the poems in random order, randomness itself being part of the appeal, Bell adopts the opposite policy, grouping the poems by genre or subgenre, and devoting a volume to each. The first seven volumes contain epistles (subdivided into 'Ethic Epistles', 'Epistles Familiar and Humorous', 'Epistles Critical and Didactic', 'Epistles Descriptive and Narrative', 'Epistles Satirical and Preceptive', and 'Epistles Heroic and Amatory'); the eighth and ninth, elegies ('Elegies Moral, Descriptive and Amatory' and 'Elegies Local, Sympathetic and Funeral; and Monodies'); the tenth, 'Poems in the Stanza of Spenser'; and the eleventh, 'Poems Imitative of Spenser, and in the Manner of Milton'. The remaining volumes are devoted to odes.

This is the 'classical arrangement' of Bell's title, 'classical' not only because the poems mostly conform to approved Greek or Roman models but also because they are arranged by genre, or 'class',[4] a time-honoured method dating back to classical antiquity. By foregrounding the organization of the collection in this way, Bell, with his customary shrewdness, manages not only to differentiate his anthology from its precursors and competitors, but also to combine the attractive unpredictability of a modern miscellany with the reassuring orderliness of the traditional genre-system. It was a combination calculated to appeal to conservative poetry readers of the 1780s and 1790s, who wanted their 'fugitive verse' in something more durable than a magazine and less chaotic than a miscellany, and would have welcomed the flattering suggestion that modern British poetry, even of the 'fugitive' variety, could still conform to 'classical' standards and possess a canon of its own.

In the event, the series failed, and publication was suspended after eighteen volumes, the last appearing in 1797. The immediate reason was Bell's bankruptcy in 1795, which Leigh Hunt later attributed to the expense of hosting a lavish party for Bell's patron, the Prince of Wales, but which probably had more to do with a libel action and financial over-commitment in Bell's rapidly expanding publishing

---

[3] Michael F. Suarez, 'Poetic Miscellanies', in Isabel Rivers (ed.), *Books and their Readers in Eighteenth-Century England: New Essays* (Leicester: Leicester University Press, 2001).

[4] This double meaning of 'classical', honorific and taxonomic, is illustrated by other poetry collections such as William Mavor and Samuel Pratt (eds), *Classical English Poetry, for the Use of Schools, and of Young Persons in General. Selected from the Works of the Most Favourite of our National Poets, with Some Original Pieces* (London, 1801); and John Pennie (ed.), *The Harp of Parnassus: A New Selection of Classical English Poetry, including Several Original Pieces never before Published. Designed for Schools and Young Readers in General* (London, 1822). The latter is organized by genre; the former contains a long introduction describing each of the principal ('classical') genres.

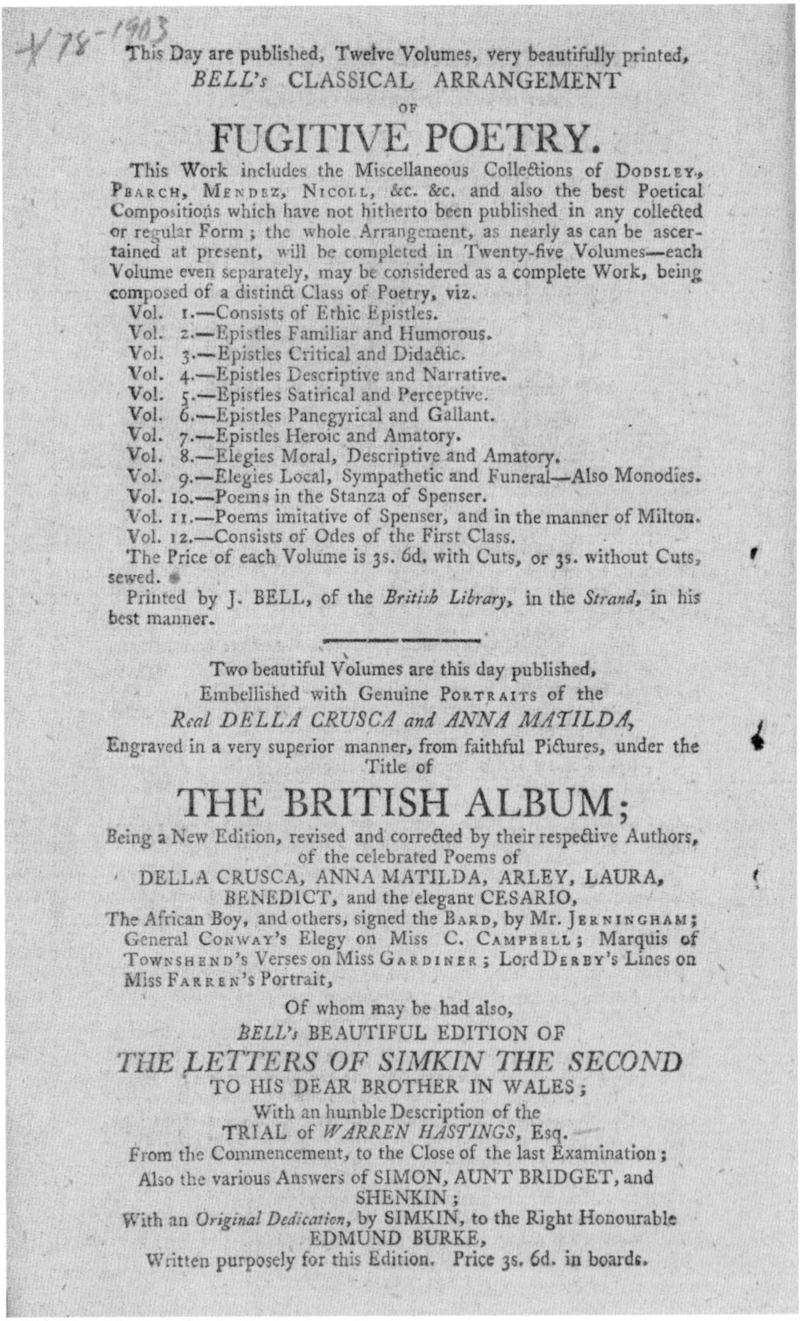

⅟ 78‑1903

This Day are published, Twelve Volumes, very beautifully printed,
*BELL's* CLASSICAL ARRANGEMENT
OF

# FUGITIVE POETRY.

This Work includes the Miscellaneous Collections of DODSLEY, PEARCH, MENDEZ, NICOLL, &c. &c. and also the best Poetical Compositions which have not hitherto been published in any collected or regular Form ; the whole Arrangement, as nearly as can be ascertained at present, will be completed in Twenty-five Volumes—each Volume even separately, may be considered as a complete Work, being composed of a distinct Class of Poetry, viz.

Vol. 1.—Consists of Ethic Epistles.
Vol. 2.—Epistles Familiar and Humorous.
Vol. 3.—Epistles Critical and Didactic.
Vol. 4.—Epistles Descriptive and Narrative.
Vol. 5.—Epistles Satirical and Perceptive.
Vol. 6.—Epistles Panegyrical and Gallant.
Vol. 7.—Epistles Heroic and Amatory.
Vol. 8.—Elegies Moral, Descriptive and Amatory.
Vol. 9.—Elegies Local, Sympathetic and Funeral—Also Monodies.
Vol. 10.—Poems in the Stanza of Spenser.
Vol. 11.—Poems imitative of Spenser, and in the manner of Milton.
Vol. 12.—Consists of Odes of the First Class.

The Price of each Volume is 3s. 6d. with Cuts, or 3s. without Cuts, sewed.

Printed by J. BELL, of the *British Library*, in the *Strand*, in his best manner.

———————

Two beautiful Volumes are this day published,
Embellished with Genuine PORTRAITS of the
*Real DELLA CRUSCA and ANNA MATILDA,*
Engraved in a very superior manner, from faithful Pictures, under the
Title of

# THE BRITISH ALBUM;

Being a New Edition, revised and corrected by their respective Authors,
of the celebrated Poems of
DELLA CRUSCA, ANNA MATILDA, ARLEY, LAURA,
BENEDICT, and the elegant CESARIO,
The African Boy, and others, signed the BARD, by Mr. JERNINGHAM;
General CONWAY's Elegy on Miss C. CAMPBELL; Marquis of
TOWNSHEND's Verses on Miss GARDINER; Lord DERBY's Lines on
Miss FARREN's Portrait,

Of whom may be had also,
*BELL's* BEAUTIFUL EDITION OF
*THE LETTERS OF SIMKIN THE SECOND*
TO HIS DEAR BROTHER IN WALES;
With an humble Description of the
TRIAL of *WARREN HASTINGS*, Esq.
From the Commencement, to the Close of the last Examination;
Also the various Answers of SIMON, AUNT BRIDGET, and
SHENKIN;
With an *Original Dedication*, by SIMKIN, to the Right Honourable
EDMUND BURKE,
Written purposely for this Edition. Price 3s. 6d. in boards.

**Figure 1.1.** Advertisement for *Bell's Classical Arrangement of Fugitive Poetry* in a John Bell marketing pamphlet (1790?)

empire.[5] Bell soon re-established himself, but in the meantime sold off this and other titles to his rival George Cawthorn, who proceeded to publish the seventeenth and eighteenth volumes, dropping Bell's name from the title and issuing cancel title pages for the preceding volumes—but then promptly discontinued the series. No explanation was given, and the decision may have been a commercial one—poor sales—or the lack of a competent editor to complete the series.

Yet there are also intellectual reasons why the *Classical Arrangement* ran into difficulties. In one sense, the whole project was based on a contradiction: the idea of classifying and canonizing the inherently unplaceable and ephemeral ('fugitive verse'). The title itself verges on paradox.[6] There are problems too with Bell's classification scheme, for the simple reason that many of the poems do not fit his chosen categories, or fit several of them simultaneously. Despite appearances, his 'classical arrangement' thus often ends up being as arbitrary as the random ordering of other miscellanies. For instance, the very first poem in the collection, Soame Jenyns's 'Essay on Virtue', opens a volume entitled 'Ethic Epistles', but could equally well have appeared among the 'Didactic Epistles' of volume iii, the 'Preceptive Epistles' of volume v, or the 'Moral Elegies' of volume viii, the distinction between epistle and elegy being largely illusory, and the subcategories of these genres overlapping so considerably as to dissolve any meaningful distinction between them (since there are 'descriptive' elegies which are also 'local', 'moral' elegies which are also 'funereal', and—one would hope—'amatory' elegies which are also 'sympathetic').

The taxonomic problems multiply when it comes to the ode, because of both the sheer number of poems that purport to belong to this category and the bewildering variety of topics on which they had been written. No fewer than seven volumes are devoted to the genre, possibly with more to come had the series continued. To preserve the symmetry of his scheme, each required a different generic label, so Bell, evidently lacking sufficient subcategories,[7] resorts to a purely numerical classification, entitling volume xii 'Odes, Class the First', volume xiii 'Odes, First, Second and Third Class', and so on up to 'Class the Tenth' in volume xviii. The logic of some of the groupings is relatively clear—odes of the first class are all addressed to personified abstractions like 'Ambition', 'Liberty', and 'Melancholy'; the seventh class covers military subjects; the ninth consists of St Cecilia's Day odes—but in others the connections are much more tenuous, and Bell provides no key to explain his thematic numbering system. Volumes x and xi, meanwhile, break the scheme entirely

---

[5] Stanley Morison, *John Bell, 1745–1831* (Cambridge: privately printed, 1930), 31–41. The Prince Regent story is mentioned in Leigh Hunt's *Autobiography* (1850).

[6] 'Classical' and 'fugitive' were sometimes paired terms, implying canonical and uncanonical respectively, as in the title of another anthology, *Flowers of British Poetry: Consisting of Fugitive and Classical Pieces of the Best Poets of Great Britain* (Newcastle upon Tyne, 1802).

[7] Neoclassical critics distinguished between the 'greater' (Pindaric) ode and the 'lesser' (Horatian) ode, sometimes recognizing the Anacreontic as a third type. Increasingly, these formal distinctions were subsumed in thematic categories, as in Hugh Blair's fourfold classification: sacred odes, heroic odes, moral and philosophical odes, festive and amorous odes (*Lectures on Rhetoric and Belles Lettres*, 2 vols (London, 1783), ii. 355). Bell's scheme required further subdivisions but lacked appropriate terminology.

by adopting the manifestly non-classical categories of 'Poems in the Stanza of Spenser' and 'Poems Imitative of Spenser, and in the Manner of Milton'. These include poetic forms otherwise missing from Bell's scheme, such as 'progress' poems, 'hymns', and 'visions'. Nowhere in the collection, however, does Bell make space for the types of 'fugitive' poem that by the 1780s and 1790s actually dominated the reviews, magazines, and newspapers, namely 'effusions', 'sketches', 'sonnets', 'anecdotes', 'ballads', and other lyric or narrative forms, many of recent invention.

The fate of Bell's anthology symbolizes the predicament this chapter will explore. In planning a selection of modern poetry along 'classical' lines, Bell demonstrated the continuing hold of traditional principles: the persistence of classical genres and labels, and the cultural prestige still associated with them. In attempting to execute that plan, however, he encountered a problem which faced many writers, editors, and publishers at the end of the eighteenth century, namely that the classical genre-system, even with all the adjustments and refinements introduced by neoclassical critics, could no longer provide an adequate map of the modern literary terrain. Classical genres and labels continued to be used, but what those terms and categories implied often bore little resemblance to their original meaning, and more and more works of literature bypassed them altogether.

The sense that the traditional classifications and methods of criticism were breaking down was frequently voiced. Henry Boyd's claim, quoted in my epigraph, that the 'old imperial code of criticism'—the neo-Aristotelian system that had dominated literary criticism since the Renaissance—was losing its intellectual authority[8] was echoed by many others. The Scottish critic John Pinkerton concluded the third of his *Letters of Literature* (1785) with the observation that Le Bossu 'and the other French critics, whom Addison followed with blind adoration, cannot be held in too sovereign contempt'.[9] George Dyer, a minor poet and Cambridge academic, remarked in his *Poetics* (1812) that just as 'the philosophy of Aristotle, to which Europe had been so long devoted, was found, at length, erroneous, and was superseded by another philosophy', so neither can 'his *Art of Poetry*, nor any Art of Poetry, be looked to as an infallible and complete dictator'.[10] Even the Poet Laureate, Henry James Pye, a staunch traditionalist who composed a fresh translation of Aristotle's *Poetics* in a bid to ensure its continued currency, conceded in 1792 that the master's influence was on the wane: 'The age of blind veneration is now over, and Aristotle, like other writers, can only be estimated by his merit.'[11]

By the turn of the century, a new theory of poetry had emerged that appeared to encapsulate the rejection of classical authority, and to advocate ways of writing and

---

[8] Henry Boyd, 'A Comparative View of the Inferno', in *A Translation of the Inferno of Dante Alighieri, in English Verse: With Historical Notes, and the Life of Dante*, 2 vols (London, 1785), i. 25–6.

[9] [John Pinkerton], *Letters of Literature. By Robert Heron* (London, 1785), 19–20.

[10] 'On Poetical Genius, and its Subjection to Rules', in George Dyer, *Poetics, or, A Series of Poems and Disquisitions on Poetry*, 2 vols (London, 1812), ii. 31.

[11] Henry James Pye, *A Commentary Illustrating the Poetic of Aristotle, by Examples Taken Chiefly from the Modern Poets. To which is Prefixed a New and Corrected Edition of the Translation of the Poetic* (London, 1792), xiii. Pye was Laureate from 1790 to 1813.

judging poetry so different from what had gone before as to inspire talk of a 'revolution in literature'. The 'new school' of poetry, together with its critical manifesto, the Preface to *Lyrical Ballads* (1800), had, in the eyes of many, rendered obsolete at a stroke the entire edifice of classical genre theory, and put an end to what Henry Fuseli sneeringly called 'the epoch of rules'.[12] 'Nothing that was established was to be tolerated', declared Hazlitt in a famous passage of his *Lectures on the English Poets* (1818):

All the common-place figures of poetry, tropes, allegories, personifications, with the whole heathen mythology, were instantly discarded; a classical allusion was considered as a piece of antiquated foppery; capital letters were no more allowed in print, than letters-patent of nobility were permitted in real life; kings and queens were dethroned from their rank and station in legitimate tragedy or epic poetry, as they were decapitated elsewhere; rhyme was looked upon as relic of the feudal system, and regular metre was abolished along with regular government.[13]

The idea that the new poetics had rejected not only traditional genre theory but genre itself receives ironic confirmation in an anonymous satire of 1814 entitled *Modern Parnassus, or, The New Art of Poetry, A Poem. Designed to Supersede the Rules of Aristotle, Horace, Longinus, Vida, Boileau, and Pope.* This versified critical treatise is both a mock-defence of what it calls the 'new poetical faith' preached in the Preface to *Lyrical Ballads* and a mock-polemic against the 'ancient critic code' represented by the roster of names in the title. Where previous Arts of Poetry had built themselves around the concept of genre, demarcating the different types of poetry and enumerating the rules that govern them, *Modern Parnassus* makes no mention of genre, except to condemn the formulaic 'epics, odes, and elegies' of poets who follow the rules but lack 'the true Promethean fire', and to show how, in the new poetical system, the poet can dance in and out of different verse forms on a line-by-line basis:

> Now in gay Lyrics trip, and now more slow,
> Linger in steps of Elegiac woe.
> Now in heroics sweep with grand array,
> And now in rapid Dactyls speed away.

In this 'golden age' of metrical spontaneity and abundance, forms can be mixed at will, and poetry is shaped by the expressive needs of the author rather than the external demands of the critic. The 'new charter' is one of total freedom:

> Our glorious day
> Grants ev'ry licence now, to ev'ry lay.
> Britons admit no rule, but their desire;
> They brook no slav'ry, even in the lyre.
> Free as the mountain breeze their numbers flow,
> And nor in word nor thought a barrier know.

---

[12] 'Aphorisms, Chiefly Relative to the Fine Arts', no. 110, in *The Life and Writings of Henry Fuseli*, ed. John Knowles, 3 vols (London, 1831), iii. 103.

[13] 'On the Living Poets', *Lectures on the English Poets* (1818), in *The Complete Works of William Hazlitt*, ed. P. P. Howe, 21 vols (London: Dent, 1930–4), v. 161–2.

> Above all law, the Muse of modern song,
> By high prerogative, can do no wrong.

The reader, too, can share this liberation: 'Bound by no rules, the courteous reader now | Is pleas'd, he knows not why, and cares not how.'

For all its pretended enthusiasm, the aim of the satire is to reveal the spuriousness of the 'new charter' by showing that total 'poetic licence' leads only to mediocrity. The difference between the 'modern' Mount Parnassus and the ancient one is that poets are content to stop halfway up it, lacking artistic ambition and revelling in their own mediocrity. Demand for poetry is greater than ever, but, far from being a sign of cultural revival, this has meant a massive drop in standards, of which both writers and readers are blissfully unaware: 'the Muse's is a thriving trade', and the 'ample profits of the well paid line' (a footnote spells out the current price—half a crown per line) are so tempting as to make quantity and speed of composition the only considerations. Hard-won artistic skill no longer matters, for 'What care the public for such needless pains? | They love alike our rough or finish'd strains.'

Confirmation that mediocrity was now an acceptable, even fashionable, poetic stance is provided by the many poetry collections of the time carrying titles like *Parnassian Trifles, Parnassian Bagatelles, A Juvenile Tour on the Borders of Parnassus, Poetical Essays, or, Short Flights Towards Parnassus*, and *Poetical Pastimes, or, Gambols Round the Base of Parnassus*, the last of which, a collection of *bouts rimés* and 'other light poetical effusions' by members of 'the Musomanick Society of Anstruther', is introduced as the work of writers content to 'flutter' like butterflies 'round the lowly heather at the foot of the Hill of Song'.[14] To these playful reworkings of the Parnassus motif must be added the dozens of other volumes of poetry describing themselves as *Poetical Attempts, Poetical Essays, Poetical Amusements*, or *Poetical Trifles*, or using some other version of the so-called 'modesty trope'—which might more properly be termed the mediocrity trope. This fashion, however, pre-dated *Lyrical Ballads*, a book which was expressly designed to counter the taste for vapid, unambitious poetry— but which clearly did not succeed in extinguishing it. The fact that the 1800 Preface had itself made identical objections to overproduction and degraded standards in the modern literary market is a measure of how complete a travesty *Modern Parnassus* is of Wordsworth's position.

The claim that the new poetics established its legitimacy by 'exploding' earlier systems is also, at best, a half-truth. The temptation for Romantic writers to think of neoclassical poetics as an *ancien régime* to their 'revolutionary poetical system',[15] and

---

[14] John C. Cross, *Parnassian Trifles: Being a Collection of Elegiac, Pastoral, Nautic, and Lyric Poetry* (London, 1792); id., *Parnassian Bagatelles: Being a Miscellaneous Collection of Poetical Attempts* (London, 1796); anon., *A Juvenile Tour on the Borders of Parnassus: By the Author of 'Christian Reflections on Moral & Sacred Subjects, in Prose and Verse'* (Bristol, 1796); J. Collett, *Poetical Essays, or, Short Flights Towards Parnassus* (Coventry, 1795); anon., *Poetical Pastimes, or, Gambols Round the Base of Parnassus* (Edinburgh, 1814), p. ix.

[15] Byron's (pejorative) phrase, in a letter to John Murray, 15 Sept. 1817, in *Byron's Letters and Journals*, ed. Leslie A. Marchand, 12 vols (London: John Murray, 1973–82), v. 265. For the context of this remark, see Hermann Fischer, 'Byron's "Wrong Revolutionary Poetical System"', in Andrew Rutherford (ed.), *Byron: Augustan and Romantic* (Basingstoke: Macmillan, 1990).

of 'the old imperial code'—with its hierarchical genre-system and armoury of generic rules—as a repressive critical ideology from which modern literature had emancipated itself, often proved irresistible; and there were few Romantic writers who did not subscribe, in part at least, to this sharply polarized view of literary history. The disagreements are real enough and the reorientation of critical attitudes sufficiently radical and far-reaching to make terms like 'revolution' and 'paradigm shift' appropriate.

These polemics, however, conceal important continuities. In the Romantic period, neoclassical and anti-classical ideas coexist: however obsolete the 'ancient critic code' seemed to supporters of the 'new poetical faith', there were still many critics willing to defend it, and it was not until the late 1820s or 1830s that the 'new charter' achieved any degree of orthodoxy. Neoclassicism itself, moreover, was by no means the static, inflexible code implied in Romantic polemic. During the eighteenth century, the neoclassical paradigm had been modified in significant ways, in response to new critical trends such as primitivism, sensibility, the aesthetics of the sublime, and various kinds of literary historicism. The received wisdom that the Romantics confronted was thus not, as their polemics suggest, the narrow, rigid doctrines propounded by Restoration critics like Thomas Rymer, a follower of French neoclassical theory, but the much more eclectic body of ideas found in Scottish Enlightenment treatises such as Hugh Blair's *Lectures on Rhetoric and Belles Lettres* (1783). Blair's *Lectures*, an ambitious synthesis of ancient and modern theories of literature, is a typical example of late eighteenth-century, modified neoclassicism, and the fact that it remained a standard university textbook until well into the nineteenth century demonstrates the resilience of the neoclassical paradigm, notwithstanding the radically different kinds of genre theory that emerged during the same period.

In this chapter, I chart the different phases of neoclassicism, and the shifting reactions to it. The first section focuses on 'high' neoclassicism, examining both its conceptual premises and the various cultural functions it serves. In the second section, I discuss critical resistance to the doctrine of 'rules', notably in the mid-eighteenth-century cult of genius and originality. The antinomian strain in Romantic poetics is a direct continuation of these critiques. My third section explores Enlightenment modifications of the neoclassical paradigm, analysing some of the intellectual currents that drive those changes. I conclude with a brief glance at an anthology of modern poetry from 1831 which reveals how critical assumptions had shifted in the turbulent years since *Bell's Classical Arrangement*—a subject to which later parts of this book will return.

## THE NEOCLASSICAL GENRE-SYSTEM

The basic premises of neoclassical genre theory can be briefly stated. A genre is a 'species of composition' (other common terms are 'kind', 'order', 'class') defined by subject matter, form, and/or purpose. There are a finite number of genres, each of which has its own 'laws' or 'rules', adherence to which is necessary for a successful performance of that genre. The rules specify permissible subject matter, external form (including metre), and type of language. These features must be internally consistent, in accordance with the principle of decorum, or 'propriety', which states that the elements of a work must match one another and fit the intended purpose of that type of writing. The rules, codified by critics, are derived from the practice of specified authors (usually ancient Greek and Roman) whose achievements are regarded as an ideal standard against which subsequent performances in that genre are measured. Genres are separate entities which should not be mixed except in special cases (or not at all, in strictest versions of the theory). All literature is an 'imitation' of nature, each genre representing its own portion of nature (a 'partition-ing of mimesis', in Emerson Marks's phrase[16]) in compliance with prescribed norms of probability.[17] The genres are hierarchically ranked, a genre's status reflecting the social class of the characters represented, the seriousness of the subject matter, and the scale and complexity of the form.

The origins of this theory lie in sixteenth-century Italian commentaries on Aristotle's newly discovered *Poetics*, and in literary criticism inspired by Aristotle's analytic method.[18] Aristotelian precepts, reinterpreted by Italian critics, and applied by extrapolation to genres left untreated in the surviving part of the *Poetics*, were combined with ideas from Horace, Cicero, Quintilian, Demetrius, Dionysus of Halicarnassus, and other classical authors to create a comprehensive genre theory and classification system, exemplified by J. C. Scaliger's masterwork *Poetices Libri Septem* (1561).[19] The new theory was then exported to other European countries, each of which produced its own version, modifying or supplementing the Italian original. The ideas were taken up with particular enthusiasm in France, which produced a formidable corpus of neoclassical theory, particularly in relation to drama, and generated what is still regarded as the definitive expression of neoclassical doctrine, Boileau's *Art poétique* (1674).[20] Loosely modelled on Horace's *Ars Poetica*, Boileau's poetic treatise was described by a later French critic, Jean-François de La

---

[16] Emerson R. Marks, *The Poetics of Reason: English Neoclassical Criticism* (New York: Random House, 1968), 92.

[17] Douglas Lane Patey, *Probability and Literary Form: Philosophic Theory and Literary Practice in the Augustan Age* (Cambridge: Cambridge University Press, 1984).

[18] Daniel Javitch, 'The Emergence of Poetic Genre Theory in the Sixteenth Century', *Modern Language Quarterly*, 59/2 (1998), 139–69; id., 'The Assimilation of Aristotle's *Poetics* in Sixteenth-Century Italy', in Glyn P. Norton (ed.), *The Cambridge History of Literary Criticism*, iii: *The Renaissance* (Cambridge: Cambridge University Press, 1999). For the broader context, see Bernard Weinberg, *A History of Literary Criticism in the Italian Renaissance*, 2 vols (Chicago: University of Chicago Press, 1961); and Paul Oskar Kristeller, 'The Modern System of the Arts' (1951), in his *Renaissance Thought and the Arts: Collected Essays* (Princeton: Princeton University Press, 1965).

[19] Rosalie L. Colie, *The Resources of Kind: Genre-Theory in the Renaissance*, ed. Barbara K. Lewalski (Berkeley: University of California Press, 1973), ch. 1. For classical genre-systems, a much-disputed topic, see James J. Donohue, *The Theory of Literary Kinds*, 2 vols (Dubuque, Iowa: Loras College Press, 1943–9); Thomas G. Rosenmeyer, 'Ancient Literary Genres: A Mirage' (1985), in Andrew Laird (ed.), *Ancient Literary Criticism* (Oxford: Oxford University Press, 2006); and Joseph Farrell, 'Classical Genre in Theory and Practice', *New Literary History*, 34/3 (2003), 383–408.

[20] Gordon Pocock, *Boileau and the Nature of Neo-Classicism* (Cambridge: Cambridge University Press, 1980); René Bray, *La Formation de la doctrine classique en France* (Paris: Hachette, 1927).

Harpe, as 'a perfect legislation, whose application is found just in every case, an indefeasible code whose decision will serve for ever to distinguish what should be condemned and what should be applauded'.[21] Where Horace's original was a poet's handbook, Boileau's was both a working poetics and a treatise on critical method, a shift of emphasis that indicates the increasingly theoretical bent of neoclassicism. The equivalent text in Germany, Johann Christoph Gottsched's *Critical Poetics* (1730), is similarly rationalistic in tendency, containing a rule-bound system of composition and evaluation intended to put literary criticism on the same basis as other theoretical disciplines such as logic and metaphysics.[22]

The earliest phase of neoclassical criticism in England was, by contrast, practical in emphasis, and works such as Puttenham's *Art of English Poesy* (1589), Sidney's *Defence of Poesy* (1595), and Jonson's *Timber, or, Discoveries* (1640) were aimed primarily at fellow writers, though they also address contemporary debates about literary value and genre.[23] At this stage, professional criticism barely existed in England, the country being 'as free from Criticks, as it is from *Wolves*', as Thomas Rymer (himself the most vulpine of critics) later remarked.[24] After 1660 this situation changed, and a more theoretical, doctrinaire form of neoclassicism came into fashion, mainly through the influence of French critics like Boileau, Le Bossu, and Rapin, and their English translators and imitators, Rymer among them.[25] The strong French influence led to neoclassicism—both the system of criticism and the school of poetry it helped to foster—being retrospectively dubbed the 'French school', a term used pejoratively by the Romantics, who perceived neoclassicism as a foreign, colonizing influence that had pushed British literature off its natural course. This may also explain Boyd's phrase 'the old imperial code': the imperium in question is clearly France, and ultimately Augustan Rome, the culture on which both France and England in their high neoclassical phase had modelled themselves. British sensitivity to the foreignness of neoclassicism became even more marked after the French Revolution of 1789, when 'French theory' of all kinds came to seem suspect and threatening, despite the fact that neoclassicism was, in essence, an international code, the intellectual attraction of which lay precisely in its cosmopolitan character, its transcendence of national boundaries, and its ability to bridge the temporal gap between ancient and modern cultures.[26]

---

[21] Jean-François de La Harpe, *Lycée ou cours de littérature ancienne et moderne*, 18 vols (Paris, 1823), vii. 324, quoted by René Wellek, *A History of Modern Criticism*, i: *The Later Eighteenth Century* (New Haven: Yale University Press, 1955), 68.

[22] Klaus L. Berghahn, 'From Classicist to Classical Literary Criticism, 1730–1806', in Peter Uwe Hohendahl (ed.), *A History of German Literary Criticism, 1730–1980* (Lincoln: University of Nebraska Press, 1988), 29–38.

[23] Gavin Alexander (ed.), *Sidney's 'The Defence of Poesy' and Selected Renaissance Literary Criticism* (Harmondsworth: Penguin, 2004), introd.

[24] *Preface to Rapin* (1674), quoted by Douglas Lane Patey, 'The Institution of Criticism in the Eighteenth Century', in H. B. Nisbet and Claude Rawson (eds), *The Cambridge History of Literary Criticism*, iv: *The Eighteenth Century* (Cambridge: Cambridge University Press, 1997), 3.

[25] A. F. B. Clark, *Boileau and the French Classical Critics in England (1600–1830)* (1925; New York: Russell and Russell, 1965); James William Johnson, *The Formation of English Neo-Classical Thought* (Princeton: Princeton University Press, 1967).

[26] On British resistance to 'French theory' post-1789, see David Simpson, *Romanticism, Nationalism, and the Revolt against Theory* (Chicago: University of Chicago Press, 1993). On the

Broadly, what distinguishes neoclassical from classical (ancient Greek and Roman) genre theory is its more systematic quality; its strengthening of the hierarchical distinctions between genres; its modification of the concept of imitation, so that what is imitated is not nature per se but an idealized world, *la belle nature*; its aspiration to the status of science; and its intensification of the prescriptive character of genre criticism.[27] It is this last feature that proved most controversial and gave the neoclassical period its subsequent notoriety as the 'epoch of rules'. The concept of generic 'rules' was indeed central to neoclassical theory, much neoclassical criticism consisting of little other than a codification of the rules governing the various genres. The guiding rationale is succinctly stated in John Baillie's *Essay on the Sublime* (1747), which describes the task of criticism as being 'to define the *Limits* of each *Kind* of Writing, and to prescribe their proper *Distinctions*. Without this there can be no legitimate Performance, which is the just *Conformity* to the Laws or Rules of that Manner of Writing in which the Piece is design'd.'[28] Pursued exhaustively, this task of codification resulted in such compendiums of generic rules as Charles Gildon's *Complete Art of Poetry* (1718), which purports to contain, in Gildon's words, 'the several Rules of Excellence in every Kind of Poetry'.[29] In reality, it is less comprehensive than it claims: where Scaliger had defined more than a hundred genres, Gildon covers no more than seven or eight (albeit with subdivisions), a restriction of the generic canon which is also characteristic of this phase of neoclassicism.

Despite talk of limits, the concept of rules was not designed to 'clip the wings of poetry', as the Romantics alleged; nor was it an expression of blind obeisance to received wisdom. At an artistic level, what motivated the search for the laws governing genres was, on the contrary, the desire to improve and modernize poetry and to find a rational basis for criticism. In the famous quarrel of the Ancients and Moderns, it was the Moderns, not the Ancients, who were the strongest supporters of the rules. 'Poetry', writes John Dennis, one of the most fervent of the Moderns, 'is either an Art, or Whimsy and Fanaticism. If it is an Art, it follows that it must propose an End to itself, and afterwards lay down proper Means for the attaining that End: For this is undeniable, that there are proper Means for the attaining every End, and those proper Means in Poetry we call the Rules.'[30] It is for want of knowing the rules that 'Poetry is fallen so low', and 'it is the laying down of those Rules alone, that can re-establish it'. Just how seriously this idea was taken is demonstrated by the poet–physician Richard Blackmore, who attributed the failure of modern attempts at epic not to 'want of

French imperium and neoclassicism, see Pascale Casanova, *The World Republic of Letters* (1999), trans. M. B. Debevoise (Cambridge, Mass.: Harvard University Press, 2004), 67–73.

[27] Walter Jackson Bate, *From Classic to Romantic: Premises of Taste in Eighteenth-Century England* (New York: Harper, 1946), ch. 1: 'Classic and Neo-Classic'; René Wellek, 'The Term and Concept of Classicism in Literary History' (1965), in his *Discriminations: Further Concepts of Criticism* (New Haven: Yale University Press, 1970); R. S. Crane, 'English Neoclassical Criticism: An Outline Sketch', in Crane (ed.), *Critics and Criticism*.

[28] John Baillie, *An Essay on the Sublime* (London, 1747), 3.

[29] Charles Gildon, *The Complete Art of Poetry*, 2 vols (London, 1718), i. 148.

[30] *The Grounds of Criticism in Poetry* (1704), in *The Critical Works of John Dennis*, ed. E. N. Hooker, 2 vols (Baltimore: Johns Hopkins University Press, 1939–43), i. 335.

*Genius*' but to ignorance of 'those incomparable Rules',[31] and proceeded to write no fewer than six epic poems to illustrate the point—a tally rivalled only by Southey.

Apologists of all hues insisted on the rationalistic quality of the neoclassical enterprise, claiming that the rules were not the arbitrary dictates of critics but a logical inference from the best practice of writers. This is Rymer's argument in his *Preface to the Translation of Rapin's Reflections on Aristotle's Treatise of Poetry* (1674), where he describes Aristotle's methods as inductive and empirical, Aristotelian axioms and theories being 'as convincing and clear as any demonstration in *Mathematicks*' ('only needful that we understand them for our consent to the truth of them').[32] The analogy with mathematics, pervasive in literary criticism of this period, underlines that fact that what was driving neoclassical discourse was not only the wish to reestablish *poetry* as an *art* but also the desire to establish *criticism* as a *science*—one that would have something of the prestige of the master discipline of the Newtonian age, mathematics. Neoclassicism was, in this sense, a professedly modern enterprise, despite being founded on ideas from classical antiquity. Other areas of knowledge—the natural sciences, philosophy—had modernized themselves by rejecting Aristotelian dogma in favour of new theories and methods. Literary criticism had done the reverse: modernize itself by rediscovering Aristotle. Neoclassical genre theory had, as a result, a curiously paradoxical status, as both a modern and an ancient discourse, authority-bound and intellectually progressive at the same time.

A purely theoretical description, however, tells us little about the true nature of neoclassical thought and the cultural imperatives that underpinned it. Pascale Casanova in her ground-breaking work on the 'world republic of letters' has stressed the importance of the neoclassical ideal as a form of symbolic capital: a set of a literary and linguistic norms through which a modern nation could achieve cultural coherence and intellectual authority.[33] In Britain as well as France (her chief example), neoclassicism was both a system of legitimization and a badge of 'politeness'. Theories of genre were integral to this cultural project. The clearest articulation of its assumptions can be found in Joshua Reynolds's theory of painting, notably in his concept of the 'central form', which expressed an artist's ability (in John Barrell's words) 'to form and to recognize general ideas, by referring all the objects of a class to the essential character by which the class is constituted'.[34] To achieve 'generic' utterance, according to this view, was to demonstrate what David Hume called 'the standard of taste', and thereby secure membership of a civic community founded on ideals of representativeness and commonality.[35]

[31] Richard Blackmore, *Prince Arthur: An Heroick Poem in Ten Books* (London, 1695), preface, [p. ix].

[32] Thomas Rymer, *Preface to the Translation of Rapin's Reflections on Aristotle's Treatise of Poetry* (1674), in J. E. Spingarn (ed.), *Critical Essays of the Seventeenth Century*, 3 vols (Oxford: Clarendon Press, 1908–9), ii. 165.

[33] Casanova, *World Republic of Letters*, 69–70.

[34] John Barrell, *The Birth of Pandora and the Division of Knowledge* (Basingstoke: Macmillan, 1992), 46. For the concept of 'central form', see Joshua Reynolds, *Discourses on Art*, ed. Robert R. Wark, 2nd edn (New Haven: Yale University Press, 1975), 45 (discourse 3, 14 Dec. 1770).

[35] 'Of the Standard of Taste', in David Hume, *Four Dissertations* (London, 1757). For Hume's place in the culture of politeness, see Adam Potkay, *The Fate of Eloquence in the Age of Hume* (Ithaca, N.Y.: Cornell University Press, 1994), ch. 4.

The social and political implications are complex. The neoclassical hierarchy of genres mirrors the social hierarchy, reinforcing class divisions by segregating literary forms and specifying what could and could not be represented in each (the same word 'decorum' denotes both social and literary protocols). In one of its manifestations, neoclassical theory is unashamedly elitist, presenting both poetry and criticism as aristocratic endeavours. Charles Gildon's *The Laws of Poetry* (1721) encapsulates this assumption by bringing together the work of three members of the House of Lords, each of whom had written a critical treatise on poetry: the Duke of Buckingham's *Essay on Poetry*, the Earl of Roscommon's *Essay on Translated Verse*, and Lord Lansdowne's essay *On Unnatural Flights in Poetry* (Figure 1.2). This is less the republic of letters than an exclusive gentleman's club, implying a direct correlation between literary and social authority.[36] 'The reader', writes Gildon in his Preface, 'is here taught the necessary rules of poetry by persons of the highest dignity, breeding and fine sense', the implication being that poetry itself should be a repository of those qualities—and criticism likewise.[37]

Not all critics agreed, however. Many saw poetry as a meritocratic art, and 'the rules' not as exclusionary borders but as pathways by which any aspirant poet, whatever their background, could ascend the slopes of Parnassus—at least, the foothills thereof (the 'higher' genres were always reserved for the social elite). This view was encouraged by popular handbooks such as John Newbery's *The Art of Poetry Made Easy* (1746), which combined simplified accounts of the rules with copious practical examples of each genre. Newbery's guide was intended for use in schools, where composition of both Latin and English verse was a staple part of the curriculum.[38] Other handbooks were aimed at a broader, adult readership. *The Beauties of Poetry Display'd* (1757), for instance, is a 'reader's digest' version of more substantial Arts of Poetry: its prefatory section consists of extracts from well-known critics, each explicating a particular genre, while the main body of the work is a dictionary of poetic quotations, arranged alphabetically by theme. The existence of such self-help guides may assist in explaining the apparently paradoxical phenomenon of working-class writers without a formal education composing elegant poems in neoclassical genres—another significant trend in eighteenth-century publishing.[39]

---

[36] The political ramifications of this critical agenda are explained by David Womersley (ed.), *Augustan Critical Writing* (Harmondsworth: Penguin, 1997), introd.

[37] Charles Gildon (ed.), *The Laws of Poetry, as Laid Down by the Duke of Buckinghamshire in his Essay on Poetry, by the Earl of Roscommon in his Essay on Translated Verse, and by the Lord Lansdowne on Unnatural Flights in Poetry, Explain'd and Illustrated* (London, 1721), preface, [p. i].

[38] A. Dwight Culler, 'Edward Bysshe and the Poet's Handbook', *Publications of the Modern Language Association of America*, 63 (1948), 858–85; Ian Michael, *Literature in Schools: A Guide to the Early Sources 1700–1830* (Swansea: Textbook Colloquium, 1999).

[39] William J. Christmas, *The Lab'ring Muses: Work, Writing, and the Social Order in English Plebeian Poetry, 1730–1830* (Newark: University of Delaware Press, 2001); Donna Landry, *The Muses of Resistance: Laboring-Class Women's Poetry in Britain, 1739–1796* (Cambridge: Cambridge University Press, 1990); Bridget Keegan, *British Labouring-Class Nature Poetry, 1730–1837* (New York: Palgrave Macmillan, 2008). For primary sources, see John Goodridge et al. (eds), *Eighteenth-Century English Labouring-Class Poets*, 3 vols (London: Pickering and Chatto, 2003).

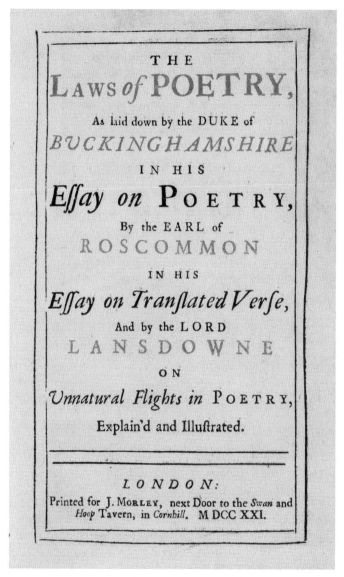

THE

L AWS *of* POETRY,

As laid down by the DUKE of

*BUCKINGHAMSHIRE*

IN HIS

*Essay on* POETRY,

By the EARL of

ROSCOMMON

IN HIS

*Essay on Translated Verse,*

And by the LORD

LANSDOWNE

ON

*Unnatural Flights in* POETRY,

Explain'd and Illustrated.

*LONDON:*

Printed for J. MORLEY, next Door to the *Swan* and *Hoop* Tavern, in *Cornhill*. M DCC XXI.

**Figure 1.2.** Title page to Charles Gildon's *The Laws of Poetry* (1721)

Other, deeper motivations may also be at work. In historical terms, the civilizing mission of neoclassical criticism, with its love of regularity and order, can be interpreted as a reaction to the chaos and fanaticism of the 1640s and 1650s, one consequence of which, in the eyes of post-Restoration writers, had been the subversion and misappropriation of traditional genres and the proliferation of new, unregulated genres like the newsbook.[40] As one recent commentator puts it, 'the classical was a kind of screen which the Augustans could place between themselves and the conceitful writing culture of the Civil War era',[41] a distancing act performed not only at a stylistic level—in the reform of poetic language and the cultivation of a harmonious realm of 'poetic diction' free from figurative excess—but also at the level of form. Restoring order to the republic of letters meant reforming its literary institutions, and the creation of a well-regulated genre-system—a canon of acceptable literary forms and rules for the proper conduct of each—was integral to that process.

Neoclassical genre theory was thus part of the 'political unconscious' of post-Restoration society:[42] an attempt to keep at bay traumatic cultural memories and defend against the threat of renewed disorder. The work of Dennis is again a good illustration. His almost messianic definition of the function of art—'to restore the Decays that happen'd to human Nature by the Fall, by restoring Order'—claims a theological rationale, but his emphasis on 'Order' suggests a social and political frame of reference: at some level, the 'Fall' is the catastrophe of the Civil War. The political connection becomes even clearer when he explains why it is that 'Poetry is fallen so low', and why the solution has to lie in strict literary decorum and generic regularity: 'for if the End of Poetry be to instruct and reform the World, that is, to bring Mankind from Irregularity, Extravagance, and Confusion, to Rule and Order, how this should be done by a thing that is in itself irregular and extravagant, is difficult to be conceiv'd'.[43] Such devotion to literary reason did not mean Dennis was averse to strong emotion in art. On the contrary, he was one of the architects of the eighteenth-century 'poetics of enthusiasm', and his view of poetry as an essentially emotive art later influenced Wordsworth. But emotion had to be regulated and kept in harmony with the other faculties of mind.[44] The function of poetic form was to achieve this harmonization, and Dennis's point is that the form itself must therefore be regular. By enforcing the rules, the neoclassical critic was thus not only preserving the health of individual genres, but also acting as a guardian of cultural order.

Another influential explanation for the poetics of 'correctness' is that it provided post-Restoration writers with a way of differentiating themselves from their Renaissance precursors and thereby escaping the sense of inferiority they felt when they measured their achievements against those of Shakespeare and his contemporaries. Such arguments are not new: Joseph Warton and others cite the famous remark of Pope, recorded in Spence's *Anecdotes*, in which Pope recalls the advice given to him by

[40] On the generic disruptions and innovations of the Civil War period, see Nigel Smith, *Literature and Revolution in England 1640–1660* (New Haven: Yale University Press, 1994).

[41] Blanford Parker, *The Triumph of Augustan Poetics: English Literary Culture from Butler to Johnson* (Cambridge: Cambridge University Press, 1998), 7.

[42] Fredric Jameson's phrase, in *The Political Unconscious: Narrative as a Socially Symbolic Act* (1981; London: Routledge, 1989).

[43] *Grounds of Criticism*, in *Critical Works*, i. 335–6.

[44] Shaun Irlam, *Elations: The Poetics of Enthusiasm in Eighteenth-Century Britain* (Stanford, Calif.: Stanford University Press, 1999), ch. 2; Jon Mee, *Romanticism, Enthusiasm and Regulation: Poetics and the Policing of Culture in the Romantic Period* (Oxford: Oxford University Press, 2003), 53–6.

his friend William Walsh 'that there was *one way left of excelling*; for though we had several great poets, we had never had any one great poet that was correct; and he desired me to make that my study and aim'.[45] The extent to which Pope heeded this advice in his own poetry is a matter for dispute, but 'correctness' is certainly the message he promulgated in his criticism, and Walter Jackson Bate plausibly interprets it as a defence mechanism: a means of negotiating an oppressively rich cultural heritage and finding new space in an overcrowded poetic tradition.[46] Warton draws a somewhat different conclusion, denouncing 'correctness', and the belief that Renaissance writers lacked it, as part of the 'nauseous cant of the French critics'.[47] Pope's mistake, according to Warton, was to fall for this cant, and to compromise his art by acting upon it—an assessment of Pope that, in turn, allows Warton to define yet another way forward for English poetry—namely, his own.

Polemics aside, it is clear that, far from being a monolithic abstraction, the neoclassical genre-system served a variety of cultural functions and a range of constituencies. For aspirant poets, it provided a convenient *gradus ad Parnassum*, breaking down a difficult art form into a series of manageable steps. For critics, it provided both a *raison d'être* and a *modus operandi*, engendering a new kind of corrective criticism which made critics (in their own minds at least) as indispensable as authors. For publishers and booksellers, it served as an effective labelling system and marketing device, ensuring that any literary product could, in principle, be generically categorized, packaged, and sold in a form that consumers could easily recognize. For librarians, it supplied a ready-made classification system, hierarchically organized into convenient overarching categories with well-defined subdivisions. For teachers, it was the perfect pedagogic tool around which to structure lectures, textbooks, and composition classes, as confirmed by the steady flow of anthologies and handbooks following some version of the 'classical arrangement'. And for ordinary readers, it offered a clear framework for the reading experience, telling them what type of material they were reading, what to expect from it, and what to say about it in their next visit to the coffee shop. The neoclassical genre-system, in other words, was not simply a set of critical theories but also a set of cultural practices deeply rooted in the society that produced it. Given this level of investment, it is not surprising that the apparent breakdown of the system at the end of eighteenth century seemed tantamount to a revolution.

## GENRE VERSUS GENIUS

The true character and timing of that revolution are not easy to define, however, and the evidence needs careful interpretation. In Romantic polemic, the neoclassical ascendancy was routinely depicted as an era of arid formalism in which a pedantic,

---

[45] Joseph Warton, *An Essay on the Genius and Writings of Pope* (London, 1756), 201.
[46] Walter Jackson Bate, *The Burden of the Past and the English Poet* (London: Chatto and Windus, 1971).
[47] *Essay on the Genius and Writings of Pope*, 202.

prescriptive criticism had produced a formulaic and unadventurous literature, and in which native originality had been displaced by the slavish imitation of Continental models. Critics like Dennis were seen as embodying all that was wrong with the 'French school', as is evident from the following critique of his work in the newly founded *Retrospective Review* (1820):

It is edifying to observe, how the canons of Mr. Dennis's criticism, which he regarded as the imperishable laws of genius, are now either exploded, or considered as matters of subordinate importance, wholly unaffecting the inward soul of poetry. No-one now regards the merits of an Epic poem, as decided by the subservience of the fable and action to the moral—by the presence or the absence of an allegory—by the fortunate or unfortunate fate of the hero—or by any other rules of artificial decorum, which the critics of former times thought fit to inculcate. We learn, from their essays, whether the works which they examine are constructed, in externals, according to certain fantastic rules; but, whether they are frigid or impassioned, harmonious or prosaic, filled with glorious imaginations, or replete with low common-places;—whether, in short, they are works of genius or mere toil—are questions entirely beneath their concern.[48]

The review strikes at the heart of neoclassical theory, or, rather, declares that it has no heart, its conception of literary form being purely 'external' and its measure of achievement—conformity to 'certain fantastic rules'—entirely arbitrary. About other neoclassical doctrines the Romantics were equally brutal. Of the theory of the dramatic unities Thomas Campbell states that the 'bare mention' of them 'is apt to excite revolting ideas of pedantry, arts of poetry, and French criticism', and he reassures purchasers of his *Specimens of the British Poets* (1819) that with none of these does he intend to 'annoy the reader'.[49] For Keats, both the French rule-makers and the English poets who obeyed them were equally blameworthy. He devotes twenty-five lines of his history of English verse in 'Sleep and Poetry' (1817) to an attack on the 'school | Of dolts' who 'blasphemed the bright Lyrist to his face' by

> Holding a poor, decrepit standard out
> Marked with most flimsy mottoes, and in large
> The name of one Boileau![50]

Like all self-serving polemics, however, Romantic constructions of neoclassicism distort a more complicated reality, concealing important continuities between neo-classical and Romantic thought, and obscuring the fact that by the turn of the century the 'old imperial code' had undergone extensive modernization. The *ancien régime* with whose dismantling Wordsworth was subsequently credited was therefore not the one he actually confronted. Nor was Wordsworth himself as hostile to neoclassical ideas as some of his disciples and detractors liked to think. He cites approvingly both Aristotle and Reynolds in the 1800 Preface, deeply admired the

[48] 'J. Dennis's Works, and the Nature and Effects of Modern Criticism', *Retrospective Review*, facs. repr., 18 vols (London: Pickering and Chatto, 1997), i/2 (1820), 309.
[49] Thomas Campbell (ed.), *Specimens of the British Poets: With Biographical and Critical Notices, and an Essay on English Poetry*, 7 vols (London, 1819), i. 151.
[50] John Keats, *The Complete Poems*, ed. John Barnard, 2nd edn (Harmondsworth: Penguin, 1997), 89–90 (lines 181–206).

ideas of Dennis, and made extensive, if idiosyncratic, use of neoclassical genre theory in the Preface to his 1815 *Poems*.[51]

These connections will be explored elsewhere in this book. In the remainder of the present chapter, I will define more precisely the modifications made to the neoclassical genre-system over the course of the eighteenth century. They can be summarized as follows: relaxation of generic rules; loosening of generic boundaries; acceptance of generic mixture; enlargement of the genre-spectrum; shifts in the hierarchy of genres; recognition of the historical variability of genres; and integration of literary genre theory into larger rhetorical or aesthetic systems. None of these changes was uncontested, and a purist stance, rejecting all such modifications, was still available throughout the period, and indeed into the nineteenth century. But the orthodoxy undoubtedly shifted, first towards a modified neoclassicism and then towards a poetics that retained the modifications but replaced the system itself.

As even the most cursory review of post-Restoration criticism reveals, opposition to 'the rules' was apparent from the start, and flexibility on this question was often seen as a defining feature of British, as distinct from French, neoclassicism. Dennis's belief that ignorance of generic rules had handicapped English poets was shared by some, but more inclined to the opposite view expressed by Leonard Welsted that most great authors had composed their works without the aid of rules, and that 'those writers have succeeded worst who have pretended to have been most assisted by them'.[52] Shaftesbury spoke for many when he declared in his *Characteristics* (1711) that 'we *Englishmen* are not ty'd up to such rigid Rules as those of the antient *Grecian*, or modern *French* Criticks'.[53] Addison took a similar position in his *Tatler* paper of 1710 on false criticism.[54] Even Pope, whose *Essay on Criticism* (1711) was regarded by the Romantics as epitomizing the spurious doctrines and defective verse of the 'French school' (De Quincey called it 'a metrical multiplication-table, of common places the most mouldy with which criticism has baited its rat-traps'[55]), wrote an anonymous article for *The Guardian* ironically undercutting the practice of judging authors by the pedantic application of narrowly interpreted rules.[56] By mid-century, Dr Johnson had published a sequence of *Rambler* essays reappraising the whole

[51] *The Prose Works of William Wordsworth*, ed. W. J. B. Owen and Jane Worthington Smyser, 3 vols (Oxford: Clarendon Press, 1974), i. 127, 156, 170–1, 183; for the 1815 Preface, see Ch. 2 below, pp. 89–94.

[52] Leonard Welsted, 'A Dissertation concerning the Perfection of the English Language, the State of Poetry, &c.' (1724), in Irène Simon (ed.), *Neo-Classical Criticism 1660–1800* (London: Arnold, 1971), 102. For earlier resistance to 'the rules', see Paul Spencer Wood, 'The Opposition to Neo-Classicism in England between 1660 and 1700', *Publications of the Modern Language Association of America*, 43 (1928), 182–97.

[53] Shaftesbury, *Characteristicks of Men, Manners, Opinions, Times*, 3 vols (London, 1711), iii. 276.

[54] *The Tatler*, ed. Donald F. Bond, 3 vols (Oxford: Clarendon Press, 1987), ii. 414–18 (no. 165, 29 Apr. 1710).

[55] Review of Schlosser's Literary History of the Eighteenth Century, *Tait's Edinburgh Magazine*, 14 (Sept.–Oct. 1847), in *The Works of Thomas De Quincey*, gen. ed. Grevel Lindop, 23 vols (London: Pickering and Chatto, 2000–3), xvi. 201.

[56] *The Guardian*, no. 40, 27 Apr. 1713, cited by James Basker, 'Criticism and the Rise of Periodical Literature', in Nisbet and Rawson (eds), *Cambridge History of Literary Criticism*, iv: *Eighteenth Century*, 321.

doctrine of rules by discriminating between those that are 'fundamental and indispensable' and those that are only 'useful and convenient', and—a more provocative distinction—between those that are 'dictated by reason and necessity' and those 'enacted by despotick antiquity'.[57]

British objections to excessively prescriptive rules reflect a long-standing respect for originality and a conception of poetry as an intrinsically transgressive medium. Sir William Temple's claim in his essay *Of Poetry* (1690) that 'there is something in the *Genius* of Poetry too Libertine to be confined by so many Rules; and whoever goes about to subject it to such Constraints loses both its Spirit and Grace'[58] typifies an antinomian strain in British literary criticism, fuelled in Temple's case by patrician disdain for commonplace rules. With the publication, half a century later, of works like Edward Young's *Conjectures on Original Composition* (1759), Alexander Gerard's *An Essay on Taste* (1759), and William Duff's *An Essay on Original Genius* (1767), this attitude intensified into a full-blown cult of genius which, in its extreme version, implied a straightforward antithesis of genre and genius, the true artist being one who transcends received ideas and forms. The German *Sturm und Drang* movement of the 1770s, with its glorification of the rebellious artist, was the fullest expression of this tendency, its critical programme being in part a radicalization of British theories of genius.[59] Johnson, writing somewhat earlier, took a more moderate line, arguing that rules exist to be broken, that actual literary texts belie the rigid separation of genres, and that writers frequently modify the genres they inhabit. 'There is', he writes, 'scarcely any species of writing, of which we can tell what is its essence, and what are its constituents; every new genius produces some innovation, which, when invented and approved, subverts the rules which the practice of foregoing authors had established.'[60]

Particular authors and genres were the focus of such counter-arguments. In their resistance to restrictive definitions, Johnson and Kames, like Addison before them, appealed to the example of Shakespeare, the supreme instance of the 'great natural Genius's that were never disciplined and broken by Rules of Art', and thus 'a Stumbling-block to the whole Tribe of these rigid Criticks'—that is, neoclassical purists.[61] Since Shakespeare was a 'genius' who used existing genres, but used them flexibly,

---

[57] *The Rambler*, no. 156, 14 Sept. 1751, quoted in the entry for 'Rules' in Joseph Epes Brown (ed.), *The Critical Opinions of Samuel Johnson* (1926; New York: Russell and Russell, 1961), 222. For Johnson's anti-dogmatic approach, see Jean Hagstrum, *Samuel Johnson's Literary Criticism* (Minneapolis: University of Minnesota Press, 1952).

[58] Temple, *Of Poetry* (1690), in J. E. Spingarn (ed.), *Critical Essays of the Seventeenth Century*, 3 vols (Oxford: Clarendon Press, 1908–9), iii. 83–4.

[59] John David Pizer, *The Historical Perspective in German Genre Theory: Its Development from Gottsched to Hegel* (Stuttgart: Hans-Dieter Heinz Akademischer Verlag, 1985), ch. 2. British influence on the *Sturm und Drang* is traced by M. H. Abrams, *The Mirror and the Lamp: Romantic Theory and the Critical Tradition* (New York: Oxford University Press, 1953), 201–2; and James Engell, *The Creative Imagination: Enlightenment to Romanticism* (Cambridge, Mass.: Harvard University Press, 1981), 80–114.

[60] *The Rambler*, no. 125, 28 May 1751, in Brown (ed.), *Critical Opinions of Johnson*, 222.

[61] Joseph Addison, *The Spectator*, ed. Donald F. Bond, 5 vols (Oxford: Clarendon Press, 1965), ii. 127 (no. 160, 3 Sept. 1711); v. 28 (no. 592, 10 Sept. 1714). Cf. Stanley Wells (ed.), *Shakespeare in the Eighteenth Century*, Shakespeare Survey, 51 (Cambridge: Cambridge University Press, 1998);

subversively, and in idiosyncratic combinations, his work posed the ultimate challenge for genre critics, and critical discussion of his plays elicited some of the period's most probing insights into the problem of genre. Though some accepted the 'French' verdict that Shakespeare's plays were seriously flawed by modern standards, and were even prepared to rewrite them to make them conform to neoclassical rules, others shared Pope's view that 'To judge . . . of *Shakespear* by *Aristotle's* rules is, like trying a man by the Laws of one Country, who acted under those of another'.[62] As will be seen in Chapter 4, it was critical analysis of Shakespeare's plays which helped to establish the distinction between 'ancient' and 'modern' versions of a genre, and to bring home the fact that modern writers use literary forms in different ways from their classical precursors. Equally, it was Shakespeare's virtuosic defiance of generic rules that raised most pertinently the question of which 'rules' were really necessary to the successful performance of a given genre. Certain rules—notably, the so-called dramatic 'unities'—lost their binding authority and were deemed by many to be inapplicable to modern, and certainly to British, writers. Generic rules as a whole came to be seen as culturally and historically relative rather than universal: that is, as conventions rather than regulations (the word 'convention' begins to enter the critical vocabulary at the end of the eighteenth century, gradually replacing the concept of 'rule'[63]).

Milton was a second crux: in this case, not a lawless creature of nature (as Shakespeare was alleged to be) but an author fully cognizant of classical theory and practice who was nonetheless willing to defy precedent and adapt genres to his own purposes. Milton's revolutionary treatment of epic in *Paradise Lost* was deemed especially controversial, since epic was not only the most prestigious of poetic genres—rivalled only by tragedy—but also the one that was most tightly regulated, the volume of critical commentary devoted to it exceeding that of any other genre.[64] As with Shakespeare, there were attempts to 'neoclassicize' Milton—Dryden's adaptation of *Paradise Lost* as a tragic opera called *The State of Innocence: And Fall of Man* (1677) is an example—but for the most part critics accepted his generic innovations and tried to make sense of them. Interpretation of Milton's work, as Donald Foerster notes, played a crucial role in the 'liberalization and extension of the whole concept of "epic"', a development that began in Addison's *Spectator* papers on the 'pleasures of the imagination' (1712) and later produced such revisionist accounts as William Hayley's *Essay on Epic Poetry* (1782), an important text for the Romantics.[65] The quotation

and Michael Dobson, *The Making of the National Poet: Shakespeare, Adaptation and Authorship, 1660–1769* (Oxford: Clarendon Press, 1992).

[62] Alexander Pope, Preface to *The Works of Shakespear* (1725), in Womersley (ed.), *Augustan Critical Writing*, 268. As Womersley notes (390 n.), the unfair-trial metaphor was a commonplace of eighteenth-century criticism, often applied to other authors besides Shakespeare.

[63] *OED* cites Hannah More in 1790 for first use of *convention* in the sense of 'a rule or practice based upon general consent', or 'recognised as valid in any particular art or study'. Literary applications emerge somewhat later. The pejorative sense of 'accepted usage become artificial and formal, and felt to be repressive of the natural' dates from the mid-nineteenth century.

[64] For representative extracts with connecting commentary, see H. T. Swedenberg, Jr, *The Theory of the Epic in England 1650–1800* (Berkeley: University of California Press, 1944).

[65] Donald M. Foerster, *The Fortunes of Epic Poetry: A Study in English and American Criticism 1750–1950* (Washington: Catholic University of America Press, 1962), 12; Dustin Griffin, *Regaining Paradise: Milton and the Eighteenth Century* (Cambridge: Cambridge University Press, 1986).

above from the *Retrospective Review* shows how far critical understanding of the genre had altered by 1820.

Dante was a third test case, the *Divine Comedy* being another work of manifest epic scope and complexity that possessed even fewer of the formal attributes of classical epic. It was in the context of a comparative study of Dante's *Inferno*, as part of an argument which cites Shakespeare and Milton as examples of other poets 'unfettered by rules', that Henry Boyd made his claim about the obsolescence of the 'old imperial code of criticism', highlighting the inability of static, formalistic definitions to capture the true nature of epic as a genre radically altered by each of its major exponents.[66] Boyd insists on a historical interpretation of both the subject matter and the form of Dante's poem, surrounding his translation of the *Inferno* with a variety of scholarly apparatuses to facilitate this. Though his methodological conclusions are less revolutionary than those of later German Romantic critics such as Schelling who saw the *Divine Comedy* as necessitating an entirely new theory of genre,[67] Boyd's dissatisfaction with traditional categories and procedures shows the strain under which the neoclassical system was placed by changes in literary taste and the growing interest in earlier literary history.

Quite apart from troublesome precursors, there was the challenge of contemporary literature, much of which operated by generic codes palpably different from those of neoclassical theory. While neoclassical critics discussed the nuances of epic and elegy, pastoral and tragedy, much of the actual poetry that was being written involved experiments with new genres, mixed genres, and anti-genres. The most enduring literary products of the Augustan period, as recent criticism has emphasized, are its 'mock forms': mock-epics such as Dryden's *Mac Flecknoe* (1682) and Pope's *The Rape of the Lock* (1712), mock-pastorals and georgics such as Swift's *A Town Eclogue* (1711) and Gay's *Trivia* (1716), and mock-elegies such as Allan Ramsay's *Elegies on Maggy Johnson, John Cowper and Lucky Wood* (1718).[68] These and other hybrid, parodic genres had no place in the neoclassical genre-system, despite the fact that parody itself had a distinguished classical lineage, and a tradition of critical interpretation (as a mode of subversive imitation if not as a genre in the normal sense) dating back to Aristotle's *Poetics*.[69] In the sphere of drama, neoclassical theory proved even more

---

For Hayley's influence, see Stuart Curran, *Poetic Form and British Romanticism* (New York: Oxford University Press, 1986), 160–1, 174.

[66] See p. 28 above. For Dante's place in contemporary debate on epic, see Foerster, *Fortunes of Epic Poetry*, ch. 2. For his broader reception in this period, see C. P. Brand, 'Dante and the Middle Ages in Neo-Classical and Romantic Criticism', *Modern Language Review*, 81/2 (1986), 327–36; and Antonella Braida, *Dante and the Romantics* (Basingstoke: Palgrave Macmillan, 2004).

[67] See Ch. 5 below, p. 170.

[68] Martin Price, *To the Palace of Wisdom: Studies in Order and Energy from Dryden to Blake* (New York: Doubleday, 1964), 249–61; Richard Terry, *Mock-Heroic from Butler to Cowper: An English Genre and Discourse* (Aldershot: Ashgate, 2005); on mock-elegy, Kenneth Simpson, 'Poetic Genre and National Identity: Ramsay, Fergusson and Burns', *Studies in Scottish Literature*, 30 (1998), 31–42; on other mock-genres, R. P. Bond, *English Burlesque Poetry, 1700–1750* (Cambridge, Mass.: Harvard University Press, 1932).

[69] Margaret Rose, *Parody: Ancient, Modern and Post-Modern* (Cambridge: Cambridge University Press, 1993).

counter-factual: the active repertoire of dramatic types and subtypes bore little relation to critical taxonomies, and such characteristic inventions as the 'ballad opera' (a term first used by Gay, for his *Beggar's Opera* of 1728) intermixed genres which most critics were yet to recognize properly as separate entities, let alone in combination.[70] The impasse of neoclassical poetics when confronted with the novel—the hybrid genre par excellence—is starker still. As Mikhail Bakhtin memorably put it, the novel lay so far outside the traditional genre-system as to seem like 'a creature from an alien species'.[71]

The 'radical restructuring' of genre theory Bakhtin deemed necessary to accommodate these changes began, retrospectively, with German Romanticism, whose ideas, as we will see in later chapters, provide the germ of Bakhtin's 'dialogic' poetics. In terms of the history of criticism, however, it is misleading to conceive of the transition from neoclassicism to Romanticism simply in terms of a liberation from the concept of rules. Objections to particular rules accumulated, exceptions were increasingly recognized, and generic definitions became more flexible, but, as Emerson Marks notes, there was 'no discernible weakening of the conviction that literature like all art was governed by certain essential laws, the discovery and propagation of which were, as Dr. Johnson thought, part of the critic's proper business'.[72] This holds true for much of the Romantic period. George Dyer's essay 'On Poetical Genius, and its Subjection to Rules' (1812) restates a long-standing British position by insisting that 'a person of genius', in 'the very act of spurning the inferior rules of critics', is 'obedient . . . to the superior laws of reason'—a principle that Dyer tried to enact in his own flamboyant but logically precise poetry.[73] His friend Coleridge, while championing originality and imaginative freedom, explicitly rejects the opposition of 'genius' to 'rules', and characterizes his whole critical project as a search for the higher-order laws governing literary creativity.[74] Wordsworth, in a cancelled passage from the 1802 Preface to *Lyrical Ballads*, also makes clear that, whatever his objections to particular generic rules, he was far from rejecting the concept of rules per se, for 'Without an appeal to laws and principles there can be no criticism', and 'What normally passes for such is little more than a string of random and extempore judgments, a mode of writing more cheap than any other, and utterly worthless.'[75]

---

[70] See Edmond McAdoo Gagey, *Ballad Opera* (New York: Columbia University Press, 1937); for other generic innovations, Richard W. Bevis, *English Drama: Restoration and Eighteenth Century, 1660–1789* (Harlow: Longman, 1988).

[71] 'Epic and Novel' (1941), in Mikhail Bakhtin, *The Dialogic Imagination: Four Essays*, ed. Michael Holquist, trans. Caryl Emerson and Michael Holquist (Austin: University of Texas Press, 1981), 4.

[72] Marks, *Poetics of Reason*, 42.

[73] Dyer, *Poetics*, ii. 29.

[74] Notably in his Shakespeare lecture of 22 or 29 Dec. 1812: 'Imagine not I am about to oppose Genius to Rules—No!—the Comparative value of these Rules is the very Cause to be tried.—The Spirit of Poetry like all other living Powers, must of necessity circumscribe itself by Rules, were it only to unite Power with Beauty' (*The Collected Works of Samuel Taylor Coleridge*, v: *Lectures 1808–1819 On Literature*, ed. R. A. Foakes, 2 vols (London: Routledge and Kegan Paul, 1987), i. 494). For other examples, see Abrams, *Mirror and the Lamp*, 223–5.

[75] *Prose Works*, i. 164.

Not only literary criticism but reading itself was understood as a rule-bound activity, amenable to investigation through the nascent science of elocution. Illustrative of this new methodology of reading is a textbook such as Daniel Staniford's *The Art of Reading: Containing a Number of Useful Rules, Exemplified by a Variety of Selected and Original Pieces, Narrative, Didactic, Argumentative, Poetical, Descriptive, Humorous, and Entertaining* (1800). 'Reading' here refers to recitation, or reading aloud, but many of Staniford's rules apply equally to silent reading, his underlying assumption being that any performance of a text—private or public—requires competence in genre-specific rules. There were certainly readers who questioned these protocols: Keats's resistance to the 'palpable designs' of didactic poetry is a case in point, and we will encounter many other examples of what could be called 'anti-generic' readings, readings which refuse to respond to texts in the manner that rule or convention dictates. But these refusals are conspicuous because the contractual nature of the reading process is increasingly recognized. It is because, to use Wordsworth's phrase, 'pre-established codes of decision' have been laid bare that authors and readers can openly challenge them.[76] In this, as in other respects, what characterizes the Romantic period is the clash between opposed systems and protocols: between established and emergent codes, generic and anti-generic tendencies.

## THE COGNITIVE TURN

Later parts of this book will explore the impact on genre theory and practice of new concepts of form, new ideas about genre-mixing, and new perceptions of literary time. To conclude the present chapter, I turn to an equally important development: the rethinking of genres as cognitive entities rather than purely formal constructs. In theoretical terms, what differentiates, say, Warton's *Essay on the Genius and Writings of Pope* (1756), an early example of the cognitive approach, from Pope's own *Essay on Criticism* is not the absence of generic categories and rules—they are, on the contrary, vital to Warton's argument, as is the notion of a generic hierarchy[77]— but, rather, his method of defining and evaluating genres in accordance with the modes of thought operative within them. Warton challenges Pope's pre-eminence in the English canon on the grounds not of the inferior quality of his poetry but of the intrinsic limitations of the genres in which he excelled. Warton's point is that didactic and satirical poetry, though strong on wit and 'sense', lack the emotive and imaginative properties that he considers the hallmark of the best or 'purest' poetry: the sublime and the pathetic.[78]

It has been said that the theory of the sublime, by foregrounding aspects of literature that defy boundaries and rules, 'shatters the conceptual framework of previous aesthetic systems' and inaugurates a subjective poetics that undermines

---

[76] Advertisement to *Lyrical Ballads* (1798), in *Prose Works*, i. 116.

[77] Paul Leedy, 'Genres Criticism and the Significance of Warton's Essay on Pope', *Journal of English and German Philology*, 45 (1946), 140–6.

[78] *Essay on the Genius and Writings of Pope*, p. x.

the traditional hierarchy of genres and erodes the mimetic paradigm on which neoclassicism is based.[79] The chronology of this argument is problematic, however, since the popularization of the Longinian theory of the sublime coincides with the rise, not the fall, of neoclassicism. The same year, 1694, in which Boileau published his famous translation of Longinus that launched the cult of the sublime also saw the publication of his definitive exposition of neoclassicism, the *Art poétique*. Dennis played a similar dual role in England, as theorist both of 'the rules' and of the sublimity which breaks the rules. The critical history of both countries suggests that the neoclassical genre-system, far from collapsing under the pressure of this potent new concept, received in the short term a tremendous boost from it.[80] As Norman Maclean notes: 'The new was not substituted for the traditional but was added to it; that is, sublimity was taken as a quality distinguishing the three genres (epic, tragedy, and the Great Ode) which throughout most of the history of criticism had been placed at the top of the poetical hierarchy.'[81] Ultimately, the logical conclusion of the theory of the sublime was indeed the sort of revolutionary attitude to genre displayed by Anna Seward, who wrote in 1790 that 'it matters little what order of composition is chosen by a highly sublimated imagination' since imaginative strength 'may be almost equally well conveyed in one form of composition as another'.[82] Few eighteenth-century writers, though, pursued the theory to its logical conclusion. A more typical response of the time was to combine the two systems by using the concept of the sublime, as John Baillie and Joseph Warton did, to redefine the 'proper Distinctions' of the various genres—and to reinforce notions of generic hierarchy.

Other new, or newly defined, concepts such as the pathetic, the beautiful, and the picturesque had similarly ambivalent effects.[83] Unlike the objective categories of neoclassical aesthetics, these were subjective concepts, part of a new science of psychological causes and effects—treated as part of 'rhetoric' in Britain, and christened 'aesthetics' in Germany—that claimed to be experimental rather than rationalistic, inductive not deductive, and that explained the workings of art in terms of the faculties of mind involved in its creation and reception. Applied to literary criticism, the new science offered a powerful alternative to the 'old imperial code': a fresh way of analysing and evaluating literary works, and a new kind of classification system that grouped works according to their emotional potencies rather

---

[79] Ernst Cassirer, *The Philosophy of the Enlightenment* (1932), trans. Fritz C. A. Koelln and James P. Pettegrove (Princeton: Princeton University Press, 1979), 329.

[80] See Samuel H. Monk, *The Sublime: A Study of Critical Theories in Eighteenth-Century England* (1935; Ann Arbor: University of Michigan Press, 1960); Peter De Bolla, *The Discourse of the Sublime: Readings in History, Aesthetics, and the Subject* (Oxford: Blackwell, 1989); and, for primary sources, Andrew Ashfield and Peter de Bolla (eds), *The Sublime: A Reader in British Eighteenth-Century Aesthetic Theory* (Cambridge: Cambridge University Press, 1996).

[81] Norman Maclean, 'From Action to Image: Theories of the Lyric in the Eighteenth Century', in R. S. Crane (ed.), *Critics and Criticism: Ancient and Modern* (Chicago: University of Chicago Press, 1952), 421.

[82] Quoted by Maclean, ibid. 460.

[83] W. J. Hipple, *The Beautiful, the Sublime and the Picturesque in Eighteenth-Century British Aesthetic Theory* (Carbondale: Southern Illinois University Press, 1957).

than their formal properties.[84] This system could operate either independently of traditional generic categories or in combination with them. Aesthetic treatises such as Edmund Burke's *Philosophical Inquiry into the Origin of our Ideas of the Sublime and the Beautiful* (1757), Archibald Alison's *Essays on the Nature and Principles of Taste* (1790), and Uvedale Price's *Essay on the Picturesque, as Compared with the Sublime and the Beautiful* (1794) are notable for their avoidance of familiar generic classifications and their foregrounding of notions of irregularity and indeterminacy. John Ogilvie's *Philosophical and Critical Observations on the Nature, Characters and Various Species of Composition* (1774), on the other hand, attempts to integrate formal and psychological approaches. Ogilvie's aim of charting the combinations of 'intellectual powers' operative in particular 'species of composition' produces fresh definitions of familiar genres like 'epic' and 'ode', and he anticipates modern genre theorists such as Jolles and Bakhtin in his overarching distinction between 'simple' and 'complex' genres[85] (a distinction based, in Ogilvie's case, on Lockean empiricism). In the second volume, however, this lucid and original classification of genres gets subsumed into a broader typology of styles, each of which is defined by a particular aesthetic attribute or mental faculty: 'perspicuous composition', 'elegant composition', 'sublime composition', 'nervous composition', and others. Though both typologies are suggestive, Ogilvie never explains the relationship between them, and his treatise ends suspended between a literary system of genres and a rhetorical system of styles.

Similar problems are encountered in George Campbell's *Philosophy of Rhetoric* (1776), another syncretic work which tries to redefine the principles of rhetoric in terms of a 'faculty' psychology. Applied to poetry, the resultant system involves no fewer than six parameters—tone (serious, facetious), psychological object (fancy, passion, will), generic function (epic, drama, satire, further differentiated by status: great versus little epic, high versus low satire, tragedy versus comedy), rhetorical means (insinuation, conformation, persuasion), and authorial stance (narrator, representer, reasoner), as represented in Campbell's diagram below:[86]

---

[84] John L. Mahoney, *The Whole Internal Universe: Imitation and the New Defense of Poetry in British Criticism, 1660–1830* (New York: Fordham University Press, 1995).

[85] John Ogilvie, *Philosophical and Critical Observations on the Nature, Characters, and Various Species of Composition*, 2 vols (London, 1774), i. 296; Mikhail Bakhtin, 'The Problem of Speech Genres' (1952–3), in his *Speech Genres and Other Late Essays*, ed. Caryl Emerson and Michael Holquist, trans. Vern W. McGee (Austin: University of Texas Press, 1986); André Jolles, *Einfache Formen* (Tübingen: Niemeyer, 1968).

[86] Reproduced from George Campbell, *The Philosophy of Rhetoric*, 2 vols (London, 1776), i. 72, by permission of Aberdeen University Special Libraries and Archives. For Campbell's contribution

Ingenious though this scheme is, the choice of emotional 'objects' seems entirely arbitrary, the genre-spectrum inexplicably truncated, and the distinction of 'means' unsustainable, quite apart from intrinsic confusion of the tabulation, which implies a comprehensiveness that the scheme plainly lacks. Campbell's relish for taxonomy does, though, produce another classification that any philosopher or teacher should take to heart, between four different species of nonsense: 'puerile nonsense' ('when an author runs on in specious verbosity'), 'learned nonsense' ('the more incomprehensible the subject is, the greater scope has the declaimer to talk plausibly without any meaning'), 'profound nonsense' ('the merest nothing, set off with an air of solemnity, as the result of very deep thought and sage reflection'), and 'marvellous nonsense' ('it astonishes and even confounds by the boldness of the affirmations, which always appear flatly to contradict the plainest dictates of common sense, and thus to involve a manifest absurdity').[87] The last variety, still much in evidence in the academic world, is yet another version of the sublime, now combined with its nearest neighbour, the ridiculous.

The ability of the new aesthetic discourse to generate alternative taxonomies can be seen even more clearly in literary anthologies, the market for which increased exponentially in the last quarter of the century. When John Adams in 1789 came to update Joshua Poole's famous handbook *The English Parnassus* (1657) with an identically titled anthology of modern verse, he replaced Poole's generic classification of poetry into six parts ('Heroick/Epick', 'Lyrick', 'Elegies, Threnodies', 'Dramatick Poesie', 'Epigram', 'Poeticall Treatises') with thematic or affective categories: 'Didactic', 'Descriptive', 'Pathetic', 'Plaintive', and 'Pastoral'.[88] Henry Headley used a similar scheme in his *Select Beauties of Ancient English Poetry* (1787), an anthology which includes a tabular classification not only of poems but also of poets, thus producing yet another taxonomy ('Epic Poets', 'Philosophical & Metaphysical', 'Dramatic Poets', 'Historical', 'Satyrical', 'Pastoral', 'Amatory, & Miscellaneous', 'Translators'). Nathan Drake's *Literary Hours* (1798) includes a similar table, in this case listing modern rather than ancient poets.[89] Such tables are a reminder that the shift from mimetic to expressive criteria and the rise of an author-based poetics did not involve the rejection of classification per se; the taxonomic method simply transferred itself from genres to authors. Not everyone was convinced: Thomas Campbell is one anthologist who rejected this approach, insisting in his multi-volume *Specimens of British Poetry* (1819) that

Poetry is of too spiritual a nature to admit of its authors being exactly grouped by a Linnaean system of classification. Striking resemblances will, no doubt, be found among poets; but the

to the 'new rhetoric', see James Engell, *Forming the Critical Mind: Dryden to Coleridge* (Cambridge, Mass.: Harvard University Press, 1989), ch. 7; and P. W. K. Stone, *The Art of Poetry 1750–1820: Theories of Poetic Composition and Style in the Late Neo-Classic and Early Romantic Periods* (London: Routledge and Kegan Paul, 1967), 80–3.

[87] *Philosophy of Rhetoric*, ii. 77–91.

[88] John Adams (ed.), *The English Parnassus: Being a New Selection of Didactic, Descriptive, Pathetic, Plaintive, and Pastoral Poetry. Extracted from the Works of the Latest and Most Celebrated Poets* (London, 1789).

[89] The author tables from Headley and Drake are reproduced in Iain McCalman (ed.), *An Oxford Companion to the Romantic Age: British Culture 1776–1832* (Oxford: Oxford University Press, 1999), 271.

shades of variety and gradation are so infinite, that to bring every composer within a given line of resemblance would require a new language in the philosophy of taste.[90]

That 'new language', or metalanguage, is, however, precisely what Enlightenment aesthetics—the 'philosophy of taste' we have been tracing—had helped to create, and there were many literary Linnaeans who were willing to use it.

The displacement of a formal metalanguage by subjective categories is apparent, too, in 'extract' collections, increasingly popular both in schools and with the general public. Marketed with titles such as *Beauties of the Poets, Flowers of British Poetry, Choice Fragments*, or—the most successful of all—*Elegant Extracts*, such anthologies either avoid generic classifications altogether, grouping the extracts into aesthetic or thematic categories, or, more typically, use some combination of the two systems.[91] Within each category, the passages are chosen to exemplify the aesthetic quality in question, the assumption being that beauty, pathos, or sublimity could be 'extracted' from the texts and genres in which the passages originated, and savoured in isolation. Selective anthologies of this kind encouraged new, more targeted (or, in Coleridge's view, lazy[92]) ways of reading—pursuant of particular aesthetic effects— and also new ways of writing, since many of them were intended for use in composition classes. The popularity of such anthologies was probably another factor that contributed in the long run to the erosion of traditional genre theory, and to the ascendancy of a poetics that favoured the short lyric over the long poem. The more that readers encountered poetry in the abbreviated, distilled form of 'lyrical gems' (as one 'extract' anthology called them[93]), the more difficult it was to sustain a taste for longer, more complex genres. The logical conclusion of the 'extracts' and 'beauties' craze was the philosophy of composition of Edgar Allan Poe, who described epic poems, or long poems of any kind, as a 'contradiction in terms', 'beauty' being 'the sole legitimate province of the poem', and intense aesthetic effects being by definition brief.[94]

The fact remains, however, that in the 'high' Romantic period a taste for lyric coexisted with a fashion for long poems; and in poetry anthologies, as in other critical discourse, formal and psychological categories were readily combined. Vicesimus Knox's *Elegant Extracts* (1789), for instance, employs aesthetic categories such as 'Descriptive' and 'Pathetic' alongside thematic categories like 'Sacred and Moral' and

[90] Quoted by Lawrence Lipking, *The Ordering of the Arts in Eighteenth-Century England* (Princeton: Princeton University Press, 1970), 470–1.

[91] Details of these and other anthologies can be found on the database maintained by Laura Mandell and Rita Raley at http://www.English.ucsb.edu/faculty/rraley/research/anthologies.

[92] In *The Collected Works of Samuel Taylor Coleridge*, vii: *Biographia Literaria*, ed. James Engell and W. Jackson Bate (London: Routledge and Kegan Paul, 1983), i. 48, Coleridge complains that periodicals and 'a shelf or two of BEAUTIES, ELEGANT EXTRACTS and ANAS, form nine-tenths of the reading of the reading public'. For other hostile comments on the fashion for literary extracts, see Richard D. Altick, *The English Common Reader: A Social History of the Mass Reading Public 1800–1900* (Chicago: University of Chicago Press, 1957), 176–7; and Leah Price, *The Anthology and the Rise of the Novel* (Cambridge: Cambridge University Press, 2000), 74–6.

[93] [Robert Malcolm (ed.)], *Lyrical Gems: A Selection of Moral, Sentimental and Descriptive Poetry from the Works of the Most Popular Modern Writers. Interspersed with Originals* (Glasgow, 1825).

[94] 'The Philosophy of Composition' (1846), in Edgar Allan Poe, *Complete Poems and Selected Essays*, ed. Richard Gray (London: Dent, 1993), 106.

presentational categories like 'Narrative' and 'Dramatic', while the fourth section reinstates the strictly generic term 'Epic' alongside the catch-all 'Miscellaneous'. The latter then subdivides into a promiscuous array of generic categories including epitaphs, epigrams, sonnets, odes, elegies, dirges, ballads, and many others.[95] Later editions adjust this schema, without obvious gain in clarity. *Roach's Beauties of the Poets* (1794–5) takes a different tack, abandoning sectional divisions but foregrounding genre in other ways, notably through the prominent display of subtitles, epigraphs, and prefaces—as if these paratextual features were part of the 'beauty' Roach is celebrating. The elaborately variegated fonts on the title page of each volume reinforce the generic diversity of the contents. The striking frontispiece to another Roach collection, *Beauties of the Modern Poets* (1793), underlines the message even more strongly. Entitled 'Taste shewing Britannia the Beauties of Modern Poets', it juxtaposes a classical iconography of poetic value—Mount Parnassus, Pegasus, a pyramid (an emblem of enlightenment)—with a fashionably dressed woman representing modern Taste, who is pointing to a banner that carries the title of the collection (Figure 1.3). It is no coincidence that the word to which her finger points is 'Arranged', since the generic organization of the collection is intended, as with Bell's collection, as a confirmation of its impeccable taste.

A further manifestation of this syncretic tendency is the proliferation of poetic subcategories such as 'elegiac sonnet', 'pathetic ballad', 'sentimental pastoral', and 'ethic epistle'. The use of generic terms with adjectival qualifiers, though not unknown in earlier periods,[96] increased markedly in the late eighteenth century, the qualifier usually being either a modal term derived from the name of a genre ('elegiac' from elegy), an aesthetic or affective term ('pathetic', 'descriptive'), or an indicator of content ('legendary', 'sacred', 'ethic'). Drake's subdivision of lyric poetry into four kinds—Sublime, Pathetic, Descriptive, and Amatory—in his *Literary Hours* is an illustration of the technique, as is *Lyrical Ballads*, a generic title Wordsworth considered distinctive enough to consider changing when Mary Robinson published her *Lyrical Tales* two years later.[97] Another example is the term 'sublime allegory', used by Thomas Warton in his *History of English Poetry* (1774–81) to describe the work of Dunbar,[98] and later adopted by Fuseli and Blake.[99] The method could be taken to comic extremes, as in Richard Graves's *The*

---

[95] [Vicesimus Knox (ed.)], *Elegant Extracts, or, Useful and Entertaining Pieces of Poetry, selected for the Improvement of Youth, in Speaking, Reading, Thinking, Composing; and in the Conduct of Life* (London, 1789).

[96] Alastair Fowler, *Kinds of Literature: An Introduction to the Theory of Genres and Modes* (Oxford: Clarendon Press, 1982), ch. 7.

[97] As noted by Dorothy Wordsworth in her letter to Jane Marshall, 10 Sept. 1800, in *The Letters of William and Dorothy Wordsworth: The Early Years, 1797–1805*, ed. Ernest de Selincourt, 2nd edn, rev. Chester L. Shaver (Oxford: Clarendon Press, 1967), 289–90.

[98] Thomas Warton, *The History of English Poetry, from the Close of the Eleventh to the Commencement of the Eighteenth Century*, 4 vols (London, 1774–81), ii. 279.

[99] Fuseli, in a Royal Academy lecture, describes epic as 'the sublime allegory of a maxim', which 'breaks the fetters of time' and 'unites with boundless sway the mythologic, feodal, local incongruities' (*Life and Writings*, ii. 193). Blake refers to his poem *Jerusalem* as a 'Sublime Allegory', defining this as 'Allegory address'd to the Intellectual powers while it is altogether hidden from the Corporeal Understanding' (letter to Thomas Butts, 6 July 1803, in William Blake, *Complete Writings*, ed. Geoffrey Keynes (London: Oxford University Press, 1966), 825).

**Figure 1.3.** 'Taste shewing Britannia the Beauties of Modern Poets', frontispiece to the second volume of *Roach's Beauties of the Modern Poets of Great Britain* (1793)

*Festoon: A Collection of Epigrams, Ancient and Modern: Panegyrical, Satyrical, Amorous, Moral, Humorous, Monumental; with An Essay on that Species of Composition* (1766), a title which hints at the playfulness of the subject matter but also ironizes the classificatory zeal of contemporary genre critics (the accompanying essay is disappointingly straightforward). On the other hand, such extremes could be entirely serious, as in the case in *Bell's Classical Arrangement*, whose prodigious array of generic subcategories represents, as we have seen, an earnest, if ultimately unsuccessful, effort of literary classification.

Even modern quasi-genres such as the 'effusion', 'fragment', or 'sketch', which Bell's 'classical' system had no way of incorporating even though these were among the commonest kinds of 'fugitive' verse, could be subjected to adjectival modification. Wordsworth's *Descriptive Sketches in Verse* (1794) is one of many works of the time which use some variant of this title ('sentimental sketches', 'poetical sketches', 'pastoral sketches', and others[100]). In the case of the 'effusion', another genre made fashionable by the new poetics of spontaneity and self-expression, the technique could produce such apparently tautologous labels as 'extempore effusion' (Wordsworth's 'Extempore Effusion upon the Death of James Hogg'), 'simple effusion' (Clare's 'A Simple Effusion Address'd to my Lame Father'), and also the multiple variants brought together in William Perfect's *Poetic Effusions: Pastoral, Moral, Amatory, Descriptive* (1796), whose prefatory claim to be reliant on 'unstudied diction, the spontaneous offspring of nature' is somewhat undermined by the title's elaborate metalanguage.[101] The 'fragment', once a purely editorial term but now functioning as a fashionable genre in its own right, was subdivided into 'pathetic fragments', 'elegiac fragments', 'sentimental fragments', 'dramatic fragments', and many other variants.[102] Helen Maria Williams's 'Part of an Irregular Fragment' (1791) shows how the fragment could be fragmented even further (in the inverted logic of the genre, her title is boastful rather than modest—the poem is intended to outdo more complete, 'regular' fragments).[103]

The 'song' too underwent adjectival subdivision, into national categories (English, Scottish, Irish, etc.) but also thematic, affective, and modal categories, as in Guy's *Songs, Consisting of Political, Convivial, Sentimental, Pastoral, Satirical, and Masonic* (1797), a title whose taxonomic exuberance runs away with its grammar. Axtell's *The British Apollo, or, Songster's Magazine* (1792) boasts an even more splendid array, describing itself as a *Choice Selection of English, Irish, and Scotch Songs, Cantatas, Duets, Trios, Catches, Glees, &c. . . . Interspersed with Many Originals, viz. Bacchanalian,*

---

[100] For a list of examples, see R. D. Mayo, 'The Contemporaneity of the *Lyrical Ballads*' (1954), in Alun R. Jones and William Tydeman (eds), *Wordsworth, Lyrical Ballads: A Casebook* (Basingstoke: Macmillan, 1972), 123.

[101] William Perfect, *Poetic Effusions: Pastoral, Moral, Amatory, Descriptive* (London, 1796), preface, quoted by John E. Jordan, *Why the 'Lyrical Ballads'? The Background, Writing, and Character of Wordsworth's 1798 'Lyrical Ballads'* (Berkeley: University of California Press, 1976), 88.

[102] Mayo, 'Contemporaneity of *Lyrical Ballads*', 123.

[103] 'Part of an Irregular Fragment, Found in a Dark Passage of the Tower', in Helen Maria Williams, *Poems*, 2 vols (London, 1786), ii. 26–56.

*Love, Hunting, Martial, Nautical, Pastoral, Political, Satirical, Humourous, &c. To which are Added, a Variety of Toasts and Sentiments.* The frontispiece depicts the figure of Taste, again in fashionable modern dress, presenting Apollo, the Greek god of music and poetry, with a copy of Axtell's collection. Meanwhile, his horse Pegasus, rearing excitedly, announces 'Song upon Song' (Figure 1.4), a punning phrase which signals both generic profusion and generic self-consciousness—features this collection shares with other works of the time, the pun possibly deriving from John Wolcot (Peter Pindar)'s satirical *Ode upon Ode* (1787).

In their conflation of old and new terminology, such publications bear witness to the eclecticism of contemporary labelling systems and genre theory. The same is true of Hugh Blair's *Lectures on Rhetoric and Belles Lettres*, the most influential of many rhetorical textbooks of the period. As holder of the new Regius Chair of Rhetoric and *Belles Lettres* at Edinburgh University, Blair was at the epicentre of the Scottish Enlightenment, and his lectures (delivered from the early 1760s and eventually published in 1783) are an impressive synthesis of ancient and modern scholarship on a range of literary and related topics. His approach to genre can be usefully compared with that of Joseph Trapp in his *Lectures on Poetry* (1742), another influential textbook in its time, originating from Oxford University. Trapp's is a neoclassical poetics in a restricted sense, similar in its basic structure to earlier 'arts of poetry' such as Gildon's, though presented more systematically and prefaced by some general philosophical remarks on *poesis* and style. Blair, by contrast, treats poetry as part of the much larger topic of rhetoric, a field which, in the Scottish university curriculum, embraced all types of composition, both oral and written, and which combined neoclassical theory with modern aesthetics.

Not until the thirty-eighth lecture does Blair start to discuss poetry, opening the topic by citing the primitivist theories of Thomas Blackwell and John Brown on the origins of poetry. Five of the seven principal 'species' into which Blair divides poetry overlap with Trapp's, but Blair differs by including 'The Poetry of the Hebrews', a new category made fashionable by Robert Lowth, and 'descriptive poetry', another broad category much discussed in recent criticism. Blair differs from Trapp, too, in foregrounding the interrelations between species: 'descriptive poetry', for instance, is defined both as a separate species in its own right and one that enters into each of the five other species—pastoral, lyric, didactic, epic, and dramatic. The sublime already figures prominently in Trapp's lectures; Blair also discusses it, and incorporates it into his generic definitions along with the beautiful, the pathetic, the sentimental, and other aesthetic concepts. Both critics take largely for granted the traditional hierarchy of poetic genres, organizing their lectures around this: the main differences are Blair's upgrading of descriptive poetry (placed between didactic and epic) and downgrading of satire (a separate category in Trapp, but a minor subset of didactic in Blair). Interestingly, lyric is ranked above didactic in Trapp, but below it in Blair, a ranking which might upset our assumptions about the critical ascendancy of lyric in this period (I take up this issue in Chapter 3). Both enumerate generic rules, Trapp exhaustively, Blair more selectively and casually.

**Figure 1.4.** 'Taste presenting Apollo with Axtell's Magazine', frontispiece to *The British Apollo, or, Songster's Magazine* (1792)

Blair's genre-system has some idiosyncratic features but it can be taken as representative of progressive critical opinion in the late eighteenth century. Neoclassical assumptions and categories supply much of its framework, but these are supplemented and modified by new categories and theories derived from Enlightenment aesthetics. The resultant synthesis proved remarkably enduring. Blair's *Lectures* remained a standard academic work in Britain and America for more than sixty years, and spawned numerous imitators.[104] Wordsworth may have read it, Coleridge certainly did, and there is evidence that Blake and Burns also knew it.[105] Simplified, Blair's arguments and definitions formed the basis of school textbooks such as William Enfield's *Familiar Treatise on Rhetoric and Belles Lettres* (1809) and—more elementary still—David Blair's *Universal Preceptor: Being an Easy Grammar of Arts, Sciences and General Knowledge* (1811), an ABC of Everything which reduces the whole of modern genre theory to a simple adjectival list: 'Poetry is classed under the heads *epic*, or heroic; *dramatic*, or representative; *lyric*, or suited to music, as odes, songs, &c.; *didactic*, or instructive; *elegiac*, or sentimental and affecting; *satirical*, *epigrammatic*, or witty and ludicrous; and *pastoral*, or descriptive of rustic life.'[106] Blair's influence can also be felt in poetry anthologies: the organization of Knox's *Elegant Extracts* owes much to Blair's critical system, as does *Bell's Classical Arrangement*, not least in its inclusion of numerous modal subcategories.

Such were its inherent contradictions, though, that Blair's system did in due course unravel. The taxonomic problems apparent in Bell's collection resurface in many other publications. When in 1831 an Aberdeen schoolmaster, David Grant, sought to produce an anthology entitled *The Beauties of Modern British Poetry, Systematically Arranged*, he turned to Blair's *Lectures* for assistance with his Introduction, citing Blair's primitivist account of the origin of poetry, while acknowledging that in matters of 'technical propriety' poetry, like other arts, has been improved 'in the progressive march of civilization' (a point also made by Blair—the familiar Scottish Enlightenment compromise). On the question of the 'aim' and 'purpose' of poetry, though, Grant turns to a more recent authority, Wordsworth's Preface to *Lyrical Ballads*, and goes on to make a claim that Blair, writing fifty years earlier, would in no way have conceded, namely that modern poetry can be as powerful and spontaneous as ancient—indeed more so. 'The present age', Grant declares, 'has been unusually prolific in poetical genius'; compared with former periods, 'in the extent and variety of genuine Poetry which it has produced, it is undoubtedly superior to them all. In proof of this, we have only to consider the depth and power of Byron, both in the delineation of natural objects and human passion— the romance, chivalry and patriotism of Scott—the oriental magnificence and lyric sweetness of Moore.'[107]

Grant's showcase of contemporary talent is notable for its high concentration of poets and poems we now think as part of the Romantic canon: not only Byron,

[104] For Blair's pedagogic legacy, see Robert Crawford, *Devolving English Literature*, 2nd edn (Edinburgh: Edinburgh University Press, 2000), ch. 1; Richard Lewis Gaillet Lynee (ed.), *Scottish Rhetoric and its Influences* (London: Routledge, 1997); and Thomas P. Miller, *The Formation of College English: Rhetoric and Belles Lettres in the British Cultural Provinces* (Pittsburgh: University of Pittsburgh Press, 1997).

[105] Duncan Wu, *Wordsworth's Reading, 1770–1799* (Cambridge: Cambridge University Press, 1993), 181–2; Liam McIlvanney, 'Hugh Blair, Robert Burns, and the Invention of Scottish Literature', *Eighteenth-Century Life*, 29/2 (2005), 25–46.

[106] David Blair [Richard Phillips], *The Universal Preceptor: Being an Easy Grammar of Arts, Sciences, and General Knowledge*, 2nd edn (London, 1811), 289–90.

[107] David Grant (ed.), *The Beauties of Modern British Poetry, Systematically Arranged* (Aberdeen, 1831), introd., p. xi.

Scott, and Moore, but also Wordsworth, Coleridge, and Southey, and the posthumously fashionable Keats and Shelley—as well as female poets like Barbauld and Hemans. As in other early anthologies of Romantic poetry, however, the emphasis is almost exclusively on lyric verse: there is little of the generic variety suggested in the Introduction, and narrative and dramatic verse is represented only by short lyrical extracts.[108] Moreover, the arrangement of the collection is purely thematic: the poems and extracts are grouped by subject matter alone. Indeed, generic categories have disappeared altogether, since, in all but one case, the poems are shorn of their original genre labels. Keats's 'Ode to a Nightingale' becomes simply 'The Nightingale' and is placed alongside Coleridge's 'The Nightingale', which in turn loses its subtitle, 'A Conversational Poem'. With extracts from longer poems, even the original titles disappear. The famous lines from *Don Juan* that begin 'Between two worlds, Life hovers like a star' appear under the editorial title 'Human Life. II' ('Human Life. I' is an extract from Joanna Baillie). In itself, this feature is not unusual: such relabelling was common practice in 'extract' anthologies, and the loss of paratextual features was often the price of inclusion in modern edited collections. Grant's anthology, however, was intended for use in schools—he was a teacher of composition—and, compared with earlier textbooks like Knox's or Mavor and Pratt's,[109] the absence of any kind of generic organization or reference marks a discernible decline in pedagogic investment in genre. The traditional genre-system is now deemed irrelevant to the understanding of modern poetry, not because the poetry itself makes no reference to genre (such references are simply ignored or erased) but because the editor is presenting it in accordance with the neo-primitivist, anti-generic poetics that supposedly produced it. The 'system' in Grant's 'systematic arrangement' is, in effect, the anti-system depicted in *Modern Parnassus*: the anthology makes visible a pseudo-Wordsworthian poetics that values spontaneity over craftsmanship, emotional content over form, and that allows one kind of lyrical exuberance to stand for all of modern poetry. Subsequent chapters of this book will attempt to reinstate what gets lost in Grant's version of the literary revolution, by showing the depth and complexity of Romantic writers' engagement with genre and the theoretical self-awareness which is an irreducible part of their 'poetical genius'.

---

[108] This is also true of Grant's earlier anthology *Elegant Selections in Verse: From the Works of Scott, Byron, Southey, and Other Popular Poets, chiefly of the Present Age* (Edinburgh, 1818), where his rationale for selection is couched in ultra-Romantic terms: 'the Compiler has...endeavoured to enrich his Collection with the most admired passages which their authors, in their happiest moments, and highest flights of inspiration, have produced:—passages "with less of Earth than Heaven:" passages so deeply impregnated with the fire of genius, and so instinct with the living spirit, as are calculated to excite a creative power, and to awaken to eloquence and to poesy, master spirits that may yet lie concealed unconscious of their strength' (advertisement, p. iii).

[109] See n. 4 above.

# 2

# Romantic Genre Theory

AMALIA. I always shudder when I open a book where the imagination and its works are classified under headings.

MARCUS. No one expects you to read such despicable books. Yet, a theory of genres is just what we lack. And what else can it be but a classification which at the same time would be a history and theory of literature?

(Friedrich Schlegel, *Dialogue on Poetry*, 1800)

## ANGLO-GERMAN DIALOGUES

The above exchange in Schlegel's *Dialogue on Poetry* marks out two extremes in attitudes to genre at the close of the eighteenth century. Amalia, Marcus, and other characters at a literary symposium have been listening to Andrea's talk on the 'Epochs of Literature', a condensed history of world poetry from its Homeric beginnings to its contemporary German renaissance in the work of Goethe. Like other 'universal histories' of literature, the talk is organized both chronologically and generically: it tells of the rise and fall of epic, the origins of drama, the birth of elegy and idyll, the emergence of parody, and the fortunes of other genres. Amalia is unimpressed. Bored and frustrated by books of critical theory that pigeon-hole works of imaginative literature into rigid categories, she calls for an abandonment of the whole misguided enterprise of generic classification, a 'dangerous, roundabout way' of thinking about literature, which, she says, 'much too frequently kills the sense for the highest things'.[1] Marcus takes the opposite view. For him, Andrea's talk was, if anything, not attentive enough to the problem of genre: what is needed, he claims, is 'a more explicit theory of the kinds of poetry', a classification 'which at the same time would be a history and a theory of literature' (p. 76).

The dispute epitomizes the gulf between ancient and modern attitudes to genre. Marcus's claim that genres are indispensable to poetry, and that generic classification is the proper basis of literary criticism, reaffirms a doctrine that dates back to Plato and Aristotle. Amalia, by contrast, sounds recognizably modern. Her strictures on the sterility of classification, and her belief that generic categories blind us to the true nature of aesthetic experience, denying the individuality of artist and artwork alike, have been echoed many times since. Resistance to genre was a rallying-cry of the

---

[1] Friedrich Schlegel, *Dialogue on Poetry and Literary Aphorisms*, trans. Ernst Behler and Roman Struc (University Park: Pennsylvania State University Press, 1968), 77.

nineteenth-century Romantic movement, and a cause that, in the twentieth century, could unite literary thinkers as diverse as the expressionist philosopher Benedetto Croce, the new critic John Crowe Ransom, and the poststructuralist theorist Jacques Derrida, all of whom regarded the 'law of genre' as a critical shibboleth that literature itself either ignores or subverts.[2]

On closer inspection, however, the polarities in Schlegel's *Dialogue* are not so clear-cut. Marcus is not simply defending traditional views: the genre theory he endorses is neither the 'old imperial code' of neoclassicism nor the Enlightenment revision of that code, where static definitions are replaced by grand historical narratives about the origins and progress of literary genres. Rather, he calls for a genre theory that does not yet exist, a classification system that would be at once historically grounded and genuinely theoretical—able to chart the history of genres while also explaining the basic concept of genre, a proper understanding of which 'is just what we lack' (p. 76). Existing generic categories, he claims, are manifestly inadequate. His own talk, the last of the four inset lectures in the *Dialogue*, focuses on literary works that challenge traditional classifications—works like Goethe's *Wilhelm Meister's Apprenticeship* (1795–6), which unites the classical and modern in so revolutionary a way as to constitute 'a new species, a new genre for itself' (p. 113).

Amalia, for her part, is objecting not to genre theory per se, but to the taxonomic obsession with separating and dividing, where what is needed is an explanation of 'the entire and indivisible poetry', 'the whole in its undivided power' (p. 79). Her position is not modern subjectivism and relativism, but a characteristically Romantic commitment to totality and organic unity. There are, moreover, other voices in the *Dialogue* which complicate the basic dichotomy of ancient and modern views. Ludovico calls for a more explicitly philosophical approach to genre, and proceeds to supply this in his 'Talk on Mythology', which outlines a new theory of poetry based on Spinozistic pantheism. Antonio, who is most scathing of all about the inadequacies of current theories of genre, proposes yet another way forward centred on a theory of the novel, an inherently mixed genre which, he claims, is to modernity what the epic was to the ancient Greeks. Even Andrea's talk, despite all the criticism it receives, refuses any simple antithesis of ancient and modern. His mini-history of literature ends, like Marcus's, by describing the synthesis achieved by Goethe, who, he says, has demonstrated how to 'explore the forms of art back to their sources in order to be able to revive or combine them' (p. 74).

Like Plato's *Symposium*, on which it is partly modelled, Schlegel's *Dialogue on Poetry* dramatizes the conversations of a real group of people, the Jena circle of Romantic writers, critics, and philosophers whose members included Friedrich and August Wilhelm Schlegel, the latter's wife, Caroline, Friedrich Schelling, Dorothea Veit, Ludwig Tieck, and Friedrich von Hardenberg (Novalis).[3] In the carefully crafted dialogues and inset lectures of Friedrich Schlegel's text, we hear echoes of the ideas and theories published by the group in *The Athenaeum* and other literary journals, and

---

[2] See David Duff (ed.), *Modern Genre Theory* (Harlow: Longman, 2000), introd., 4–6.
[3] For the biographical basis of the *Dialogue on Poetry*, see Philippe Lacoue-Labarthe and Jean-Luc Nancy, *The Literary Absolute: The Theory of Literature in German Romanticism*, trans. Philip Barnard and Cheryl Lester (New York: State University of New York Press, 1988), preface.

expounded in unpublished lectures, notebooks, and letters. We see, too, in embryonic form, the philosophical and historical investigations which would later produce such masterworks of German criticism as Schelling's *Philosophy of Art* (1801–4), Jean Paul Richter's *School for Aesthetics* (1804), A. W. Schlegel's *Lectures on Dramatic Art and Literature* (1809), and Friedrich Schlegel's *Lectures on the History of Literature, Ancient and Modern* (1815). The topics discussed in the *Dialogue* range widely across authors, periods, national traditions, and critical methods, but the pivotal issue is genre, just as the central theme of Plato's *Symposium* is love. A satisfactory theory of genre—one that, in Schlegel's words, 'would then be the true aesthetics of literature' (p. 78)—is the holy grail of German Romantic theory, and the *Dialogue* shows how some of the best literary minds of the time went in quest of it.

The period of most intensive German discussion, 1797 to 1805, coincides exactly with the emergence of a 'new school of poetry' in England, whose theoretical manifesto, Wordsworth's Preface to *Lyrical Ballads*, was published in the same year as Schlegel's *Dialogue*.[4] Despite the similar chronology, and the many parallels between the two 'new schools', genre theory has usually been considered marginal to the British programme. The apparent neglect of genre in Wordsworth's Preface was noted from the start, attracting disapproval from neoclassically minded reviewers like Francis Jeffrey, and making possible the kind of anti-generic interpretation of the new poetics we found in *Modern Parnassus* (1814). Later anti-formalist definitions of poetry such as John Stuart Mill's ('the thoughts and words in which emotion spontaneously embodies itself') or John Henry Newman's (the 'free and unfettered effusion of genius') also claim descent from Wordsworth,[5] and were taken as accurate descriptions of Romantic poetry for much of the nineteenth and early twentieth century.

There is, unquestionably, a strain of anti-formalism in Romantic poetics, and the Preface to *Lyrical Ballads* is the canonical expression of it. Wordsworth's description of poetry as 'the spontaneous overflow of powerful feelings'[6] crystallizes the subject-ive, emotionalist theory of poetry that had been gaining favour since the mid-eighteenth century, and takes it one step further by applying to poetry as a whole the norms that had previously applied to one variety of it, the lyric.[7] The notion of 'spontaneous overflow' seems antithetical to the idea of rule-bound creativity on

---

[4] The phrase 'new school of poetry' originated in an *Anti-Jacobin* article (20 Nov. 1797) about the Southey–Coleridge circle; Jeffrey's review of *Thalaba* in the *Edinburgh Review* (Oct. 1802) added Wordsworth to the 'sect' and claimed that its 'doctrines are of *German* origin', though without connecting it to the Jena circle, which German critics also referred to as a 'new school'. See Peter A. Cook, 'Chronology of the "Lake School" Argument: Some Revisions', *Review of English Studies*, new ser., 28 (1977), 175–81; and Ernst Behler, *German Romantic Literary Theory* (Cambridge: Cambridge University Press, 1993), 30.

[5] John Stuart Mill, 'Thoughts on Poetry and its Varieties' (1859), and John Henry Newman, 'Poetry, with Reference to Aristotle's Poetics' (1829), in Edmund D. Jones (ed.), *English Critical Essays: Nineteenth Century* (1916; Oxford: Oxford University Press, 1971), 355, 197.

[6] Preface to *Lyrical Ballads* (1800), in *The Prose Works of William Wordsworth*, ed. W. J. B. Owen and Jane Worthington Smyser, 3 vols (Oxford: Clarendon Press, 1974), i. 126, 148. Subsequent references to the *Prose Works* are given parenthetically in the text by volume and page number.

[7] M. H. Abrams, *The Mirror and the Lamp: Romantic Theory and the Critical Tradition* (New York: Oxford University Press, 1953), ch. 4.

which neoclassical theories of genre had rested, and Wordsworth appears to undercut the very basis of generic distinction by advocating a linguistic primitivism that sees no essential difference between literary language and ordinary speech, or between poetry and prose. His insistence that the emotional life of country people is the most authentic subject matter for poetry appears to remove a further basis of generic distinction (all poetry becomes in effect a version of pastoral), and his declared aim of tracing 'the fluxes and refluxes of the mind' (i. 126) makes poetry sound little different from any other psychological discourse.

Yet, the relation of *Lyrical Ballads* to genre is actually much more complex. If parts of the Preface appear to ignore questions of genre, the title of the book ostentatiously foregrounds them, the unusual designation 'lyrical ballads' coming into sharper relief (in the 1798 edition) through contrast with the throwaway subtitle, *With a Few Other Poems*. Far from neglecting genre in the 1800 Preface, moreover, Wordsworth makes it pivotal to his argument. Part of the rationale for his defence of poetry is the perceived threat from 'frantic novels, sickly and stupid German Tragedies, and deluges of idle and extravagant stories in verse' (i. 128). In articulating this threat, Wordsworth enters a heated public discussion about the cultural effects of populist, mass-marketed genres (some of them imported) and voices a widely held concern that the aesthetic hierarchy of genres was being displaced by a purely commercial one.[8] His treatment of the poetry–prose crux, likewise, is not the product of an eroded sense of generic distinction, but a contribution to an ongoing debate about whether or not verse is essential to poetry, a thorny critical issue to which Words-worth brings fresh clarity with his innovative theory of metrical 'contract' (i. 122).[9] Equally timely are his remarks on reading. His challenge in the 1798 Advertisement to 'pre-established codes of decision', 'that most dreadful enemy to our pleasures', restates a familiar objection to neoclassical rules, but adds force to it by stressing that we are our own worst enemy since we internalize restrictive reading practices: they are '*our own* pre-established codes' (i. 116; my italics).

Wordsworth's discussion of the psychological 'purpose' of his poetry strikes another topical note. The distinction he claims between his and other contemporary poetry—that feeling has primacy over action, not the other way round—is usually interpreted as a reference to his lyricizing of the ballad form, and thus an implicit explanation of his title. But it is an intervention, too, in a broader debate about literary function, an issue which had acquired enormous urgency in the 1790s for reasons I will explain in the next chapter. Wordsworth's remarks in the 1802 Preface about the relationship between poetry and science extend this argument, addressing the deepening controversy about the relative value and use of different forms of

---

[8] G. Kim Blank, 'The "Degrading Thirst After Outrageous Stimulation": Wordsworth as Cultural Critic', *Journal of Popular Culture*, 39/3 (2006), 365–82; Andrew Franta, *Romanticism and the Rise of the Mass Public* (Cambridge: Cambridge University Press, 2007), ch. 2; Jon P. Klancher, *The Making of English Reading Audiences, 1790–1832* (Madison: University of Wisconsin Press, 1987), ch. 5. For the perceived foreign threat, see Peter Mortensen, *British Romanticism and Continental Influences: Writing in an Age of Europhobia* (New York: Palgrave Macmillan, 2004).

[9] John Hollander, 'Romantic Verse Form and the Metrical Contract', in Harold Bloom (ed.), *Romanticism and Consciousness: Essays in Criticism* (New York: Norton, 1970).

knowledge. His discussion of poetic language has an even sharper public resonance, in that it links the reform of literary diction to the representation of working people, thus turning on its head the traditional concept of decorum (which specifically excludes this class from serious poetry) and making literary primitivism an explicitly political issue.[10] This removes any doubt that his strategic conjunction of 'high' and 'low' genres—the classical lyric and the popular ballad—was intended as an exercise in literary democratization as well as an experiment in linguistic barrier-breaking.

Despite Wordsworth's continuous use of the first person singular, the Preface to *Lyrical Ballads* is thus a profoundly dialogic text, enacting a series of implicit conversations: with Coleridge, most obviously, who described the Preface as 'half a child of my own Brain'[11] (while strenuously objecting to the other half of it); with other poets and critics, named and unnamed, with whom Wordsworth establishes his agreement or disagreement; with prospective reviewers, against whom the Preface enacts some carefully judged pre-emptive manoeuvres; with ordinary readers, actual and imagined, whose edification and pleasure Wordsworth's prefatory remarks are intended to enhance; and, finally, with the poems themselves, whose concrete achievements modify and are modified by his theoretical preliminaries.

This last point is particularly important, because the effect of the Preface, and to a lesser extent the original Advertisement, is to weld poetry and theory together in an inseparable mixture. However problematic the relation between the two, the poems and the theoretical prose became part of one another, functioning as a composite entity—a mixed genre in its own right (as if the volume had been called, say, *Philosophical Ballads*[12]). It is this that makes *Lyrical Ballads* so suggestive a parallel to the genre theory of German Romanticism: Wordsworth and Coleridge's book, taken as a whole, enacts in its own fashion precisely that fusion of poetry and criticism, verse and prose, art and science, which Friedrich Schlegel was calling for in the pages of *The Athenaeum* and *The Lyceum*. In Paul Hamilton's sense, *Lyrical Ballads* is a 'metaromantic' text, a literary work that conceptualizes its own perform-ance;[13] and the evidence of the reviews and other contemporary responses confirms that it was the juxtaposition of theory and practice, not just the poetic innovations themselves, that made this such a controversial publication—so far-reaching in its implications as to inspire talk (both enthusiastic and hostile) of a 'revolution in literature'.

This chapter explores the place of genre theory in that revolution. The first section concentrates on the 1790s, highlighting the politicization of genre in the wake of the

[10] See Olivia Smith, *The Politics of Language, 1791–1819* (Oxford: Clarendon Press, 1984); William Keach, *Arbitrary Power: Romanticism, Language, Politics* (Princeton: Princeton University Press, 2004); and Susan Manly, *Language, Custom and Nation in the 1790s: Locke, Tooke, Words-worth, Edgeworth* (Aldershot: Ashgate, 2007).

[11] To Robert Southey, 29 July 1802, in *Collected Letters of Samuel Taylor Coleridge*, ed. Earl Leslie Griggs, 6 vols (Oxford: Clarendon Press, 1956–71), ii. 830.

[12] Cf. Thomas Love Peacock's chapter 'The Philosophy of Ballads' in his novel *Melincourt* (1817), which satirizes the spurious theorization of simple ballads as part of the intellectual inflation for which the Lake poets were responsible.

[13] Paul Hamilton, *Metaromanticism: Aesthetics, Literature, Theory* (Chicago: University of Chicago Press, 2003).

French Revolution. I show how, in the revolutionary decade, the forms and functions of literature were debated alongside the forms and functions of government, and how genericity itself—the display of generic affiliation—acquired a strong political colouring. Setting *Lyrical Ballads* against other 1790s texts, I consider the complexities of this intersection of literature and politics, and its implications for later conceptualizations of genre. The second section examines new theories of form, taking German poetics as a point of departure. My focus here is Coleridge, the most influential exponent of German doctrines of organic form and also the shrewdest interpreter of the earlier British aesthetic tradition to which German theory was, in turn, a response. The contradictory attitudes that Coleridge displays towards concepts of form and genre, and critical methodologies derived from them, are, I argue, illustrative of an ambivalence that characterizes the Romantic movement as a whole. In my final section, I turn to an even more contradictory text, Wordsworth's Preface to his collected *Poems* of 1815, whose multiple classification systems dramatize in a peculiarly stark way the tensions and confusions in contemporary approaches to genre and the difficulties faced by Romantic writers when trying to organize and theorize their work.

## THE REVOLUTIONARY CONTEXT

The decline of the neoclassical genre-system, once a cornerstone of the 'republic of letters', was an important factor in what Paul Keen terms the 'crisis of literature' of the 1790s.[14] Although, as we saw in the previous chapter, neoclassical genre theory survived well into the nineteenth century in the modified form of Enlightenment treatises such as Hugh Blair's much-reprinted *Lectures on Rhetoric and Belles Lettres* (1783), its limitations and blind spots became ever more apparent, as was demonstrated by the increasingly frequent denunciations of the 'French school' and the growing support for alternative theories of literature. Henry Boyd's argument, quoted previously, about the non-applicability of the 'old imperial code' to a medieval writer like Dante, and similar comments by others about Shakespeare, Spenser, and Milton, expressed a widely held conviction that large parts of the European literary tradition were governed by principles fundamentally different from those found in neoclassical handbooks. The emergence in contemporary literature of new ways of writing that eluded traditional poetic categories altogether—compositions entitled 'fragments', 'sketches', or 'effusions', or carrying no generic designation at all—put further pressure on the neoclassical genre-system, which seemed incapable too of dealing with the period's most conspicuous literary phenomenon, the rise of the novel. Attempts were made to integrate these new genres or quasi-genres into existing taxonomies, but many writers and critics were coming

---

[14] Paul Keen, *The Crisis of Literature in the 1790s: Print Culture and Public Sphere* (Cambridge: Cambridge University Press, 1999), ch. 1. Cf. Jon Klancher, 'The Vocation of Criticism and the Crisis of the Republic of Letters', in Marshall Brown (ed.), *The Cambridge History of Literary Criticism*, v: *Romanticism* (Cambridge: Cambridge University Press, 2000).

to the conclusion that, where matters of genre was concerned, the neoclassical paradigm was irretrievably flawed and obsolete.

The perception that the traditional genre-system was under serious threat may, paradoxically, explain the exaggerated classicism of a project like *Bell's Classical Arrangement of Fugitive Poetry* (1789–96), which attempts to satisfy the demand for new modes of expression while remaining faithful to established categories.[15] Another, more successful example of the same strategy is John Wolcot's *Pindariana, or, Peter's Portfolio, containing Tale, Fable, Translation, Ode, Elegy, Epigram, Song, Pastoral, Letters, with Extracts from Tragedy, Comedy, Opera, &c.* (1794). Wolcot, a brilliant self-inventor whose ultra-classical pseudonym 'Peter Pindar' conceals complex literary and political loyalties, exploits contemporary ambivalence about genre to clever satirical effect. The ostentatious array of genres on his title page (Figure 2.1), reinforced by a part-quotation from Horace's *Ars Poetica*, '*Non satis est* pulchra *esse poemata*—' ('It is not enough for poems to be *beautiful*—'), is calculated to appeal to a classically minded readership for whom the reading experience is an exercise in advanced literary competence. It soon becomes clear, though, that what is being offered is not pure classicism but a set of irreverent variations upon it. Wolcot completes the Horace quotation with six supplementary lines of his own which compare the writing of poetry to a game of cards, with the four suits (rendered in Italian) mirroring his classification of genres: 'The game is in the Poet's hand— | SPADILLIO, and MANNILLIO, BASTO, PUNTO').[16] This celebration of generic diversity continues in the prefatory address 'To the Public', which contains an apostrophe to 'Versatility' intended to whet the reader's appetite for the even more eclectic array of genres found in the collection itself. These include, in addition to the genres listed on the title page, a 'complaint', a 'panegyric', a 'druid hymn', an 'anacreontic song', a 'stable cantata', a 'madrigal', an 'elegiac ballad', a 'sketch', various kinds of 'fragment', and a poem in praise of 'anecdote'.

In his use of pseudo- or mock-genres Wolcot is working in the tradition of Augustan satire, and the collection as a whole is reminiscent of the Scriblerian miscellanies of the 1720s and 1730s.[17] But Wolcot is also exploiting the expanded generic repertoire of the 1790s, ironizing the current fashion for new quasi-genres like the fragment, anecdote, or sketch. His inclusion of 'delicious scraps of Criticism' underlines the work's playful self-consciousness, signalling that criticism too has become another fashionable genre in its own right. The hyper-classicism of *Pindariana* is not, then, the conservative gesture it purports to be, but a more subversive engagement with contemporary literary taste which taps competing trends simultaneously.

---

[15] See Ch. 1 above, pp. 24–8.

[16] [John Wolcot], *Pindariana, or, Peter's Portfolio, Containing Tale, Fable, Translation, Ode, Elegy, Epigram, Song, Pastoral, Letters; with Extracts from Tragedy, Comedy, Opera, &c. By Peter Pindar* (London, 1794), title page. Horace's original reads 'Non satis est pulchra esse poemata, dulcia sunto' ('It is not enough for poems to be beautiful; they must also be pleasing'; *Ars Poetica*, line 99).

[17] For Wolcot's connection with this tradition, see Thomas Lockwood, *Post-Augustan Satire: Charles Churchill and Satirical Poetry, 1750–1800* (Seattle: University of Washington Press, 1979); Howard D. Weinbrot, *Eighteenth-Century Satire: Essays on Text and Context from Dryden to Peter Pindar* (Cambridge: Cambridge University Press, 1988), 199–202; and Robert L. Vales, *Peter Pindar* (New York: Twayne, 1973).

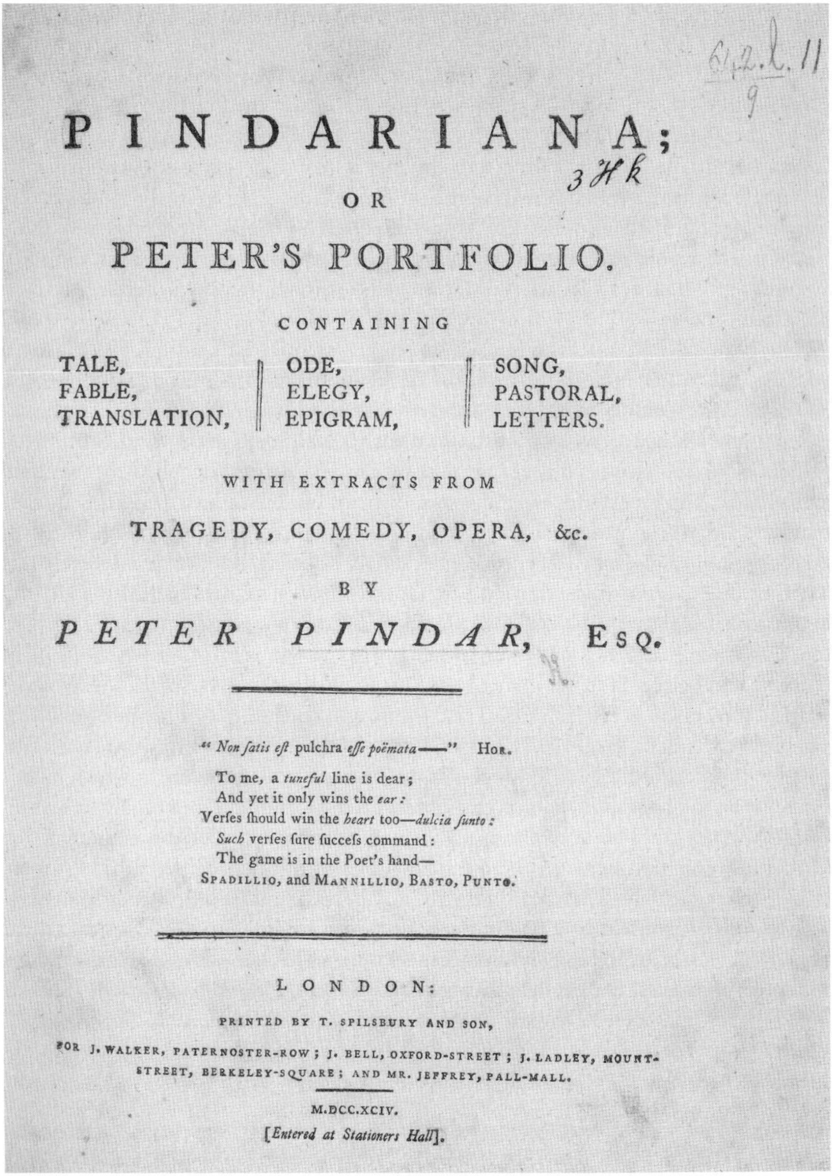

6,2.l. 11
9

# PINDARIANA;

3 H k

### OR

## PETER'S PORTFOLIO.

CONTAINING

| TALE, | ODE, | SONG, |
|---|---|---|
| FABLE, | ELEGY, | PASTORAL, |
| TRANSLATION, | EPIGRAM, | LETTERS. |

WITH EXTRACTS FROM

TRAGEDY, COMEDY, OPERA, &c.

BY

## PETER PINDAR, Esq.

"*Non fatis eft* pulchra *effe poëmata*——" Hor.

To me, a *tuneful* line is dear;
And yet it only wins the *ear:*
Verfes fhould win the *heart* too—*dulcia funto:*
Such verfes fure fuccefs command:
The game is in the Poet's hand—
Spadillio, and Mannillio, Basto, Punto.

LONDON:

PRINTED BY T. SPILSBURY AND SON,

FOR J. WALKER, PATERNOSTER-ROW; J. BELL, OXFORD-STREET; J. LADLEY, MOUNT-
STREET, BERKELEY-SQUARE; AND MR. JEFFREY, PALL-MALL.

M.DCC.XCIV.

[*Entered at Stationers Hall*].

**Figure 2.1.** Title page to John Wolcot's *Pindariana, or, Peter's Portfolio* (1794)

In contrast to *Bell's Classical Arrangement*, the editorial rationale of which is to impose order on its 'fugitive' contents, Wolcot presents heterogeneity as an end in itself: 'Let me inform thee, Reader, that no order will be observed with respect to the various pieces. Thou wilt receive them as they leap from the Portfolio' (p. vi). Yet, if 'order' has been abandoned, genre clearly has not. Indeed, what both Wolcot's collection and Bell's bring home very forcibly is that genericity—the overt display of generic affiliation—had now become, in the technical sense, 'marked'. In face of the anti-generic and anti-classical tendencies that were gaining ground in other quarters, for a poet or editor to highlight genre was no longer a neutral, innocent gesture, as it had been in the heyday of neoclassicism. It was a deliberate, even polemical, stance.

The political resonances of such a stance are complex. By adopting a classicist persona and positioning himself within the tradition of Pope, Gay, and Churchill, Wolcot might seem to be aligning himself with the literary *ancien régime*—the so-called 'French school'. Wolcot, however, detaches his classicism from the outmoded poetics of neoclassicism. His reworkings of classical genres are unpredictable and iconoclastic, and he extends the Augustan tactic of burlesque imitation into an even freer style of ironic variation, introducing his bizarre compositions with a critical rhetoric that is gleefully eccentric. His actual political opinions, moreover, are anything but conservative. A friend of Godwin and a known radical (albeit of a highly individual cast), Wolcot opens *Pindariana* with a mock-reverential 'Hymn to the Guillotine', and includes many other poems in the vein of anti-establishment satire he had perfected in his *Lyric Odes to the Royal Academicians* (1782).[18] Wolcot's satirical targets are as varied as his verse forms, the consistency of his position lying not in his adherence to any party or faction but in his rejection of spurious authority, whether political or literary. The fact that the Pindaric ode, the genre in which he had (literally) made his name, had recently been used for public ceremonials in revolutionary France only adds to the irony in which his poetry delights, complicating further any equation between literary classicism and political conservatism.

Nor is there, at this historical moment, any necessary connection between genericity and classicism. Conspicuous generic affiliation could be to non-classical as well as classical genres, or to both simultaneously, as in John Thelwall's *The Peripatetic, or, Sketches of the Heart, of Nature and Society; in a Series of Politico-Sentimental Journals, In Verse and Prose, of the Eccentric Excursions of Sylvanus Theophrastus, Supposed to be Written by Himself* (1793). Aptly described by Judith Thompson as an 'exercise in applied genre theory',[19] Thelwall's strange book exceeds even Wolcot's in its display

---

[18] Gary Dyer, *British Satire and the Politics of Style, 1789–1832* (Cambridge: Cambridge University Press, 1997), ch. 1. See also Benjamin Colbert, 'Petrio-Pindarics: John Wolcot and the Romantics', *European Romantic Review*, 16/3 (2005), 311–28; and H. J. Jackson, 'England's Populist Pindars', *Electronic British Library Journal* (2002), available at http://www.bl.uk/eblj/2002articles/article4.html.

[19] Judith Thompson, ' "A Voice in the Representation": John Thelwall and the Enfranchisement of Literature', in Tilottama Rajan and Julia M. Wright (eds), *Romanticism, History, and the Possibilities of Genre: Re-forming Literature 1789–1837* (Cambridge: Cambridge University Press, 1998), 124.

of generic abundance, but does so in ways that are recognizably Romantic: first, by calling attention to its promiscuous mixture of genres; secondly, by describing its miscellaneous contents as 'sketches', thereby invoking the emergent poetics of indeterminacy and incompleteness; thirdly, by harnessing the fashionable cult of sentiment, now strongly politicized through its association with French revolutionary psychology; and fourthly, by presenting his generic experiment in the first person, as a piece of confessional writing in the tradition of Rousseau, albeit mediated here by a pseudo-classical persona, 'Sylvanus Theophrastus'. In his Preface, Thelwall underlines his commitment to generic hybridity, explaining that he wrote *The Peripatetic* with the aim of 'uniting the different advantages of the novel, the sentimental journal, and the miscellaneous collection of essays and poetical effusions'.[20] Formally, the work's most distinctive feature is the continuous interspersal of verse and prose, especially critical prose, as in the sections 'The Epic Poem' and 'The Sonnet', each of which theorizes a genre while also generating original samples of it. Foregrounding genre both in its subject matter and its construction, the whole book becomes what Thompson calls an 'intergeneric conversation' in which the author 'revolutionizes literature not by escaping convention but by highlighting it'.[21]

If the extreme foregrounding of generic affiliation is one manifestation of contemporary hyperconsciousness about genre, another is what Jon Klancher calls the ideologically driven 'genre-reform programmes' which transformed many genres in the 1790s.[22] A good example is Southey's reworking of the eclogue. As Stuart Curran has shown, Southey's 'Botany-Bay eclogues' in his *Poems* (1797) exploit a fashion for territorial adaptations of the eclogue that had begun with William Collins's *Persian Eclogues* (1742) and by now included such variants as 'Asiatic eclogues', 'American eclogues', 'Arabian eclogues', 'East-Indian eclogues', 'Chinese eclogues', 'African eclogues', 'European eclogues', and many others.[23] Southey supplements and ironizes this generic imperialism by relocating the pastoral ideal among the transported felons of Botany Bay, a manoeuvre which plays on the theme of exile already present in Virgil's eclogues while simultaneously allowing Southey to expose pastoral's ideological 'trick', as Empson called it, of mystifying class divisions by depicting gentlemen dressed up in proletarian clothes enjoying idealized country landscapes.[24] Southey was not the first to expose this generic trick—he is part of a tradition of radical anti-pastoral that goes back through Crabbe and Churchill to Stephen Duck's *The Thresher's Labour* (1730), a genuinely proletarian pastoral[25]—but he does so in a new and uncompromising way

[20] John Thelwall, *The Peripatetic*, ed. Judith Thompson (Detroit: Wayne State University Press, 2001), 72.

[21] Ibid., introd., 43. For a similar reading of this text, see Gary Kelly, 'The Limits of Genre and the Institution of Literature: Romanticism between Fact and Fiction', in Kenneth Johnston et al. (eds), *Romantic Revolutions: Criticism and Theory* (Bloomington: Indiana University Press, 1990).

[22] Jon Klancher, 'Godwin and the Genre Reformers: On Necessity and Contingency in Romantic Narrative Theory', in Rajan and Wright (eds), *Romanticism, History, and the Possibilities of Genre*.

[23] Stuart Curran, *Poetic Form and British Romanticism* (New York: Oxford University Press, 1986), 95–9.

[24] William Empson, *Some Versions of Pastoral* (1935; London: Hogarth Press, 1986), 11–12.

[25] For examples and commentary, see John Barrell and John Bull (eds), *The Penguin Book of English Pastoral Verse* (Harmondsworth: Penguin, 1974), section entitled 'Some Versions of Anti-Pastoral'.

that pushes the genre beyond topical satire towards outright political propaganda. Like Southey's controversial adaptation of epic, whose nationalist premiss he subverts in *Joan of Arc* (1796) by taking as his subject 'the defeat of my country', this open challenge to the ideological foundations of his chosen form shows how central genre theory was to the literary politics of the revolutionary decade.[26]

Drama provides other examples. One of the most impressive attempts at genre-reform is Joanna Baillie's *Plays on the Passions* (1798), an experimental work whose originality, like that of *Lyrical Ballads*, lies partly in its synthesis of precept and practice (Baillie's Introductory Discourse may indeed have influenced Wordsworth's Preface[27]). In purely theoretical terms, Baillie's most significant innovation was to develop Adam Smith's concept of sympathy into a dramaturgical principle of 'sympathetick curiosity', a move which allows her to re-examine the psychodynamics of audience response while avoiding the usual Aristotelian clichés about catharsis.[28] Crucial, too, to her case for generic reform is her historical relativizing of the 'rules' of drama. The 'taste for drama', she argues, is 'universal', but the forms in which it exists are culturally specific. Critics err in deriving universally binding rules from the practice of the ancient Geeks, for

> Had the Drama been the invention of a less cultivated nation, more of action and of passion would have been introduced into it. It would have been more irregular, more imperfect, more varied, more interesting. From poor beginnings it would have advanced in a progressive state; and succeeding poets, not having those polished and admired originals to look back upon, would have presented their respective contemporaries with the produce of a free and unbridled imagination.[29]

This is not the usual libertarian attack on Aristotle and his disciples, but an astute application of the historical methods of the Scottish Enlightenment. In Baillie's hands, conjectural history becomes virtual history as she imagines an evolution of European drama entirely different from the one that actually occurred. Her own dramas are offered as illustrations of this imagined alternative tradition: their formal and thematic innovations are intended to demonstrate unexplored possibilities in tragedy and comedy, not only in the realm of character psychology but also in sociological matters, a central feature of the plays being their subtle investigation of gender and class.[30]

---

[26]  Robert Southey, *Joan of Arc: An Epic Poem* (1796), preface, p. vii. For his subversion of epic, see Curran, *Poetic Form and British Romanticism*, 167–8; and Lynda Pratt, 'Patriot Poetics and the Romantic National Epic: Placing and Displacing Southey's *Joan of Arc*', in Peter J. Kitson (ed.), *Placing and Displacing Romanticism* (Aldershot: Ashgate, 2001).

[27]  Marlon Ross, *The Contours of Masculine Desire: Romanticism and the Rise of Women's Poetry* (New York: Oxford University Press, 1989), 257–9.

[28]  As noted by Peter Duthie in his introduction to Joanna Baillie, *Plays on the Passions (1798 Edition)* (Peterborough, Ont.: Broadview, 2001), 28. All subsequent references are to Duthie's edition.

[29]  *Plays on the Passions*, introductory discourse, 84 n.

[30]  Daniel P. Watkins, *A Materialist Critique of English Romantic Drama* (Gainesville: University Press of Florida, 1993), ch. 3; Catherine B. Burroughs, *Closet Stages: Joanna Baillie and the Theater Theory of British Romantic Women Writers* (Philadelphia: University of Pennsylvania Press, 1997).

The political subtext of Baillie's Introductory Discourse becomes even clearer when she turns to the question of audience response, and quotes the famous saying recorded by her countryman Andrew Fletcher of Saltoun: 'let who will make the laws of the nation, if I have the writing of its ballads'.[31] Baillie promptly extends this striking idea to drama:

Its lessons reach not, indeed, to the lowest classes of the labouring people, who are the broad foundation of society, which can never be generally moved without endangering every thing that is constructed upon it, and who are our potent and formidable ballad readers; but they reach to the classes next in order to them, and who will always have over them no inconsiderable influence. The impressions made by it are communicated, at the same instant of time, to a greater number of individuals, than those made by any other species of writing; and they are strengthened in every spectator, by observing their effects upon those who surround him. (pp. 103–4)

Baillie's confidence that theatre audiences were drawn only from the lower middle class and above was probably misplaced. This may have been true of the 'legitimate' dramas staged at Covent Garden and Drury Lane, but 'illegitimate' theatre was available to all comers in the minor playhouses, and the history of theatre in this period shows a steady downward mobility in theatre audiences both in London and in the provinces.[32] Such developments, however, are precisely what worry her. Her point about the contagion of emotion in a theatre audience is presented as part of an argument about the positive effects of drama, but it betrays an undercurrent of anxiety about crowd psychology that almost certainly reflects the political experience of the 1790s. The tightening of censorship controls over spoken drama was a product of the same political paranoia that led to bans on political associations. Baillie's proposals for generic reform can thus be seen in part as an attempt to harness the ideological power of drama while guarding against its misuse—and thereby forestalling government interference.

Her comments about 'potent and formidable ballad readers' illustrate a similar nervousness, widely shared at the time, about the spread of political literacy. The special danger believed to be posed by ballads is pinpointed by the definition of the genre that appears in the third edition of the *Encyclopaedia Britannica* (1797):

BALLAD, a kind of song, adapted to the capacity of the lower class of the people; who being mightily taken with the species of poetry, are thereby not a little influenced in the conduct of their lives. Hence we find, that seditious and designing men never fail to spread ballads among the people, with a view to gain them over to their side.[33]

Although the borrowing is unacknowledged, the first sentence of this definition is copied verbatim from an earlier dictionary published in 1778.[34] The second

---

[31] *Plays on the Passions*, introductory discourse, 103. For the Fletcher quotation, see Ch. 3 below, p. 107.

[32] Jane Moody, *Illegitimate Theatre in London 1770–1840* (Cambridge: Cambridge University Press, 2000); David Worrall, *Theatric Revolution: Drama, Censorship and Romantic Period Subcultures 1773–1832* (Oxford: Oxford University Press, 2006).

[33] *Encyclopaedia Britannica, or, A Dictionary of Arts, Sciences, and Miscellaneous Literature*, 18 vols (Edinburgh, 1797), ii/2. 768.

[34] Entry for 'Ballad' in *The New Complete Dictionary of Arts and Sciences, or, An Universal System of Useful Knowledge* (London, 1778).

sentence, however, is new, and it is without doubt a disapproving allusion to the radical broadside ballads currently being circulated in large numbers by working-class reform organizations. Such propagandistic deployments of the popular ballad are as much part of 1790s genre-reform as the more subtle innovations of the Wordsworthian 'lyrical' ballad; and so too are their ideological adversary, the loyalist pseudo-ballad produced, in equally large numbers, by Hannah More at the Cheap Repository.[35] The proliferation of these ideological variants is symptomatic of a period in which transformations of generic function and status were as rapid and as contentious as transformations of form.

The wholesale politicization of genre in the 1790s is nowhere better captured than in James Gillray's famous cartoon 'New Morality', published in the *Anti-Jacobin Review and Magazine* in 1798 (Figure 2.2). Inspired by George Canning's poem of the same name, a satire on both 'Modern Philosophy' and the 'new school of poetry', Gillray's scene depicts an imaginary inauguration ceremony in St Paul's Cathedral following a successful French invasion, in which British Jacobins pay homage to the new secular gods of revolutionary France and their high priest Lépeaux. Southey and Coleridge lead the procession, carrying a large 'Cornucopia of Ignorance' and brandishing their 'Sapphics' and 'Dactylics' respectively. Thelwall sits on the head of Leviathan in an oratorical posture, holding his 'Lectures'. Charles Lloyd and Charles Lamb, represented as a toad and a frog, carry their 'Blank Verse' (the title of their co-authored volume of 1798). Elsewhere, held aloft or deposited in a heap at the altar, we find 'Priestley's Political Sermons', 'Tooke's Speeches', 'Curwen's Speeches', 'Tierney's Address', 'Morris's Bawdy Songs', 'Mrs Godwin's Memoirs', 'Whig Toasts and Sentiments', 'Letter to the Peers of Scotland', and other offerings, each alluding to a recent publication.[36] This heterogeneous array of titles underlines Canning's declared aim of stamping out Jacobinism 'in all its shapes, and in all its degrees, political and moral, public and private',[37] but equally telling is Gillray's round-up of all its *forms*, from parliamentary speeches and political lectures to poems, novels, and newspapers. The French Revolution debate is often referred to as a 'pamphlet war', but it was, generically speaking, much more diverse than that.[38] Indeed, the generic diversity of the Revolution controversy—the ability of political theory to metamorphose into other forms, and to infiltrate and

---

[35]  Gary Kelly, 'Revolution, Reaction, and the Expropriation of Popular Culture: Hannah More's "Cheap Repository"', *Man and Nature*, 6 (1987), 147–59; Kevin Gilmartin, *Writing against Revolution: Literary Conservatism in Britain, 1790–1832* (Cambridge: Cambridge University Press, 2007), ch. 2.

[36]  For an analysis of Gillray's cartoon and its textual allusions, see M. Dorothy George, *Catalogue of Political and Personal Satires Preserved at the Department of Prints and Drawings in the British Museum*, vi: *1784–92* (London: British Museum, 1938), 468–72 (no. 9240).

[37]  *Anti-Jacobin, or, Weekly Examiner*, prospectus [by George Canning] (1797), in Marilyn Butler (ed.), *Burke, Paine, Godwin, and the Revolution Controversy* (Cambridge: Cambridge University Press, 1984), 216.

[38]  Some indication of the generic range is given by Butler's anthology (see previous note) and two other influential collections: Alfred Cobban (ed.), *The Debate on the French Revolution 1789–1800*, 2nd edn (London: A. and C. Black, 1960); and David Bindman, *The Shadow of the Guillotine: Britain and the French Revolution*, exhibition catalogue (London: British Museum, 1989).

**Figure 2.2.** Detail from James Gillray's *New Morality*, published in the *Anti-Jacobin Review and Magazine* on 1 August 1798

pamphletize a huge range of genres—is an aspect of the revolutionary phenomenon that Burke and other conservatives found deeply disturbing, however much they exploited this technique themselves. Genres, verse forms, aesthetic categories, para-textual devices, publishing formats, even typefaces, all acquired specific political resonances, and were fought over almost as vehemently as the political ideas themselves. Just as the French Revolution debate established a model for the intensely discursive and intertextual form of literariness that characterizes British Romanticism, so it helped shape the ideological sensitivity to genre that is another defining feature of the period.

When Coleridge in 1800 told Humphry Davy of his intention to write an 'Essay on the Elements of Poetry' which 'would in reality be a disguised System of Morals & Politics',[39] he was thus making explicit an assumption that at the time was widely accepted, namely that literary theory and politics had become inseparably connected. Rediscovery of this connection, and of the literary–political codes that govern it, has transformed scholarly interpretation of Romantic-era criticism, including its best-known text, the Preface to *Lyrical Ballads*. Previously regarded as the blueprint for an expressive, transcendental poetics that would abstract poetry from the world of revolutionary politics and current affairs, the Preface is now seen once again as an irreducibly political document. Had it been published in 1798, 'Wordsworth's Preface' might well have found itself in Gillray's pile of subversive pamphlets. The pamphlet-like quality of the Preface is, indeed, one of its most controversial features, since the Preface is not simply an introduction to a collection of poems, but a statement of fundamental principles that is knowingly polemical both in its fore-grounding of 'theory'—another anti-Jacobin bugbear—and in the theoretical posi-tions themselves. Wordsworth disclaims the idea that the Preface is 'a systematic defence of the theory upon which these poems are written' (i. 148), but it is precisely that, so much so that it gave new impetus to the word 'system', thereafter inextricably associated in British critical discourse with the kind of theory-driven, experimental poetry that *Lyrical Ballads* made fashionable.[40] Stylistically, too, the Preface is pamphlet-like. Wordsworth's defensive posture, while reminiscent of earlier critical treatises such as Sidney's *Defence of Poesy* (1595), is shaped by the rhetoric of vindication fashioned by James Mackintosh, Mary Wollstonecraft, and other de-fenders of the French Revolution, a rhetoric which is more self-justificatory than apologetic, and which modulates easily into the even more assertive rhetoric found in the many 'Rights of' pamphlets of the 1790s. The prototype for the latter was the French *Declaration of the Rights of Man and of the Citizen*, reprinted in Paine's *Rights of Man* (1791). Wordsworth's Preface is, in effect, a British *Declaration of the Rights of the Poet*. The 1802 additions amplify the declamatory, manifesto-like quality of the Preface, introducing the demotic 'man speaking to men' passages, and claiming for the poet an ever more exalted role as universal educator and healer, he who 'binds

---

[39] *Collected Letters*, i. 632.
[40] Scott Hess, 'Wordsworth's "System", the Critical Reviews, and the Reconstruction of Literary Authority', *European Romantic Review*, 16/4 (2005), 471–97.

together by passion and knowledge the vast empire of human society, as it is spread over the whole earth, and over all time'.[41]

The subsequent history of Romantic theory in Britain is, to no small degree, a history of responses to this foundational document. The distinctive emphases, omissions, and tactical concealments in Wordsworth's treatment of genre are thus of the greatest consequence in establishing the terms of subsequent debate. A brief comparison with Schlegel's *Dialogue on Poetry* and other German texts will highlight salient features both of Wordsworth's Preface and of the British debate as a whole. Broadly, the genre theory of British Romanticism is less abstract and speculative, more empirical and descriptive, than its German counterpart. With the notable exception of Coleridge, British discussion of genre proceeds at a lower level of abstraction and generalization, and outside the philosophical framework of transcendental idealism that underpins German critical discourse of the period. In his *Critical Fragments* (1797), Friedrich Schlegel remarks: 'We already have so many theories about poetical genres. Why have we no concept yet of poetical genre? Perhaps then we would have to make do with a single theory of poetical genres.'[42] His own theoretical work, like that of other German critics and philosophers, was an attempt to supply that missing concept, and with it to build a new kind of genre theory that would be 'the true aesthetics of literature'.[43] In Britain, such questions did not arise. At the close of the eighteenth century, individual 'species of composition' were regularly defined and discussed, as they had been since the Renaissance, but theoretical discussion rarely progressed from the species to the genus. When it did, the genus was 'poetry in general', or 'literature' as a whole, rather than 'genre', a word that only entered English in the twentieth century. The philosophical issues posed by German theorists— whether genre was a metaphysical category or a taxonomic convenience, a product of mind or a product of history—were rarely addressed in Britain.

Another plane of generalization, concerned with the three presentational modes— epic, lyric, and dramatic—is also largely absent from British theory of this period. The 'seductive triad' (derived, as Gérard Genette explains in his indispensable history of the topic, from a misreading and conflation of Plato and Aristotle[44]) was the focus of endless speculative discussion in Germany, inaugurating a tradition of *Gattungstheorie* that lasted for more than a century and a half.[45] The triadic genre theories of Goethe, the Schlegels, Hölderlin, Novalis, Schelling, Jean Paul, Humboldt, Hegel, and others, with their ingenious but mutually incompatible allocations of different temporalities, and different levels of 'subjectivity' and 'objectivity', to the three modes (and combinations thereof) have no real equivalent in British Romantic

---

[41] *Prose Works*, i. 138, 141.

[42] *Critical Fragments* (1797), no. 62, in Friedrich Schlegel, *Philosophical Fragments*, trans. Peter Firchow (Minneapolis: University of Minnesota Press, 1991), 8.

[43] *Dialogue on Poetry*, 78.

[44] Gérard Genette, *The Architext: An Introduction* (1979), trans. Jane E. Lewin (Berkeley: University of California Press, 1992), 38.

[45] For modern appraisals of this tradition, see ibid.; Paul Hernadi, *Beyond Genre: New Directions in Literary Classification* (Ithaca, N.Y.: Cornell University Press, 1972); and René Wellek, 'Genre Theory, the Lyric and *Erlebnis*' (1967), in his *Discriminations: Further Concepts of Criticism* (New Haven: Yale University Press, 1970).

theory. Nor do the equally persistent attempts by German theorists, beginning with Friedrich Schlegel, to establish a dialectical relationship between the three modes by equating them with 'thesis', 'antithesis', and 'synthesis' (though, again, there is little agreement about which goes with which). There are occasional echoes of these ideas in Coleridge and De Quincey, but in general, by comparison with the German, British Romantic theory seems stubbornly unsystematic, and more concerned with the empirical characteristics of genres than with their logical relationship to one another.

Missing, too, from most British theory is the classical–romantic antithesis, described by Hazlitt as 'the *nucleus* of the prevailing criticism of German criticism'.[46] The English translation (1813) of Madame de Staël's *De l'Allemagne* gave some currency to this distinction, as did translations of A. W. Schlegel's *Lectures on Dramatic Art and Literature* (1815) and Friedrich Schlegel's *Lectures on the History of Literature, Ancient and Modern* (1818), both of which (the former especially) were widely reviewed.[47] But, as Byron noted in 1820, the 'great struggle' that took place in Germany and Italy 'about what they call "*Classical and Romantic*"' never happened in England, and these terms 'were not subjects of Classification' when he left the country in 1816.[48] Indeed, the English word 'romantic', for all its many meanings, was rarely used except by Coleridge in anything resembling the German sense; and when British critics spoke of 'romantic poetry', they were generally referring to medieval or Renaissance literature, not modern. Only much later, in the 1880s, did the term start to be applied, retrospectively, to poetry of the late eighteenth and early nineteenth century, and the 'classical–romantic' binary be used to differentiate ancient and modern literature.[49]

To speak of 'Romantic genre theory' in the British context thus entails a degree of anachronism: in the period we now designate Romantic, the adjective 'romantic' meant something different, the term 'genre' did not exist, and the word 'theory' was generally avoided. Nevertheless, on its own terms the British debate on genre was as profound and far-reaching as the German. The preoccupations that mark the Preface to *Lyrical Ballads*—generic rivalry, the value and 'purpose' of poetry, the relationship between poetry and prose, the function of metre, the psychology of composition, generic decorum, the author–reader contract—continue to shape British critical

---

[46] 'Schlegel on the Drama', *Edinburgh Review*, 26 (Feb. 1816), in *The Complete Works of William Hazlitt*, ed. P. P. Howe, 21 vols (London: Dent, 1930–4), xvi. 60.

[47] Thomas G. Sauer, *A. W. Schlegel's Shakespearean Criticism in England, 1811–1835* (Bonn: Bouvier Verlag H. Grundmann, 1981). For the British reception of Friedrich Schlegel's *Lectures* (in Lockhart's 1818 translation), see Ian Duncan, *Scott's Shadow: The Novel in Romantic Edinburgh* (Princeton: Princeton University Press, 2007), 47–8; and Daniel Wall, 'Countering Cultural Maladies: The Writings of John Gibson Lockhart', Ph.D. diss. (University of Aberdeen, 2008), 10–25.

[48] Epistle to Goethe, cancelled Dedication to *Marino Falieri*, in Lord Byron, *The Complete Poetical Works*, ed. Jerome J. McGann, 7 vols (Oxford: Clarendon Press, 1980–93), iv. 546.

[49] See George Whalley, 'England: Romantic-Romanticism', in Hans Eichner (ed.), *'Romantic' and its Cognates: The European History of a Word* (Manchester: Manchester University Press, 1972); Herbert Weisinger, 'English Treatment of the Classic–Romantic Problem', *Modern Language Quarterly*, 7 (1946), 477–88; René Wellek, 'The Concept of Romanticism in Literary History' (1949), in his *Concepts of Criticism*, ed. Stephen G. Nichols (New Haven: Yale University Press, 1963); and David Perkins, 'The Construction of "the Romantic Movement" as a Literary Classification', *Nineteenth-Century Literature*, 45/2 (1990), 129–43.

theory for several decades. Typically, reflection on genre is framed within larger debates about rhetoric, the arts, or knowledge in general. Lacking a concept of 'aesthetics' as a separate branch of philosophy (as it had been in Germany since the 1750s), British genre theory is eclectic and interdisciplinary: geography and history, philosophy and politics, psychology and rhetoric, are as much part of its remit as questions of language and form. A characteristic feature is the conjunction of idealist and materialist premises: interest in the internal workings of genre is complicated by the realization, often reluctant, that literature was now a commodity, its fortunes regulated by a sophisticated book trade with its own generic hierarchies and classification systems. Where neoclassical critics had agonized over generic rules and definitions, Romantic theorists struggle with the knowledge that literary genres are subject not only to artistic laws but also to commercial laws of supply and demand, which are dependent in turn on the rapidly shifting demography of the reading public. Economic and social factors surface constantly in British critical writing of the period, and Friedrich Schlegel's Antonio is not wide of the mark when he observes that 'the basic principles of English criticism' should be sought in Adam Smith's *Wealth of Nations*.[50]

It is no accident, then, that parts of Shelley's *Defence of Poetry*, including its famous final paragraph about poets as 'the unacknowledged legislators of the world', originate in an unfinished political tract entitled 'A Philosophical View of Reform', or that Peacock and Jeffrey link their analysis of the rise and fall of poetry to a Scottish-Enlightenment-style history of civil society organized around shifts in the division of labour.[51] Shelley, Hazlitt, Lamb, De Quincey, and Barry Cornwall all follow Wordsworth's lead in treating poetry as a form of 'power' and investigating its connection with other forms of power, political included.[52] In their essays, reviews, and prefaces, Leigh Hunt and Hazlitt write constantly about the politics and sociology of genres, an approach already popularized by Isaac D'Israeli, whose best-selling *Curiosities of Literature* books include, alongside quirky literary anecdotes, penetrating historical studies of marginal genres such as masques, royal proclamations, pamphlets, proverbs, anagrams and echo verses, and 'secret histories'.[53] The fact that informal works

---

[50] *Dialogue on Poetry*, 58.

[51] See Chs 4 and 5 below, pp. 142–5, 195.

[52] For 'power' as a keyword in Romantic critical discourse, see Patrick Parrinder, *Authors and Authority, English and American Criticism 1750–1990*, 2nd edn (New York: Columbia University Press, 1991), 56–63. Another example is Barry Cornwall [Bryan Procter]'s *Defence of Poetry* (1828), which, like Shelley's *Defence*, rebuts the utilitarian charge that poetry is useless, describing the poetic imagination as 'a POWER (and no mean one) not be despised or neglected, but to be cherished and used like any other power, for purposes beneficial to mankind'; *Essays and Tales in Prose*, 2 vols (Boston, 1853), ii. 176.

[53] Isaac D'Israeli, *Curiosities of Literature: Consisting of Anecdotes, Characters, Sketches, and Observations, Literary, Critical, and Historical* (London, 1791; additional vols, 1793, 1817); *A Second Series of Curiosities of Literature: Consisting of Researches in Literary, Biographical, and Political History; of Critical and Philosophical Inquiries; and of Secret History*, 3 vols (London, 1823). For D'Israeli's distinctive brand of historical criticism, see April London, 'Isaac D'Israeli and Literary History: Opinion, Anecdote, and Secret History in the Early Nineteenth Century', *Poetics Today*, 26 (2005), 351–86; and Ina Ferris, 'Antiquarian Authorship: D'Israeli's Miscellany of Literary Curiosity and the Question of Secondary Genres', *Studies in Romanticism*, 45/4 (2006), 523–42.

like D'Israeli's, intended for the coffee table rather than the lecture hall, could include substantial essays on such topics as 'The Political Influence of Authors' (1795), 'The Spirit of Literature and the Spirit of Society' (1818), and 'Expression of Suppressed Opinion' (1823)[54] shows how receptive the British public was to the sociological approach. One reason for this, as D'Israeli himself points out,[55] was the recent experience of the French Revolution, which had demonstrated all too clearly the political effects of literature and ideas (Hazlitt later called it 'the only match that ever took place between philosophy and experience'[56]).

For Madame de Staël, herself a pioneer of literary sociology and author of an influential book about the intellectual origins of the French Revolution, this ubiquitous political awareness was a key difference between England and Germany. 'The powerful English interest in public affairs', she writes, 'is almost nonexistent' in Germany, where writers turn instead 'towards self-examination and the contemplation of nature' or, more worryingly, 'surrender to systematic theories' and 'the random action of their thoughts'.[57] Her conclusion hardly does justice to the political undercurrents in German theory,[58] but the 'public' emphasis of British literary criticism is indeed unmistakable, and it persisted long after the supposed internalization of Romantic poetics that took place at the close of the revolutionary decade. Rewriting his 'Political Influence of Authors' essay in 1822, D'Israeli was more convinced than ever: 'The public mind is the creation of the public writer; an axiom as demonstrable as any in England, and a principle as sure in its operation as any in mechanics.'[59]

## THE LANGUAGE OF FORMS

None of this can be easily reconciled with the familiar claim that the central concept of Romantic poetics was the theory of organic form. According to this view, the organic theory, with its distinction between 'organic' and 'mechanical form', was

---

[54] In, respectively, *An Essay on the Manners and Genius of the Literary Character* (London, 1795); *The Literary Character, Illustrated by the History of Men of Genius, Drawn from their Own Feelings and Confessions* (London, 1818); *A Second Series of Curiosities of Literature* (1823). See also D'Israeli's poem 'A Defence of Poetry', prefixed to his *Specimens of a New Version of Telemachus* (London, 1791), which laments the 'feeble' condition of contemporary poetry and calls on poets to be both more socially engaged and more artistically ambitious.

[55] 'Of the Political Influence of Authors', in *Essay on the Manners and Genius of the Literary Character*, 178. See also Ch. 3 below, p. 106.

[56] *Memoirs of the Late Thomas Holcroft* (1816), in Hazlitt, *Complete Works*, iii. 156.

[57] *On Literature Considered in its Relationship to Social Institutions* (1800), in *Major Writings of Germaine de Staël*, trans. Vivian Folkenflik (New York: Columbia University Press, 1987), 182–3; first trans. in 1803 as *A Treatise on Ancient and Modern Literature: Illustrated by Striking References to the Principal Events and Characters that have Distinguished the French Revolution*.

[58] On which, see Behler, *German Romantic Literary Theory*, 54–71; Frederick C. Beiser, *The Romantic Imperative: The Concept of Early German Romanticism* (Cambridge, Mass.: Harvard University Press, 2004), ch. 10; and id., *Enlightenment, Revolution, and Romanticism: The Genesis of German Political Thought* (Cambridge, Mass.: Harvard University Press, 1992).

[59] *The Literary Character, Illustrated by the History of Men of Genius*, 3rd edn, 2 vols (London, 1822), ii. 301.

developed in Germany in the late eighteenth century and imported into Britain by Coleridge. By conceiving of poetic form as the product of internally generated 'laws of growth' rather than externally imposed 'rules of construction', organic poetics posed a direct challenge to neoclassical genre theory, ultimately undermining the very concept of genre. Poetic form is individual not generic, and literary criticism must concern itself with the internal structure of a poem and the relation of its parts to the whole, not with its external shape or its conformity to some abstract generic model. Thus defined, the Romantic theory of organic form finds its logical conclusion in twentieth-century 'new criticism' or 'practical criticism', a critical methodology acutely attentive to poetic form but largely unconcerned with questions of genre, an aspect of poetry it regards as contingent and subsidiary.

Though frequently invoked, this account is misleading in several respects. First, there is no single organic theory of literature. Organic metaphors abound in Romantic criticism, and there are a number of distinct theories which elaborate the organic analogy.[60] The most significant of these are the organic–mechanical distinction developed by A. W. Schlegel in his work on dramatic form; Schelling's idea of 'self-enclosed', internally consistent art forms; Friedrich Schlegel's conception of the organic 'indivisibility' of literature as a whole; the notion of organic 'fusion' in mixed-genre works, a recurrent theme in German criticism; and the 'morphological' poetics devised by Goethe and Humboldt. Of these, none antithesizes form and genre in quite the manner suggested above. A. W. Schlegel rejects many aspects of neoclassical genre theory, especially the French doctrine of the dramatic unities, but what he proposes instead is not an anti-generic approach but a new kind of genre theory that respects the uniqueness of individual artworks and acknowledges the transformation of genres across time. His new theory of formal unity is first sketched in his 1797 essay 'Romeo and Juliet', where he seeks to resolve the sterile neoclassical dispute over tragicomedy by arguing that Shakespeare's work was *sui generis*, not least in its capacity to create unity out of contradiction.[61] In his *Lectures on Dramatic Art and Literature* (1809), he returns to this idea, developing it with his new distinction between organic and mechanical form.[62] Coleridge recapitulates these arguments in his own lectures on drama, insisting, like Schlegel, that 'we must emancipate ourselves of a false association from misapplied names—& find a new word for the Plays of Shakespear—they are in the ancient sense neither Tragedies nor Comedies,

---

[60] Abrams, *Mirror and the Lamp*, ch. 7; G. S. Rousseau (ed.), *Organic Form: The Life of an Idea* (London: Routledge and Kegan Paul, 1972); Frederick Burwick (ed.), *Approaches to Organic Form: Permutations in Science and Culture* (Dordrecht: Reidel, 1987); G. N. G. Orsini, 'The Organic Concepts in Aesthetics', *Comparative Literature*, 21 (1969), 1–30; Charles Armstrong, *Romantic Organicism: From Idealist Origins to Ambivalent Afterlife* (New York: Palgrave Macmillan, 2003).

[61] Behler, *German Romantic Literary Theory*, 93–5. First published in Schiller's journal *Die Horen*, this essay may have been read by Coleridge. An anonymous translation appeared alongside Peacock's *Four Ages of Poetry* in *Ollier's Literary Miscellany*, 1 (1820), which means that Shelley too probably saw it, though for both Coleridge and Shelley the key A. W. Schlegel text is *Lectures on Dramatic Art and Literature*.

[62] René Wellek, *A History of Modern Criticism: 1750–1950*, ii: *The Romantic Age* (New Haven: Yale University Press, 1955), 64–5.

nor both in one—but a different genus, diverse in kind not merely different in Degree—romantic Dramas, or dramatic Romances'.[63]

Goethe's description of lyric, epic, and drama as the 'three genuine natural forms of poetry' (*drei echte Naturformen der Poesie*), in contrast to the ordinary 'poetic species' (*Dichtarten*) such as ballad, elegy, epigram, and ode, represents a further extension of the organic analogy, though the precise relation between *Naturformen* and *Dichtarten* is resolved neither by Goethe nor by his successors.[64] Even more important for the history of generic thought is Goethe's theory of 'morphology', a term he coined in his botanical work to define 'the structure, the formation, and the transformation of organic bodies'.[65] Contrary to some accounts, Goethe himself did not apply his morphological model to the study of literary forms, but an attempt to do so was made by his fellow polymath Wilhelm von Humboldt, who developed a poetics based on what Lubomír Doležel calls the 'double aspect of the poetic work', its 'specific individuality and its generic form'.[66] Humboldt's 'zigzag method' of moving between individual poetic structures and universal categories represents, as Doležel notes, a highly distinctive realization of the Schlegelian goal of a new aesthetics that is both empirical and genuinely theoretical.

It was not until a century later, though, that literary theorists grasped the full implications of Goethe's dual concept of metamorphosis and of the 'Ur-type' for an understanding of genre. The breakthrough came in Vladimir Propp's *Morphology of the Folk Tale* (1928), which took as its epigraph Goethe's axiom that 'The study of forms is the study of transformations' (*Gestaltenlehre ist Verwandlungslehre*) and developed an approach to genre based on the analysis of invariants and variables.[67] Though sometimes misleadingly labelled 'formalist', Propp's methodology has little in common with Anglo-American 'new criticism', with which it is exactly contemporary, being theoretical rather than practical in emphasis, and concerned with the underlying structures of literature and their laws of transformation rather than the surface form of individual works. That such opposed critical methodologies should both derive from Romantic theories of organic form—Goethe's in the one case, Coleridge's in the other—is a reminder of the latent contradictions within this ubiquitous episteme. If we set these approaches alongside other modern theories of genre which have their roots in Romantic theory—Russian Formalism, the dialogic

[63] *The Collected Works of Samuel Taylor Coleridge*, v: *Lectures 1808–1819 On Literature*, ed. R. A. Foakes, 2 vols (London: Routledge and Kegan Paul, 1987), i. 466 (1812 series, 1st course, lecture 5, 2 June 1812; cancelled words omitted).

[64] Note to *West-österlicher Divan* ('West–East Divan'; 1819), quoted by Genette, *Architext*, 62–3, who charts the problematic legacy of this distinction.

[65] 'Vorarbeiten zu einer Physiologie der Pflanzen' ('Prolegomenon to a Physiology of Plants'; 1795), quoted by Lubomír Doležel, *Occidental Poetics: Tradition and Progress* (Lincoln: University of Nebraska Press, 1990), 56. See also Elizabeth M. Wilkinson, 'Goethe's Conception of Form', in *Goethe: Poet and Thinker: Essays by Elizabeth M. Wilkinson and L. A. Willoughby* (London: Edward Arnold, 1962); and, for the scientific context of morphological theory, Helmut Müller-Sievers, *Self-Generation: Biology, Philosophy and Literature around 1800* (Stanford, Calif.: Stanford University Press, 1997).

[66] Doležel, *Occidental Poetics*, 66–7.

[67] Vladimir Propp, *Morphology of the Folktale*, trans. Laurence Scott, 2nd edn (Austin: University of Texas Press, 1968).

poetics of Bakhtin, German *Gattungstheorie*, Bloom's theory of internalization, Marxist sociology of genres—the richness and complexity of the Romantic legacy begin to be apparent. Later chapters will explore some of these connections.

One reason for the remarkable diversity of Romantic thinking about genre was the range of critical traditions to which the Romantics were themselves responding. Historians of literary criticism are right to emphasize the innovatory character of the philosophical genre theory of German Romanticism,[68] and the pioneers were not slow to declare the originality of their aims and methods. Friedrich Schlegel's claim to be participating in an 'aesthetic revolution' analogous to the political revolution in France and Kant's 'Copernican Revolution' in philosophy[69] is no mere rhetorical gesture: the methodological shift was of that order. Yet, for Schlegel as for Kant, the stimulus—antithetical or otherwise—often came from earlier intellectual traditions, including British ones. In his *Lectures on the History of Literature, Ancient and Modern* (1812), Schlegel remarks on the 'greater freedom, originality, and knowledge of the antique' of English as compared with French critics, and acknowledges that 'German criticism certainly received its first impulse from the study of the English works of Harris, Home, Hurd, Watson, &c.'—a process assisted by the rapid flow of translations (sometimes in multiple versions) of all the major British treatises on aesthetics and literary criticism.[70]

The strength of this 'impulse', and the radical transformation British ideas undergo in German hands, can be demonstrated by some well-known examples. An important influence on A. W. Schlegel's organic–mechanical distinction was Edward Young's *Conjectures on Original Composition* (1759, translated twice into German by 1761), whose argument pivots on a contrast between 'Originals' and 'Imitations', and the different kinds of creativity they represent: 'An *Original* may be said to be of a *vegetable* nature; it rises spontaneously from the vital root of Genius; it *grows*, it is not *made*: *Imitations* are a sort of Manufacture wrought by those *Mechanics*, *Art*, and *Labour*, out of pre-existent materials not their own.'[71] Schlegel develops this comparison, substituting 'organic' for 'vegetable', introducing an internal–external distinction, and transposing the principle of growth from the artistic creator ('genius') to his artistic material ('form'). The result is the binary opposition which so impressed Coleridge, between 'organical form', which 'is innate; it unfolds itself from within, and acquires its determination along with the complete development of the

[68] Cyrus Hamlin, 'The Origins of a Philosophical Genre Theory in German Romanticism', *European Romantic Review*, 5/1 (1994), 3–14; Tilottama Rajan, 'Theories of Genre', in Brown (ed.), *Cambridge History of Literary Criticism*, v: *Romanticism*.

[69] Quoted by Behler, *German Romantic Literary Theory*, 55.

[70] Friedrich Schlegel, *Lectures on the History of Literature, Ancient and Modern*, [trans. J. G. Lockhart], 2 vols (Edinburgh, 1818), ii. 220 (lecture 14). For the flow of translations, see David Simpson (ed.), *German Aesthetic and Literary Criticism: Kant, Fichte, Schelling, Schopenhauer, Hegel* (Cambridge: Cambridge University Press, 1984), introd., 20–4; and Lawrence Marsden Price, *English Literature in Germany* (Berkeley: University of California Press, 1953).

[71] Edward Young, *Conjectures on Original Composition. In a Letter to the Author of Sir Charles Grandison* (London, 1759), 12. For German development of Young's 'vegetable genius' analogy, see Abrams, *Mirror and the Lamp*, 201–13.

germ', and 'mechanical' form, which 'through external influence...is communicated to any material merely as an accidental addition without reference to its quality'.[72]

Schlegel's application of this theory to Shakespeare develops another distinction already found in British criticism: between two different structuring principles, the classical and the gothic. Applied to literature, this distinction dates back at least as far as Pope, who concluded his *Preface to Shakespeare* (1725) with the admission 'that with all his faults, and with all the irregularity of his *Drama*, one may look upon his works, in comparison of those that are more finish'd and regular, as upon an ancient majestick piece of *Gothick* Architecture, compar'd with a neat Modern building: The latter is more elegant and glaring, but the former is more strong and more solemn'[73] (by 'Modern' here, we should understand neoclassical, the prevailing architectural idiom in Pope's time). Purged of its normative assumptions, Pope's remarks contain the germ not only of Richard Hurd's famous distinction between 'Gothic' and 'Grecian' form in his *Letters on Chivalry and Romance* (1762), which recognizes the gothic as a 'regular' form in its own right, with 'its own rules' and its own kind of 'unity',[74] but also of A. W. Schlegel's distinction between the 'classical' and the 'romantic', which, again, hinges on contrasting principles of structural unity—and makes Shakespeare, the supreme exponent of gothic–organic form, the touchstone of romantic art.

A third key influence on German theories of form was Shaftesbury, whose work Goethe was studying at the time of his Italian journey, as he developed his morphological theory.[75] Shaftesbury's analogy between the creative imagination and 'universal Plastic Nature', his idea of the artist as 'a second Maker: a just Prometheus, under Jove', and, most important of all, his notion of 'inward Form', all have direct echoes in the writings of Herder, Goethe, and their successors.[76] Shaftesbury's influence, however, extends beyond particular concepts and metaphors. By applying Plato's concept of ideal Form (*eidos*) to the forms of art, and by analysing the properties of different artistic media (poetry, painting, sculpture), Shaftesbury helped to lay the

---

[72] A. W. Schlegel, *A Course of Lectures on Dramatic Art and Literature*, trans. John Black, 2 vols (London, 1815), ii. 94–5 (lecture 12). Coleridge rephrases as follows: 'The form is mechanic when on any given material we impress a predetermined form, not necessarily arising out of the properties of the material—as when to a mass of wet clay we give whatever shape we wish it to retain when hardened—The organic form on the other hand is innate, it shapes as it developes itself from within, and the fullness of its developement is one & the same with the perfection of its outward Form' (*Lectures 1808–1819*, i. 495: 1812–13 series, lecture 8, 22 or 29 Dec. 1812).

[73] Alexander Pope, Preface to *The Works of Shakespear* (1725), in David Womersley (ed.), *Augustan Critical Writing* (Harmondsworth: Penguin, 1997), 278.

[74] Richard Hurd, *Letters on Chivalry and Romance* (London, 1762), 61–2 (letter 8).

[75] Price, *English Literature in Germany*, 99.

[76] The concept of 'inward Form' first appears, somewhat inconsequentially, in Shaftesbury's *Characteristicks of Men, Manners, Opinions, Times*, 3 vols (London, 1711), iii. 222. Goethe adopts it in a commentary on French theatre theory (1773), excerpted in Timothy J. Chamberlain (ed.), *Eighteenth Century German Criticism* (New York: Continuum, 1992), 180. For this and other German borrowings from Shaftesbury, see René Wellek, *A History of Modern Criticism: 1750–1950*, i: *The Later Eighteenth Century* (New Haven: Yale University Press, 1955), 188, 203; Abrams, *Mirror and the Lamp*, 201; Price, *English Literature in Germany*, 88–102; and Kathleen Wheeler (ed.), *German Aesthetic and Literary Criticism: The Romantic Ironists and Goethe* (Cambridge: Cambridge University Press, 1984), introd., 1.

foundations of German aesthetics.[77] Shaftesbury's *magnum opus*, left unfinished at his early death in 1712, was to have been subtitled *The Language of Forms*, a phrase that encapsulates this new, form-sensitive aesthetic discourse. Shaftesbury's own forms of expression were as influential as his ideas. As well as reviving the genre of the philosophical dialogue, he cultivated a self-consciously elliptical and playful style which embodied his belief that the most effective way of communicating was to write 'darkly or pleasantly with raillery upon self; or some such indirect way as in Miscellany'.[78] One important legacy of his work, as Michael Prince has shown, was to create a new critical language (absent from mainstream neoclassicism) for the emergent form of the novel, particularly the comic novel which was soon to occupy so prominent a place in British literature.[79] A second legacy was to inspire the philosophical genre theory of German Romanticism, another critical discourse in which theorization of the novel played a central role, and which, in the case of Friedrich Schlegel, Novalis, and Jean Paul, employed a mode of self-reflexive, ironic expression often strikingly similar to Shaftesbury's. Shaftesbury's self-contradictions—for all his proto-Romantic irony and theories of creativity, as a practical critic he spoke as an 'Ancient', invoking neoclassical criteria of order, regularity, and proportion—only added to his attraction for the German Romantics, since it was a mirror of their own. Yet, while reproducing some of the contradictions in Shaftesbury's approach to form, German theorists also sought to resolve them, by using transcendental philosophy to synthesize empiricist and idealist strands in his aesthetics.

Coleridge's thinking on organic form draws on both German and British sources, and much scholarly effort has been expended in establishing the provenance of his ideas and debating the intellectual honesty or otherwise of his borrowings.[80] On the latter question, opinion remains divided, but few doubt the skill with which Coleridge assimilated the diverse strands of organic theory, or the subtlety and eloquence of his reformulations. Conceptually, his most original contribution was to link the Schlegelian organic–mechanical distinction to the British imagination–fancy antithesis, a move that enabled him to make a decisive break with associationist theories of literary invention (which he equated with the mechanical fancy) and to establish a new account of the creative process centred in the 'blending, fusing power' of the imagination, the 'co-adunating faculty' that impels separate entities to 'grow together into one'.[81] Coleridge's theory of imagination sharpens further Schlegel's

---

[77] On Platonic and Neoplatonic elements in Shaftesbury's aesthetics, see R. L. Brett, *The Third Earl of Shaftesbury: A Study in Eighteenth Century Literary Theory* (London: Hutchinson, 1951).

[78] Shaftesbury, *Second Characters, or, The Language of Forms*, ed. Benjamin Rand (Cambridge: Cambridge University Press, 1914), 6.

[79] Michael Prince, *Philosophical Dialogue in the British Enlightenment: Theology, Aesthetics, and the Novel* (Cambridge: Cambridge University Press, 1996), 28–46.

[80] For present purposes, the most helpful commentaries are: Gordon McKenzie, *Organic Unity in Coleridge* (1939; New York, AMS Press, 1977); Abrams, *Mirror and the Lamp*, 218–25; R. H. Fogle, *The Idea of Coleridge's Criticism* (Berkeley: University of California Press, 1962); G. N. G. Orsini, 'Coleridge and Schlegel Reconsidered', *Comparative Literature*, 16/2 (1964), 97–118; and Daniel Stempel, 'Coleridge and Organic Form: The English Tradition', *Studies in Romanticism*, 6/2 (1966), 89–97.

[81] Phrases from *Biographia Literaria* and elsewhere, quoted by Abrams, *Mirror and the Lamp*, 168–9. For the history of the imagination–fancy distinction, see James Engell, *The Creative Imagination: Enlightenment to Romanticism* (Cambridge, Mass.: Harvard University Press, 1981), 172–83.

contrast between the neoclassical idea of unity—a harmonious and regular assemblage of parts—and the Romantic notion of organic unity: a 'balance or reconcilement of opposite or discordant qualities', and an interdependence of parts so complete that (to use one of his most vivid similes) to extract a single element would be as difficult as removing a stone from a pyramid with one's bare hands.[82] His account of the imagination's power to synthesize discordant materials results in a new evaluative scale whereby the beauty of an artwork is measured 'in proportion to the variety of parts which it holds in unity'.[83] The more diverse the materials, the greater the artwork that holds them together, the perfection of form consisting in what he calls, in a resonant phrase, 'harmonized Chaos'.[84] As with Schlegel, his supreme example is Shakespeare, whose plays he praises for the very qualities—heterogeneity, irregularity—for which neoclassical critics had condemned them, their unity being of a 'romantic' and 'organic' kind, residing in 'the balance, counteraction, intermodification, & final Harmony of Differents'.[85]

Coleridge's desynonymization of fancy and imagination, and his further differentiation between the 'primary' and 'secondary imagination', are, as M. H. Abrams notes, 'part of his all-out war against the "Mechanico-corpuscular Philosophy"'.[86] But they are also part of his drive to clarify aesthetic terminology, another abiding concern throughout his career. In a letter of 1811, Coleridge defends himself against the charge of having plagiarized from A. W. Schlegel in his Shakespeare lectures by pointing out that both he and Schlegel had studied the philosophy of Kant, 'the distinguishing feature of which [is] to treat every subject in reference to the operation of the mental Faculties, to which it specially appertains'.[87] He reiterates on many occasions his adherence to what he calls the 'psychological Method', helping to give currency to the new word 'psychology', and to psychologically based criticism, while always insisting that such criticism should be grounded in a 'Philosophy of the Human Mind', not simply in the casual observation of mental processes.[88] His most far-reaching proposal comes in a Bristol lecture in 1813, where he is recorded as saying that 'the only nomenclature of criticism should be the classification of the

---

[82] *The Collected Works of Samuel Taylor Coleridge*, vii: *Biographia Literaria*, ed. James Engell and W. Jackson Bate, 2 vols (London: Routledge and Kegan Paul, 1983), ii. 16, 23. Except where indicated, all references are to this edition.

[83] 'On Poesy or Art' (1818), in *Biographia Literaria; with his Aesthetical Essays*, ed. J. Shawcross, 2 vols (Oxford: Clarendon Press, 1907), ii. 255. This phrasing does not appear in the transcription included as part of lecture 13 of the 1818 series in the *Collected Coleridge* (*Lectures 1808–1819*, ii. 218).

[84] *Lectures 1808–1819*, ii. 224 (1818 series, lecture 13, 10 Mar. 1818).

[85] Marginal note to *Anderson's British Poets*, in *The Collected Works of Samuel Taylor Coleridge*, xii: *Marginalia*, i: *A to B*, ed. George Whalley (London: Routledge and Kegan Paul, 1980), 72.

[86] Abrams, *Mirror and the Lamp*, 169, quoting a phrase from Coleridge's *Aids to Reflection* (1825).

[87] To an unknown correspondent, *c.* 15–21 Dec. 1811, in *Collected Letters*, iii. 360.

[88] *Treatise on Method* (1818), in *The Collected Works of Samuel Taylor Coleridge*, xi: *Shorter Works and Fragments*, ed. H. J. and J. R. de J. Jackson, 2 vols (London: Routledge and Kegan Paul, 1995), i. 655. Here Coleridge applies 'psychological' to Shakespeare's method of character delineation, apologizing for using a newfangled word. In his lecture of 28 Nov. 1811, he applies the term to his own critical method, declaring his intention 'to pursue a psychological, rather than a historical, mode of reasoning' (*Lectures 1808–1819*, i. 253, 257).

faculties of the mind, how they are placed, how they are subordinate, whether they do or not appeal to the worthy feelings of our nature'.[89] If reported correctly, the idea of *totally* replacing established critical terminology with a psychological–philosophical vocabulary goes beyond even the most radical German practice: Schiller's, for example, where psychological terms coexist, however uneasily, with traditional generic categories.

In practice, Coleridge's reform of the critical lexicon involves both the introduction of new terms and the redefinition of existing ones. His redefinitions often entail the desynonymizing of closely related words, a famous example being 'form' and 'shape', in the contradistinction he draws in an 1818 lecture between 'Form as proceeding' and 'Shape as superinduced'.[90] The antithesis derives from Schelling, but Coleridge's juxtaposition of the English words 'form' and 'shape' crystallizes the comparison on which Schelling's theory rests: between the type of form (external, mechanical, generic) produced by 'lifeless technical Rules' and the type (internal, organic, text-specific) created by the artist 'out of his own mind . . . according to the several Laws of the Intellect'. A given artwork may possess both kinds, but it is through inner 'form' not outer 'shape' that the work's true artistry and, in Schelling's term, its 'freedom' are revealed, 'shape' being 'either the Death or the imprisonment of the Thing', and 'form' being what Coleridge, in another brilliant rephrasing of Schelling, calls the poem's 'self-witnessing, and self-effected sphere of agency'.[91]

In his 'Essays on the Principles of Genial Criticism' (1814), Coleridge makes a more sustained attempt to establish an alternative critical terminology, based in this case on the psychological categories of Kant's *Critique of Judgment*, but formulated in such a way as to make all aesthetic descriptors ('the agreeable', 'the beautiful', 'the picturesque', etc.) variant kinds of form, specifying different relations of parts to whole.[92] That Coleridge's system is essentially a typology of forms, or of formal relationships, is brought out even more clearly in a related fragment, where he draws up an eight-point list of aesthetic categories, hierarchically ranked according to the extent to which 'a Whole' is perceptible alongside 'the constituent Parts'.[93] At one extreme is 'the *Shapely*' (a term that, confusingly, carries here an opposite meaning to the one assigned to 'shape' in the 1818 lecture[94]), where there is a full and 'distinct'

[89] *Lectures 1808–1819*, i. 564 (1813 series, lecture 5, 11 Nov. 1813; from a report in the *Bristol Gazette*).

[90] *Lectures 1808–1819*, ii. 224 (1818 series, lecture 13, 10 Mar. 1818). On Coleridge's method of desynonymy, see Paul Hamilton, *Coleridge's Poetics* (Oxford: Blackwell, 1983), ch. 3.

[91] *Lectures 1808–1819*, ii. 222. For Coleridge's reworking of Schelling, see Nigel Leask, *The Politics of Imagination in Coleridge's Critical Thought* (Basingstoke: Macmillan, 1988), ch. 11.

[92] For the Kantian influence, see G. N. G. Orsini, *Coleridge and German Idealism* (Carbondale: Southern Illinois University Press, 1969), 168–9; D. M. McKinnon, 'Coleridge and Kant', in John Beer (ed.), *Coleridge's Variety: Bicentenary Studies* (London: Macmillan, 1974); and René Wellek, *Immanuel Kant in England, 1793–1838* (Princeton: Princeton University Press, 1931), 111–14.

[93] 'Definitions of Aesthetic Terms' (1814?), in *Shorter Works and Fragments*, i. 350–1.

[94] In a related fragment (1814?), Coleridge defines 'shapeliness' as the 'perfection of *form*', where 'the Whole and the Parts are seen as mutually producing and explaining each other, as Unity in Multëity', to be distinguished from 'THE FORMAL', where 'there is a deficiency of Unity in the line forming the Whole' ('On the Distinction between the Picturesque and the Sublime', in *Shorter Works and Fragments*, i. 352). The inconsistency between his 1814 and 1818 definitions of 'shape' is

perception of all parts simultaneously with the whole; at the opposite extreme is 'the SUBLIME', where 'neither Whole, or Parts' is perceived and 'the Comparative Power' is suspended. In between come the Beautiful, the Picturesque, the Lovely, the Grand, the Statuesque, and the Majestic. Four of these categories disappear, while another ('the Agreeable') is added, in the published texts on 'Genial Criticism', which reworks the schema of the fragment into what is clearly intended to be a comprehensive aesthetic classification system. Like Shaftesbury's, Coleridge's typology of forms, though presented here in terms of the visual and plastic arts, is intended to be applicable to every sphere of art. 'All the Fine Arts', he says, 'are different species of Poetry,' their 'common essence' consisting in 'the excitement of emotion for the immediate purpose of pleasure thro' the medium of beauty.'[95]

If implemented in full, Coleridge's project of 'genial criticism' would render redundant traditional distinctions of genre, and rewrite literary criticism (and art criticism in general) as a science of mental causes and effects, with its own classification system, its own criteria of evaluation, and its own hierarchy of forms. It would replace the mechanistic neoclassical conception of artistic structure and unity with a Romantic notion of inward form and organic unity. The rules of genre would be abolished, and the task of theoretical criticism would, instead, be to discover 'the *rules* of the IMAGINATION', which 'are themselves the very powers of growth and production'.[96] Applied criticism, meanwhile, would concern itself not with generic but with individual form, and judge each work of art according to the extent to which it achieves a harmonious synthesis of conflicting elements.

In the event, 'genial criticism' is just one of many critical ventures initiated by Coleridge. The type of applied criticism for which he is best known is not the Kantian variety described in the 1814 essays but the more technical style of 'practical criticism' exemplified in parts of *Biographia Literaria*, which involves appraisal of the qualities in a poem 'which may be deemed promises and specific symptoms of poetic power'.[97] Despite the adoption of Coleridge's phrase, this is a method of close reading very different from the 'practical criticism' inaugurated a century later by I. A. Richards, which retains Coleridge's organic particularism but outlaws consideration of a work's imaginative genesis.[98] Other parts of *Biographia*, meanwhile, are purely theoretical, offering the distinctive synthesis of German and British 'philosophical criticism' for which the work has become famous. To these must be added the rhetorical criticism of his journal *The Friend* (1809–10); the comparative criticism of his 1818 lecture series (advertised as 'Lectures on the Principles of Judgement, Culture and European Literature'); the sociological criticism of the *Lay*

a reminder of the slipperiness of this vocabulary, and the challenge Coleridge faced in trying to forge a technical terminology out of everyday words.

[95] 'Essays on the Principles of Genial Criticism', in *Shorter Works and Fragments*, i. 358. 'Poetry' here is Coleridge's collective term for the arts; elsewhere (in the 1818 lecture, for instance), he uses 'poesy' as 'the generic or common term' for the arts, reserving 'poetry' for the art based on 'articulate Speech', as distinct from the 'mute' arts (*Lectures 1808–1819*, ii. 218–19).

[96] *Biographia Literaria*, ii. 84.

[97] Ibid. ii. 19.

[98] I. A. Richards, *Practical Criticism: A Study of Literary Judgment* (London: Routledge and Kegan Paul, 1929).

*Sermons* (1817) and *On the Constitution of Church and State* (1830); and the as yet unnamed form of criticism promised in his (unwritten) 'Essay on the Metaphysics of Typography', to which he refers in a letter of 1798.[99] Coleridge moves in and out of all these methodologies, enacting his own Schlegelian dialogue on poetry by assimilating all the major currents of British and Continental criticism and conducting an ongoing metacommentary on his own varying positions.

On the more specific issue of the role of genre in literary evaluation, Wellek concludes that Coleridge is 'of two minds'.[100] This is an understatement (Coleridge was rarely in as few as two minds on anything). As we have seen, the aesthetic categories outlined in his 'Genial Criticism' essays cut across traditional generic distinctions, tending to make the concept of genre redundant. Yet elsewhere, speaking of Milton's poems, Coleridge defines the role of 'the genial Judgement' as being 'to distinguish accurately the character & characteristics of each poem, praising them according to their force & vivacity *in their own kind*' (my italics)—a statement which suggests, as the Bollingen editors note, that 'genial' criticism should combine sympathy for authorial intention with sensitivity to genre.[101] 'Practical criticism', we are told, should investigate 'symptoms of poetic power' in specific poems. Yet before embarking on his practical criticism of Wordsworth, Coleridge defines as 'fair and philosophical' that investigation 'in which the critic announces and endeavours to establish the principles which he holds for the foundation of poetry in general, with the specification of these in their application to the different *classes* of poetry'.[102] At one moment he declares how 'absurd' it is 'to pass judgement on the works of a Poet on the mere ground that they have been called by the same class-name with the works of other poets of other times & circumstances';[103] at another, that it is 'far better to distinguish Poetry into different Classes: & instead of *fault*-finding to say, this belongs to such or such a class—thus noting inferiority in the *sort* rather than censure in the particular poem or poet'.[104] He searches endlessly for a universal criterion to distinguish good from bad poetry, but as soon as he gets near one, he immediately concedes that features 'which would be worthy of admiration in an empassioned Elegy, or a short indignant Satire, would be a blemish & proof of vile Taste in a Tragedy or Epic Poem'—a return to the neoclassical idea of decorum.[105]

There are inconsistencies, too, in Coleridge's ranking of genres. Like Wordsworth, Keats, and other Romantic poets, Coleridge retains a strong sense of generic hierarchy, displaying a traditional veneration for epic, tragedy, and the 'greater ode'. Yet he also participates enthusiastically in the revival of 'lesser' forms like the sonnet, and experiments with uncanonical, emergent genres such as the effusion and sketch. Towards certain genres, he shows decidedly mixed opinions. Having

---

[99] To Joseph Cottle, 28 May 1798, in *Collected Letters*, i. 412.

[100] Wellek, *History of Modern Criticism*, ii. 179.

[101] *Shorter Works and Fragments*, 356; marginal note to Milton's *Poems upon Several Occasions*, ed. Thomas Warton, 2nd edn (London, 1791), in *Marginalia*, iii. 886.

[102] *Biographia Literaria*, ii. 107.

[103] *Lectures 1808–1819*, i. 465 (1812 series, 1st course, lecture 5, 2 June 1812).

[104] *Marginalia*, iii. 886.

[105] *Lectures 1808–1819*, i. 218 (1811–12 series, lecture 3, 25 Nov. 1811).

co-authored a collection entitled *Lyrical Ballads*, he might be expected to have critical respect for the genre of the ballad. Yet in his published work he rarely speaks approvingly of it. Of the more simple ballads by Wordsworth like 'Anecdote for Fathers' and 'Simon Lee', he observes in *Biographia* that some of them 'would have been more delightful to me in prose',[106] a view that comes close to endorsing the common criticism of Wordsworth's poetry as already far too prosaic. Coleridge's own attempt at a simple ballad 'The Three Graves' (begun by Wordsworth) is introduced in *Sibylline Leaves* as 'the fragment, not of a Poem, but of a common Ballad-tale . . . Its merits, if any, are exclusively Psychological.'[107] Besides reinstating the very distinction between poetry and ballad that *Lyrical Ballads* was intended to overcome, his remark is open to the charge of further inconsistency since, according to his own aesthetic system, poetry and psychology were not separate domains: one was a subset of the other. This is precisely the point of the 'psychological' method of criticism, as is made diagrammatically explicit by the tree of knowledge in his 1817 Prospectus to the *Encyclopaedia Metropolitana*, where 'Poetry, introduced by Psychology' appears as a branch of 'the Fine Arts', itself a part of the 'Applied Sciences'.[108]

Inconsistent or not, Coleridge's criticism is full of astute psychological descriptions of genres, whether inspired by contemporary German theory or by the older British tradition of cognitive aesthetics. His Schlegelian definition of 'romantic Dramas, or dramatic Romances', quoted earlier, is couched entirely in mentalistic terms, the distinguishing feature of the genre being that it 'appealed to the Imagination rather than to the Senses', and demonstrated the mind's control over 'Time & Space'.[109] He is referring here to Shakespearean romance, but elsewhere he describes Spenserian romance in similar terms, referring to 'the Land of Faery' as 'mental space', characterized by a 'marvellous independence or true imaginative absence of all particular place & time'.[110] The antithesis to romance is found in 'the common modern novel', a genre in which he claims 'there is no imagination, but a miserable struggle to excite and gratify mere curiosity', plus a persistent, disabling confusion between fact and fiction.[111] Elegy is another genre which he defines in psychological terms, drawing on the German subjective–objective distinction and extending the category, as Schiller had done, to expressions of either 'regret for the Past or desire for the Future'. Elegy, says Coleridge, 'presents everything as lost and gone or absent and future'; it is 'the natural poetry of the reflective mind; it *may* treat of *any* subject but it must treat no subject for itself, but always and exclusively with reference to the poet himself'. It is thus 'the exact opposite of the Homeric Epic, in which all is purely external and objective'.[112] Like Schiller, too,

---

[106] *Biographia Literaria*, ii. 67.

[107] *Sibylline Leaves* (London, 1817), 217.

[108] Prospectus to the *Encyclopaedia Metropolitana*, in *Shorter Works and Fragments*, i. 584.

[109] *Lectures 1808–1819*, i. 467 (1812 series, 1st course, lecture 5, 2 June 1812).

[110] *The Notebooks of Samuel Taylor Coleridge*, iii: *1808–19*, ed. Kathleen Colburn (London: Routledge and Kegan Paul, 1973), no. 4501.

[111] *Lectures 1808–1819*, ii. 193 (1818 series, lecture 11).

[112] *The Collected Works of Samuel Taylor Coleridge*, xiv: *Table Talk*, ed. Carl Woodring, 2 vols (London: Routledge and Kegan Paul, 1990), i. 444–5 (entry for 28 Oct. 1833). Cf. Schiller, *On Naïve and Sentimental Poetry* (1795–6), in H. B. Nisbet (ed.), *German Aesthetic and Literary Criticism: Winckelmann, Lessing, Hamann, Herder, Schiller, Goethe* (Cambridge: Cambridge University Press, 1985), 200–2.

Coleridge uses poetic labels in both a modal and a generic sense, treating elegy, epic, and romance as discrete genres, but sometimes also referring to their modal manifestations, as, for example, in his proposed discussion of 'the Epic and Romantic of Shakespear'.[113] As Seamus Perry observes, such informal typologies of imaginative division are where much of Coleridge's most suggestive literary thinking occurs.[114]

Most suggestive of all are those definitions which directly link formal and psychological factors. An example is Coleridge's description of the sonnet, a poetic form whose fixed length and strict formal patterning he interprets not as ends in themselves but as means to 'generate' a particular 'habit of thought'.[115] The short length and intricate rhyme pattern impose a mental discipline which allows the author to overcome his emotional distress (the agitated feelings that typically give rise to a sonnet) and to 'methodize his thought'.[116] On the reader's part, the fixed length operates as an arousing and fulfilling of expectations, permitting an experience of unity which is both psychological and formal: 'the reader's mind having expected the close at the place in which he finds it, may rest satisfied; and that so the poem may acquire, as it were, a *Totality*—in plainer phrase, may become a *Whole*'. This early attempt by Coleridge to describe the mind's perception of aesthetic unity pre-dates his acquaintance with German theories of organic form, and has many echoes in his later work. Commenting on Joseph Cottle's rambling poem *Messiah* (1815), he pinpoints what it lacks: 'The common end of all *narrative*, nay, of *all* Poems is, to convert a *series* into a *Whole*: to make those events, which in real or imagined History, move on in a *strait* line, assume to our Understandings a *circular* motion—the snake with it's Tail in it's Mouth.'[117] The conversion of linearity into circularity, and the 'methodizing' of thought through poetic structure, are at the heart of Coleridge's thinking about organic unity, insights crystallized here in his favourite metaphor of the *ouroboros*, the snake with its tail in its mouth.

An even earlier discovery that becomes fundamental both to Coleridge's critical philosophy and to his artistic practice concerns the imaginative 'logic' of poetry. In *Biographia*, Coleridge recalls his gruelling initiation in poetics at the hands of James Boyer, the disciplinarian headmaster of Christ's Hospital, who taught him that 'Poetry, even that of the loftiest and, seemingly, that of the wildest odes, had a

---

[113] A topic for future inquiry mentioned at the close of his 1813 lecture series: *Lectures 1808–1819*, i. 595 (23 Nov. 1813).

[114] Seamus Perry, *Coleridge and the Uses of Division* (Oxford: Clarendon Press, 1999), 212.

[115] 'Introduction to the Sonnets', in *Poems, by S. T. Coleridge, Second Edition. To which are now Added Poems by Charles Lamb, and Charles Lloyd* (Bristol, 1797), 71–4. This is a reworking of the introduction to his unpublished anthology of sonnets, on which, see David Fairer, 'Coleridge's Sonnets from Various Authors (1796): A Lost Conversation Poem?', *Studies in Romanticism*, 41/4 (2002), 585–604.

[116] Coleridge is quoting, slightly inaccurately, William Preston's Preface to his 'Sonnets, Elegies, and Amatory Poems', in *The Poetical Works of William Preston, Esq.*, 2 vols (Dublin, 1793), i. 268. His misquotation has the effect—doubtless deliberate—of reversing Preston's meaning and making a more powerful claim for the sonnet. Preston's point is that the emotionally agitated man chooses the short form of the sonnet to vent his feelings because he lacks sufficient composure 'to methodize his thoughts, and undertake a work of length'. In Coleridge's version, the implication is that sonnet form itself performs that methodizing.

[117] To Joseph Cottle, 7 Mar. 1815, in *Collected Letters*, iv. 545.

logic of its own, as severe as that of science; and more difficult, because more subtle, more complex, and dependent on more, and more fugitive causes.'[118] The actual source of this idea is a critical text Coleridge knew well, Edward Young's 'Essay on Lyrick Poetry' (1728), where Young, in a brilliantly perceptive discussion of the Pindaric ode, overturned current misconceptions by arguing that lyric poetry of this kind 'has as much Logick at the bottom, as *Aristotle*, or *Euclid*', though 'to some Criticks' it 'has appear'd as mad'.[119] The 'logic' in question was emotional rather than rational, the secret of the ode (or of 'Ode', as Young calls it, without an article) being its ability to appear imaginatively chaotic while in fact retaining an underlying order and control. The more seemingly chaotic, the more impressive the actual control, a point Young brings home through two analogies which would have delighted Coleridge (though possibly not Mrs Coleridge). Defining 'Judgment' as 'the masculine power of the mind', which should hold supreme sway over Imagination, 'its Mistress', he points out what is distinctive about this genre:

in Ode, there is this difference from other kinds of Poetry; That, *there*, the *Imagination*, like a very beautiful Mistress, is indulged in the appearance of domineering; tho the *Judgment*, like an Artful Lover, in reality carries its point; and the less it is suspected of it, It shews the more masterly conduct, and deserves the greater commendation.

It holds true in this Province of writing, as in war, 'The more danger, the more honour'. It must be very Enterprizing, it must (in *Shakespear*'s style) have hair-breadth 'Scapes; and often tread the very brink of Error: Nor can It ever deserve the applause of the *real* Judge, unless It renders itself Obnoxious to the misapprehensions of the *Contrary*. (pp. 21–2)

In terms of poetic structure, this art of erotic subterfuge and military brinkmanship is embodied in the abrupt 'transitions' for which the Pindaric ode was notorious. Young's argument, which builds on Congreve's discovery that Pindar's odes were not, as previously thought, formally irregular, but, rather, regular in a complex way,[120] makes structural tension (apparent conflict concealing actual harmony) the essence of the genre. Coleridge goes one step further, dovetailing Young's insight with recent theories about organic unity to produce a dialectical definition not only of lyric poetry, but of the poetic imagination itself: as the 'power, first put in action by the will and understanding, and retained under their irremissive, though gentle and unnoticed, controul', which 'reveals itself in the balance or reconciliation of opposite or discordant qualities' and 'a more than usual state of emotion, with more than usual

---

[118] *Biographia Literaria*, i. 9. The implications of this idea for Coleridge's broader theory of method are explored by H. J. Jackson, 'Coleridge's Lessons in Transition: The "Logic" of the "Wildest Odes" ', in Thomas Pfau and Robert F. Gleckner (eds), *Lessons of Romanticism: A Critical Companion* (Durham, N.C.: Duke University Press, 1998).

[119] 'On Lyric Poetry', in Edward Young, *Ocean: An Ode. Occasion'd by His Majesty's Late Royal Encouragement of the Sea-Service. To which is Prefix'd, an Ode to the King; and a Discourse on Ode* (London, 1728), 20. Coleridge had taken notes from Young's essay in 1795 and refers to it again in a letter of 1802: see *Biographia Literaria*, i. 9 n. 2.

[120] William Congreve, 'A Discourse on the Pindarique Ode', prefixed to his *A Pindarique Ode, Humbly Offer'd to the Queen* (London, 1706). For eighteenth-century theories of 'transition' and their relevance to Romantic poetry, see Jane Stabler, *Burke to Byron, Barbauld to Baillie, 1790–1830* (Basingstoke: Palgrave, 2002), ch. 3.

order; judgement ever awake and steady self-possession, with enthusiasm, and feeling profound or vehement'.[121] Psychology and form merge in Coleridge's famous definition, and a theory of genre becomes a theory of poetry in general, the closest British criticism comes to a properly conceptualized 'language of forms', the 'true aesthetics' for which Romanticism strives.

## WORDSWORTH IN 1815

Though successful on occasion in combining formal and psychological theories of genre, Coleridge rarely managed to integrate these with the historical and socio-logical approaches which, at other moments, he also pursued. In terms of his long-term legacy, Coleridge was as influential in the nineteenth century as a cultural critic of literature as he was in the twentieth century as a practical critic, but he left few examples of how to combine these methodologies, and it is significant that his projected 'Essay on the Elements of Poetry' which 'would in reality be a disguised System of Morals & Politics'[122] remained unwritten. In fact, the disguised morality and politics of his later criticism are not radical but conservative. As David Simpson has shown, the ideological implications of his theory of organic form are essentially Burkean, and his theory of the imagination, with its emphasis on 'balance and reconciliation', is couched in phrasing strikingly reminiscent of Burke's description of the body politic.[123] It is this conservative organicism, among other things, that Shelley takes issue with in *A Defence of Poetry*, the one British theoretical text of the period which does attempt, in a sustained way, to combine political, psychological, and formal approaches to genre. As we will see in Chapter 5, however, Shelley's theory of genre contains its own contradictions, and its idiosyncratic blend of Plato, Coleridge, A. W. Schlegel, Adam Smith, and others produces a philosophy of genre whose critical legacy is as tangled as Coleridge's. To conclude the present chapter, however, I turn to another text which illustrates even more starkly the tensions in Romantic genre theory, and the challenge Romantic authors faced when attempting to put theory into practice in relation to their own work: Wordsworth's Preface to *Poems* (1815).

Given the controversy provoked by the Preface to *Lyrical Ballads*, one might have expected Wordsworth to omit a preface from his 1815 collection, as he had from *Poems, in Two Volumes* (1807);[124] and this indeed appears to have been his original intention. In the event, though, he includes *two* prefaces—the 'Preface' proper and an 'Essay, Supplementary to the Preface'—and reprints, as further supplements, the Preface to *Lyrical Ballads* together with its Appendix on 'poetic diction'. These four

---

[121] *Biographia Literaria*, ii. 16–17.

[122] *Collected Letters*, i. 632.

[123] David Simpson, 'Coleridge and Wordsworth on the Form of Poetry', in Christine Gallant (ed.), *Coleridge's Theory of Imagination Today* (New York: AMS Press, 1989), 222–3.

[124] A short prefatory Advertisement, now lost, was set in proof but deleted from the published text of 1807.

texts surround and guard the 1815 edition, opening and closing the first volume, and ending the second.[125] The prefatory abundance of the collection can be interpreted in a number of ways. There is a revealing remark in the Preface (the Preface proper— the *prefatory* Preface) that 'Poems . . . cannot read themselves.'[126] The reference is to reading aloud—the 'impassioned recitation' which lyrical poetry ideally requires— but Wordsworth's comment also applies to reading in general, since the whole thrust of the 1815 Preface is to tell us how to read, and *not* to read, the poems: what to look for, where to find it, how to judge. The same is true of the 'Essay, Supplementary', which begins with an explicit attack on misjudging readers and critics, and ends with Wordsworth's discussion—expanding an idea of Coleridge's—of how 'every author, as far as he is great and at the same time *original*, has the task of *creating* the taste by which he is to be enjoyed' (iii. 80). The extensive critical apparatus of the 1815 edition is, in part, a fulfilment of that task: a means of accelerating the creation of an appropriate taste by explaining the principles on which the poems were written.

Wordsworth's stance, however, is defensive as well as assertive. His explanations are clearly intended not only to enhance enjoyment but also to forestall criticism and prevent misreading. His defensive posture is hardly surprising given the mixed reception of his previous publications,[127] the proven hostility to his poetry of reviewers like Jeffrey, and the continuing controversy over his poetic 'system' that was still producing satires like *Modern Parnassus*. The fact that, in some cases, Wordsworth was republishing poems originally written in the 1790s, under very different historical circumstances and with different ideological motives, added to the possibility of misreading. This was, moreover, the first collected edition of his poems, an important moment in any writer's life, but especially so in the case of Wordsworth, who had been brooding on this moment for many years, who had such strong ambitions to be the exemplary poet of his time. All these factors contribute to what Lucy Newlyn identifies as an 'anxiety of reception' in the 1815 edition, a syndrome evident in many Romantic texts but here displayed to an extreme degree. The 'Essay, Supplementary' is, indeed, the *locus classicus* of reception-angst, with its strangely distorted history of poetic popularity, its 'almost paranoid fear that poets were at the mercy of a hostile reading-public',[128] and its abstraction of actual readers into what Wordworth calls 'the People, philosophically characterized' (iii. 84)—in his eyes, a more reliable arbiter of his work. The multiplication of prefaces could be interpreted as further evidence of the same anxiety, a reaction-formation to a perceived crisis in author–reader relations.

The 'supplementary' quality of the 1815 edition—metaphorically described in the Preface to *The Excursion* as a network of 'little cells, oratories, and sepulchral recesses' annexed to the 'gothic church' of *The Recluse*[129]—may, however, have another

[125] *Poems by William Wordsworth: Including Lyrical Ballads, and the Miscellaneous Pieces of the Author. With Additional Poems, A New Preface, and a Supplementary Essay. In Two Volumes* (London, 1815). A third volume was added in 1820; the composite 1815–20 edition became the basis for subsequent lifetime editions.

[126] *Prose Works*, iii. 29.

[127] Stephen Gill, *William Wordsworth: A Life* (Oxford: Clarendon Press, 1989), 300–4.

[128] Lucy Newlyn, *Reading, Writing, and Romanticism: The Anxiety of Reception* (Oxford: Oxford University Press, 2000), 92.

[129] *Prose Works*, iii. 5–6.

explanation, exemplifying once again the 'metaromantic' impulse we saw in the Preface to *Lyrical Ballads*. Like the earlier text, the 1815 Preface and 'Essay, Supplementary' go far beyond mere introduction: they interpose between author and reader a formidable body of critical theory, turning the whole collection into an extended theoretical experiment. Between them, the two 1815 essays incorporate a comprehensive genre-system, a history of poetry, a theory of reading, a commentary on the distinction between fancy and imagination, and a discussion of the fashionable theory of organic unity (an idea which Wordsworth attributes to 'the Germans'[130]). These theories are integral to the collection. Unity, Wordsworth argues in the 'Essay, Supplementary', is an essential criterion of poetic greatness: unity not just of the individual text but of a complete œuvre. His chief example is Shakespeare, whose works, he claims, 'heterogeneous as they often are, constitute a unity of their own, and contribute all to one great end' (iii. 69). In collecting his own heterogeneous poems, Wordsworth goes to extreme lengths to demonstrate a similar unity in his own œuvre. The entire edition, in this sense, is an exercise in Romantic organicism, mixing the theory and practice of it in a unique way.

The uniqueness lies partly in Wordsworth's complex organization of the 1815 edition, which brings together no fewer than three classification systems, each with its own notion of unity.[131] The first is based on subject matter, and involves the grouping and ordering of poems so as to chart the human life cycle, with an ascending 'scale of imagination' in each class. This plan, first sketched in a letter to Coleridge in 1809, supplies such categories as 'Juvenile Poems', 'Poems Referring to the Period of Childhood', and 'Poems Referring to the Period of Old Age'. The second plan, discussed with Henry Crabb Robinson in 1812, involves the arrangement of poems 'with some reference either to the fancy, imagination, reflection, or mere feeling contained in them'.[132] Elements of this psychological or (as Crabb Robinson terms it) 'philosophical' scheme are retained in categories such as 'Poems Founded on the Affections', 'Poems of the Fancy', 'Poems of the Imagination', and 'Poems Proceeding from Sentiment and Reflection'. The third scheme, dating back to 1811, is formal: classification by genre, or, in Wordsworth's 'casting' metaphor, 'by means of various moulds, into divers forms' (iii. 27). This produces such categories as 'Epitaphs and Elegiac Pieces', 'Inscriptions', and 'Miscellaneous Sonnets'. The 1815 edition employs all three methods of classification, and also includes one further, purely thematic category, 'Poems on the Naming of Places' (carried over from the 1800 edition of *Lyrical Ballads*).

Wordsworth's Preface attempts to explain and justify his complicated taxonomy, claiming that 'for him who reads with reflection, the arrangement will serve as a commentary unostentatiously directing his attention to my purposes, both particular and general' (iii. 28). But many readers, both then and now, have found his explanation unconvincing. The *Monthly Review* set the tone, describing the Preface

---

[130] Ibid. iii. 69. As the editors note, Coleridge resented this comment as a slight on his own organicist Shakespeare criticism.

[131] For the evolution of the 1815 classification scheme, see William Wordsworth, *Shorter Poems*, ed. Carl H. Ketcham (Ithaca, N.Y.: Cornell University Press, 1989), introd., 19–32.

[132] *The Correspondence of Henry Crabb Robinson with the Wordsworth Circle, 1808–1866*, ed. E. J. Morley, 2 vols (Oxford: Clarendon Press, 1927), i. 89–90.

as obscure and condescending, and interpreting the organization of the collection as an attempt to give an 'air of invention and novelty' to ordinary and insignificant compositions; 'in short, we have here such a pompous classification of trifles, for the most part obvious and extremely childish, that we do not remember to have ever met with so "Much Ado about Nothing" in any other author'.[133] Coleridge, despite being privy to Wordsworth's plan, criticized his execution of it, taking issue in *Biographia Literaria* with Wordsworth's long and, in Coleridge's view, confused account of the difference between fancy and imagination (*Biographia* as a whole appears to have originated as a preface, intended to rival and correct Wordsworth's, to Coleridge's own collected poems, *Sibylline Leaves*, published in 1817).[134] Though some modern editions retain vestiges of Wordsworth's arrangement, his idiosyncratic taxonomy has found few defenders, and the psychological aspect in particular is considered by most critics to be innovative but seriously flawed.[135]

By contrast, the generic dimension of Wordsworth's scheme is usually regarded as unproblematic, even 'conventional'.[136] In fact, though, even here there are innovations and anomalies. Wordsworth posits six (or seven) broad categories: 'The Narrative', 'The Dramatic', 'The Lyrical', 'The Idyllium', 'Didactic', 'philosophical Satire', plus a 'composite species' (amended in later editions to 'composite order') compounded out of the last three. Some of these categories are then subdivided. Though apparently straightforward, this classification has two unusual features. The first is the category of 'composite species'. As we will see in Chapter 5, the concept of mixed genres has a long history, but very few genre-systems explicitly included such a category as a genre in its own right. Although Wordsworth defines the 'composite species' restrictively, limiting it to a very specific combination of genres and ignoring many other examples (including his own), his formalization of the concept of genre-mixing is highly significant in light of contemporary German theories of the *Mischgedicht*.

Unusual, too, is Wordsworth's category of 'Idyllium', a type of poetry he defines as

descriptive chiefly either of the processes and appearances of external nature, as the Seasons of Thomson; or of characters, manners, and sentiments, as are Shenstone's Schoolmistress, The Cotter's Saturday Night of Burns, The Twa Dogs of the same Author; or of these in conjunction with the appearances of Nature, as most of the pieces of Theocritus, the Allegro and Penseroso of Milton, Beattie's Minstrel, Goldsmith's Deserted Village. (iii. 28)

Superficially, this might seem equivalent to standard neoclassical definitions of 'Descriptive' poetry, such as Nathan Drake's in his *Literary Hours* (1798). Etymologically, 'idyllium' actually means 'little picture' (Greek, *eidyllion*). But the term

---

[133] *Monthly Review* (Nov. 1815), in Donald H. Reiman (ed.), *The Romantics Reviewed: Contemporary Reviews of British Romantic Writers*, 9 vols (New York: Garland, 1972), A ii. 734.

[134] For Coleridge's 'near obsession' with Wordsworth's 1815 Preface, which he planned to emulate even to the extent of using the same typeface, see *Biographia Literaria*, introd., pp. l–li.

[135] See e.g. Gene W. Ruoff, 'Critical Implications of Wordsworth's 1815 Categorization, with Some Animadversions on Binaristic Commentary', *Wordsworth Circle*, 9/1 (1978), 75–82; Judith R. Herman, 'The Poet as Editor: Wordsworth's Edition of 1815', *Wordsworth Circle*, 9/1 (1978), 82–7; and Donald Ross, 'Poems "Bound Each to Each" in the 1815 Edition of Wordsworth', *Wordsworth Circle*, 12 (1981), 133–40.

[136] Ketcham, introd. to Wordsworth, *Shorter Poems*, 29.

'idyllium', or (its more typical form) 'idyll', had previously been applied more or less exclusively to pastoral poems in the tradition of Theocritus, whereas Wordsworth extends it to all kinds of pastoral poetry, whether descriptive or not, and to all kinds of descriptive poetry, whether pastoral or not. His list of examples, and the range of poetic forms that he includes as subsets of the idyllium (namely, 'the Epitaph, the Inscription, the Sonnet, most of the epistles of poets writing in their own persons, and all loco-descriptive poetry') show just how broad his definition is, without making at all clear what these various types of poetry have in common.

Wordsworth's unorthodox expansion of the category of idyllium may owe something to Schiller's *On Naïve and Sentimental Poetry* (1795–6), an essay he may have discussed with Coleridge or Crabb Robinson.[137] Schiller treats idyll, along with elegy and satire, as one of the three types of 'sentimental' poetry, each of which expresses in a different way the gap between the ideal and the actual. Traditionally, idyll projects its ideal backwards, to an Arcadian golden age set in the distant past. As with elegy, though, Schiller calls on poets to extend the genre forwards, 'so as to display that pastoral innocence even in creatures of civilization', under conditions 'of expansive thought, of the subtlest art, the highest social refinement'.[138] Thus redefined, idyll comes close to Wordsworth's conception of the pastoral ideal as a model for civilization in works like *The Excursion*.[139] Schiller's claim that he is defining idyll and other genres not in their customary sense but in terms of 'the modes of perception [*Empfindunsgsweise*] predominant in these poetic categories'[140] is also strikingly similar to Wordsworth's proposal to classify his poems according to 'the powers of mind *predominant* in the production of them' (iii. 28). The difference is that Schiller's 'modes of perception' are part of his redefinition of genre, whereas Wordsworth's *perceptual* classification system is entirely separate from his *generic* classification system. The two systems stand side by side in the 1815 edition, but there is no attempt to integrate them—no sense that it might be possible to conceive of genres themselves as forms of consciousness. When speaking of genre, Wordsworth seems to reject the notion of organic form, reverting instead to the old mechanistic metaphor of genres as 'moulds' into which 'content' is poured; whereas, when explaining his psychological categories, he adopts a theory of composition that is so subjective as to dispense with form altogether.

The result of Wordsworth's failure to integrate these two systems—or even to recognize their incompatibility—is major confusion, especially for the poor reader, who is being told so emphatically such contradictory things about how to read the poems. But the confusion is not wholly of Wordsworth's making. The contradictions of the 1815 edition are characteristic of their time. We have already seen similar

[137] For Coleridge's and Crabb Robinson's knowledge of this essay, see Michael J. Kooy, *Coleridge, Schiller and Aesthetic Education* (Basingstoke: Palgrave, 2002); and J. M. Baker, *Henry Crabb Robinson* (London: Allen and Unwin, 1937), 210–11. For Wordsworth's more limited acquaintance with Schiller's work, see L. A. Willoughby, 'Wordsworth and Germany', in *German Studies Presented to Professor H. G. Fiedler* (Oxford: Clarendon Press, 1938), 443–7.
[138] *On Naïve and Sentimental Poetry*, in Nisbet (ed.), *German Aesthetic and Literary Criticism*, 213.
[139] Herbert Lindenberger, 'The Idyllic Moment: On Pastoral and Romanticism', *College English*, 34/3 (1972), 335–51.
[140] *On Naïve and Sentimental Poetry*, 292 n. k (Schiller's); see also 294 n. r.

discontinuities in Coleridge's thinking, tensions writ large in *Biographia Literaria* and other critical works of 1814–18. To set these and the 1815 Preface against the Preface to *Lyrical Ballads* is to realize that the issues raised by Wordsworth in 1800, far from being resolved, had grown steadily more problematic. Generic rivalry, public taste, the poetry–prose crux, generic decorum, the metrical contract, poetic 'purpose': these and other topics now loom larger than ever, and to the technical and social concerns of the 1800 Preface have been added a new set of theoretical (and terminological) problems reflecting the vigorous critical controversies of the intervening period. These include debates about organic form, about neoclassicism and the 'French school', about literary history, and about the Lake School itself, not least its relationship to the political revolution in France and the aesthetic revolution in Germany.

The ironic account of the British literary revolution in *Modern Parnassus* (1814) presents it as a fait accompli: the old rules have been annulled, the neoclassical genre-system has been abolished, and a new poetics of spontaneous overflow is now dominant. In reality, the new poetics is a more complex, contradictory phenomenon, and its trajectory is more ambiguous. By 1815 many writers had embraced something resembling the 'new charter' of *Modern Parnassus*: the age of the effusion, the 'poem affecting not to be poetry', the 'fragment of an irregular sketch' had begun (in fact, well before *Lyrical Ballads*). Others, though, still cleaved to the old system, using traditional genres and generic terminology, and presenting their work in some version of the 'classical arrangement'. The most advanced writers of the time, such as Wordsworth and Coleridge, moved between the two systems, weaving in and out of genres, inviting attention to their generic affiliations at one moment, then insisting on their uniqueness, their spontaneity, their defiance of 'pre-established codes' at another. In this sense, the theoretical contradictions of the 1815 edition mirror the conflicting messages of the poetry. As first attempts, by the architects of the new poetics, to collect, classify, and unify their œuvre, Wordsworth's *Poems* (1815), Coleridge's *Sibylline Leaves* and *Biographia Literaria*—to which we might add Southey's *Minor Poems*, another collected edition by a Lake School poet published in 1815—provide a snapshot of the Romantic 'dialogue on poetry' a decade and a half after the watershed of *Lyrical Ballads*. What that dialogue tells us is that the Romantic literary revolution, in its most creative phase, involves not the displacement of one literary paradigm (mimetic, objective, generic) by another (expressive, subjective, organic), but a prolonged and fertile conflict between the two.

# 3

# (Anti-)Didacticism

We hate poetry that has a palpable design upon us—and if we do not agree, seems to put its hand in its breeches pocket. Poetry should be great & unobtrusive...

(John Keats, letter to J. H. Reynolds, 3 February 1818)

We are on a *mission*. Our vocation is the education of the earth.

(Novalis, *Miscellaneous Observations* (1797), no. 32)

If the Russian Formalists are right in claiming that shifts in the hierarchy of genres are the deepest indicators of literary change, a crucial sign of the 'revolution in literature' that we call Romanticism was the relegation of didactic poetry. A 'species of composition' that, in Addison's eyes, had produced 'the most compleat, elaborate, and finisht Piece of all Antiquity'—Virgil's *Georgics*[1]—and that Thomas Tickell in 1711 could rank 'second to Epic alone' in the hierarchy of poetic forms,[2] became for the Romantics a byword for mediocrity or a simple contradiction in terms. The reorientation of literary values signalled by Joseph Warton's *Essay on the Genius and Writings of Pope* (1756), which damned Pope with the faint praise of having excelled in poetry 'of the *didactic*, *moral*, and *satyric* kind; and, consequently, not of the most *poetic* species *of poetry*',[3] was extended half a century later by the literary theory and practice of the Romantics, who favoured genres marginalized by the 'French school' of Dryden and Pope, and developed a poetics based on expressly anti-didactic premises. William Lisle Bowles's presumed victory over Byron and others in the long-running 'Pope controversy'[4] was critical confirmation of the new literary order, whose anti-didactic stance is exemplified by many of the period's most famous critical pronouncements. Blake's 'The tygers of wrath are wiser than the horses of instruction' and 'cast aside from Poetry all that is not Inspiration',[5] Keats's 'We hate poetry

---

[1] [Joseph Addison], 'An Essay on the Georgics' (1697), in *The Works of Virgil: Containing his Pastorals, Georgics and Aeneis, Translated into English Verse by Mr Dryden*, 5th edn, 3 vols (London, 1721), i. 210.

[2] Thomas Tickell, 'De Poesi Didactica', unpub. lecture (1711), trans. J. L. Austin, in Richard Eustace Tickell, *Thomas Tickell and the Eighteenth Century Poets* (London: Constable, 1931), 199. Tickell refers to didactic poetry as a 'neglected' topic in literary criticism—something it was not to remain.

[3] This wording appears in the fourth, expanded edition, 2 vols (London, 1782), ii. 408.

[4] See Jacob Johan Van Rennes, *Bowles, Byron and the Pope Controversy* (Norwood: Norwood Editions, 1927); Upali Amarasinghe, *Dryden and Pope in the Early Nineteenth Century: A Study of Changing Literary Taste* (Cambridge: Cambridge University Press, 1962); and James Chandler, 'The Pope Controversy: Romantic Poetics and the English Canon', *Critical Inquiry*, 10 (1984), 481–509.

[5] *The Marriage of Heaven and Hell* (1790–3), pl. 9; *Milton: A Poem* (c.1804–11), book 2, pl. 41, in William Blake, *Complete Writings*, ed. Geoffrey Keynes (London: Oxford University Press, 1966), 152, 533.

that has a palpable design on us' and his insistence that '*an artist*' must serve the 'Mammon' of 'Poetry, and dramatic effect' rather the 'God' of 'purpose',[6] Shelley's 'didactic poetry is my abhorrence',[7] and De Quincey's contradistinction between the 'literature of knowledge' and the 'literature of power',[8] are all indicative of the new poetic, which has exact parallels in Germany and France in the elaboration of the concepts of disinterestedness and aesthetic autonomy, and the emergence of a full-blown theory of 'art for art's sake'.[9]

Such is the familiar story, a tale of decanonization and displacement whose continued presence in literary histories of the period reflects not only the abundance of evidence that appears to support it but also the fact that the anti-didactic criteria promoted by the Romantics and their successors remain integral to our own sense of literary worth. Though 'art for art's sake' is a cause few would still want to fight for, Edgar Allan Poe's strictures on 'the heresy of *The Didactic*' has as much relevance now as they did a hundred years ago.[10] A poet today would no more think to versify a farming manual (as Virgil did) than a composer would wish to set to music a telephone directory. The word 'didactic' itself, except in certain specialized contexts, retains the pejorative connotations it acquired in the Romantic period (as in Leigh Hunt's scornful reference to 'another didactic little horror of Mr. Wordsworth's', *Peter Bell*[11]), and poetic forms such as the georgic, 'moral essay', and 'didactic' or 'philosophical poem' seemingly have no place in the modern literary repertoire.

As an account of Romanticism, however, there are several problems with this argument. The idea of a comprehensive rejection of didacticism (the 'fashion of moralizing in verse', as Joseph Warton called it[12]) has always lain uneasily alongside other aspects of Romantic aesthetics where contrary impulses seem to be in play. Ezra Pound was thinking of his own poetry when he wrote, 'It's all rubbish to pretend that art isn't didactic. A revelation is always didactic.'[13] But the comment could apply equally well to Blake, Wordsworth, Coleridge, or Shelley, all of whom defined poetry as a 'visionary' art, comparing it to biblical prophecy or claiming for it some similarly exalted cognitive or social function. The famous statement that ends Shelley's *Defence*

---

[6] To J. H. Reynolds, 3 Feb. 1818; to P. B. Shelley, 16 Aug. 1820, in *The Letters of John Keats*, ed. Hyder E. Rollins, 2 vols (Cambridge, Mass.: Harvard University Press, 1958), i. 224, ii. 332–3.

[7] Preface to *Prometheus Unbound* (1820), in *Shelley's Poetry and Prose*, 2nd edn, ed. Donald H. Reiman and Neil Fraistat (New York: Norton, 2002), 209.

[8] Review of *The Works of Alexander Pope*, ed. W. Roscoe (1847), *North British Review*, 9 (Aug. 1848) in *The Works of Thomas De Quincey*, gen. ed. Grevel Lindop, 23 vols (London: Pickering and Chatto, 2000–3), xvi. 336.

[9] Rose Frances Egan, *The Genesis of the Theory of 'Art for Art's Sake' in Germany and England*, Smith College Studies in Modern Languages, 2/4 (1921); John Wilcox, 'The Beginning of l'Art pour l'Art', *Journal of Aesthetics and Art Criticism*, 11 (1953), 360–77; Frederick Burwick, *Mimesis and its Romantic Reflections* (University Park: Pennsylvania State University Press, 2000), ch. 1.

[10] 'The Poetic Principle' (1850), in Edgar Allan Poe, *Complete Poems and Selected Essays*, ed. Richard Gray (London: Dent, 1993), 158.

[11] *The Examiner* (2 May 1819), in Donald H. Reiman (ed.), *The Romantics Reviewed: Contemporary Reviews of British Romantic Writers*, facs. repr., 9 vols (New York: Garland, 1972), A ii. 538.

[12] Joseph Warton, *Odes on Various Subjects* (London, 1746), advertisement.

[13] To Felix E. Schelling, 8 July 1922, in *The Selected Letters of Ezra Pound 1907–1941*, ed. D. D. Paige (London: Faber and Faber, 1950), 180.

*of Poetry*, 'Poets are the unacknowledged legislators of the World',[14] is not the credo of a writer who has renounced all didactic pretensions, if we use 'didactic' in the broad sense of 'having the giving of instruction as its aim or object' (*OED*)—for what is 'legislation', unacknowledged or otherwise, if not a type of instruction?

It is a striking fact, too, that many of the anti-didactic anathemas of the Romantics are provoked not by the moralizing habits of their Augustan precursors but by similar tendencies in their contemporaries. Keats's dictum about God and Mammon is a piece of critical advice offered to his friend and rival Shelley, following a reading of *The Cenci*: it is the idea that 'a *modern* work . . . must have purpose' (my italics) with which Keats takes issue. The 'abhorrence' of didactic poetry Shelley professes in the Preface to *Prometheus Unbound* (1820) was, in part, a reaction against his own earlier work, notably his 'philosophical poem' *Queen Mab*. De Quincey's deconstruction of 'didactic poetry'—which he calls a contradiction in terms—is best known from his 1848 essay on Pope, but he had first made this case in his *Letters to a Young Man Whose Education Has Been Neglected* (1823), in response to *current* abuses of the word 'literature' and to the ongoing problems caused by the 'wretched antithesis' of Horace that poets must either instruct or amuse (*aut prodesse volunt, aut delectare poetae*).[15] De Quincey acknowledges on this occasion that his literature of power– knowledge distinction (here glossed as 'literature as art, or polite literature, as opposed to didactic or educational literature', or simply 'literature' versus 'anti-literature'), like 'most of the sound criticism on poetry', originated in his conversations with Wordsworth. Yet Wordsworth himself was often accused of didacticism in his poetry, even by those (like Leigh Hunt) who otherwise admired his writing. This, among other things, is what Byron was complaining about when he recalled how 'Shelley, when I was in Switzerland, used to dose me with Wordsworth physic even to nausea'[16]—a witty inversion of the Lucretian metaphor for didactic verse, a dose of wormwood sweetened with honey.

Critics have tried to explain away the didactic strain in Romantic writing by defining as properly 'Romantic' only those 'mature' texts that resist or transcend it, implying that didacticism is something the Romantics grew out of, or fell into in spite of themselves. This might seem a plausible way of differentiating, say, *Prometheus Unbound* from *Queen Mab*, or 'Kubla Khan' from 'Religious Musings', but it ignores the didactic element in canonical texts like *Childe Harold's Pilgrimage* and *Jerusalem*, and fails to explain why Wordsworth was seen to get more rather than less didactic as he grew older, or why Shelley ends the supposedly undidactic *Prometheus*

---

[14] *Shelley's Poetry and Prose*, 535.

[15] *Works*, xvi. 359; 'Letters to a Young Man whose Education has been Neglected', *London Magazine* (1823), in *Works*, iii. 70. See also 'Postscript on Didactic Poetry' appended to De Quincey's essay on Lessing, *Blackwood's Magazine*, 20 (Jan. 1827), in *Works*, vi. 67–72. For commentary on the power–knowledge distinction, see Jonathan Bate, 'The Literature of Power: Coleridge and De Quincey', in Tim Fulford and Morton D. Paley (eds), *Coleridge's Visionary Languages: Essays in Honour of J. B. Beer* (Cambridge: Brewer, 1993); and Frederick Burwick, *Thomas De Quincey: Knowledge and Power* (New York: Palgrave, 2001).

[16] *Medwin's 'Conversations of Lord Byron'*, ed. Ernest J. Lovell, Jr (Princeton: Princeton University Press, 1966), 194, quoted by Charles E. Robinson, *Shelley and Byron: The Snake and Eagle Wreathed in Fight* (Baltimore: Johns Hopkins University Press, 1976), 18.

*Unbound* with a speech by Demogorgon summarizing the moral lessons of the drama. The presence of a didactic component in Romantic texts that are mainly governed by other generic codes (often of a highly complex kind) does not, of course, prove that the hierarchy of genres has not altered, or that anti-didactic tendencies are not operative too. But it is a simplification to suggest that the Romantics liberated themselves in any consistent way from the temptations (if that is the right word) of didacticism.

This becomes even clearer if we turn our attention from moral to political didacticism. Here, very different criteria tend to be applied, and modern critics are liable to excuse or even commend in a politically motivated text a level of didacticism they might condemn in a morally didactic work—especially if the political views happen to coincide with their own. Indeed, evidence of ideological engagement, overt or covert, in a Romantic text has become for many scholars a virtual precondition of critical approval, and Romanticism (the British variety at least) is now studied less for its intermittent aspirations to aesthetic autonomy than for its self-conscious politicization of literature. In the same way, current work on the importance of education in Romanticism, manifested most visibly in the emergence of genres such as the *Bildungsroman* and in the growth of pedagogic writing, have changed the terms of the debate about didacticism—or would have done had the appropriate connections been made. In general, however, these links have not been made, so we continue to apply double standards, reserving the term 'didactic' for texts whose palpable designs we disagree with, and calling by some other name those whose ideological motivations we approve.

A more satisfactory approach might be to face these contradictions head on, recognize the ambivalence of Romantic attitudes to didacticism, and seek to understand what M. H. Abrams calls the 'conscious and persistent conflict' in Romantic literature and theory 'between the requirements of social responsibility and of aesthetic detachment'.[17] To acknowledge such tensions is not to underestimate the strength of the anti-didactic impulses displayed by Keats and others, nor to deny that these may inhere, in some deep sense, in the aesthetic logic of Romanticism (though the ground on which this claim might be made is something I wish to reconsider). It is, rather, to see these intuitions and arguments as part of a dialectic that also produced, in the same period and often from the same writers, some of the boldest claims ever made for the social and political efficacy of art.

My aim in this chapter is to explore this dialectic, first by tracing the origins of the anti-didactic aesthetic and analysing the arguments that produced it; secondly, by showing that the Romantic period experienced its own fashion for moralizing, and, more important, for philosophizing and polemicizing in verse, as witnessed by the currency of didactic genres such as the georgic and 'philosophical poem', and by didactic tendencies in other Romantic genres; and thirdly, by explaining how the question of didacticism connects with broader debates about literary function, including its ideological aspects and its connection to what German theorists called

---

[17] M. H. Abrams, *The Mirror and the Lamp: Romantic Theory and the Critical Tradition* (New York: Oxford University Press, 1953), 328.

'aesthetic education'. These are large topics and they can be treated only briefly, but I hope they will shed light on what Hazlitt meant when he listed 'didactic' as one of the defining characteristics of the spirit of the age ('The age we live in is critical, didactic, paradoxical, romantic'[18]) and why, conversely, many later interpretations of Romanticism have identified as its central aesthetic principle the notion that art is fundamentally *anti*-didactic.

## PURE AND APPLIED POETRY

As is often the case in critical controversy, linguistic confusion played a part in the didacticism debate, and still does. The confidence with which the Romantics, on occasion, condemned 'didactic poetry' and the 'didactic way' of writing, and the readiness with which modern critics echo this judgement, belie the vagueness with which these terms were defined, and the inconsistency with which they were applied. The impression sometimes given that this was an ancient genre whose character and boundaries were settled is false. As an active compositional label, 'didactic poem' dates only from the 1760s, the first English poem to describe itself thus being Richard Shepherd's *The Nuptials: A Didactick Poem* (1761). As a critical category, applied retrospectively to poems that had originally called themselves something else, the term goes back further, but what that category was deemed to include varied enormously. Trapp, in his *Lectures on Poetry* (1742), defines 'didactic poems' as 'Precepts delivered in Verse', dividing them into four types according to the nature of the subject matter: 'those that relate to moral Duties; or philosophical Specula-tions; or the Business or Pleasures of Life; or, lastly, to Poetry itself'.[19] Of the first type, he says little; Lucretius' *De Rerum Natura* is his chief example of the second, Virgil's *Georgics* of the third, and Horace's *Ars Poetica* of the fourth—a predictable enough canon, though he also admits modern works and ends his lecture with an appeal for more didactic poems to be written, even suggesting possible topics. Purely descriptive verse, however, he excludes, and he differentiates didactic poetry from satire as well from epigrams, elegies, epistles, and other types of moral or philosoph-ical—but not explicitly 'preceptive'—verse.

Other critics, though, made didactic poetry a much broader category. Blair's *Lectures on Rhetoric and Belles Lettres* (1783) extends 'this numerous Class of Writings' to include not just formal philosophical poems like Pope's *Essay on Man* (1734) but also reflective and meditative verse like Young's *Night Thoughts* (1742) and various kinds of verse satire.[20] Joseph Warton, as we have seen, makes 'didactic poetry' synonymous with 'moralizing in verse', an even wider category. Robert Lowth, in his *Lectures on the Sacred Poetry of the Hebrews* (1753), gives an equally broad

[18] 'The Drama: No. IV', *London Magazine* (Apr. 1820), in *The Complete Works of William Hazlitt*, ed. P. P. Howe, 21 vols (London: Dent, 1930–4), xviii. 302.

[19] Joseph Trapp, *Lectures on Poetry: Read in the Schools of Natural Philosophy at Oxford* (1742), 187–9 (lecture 15: 'Of Didactic or Preceptive Poetry').

[20] Hugh Blair, *Lectures on Rhetoric and Belles Lettres*, 2 vols (London, 1783), ii. 361–70 (lecture 40: 'Didactic Poetry').

definition,[21] as does Charles Batteux in his *Course of the Belles Lettres* (1753),[22] a follow-up to his famous treatise on the *beaux arts*. Batteux, interestingly, treats didactic poetry not simply as one genre among many but as one of the four fundamental poetic types, alongside the more familiar triad of narrative, dramatic, and lyrical poetry. Wordsworth, in his 1815 Preface, proposes yet another classification, reinstating the distinction between 'didactic poetry' and 'philosophical satire' but also devising another, hybrid category, the 'composite species', and assigning Young's *Night Thoughts* to this.[23]

Such demarcation disputes were not uncommon in genre theory, but 'didactic' was a particularly unstable category not only because its boundaries were hard to define but also because an influential strand of critical opinion had come to doubt whether it was a legitimate poetic genre at all. Such doubts had been expressed before. Sidney in his *Defence of Poesy* (1595) had questioned whether writers of philosophical verse like Lucretius 'properly be poets or no';[24] Shaftesbury in 1712 had denounced the 'didactick or preceptive way' as 'un-artificial, un-masterly, and un-poetic';[25] and even Batteux, while broadly endorsing the genre, had wondered whether it was 'a kind of usurpation of poetry on prose'.[26] By the end of the eighteenth century, these doubts, fuelled by new trends in literary criticism and aesthetic psychology, had developed into a fully fledged anti-didacticism that commanded widespread support. In its extreme form, this meant excluding didactic verse altogether from the poetic canon. More typically, it meant downgrading didactic poetry in the hierarchy of genres and measuring it against criteria of literariness derived from other, more favoured genres.

The criterion most often applied was that of poetic 'purity', a somewhat nebulous concept that was interpreted in a variety of ways.[27] Warton, who gave this idea currency in his essay on Pope, defined 'PURE POETRY', or the 'essentially poetical', as the product of 'a creative and glowing IMAGINATION', ranking different genres according to the extent to which they display this quality.[28] The notion of a poetic

---

[21]   Robert Lowth, *Lectures on the Sacred Poetry of the Hebrews* (1753), trans. G. Gregory, 3 vols (London, 1787), ii. 162–88 (lecture 24: 'Of the Proverbs, or Didactic Poetry of the Hebrews').

[22]   Charles Batteux, *A Course of the Belles Lettres, or, The Principles of Literature*, trans. John Miller, 4 vols (London, 1761), iii. 110–26 (sect. 4: 'Of Didactic Poetry in General').

[23]   See Ch. 5 below, pp. 166–7.

[24]   Gavin Alexander (ed.), *Sidney's 'The Defence of Poesy' and Selected Renaissance Literary Criticism* (Harmondsworth: Penguin, 2004), 11. Sidney echoes the doubts of Italian critics such as Castelvetro, who had questioned the legitimacy of didactic poetry by rejecting the Horatian formula of 'dulce et utile' and arguing that the aim of poetry is simply to give delight, 'without meddling with utility, which ought to be of no account whatever'; James Harry Smith and Edd Winfield Parks (eds), *The Great Critics: An Anthology of Literary Criticism*, 3rd edn (New York: Norton, 1951), 149.

[25]   Shaftesbury, *Second Characters, or, The Language of Forms*, ed. Benjamin Rand (Cambridge: Cambridge University Press, 1914), 97. Cf. his earlier remark in *Characteristicks*, 3 vols (London, 1711), i. 258, that 'the *didactic* or *preceptive* Manner…has so little force towards winning our Attention, that it is apter to tire us than the Metre of an old Ballad'.

[26]   *Course of the Belles Lettres*, 104.

[27]   For the evolution of this concept, see Abrams, *Mirror and the Lamp*, 133–8; P. W. K. Stone, *The Art of Poetry 1750–1820: Theories of Poetic Composition and Style in the Late Neo-Classic and Early Romantic Periods* (London: Routledge and Kegan Paul, 1967), 78–82; and Walter Jackson Bate, *The Burden of the Past and the English Poet* (London: Chatto and Windus, 1971), 75–6.

[28]   *Essay on the Genius and Writings of Pope*, dedication, pp. iv–vii. For Warton's revisionist hierarchy of genres, see Paul Leedy, 'Genres Criticism and the Significance of Warton's Essay on Pope', *Journal of English and German Philology*, 45 (1946), 140–6.

'essence' and of a scale of 'poeticalness' became a Romantic commonplace, an example being Hunt's essay 'What is Poetry?' (1844), with its elaborate typology of seven 'different kinds and degrees of imagination' replacing the traditional hierarchy of genres.[29] Emotional intensity was a second measure of poetic 'purity', and metaphoric inventiveness a third. Taken together, these vague but potent ideas gave rise to the kind of revolutionary classification proposed in 1797 by Anna Barbauld, who suggested that the 'different species of Poetry may be reduced under two comprehensive classes': the first includes all those genres 'in which the charms of verse are made use of to illustrate subjects which in their own nature are affecting or interesting', such as epic, dramatic, descriptive, or didactic poetry; the second

consists of what may be called pure Poetry, or poetry in the abstract. It is conversant with an imaginary world, peopled with beings of its own creation. It deals in splendid imagery, bold fiction, and allegorical personages. It is necessarily obscure to a certain degree; because, having to do chiefly with ideas generated within the mind, it cannot be at all comprehended by any whose intellect has not been exercised in similar contemplations; while the conceptions of the Poet (often highly metaphysical) are rendered still more remote from common apprehension by the figurative phrases in which they are couched.[30]

Skilfully combining the theory of romance developed by critics like Richard Hurd with concepts of lyric derived from the theory of the sublime, Barbauld turns 'pure poetry' into the quintessential poetic category, a supra-genre that transcends ordinary distinctions of genre while still retaining the essence of the genres it subsumes.[31]

Judged by these criteria, didactic poetry—a genre grounded in fact rather than fiction, and on accuracy and elegance of expression rather than 'splendid imagery'— was inevitably found wanting. Such definitions, revealing as they are about shifting critical values, do not, however, fully explain Romantic hostility to didactic writing: why, that is, didactic verse seemed not just marginal but antithetical to Romantic conceptions of poetry. Three further factors need to be considered. The first is the vexed issue of aesthetic autonomy. Implicit in the notion of 'pure poetry' is the idea that the application of poetry to some ulterior purpose is a corruption of its nature. By definition didactic poetry is guilty of this, since what distinguishes this genre from others is its reversal of the priority normally accorded in poetry to 'pleasure' over 'truth'. 'Information', 'truth', 'knowledge' are permissible as 'secondary' or 'ultimate' aims of poetry, but the 'immediate' or 'primary' end must be to give pleasure. So basic an article of faith was this that it entered into almost all Romantic definitions of

---

[29] Leigh Hunt, *Selected Writings*, 6 vols (London: Pickering and Chatto, 2003), iv: *Later Literary Essays*, ed. Charles Mahoney, 8.

[30] Anna Letitia Barbauld (ed.), *The Poetical Works of Mr William Collins, with a Prefatory Essay* (London, 1797), preface, p. iv.

[31] Norman Maclean, 'From Action to Image: Theories of the Lyric in the Eighteenth Century', in R. S. Crane (ed.), *Critics and Criticism* (Chicago: University of Chicago Press, 1952), 440; Steven Shankman, 'The Pindaric Tradition and the Quest for Pure Poetry', *Comparative Literature*, 40 (1988), 219–44: 230; Douglas Lane Patey, '"Aesthetics" and the Rise of Lyric in the Eighteenth Century', *Studies in English Literature 1500–1900*, 33/3 (1993), 587–608. For romance theory, see Arthur Johnston, *Enchanted Ground: The Study of Medieval Romance in the Eighteenth Century* (London: Athlone Press, 1964).

poetry, including the Preface to *Lyrical Ballads* and chapter 14 of *Biographia Literaria*, where the whole division of knowledge rests on this one distinction. It is, says Coleridge, by 'proposing for its *immediate* object pleasure, not truth' that poems are distinguished from 'works of science';[32] and it is 'the necessity of giving immediate pleasure' that, for Wordsworth, differentiates the poet from the biographer, the historian, and the natural philosopher.[33] Since 'the principal object' of didactic poetry, as Wordsworth and others defined it, 'is direct instruction',[34] either it is *not* poetry—the conclusion drawn by some—or one of these definitions must be wrong: the view taken by De Quincey, who demonstrates, with an ostentatious show of philosophic rigour, that didactic poetry, as traditionally defined, is a pseudo-category, a logical impossibility.

More subtle but no less powerful than the philosophical objection to didactic poetry is what might be called the psychological resistance. Such forces are hard to quantify, but it is clear that the level of aversion displayed in Keats's 'hatred' and Shelley's 'abhorrence' of didactic poetry goes beyond mere matters of taste or terminological quibbles about what is or is not poetry. To compare remarks like these with the kind of enthusiasm for didactic poetry expressed by Trapp—the positive relish for 'Precepts delivered in Verse...imbibed with so much Pleasure; and...held in so great Esteem'[35]—is to register a profound shift in sensibility. In part, didactic poetry is compromised for the Romantics by its association with a cultural tradition of subordination, of deference to received wisdom and authority, or what Blake called the 'horses of instruction' (an allusion to Swift's Houyhnhnms, the ultimate culture of subordination). The Romantics seek from poetry a different kind of wisdom, a kind that does not come in the form of precepts and instructions, of being told what and what not to do. For Blake and Shelley, anti-didacticism meant anti-authoritarianism—opposing other men's systems, and laying aside, as Shelley put it, 'the presumptuous attitude of an instructor'.[36] Keats, too, felt poetic didacticism to be a form of coercion: 'Are we to be bullied into a certain philosophy engendered by the whims of an egotist?' is his indignant reaction to a reading of Wordsworth—probably *The Excursion* (1814).[37] Lamb makes a similar complaint about 'The Old Cumberland Beggar', pointing out to Wordsworth that 'the instructions conveyed in it are too direct and like a lecture: they don't slide into the mind of the reader, while he is imagining no such matter.—An intelligent reader finds a sort of insult in being told, I will teach you how to think upon this subject.'[38]

---

[32] *The Collected Works of Samuel Taylor Coleridge*, vii: *Biographia Literaria*, ed. James Engell and W. Jackson Bate, 2 vols (London: Routledge and Kegan Paul, 1984), ii. 13. Cf. George Dyer, 'On the Primary and Ultimate End of Poetry', in his *Poetics, or, A Series of Poems and Disquisitions on Poetry*, 2 vols (London, 1812).

[33] Preface to *Lyrical Ballads* (1802), in *The Prose Works of William Wordsworth*, ed. W. J. B. Owen and Jane Worthington Smyser, 3 vols (Oxford: Clarendon Press, 1974), i. 139.

[34] Preface to *Poems* (1815), in *Prose Works*, iii. 28.

[35] *Lectures on Poetry*, 187.

[36] 'Dedication to Leigh Hunt', *The Cenci* (1820), in *Shelley's Poetry and Prose*, 140.

[37] To J. H. Reynolds, 3 Feb. 1818, in *Letters*, i. 223–4.

[38] To William Wordsworth, 30 Jan. 1801, in *The Letters of Charles and Mary Lamb*, ed. Edwin W. Marrs, Jr, 3 vols (Ithaca, N.Y.: Cornell University Press, 1975–8), i. 265.

Given that Wordsworth was the founder of a radical poetics which placed a premium on spontaneity and expressive freedom, it is ironic that his own poetry provoked such strong anti-didactic reactions.[39] But Lamb's appeal to the experience of the 'intelligent reader' suggests another factor in the cultural shift we are examining: the emergence of new reading practices, and a new understanding of the psychology of reading. Some of the most robust anti-didactic comment of the Romantic period is uttered from the standpoint of the reader rather than the writer. Blake's marginalia are a case in point. The bone of contention in his famously antagonistic readings is often the intended moral of a passage which he interprets in a different way from the author. 'Unity & Morality', he declares, 'are secondary considerations, & belong to Philosophy & not to Poetry, to Exception & not to Rule, to Accident & not to Substance.'[40] William Godwin's objection to the crude and counter-productive didacticism of his fellow novelist Thomas Holcroft is in the same vein: 'If you wished to impress on your countrymen an abhorrence of the very name of Political Philosophy, you could not have done your business in any way so effectually, as by obtruding it upon them, when their passions were roused, and imagination was on tip toe for events.'[41] The distinction Godwin draws, in an essay on reading, between the 'moral' and the 'tendency' of a work reinforces the point that the 'actual effect' of a literary text may not coincide with the author's intended message, partly because the former depends on the reader's 'previous state of mind'.[42] Walter Scott, a novelist of a very different political stamp, makes a similar point with a brilliant analogy: 'The professed moral of a piece is usually what the reader is least interested in; it is like the mendicant, who cripples after some gay procession, and in vain solicits the attention of those who have been gazing upon it.'[43] Once again, an objection to didacticism is grounded in reader psychology, the claim being that direct moral or political instruction demands a type of response inconsistent with, and even antithetical to, the imaginative attention which *poesis*, or fiction, requires.

Taken to their logical extreme, such arguments lead to De Quincey's distinction between 'moral' and 'aesthetic' interpretation, playfully applied to the topic of homicide in his famous essays 'On Murder Considered as One of the Fine Arts' (1827, 1839). Like Coleridge's 'Essays on the Principles of Genial Criticism' (1814), discussed in Chapter 2, De Quincey's 'Murder' essays are landmarks in the assimilation of Kant's theory of the aesthetic, which defines aesthetic pleasure as contemplative rather than moral and severs the traditional link between the beautiful and the

---

[39] Cf. Stephen Gill, 'Wordsworth's Breeches Pockets: Attitudes to the Didactic Poet', *Essays in Criticism*, 19 (1969), 385–401.

[40] 'On Homer's Poetry', in *Complete Writings*, 778.

[41] Bodleian Library, Abinger Dep. b. 227/6, quoted by Katherine Binhammer, 'The Political Novel and the Seduction Plot: Thomas Holcroft's *Anna St Ives*', *Eighteenth-Century Fiction*, 11/2 (1999), 205–22: 212. Illustrative of Holcroft's baldly didactic approach is the statement in his Preface to *Memoirs of Bryan Perdue* (1805): 'Whenever I have undertaken to write a novel, I have proposed to myself a specific moral purpose' (quoted by Joseph F. Bartolomeo, *A New Species of Criticism: Eighteenth-Century Discourse on the Novel* (Newark: University of Delaware Press, 1994), 96).

[42] 'Of Choice in Reading', in William Godwin, *The Enquirer: Reflections on Education, Manners, and Literature. In a Series of Essays* (London, 1797), 136.

[43] 'Fielding', *Lives of the Novelists* (1827), in Miriam Allott (ed.), *Novelists on the Novel* (London: Routledge and Kegan Paul, 1965), 92.

good. As well as invoking Kant, though, De Quincey also cites Wordsworth, and the 'Murder' essays can be read as yet another reworking of the power–knowledge distinction and of De Quincey's deconstruction of the didactic. 'Knowledge', in this context, is represented by the self-evident truth that murder is bad, but the startling claim of the essays is that murder cases 'may also be treated *aesthetically*, as the Germans call it, that is, in relation to good taste'.[44] This macabre connoisseurship involves applying to the art of murder the same criteria used in the criticism of other art forms, namely originality, importance of subject matter (the status of the victim), quality of execution (including concealment of method), sublimity—whatever it is about a murder that can, as he puts it, 'excite our wonder'. Underlying De Quincey's mock-argument is the serious point that the imagination is an independent faculty, with its own logic, and the aesthetic an autonomous mode of cognition which can act separately from and even antithetically to the moral sense. This leaves little room for didactic art, if by that we mean art which serves a predetermined moral purpose, but plenty of room for the dark art that is De Quincey's subject.

Compelling though these arguments are, there was, however, an even more basic objection to didacticism—in poetry especially—which was linguistic. Reading Romantic criticism of didactic poetry, it is sometimes difficult to understand how this genre could ever have been found aesthetically appealing, or to appreciate the grounds on which it was once placed so high in the hierarchy of poetic forms. The best answer can be found in Addison's 'Essay on the Georgics' (published in 1697 as an appendix to Dryden's translation of Virgil), a piece of criticism so lucid in its arguments and so eloquent in its advocacy of the genre that it set the terms for discussion of georgic for over a century (even Joseph Warton, elsewhere an opponent of didactic poetry, approvingly quotes large chunks of Addison's essay in the introduction to his own translation of Virgil). For Addison, writing a georgic—that is, a didactic poem on the science of farming (or, by extension, other practical topics)—is the supreme test of a poet's skill, because it involves elevating 'low', unpoetic subject matter into high art, a metamorphosis which must be achieved through the power of language alone, by a careful process of selection and embellishment:

I think nothing which is a Phrase or Saying in common Talk, shou'd be admitted into a serious Poem; because it takes off from the Solemnity of the Expression, and gives it too great a turn of Familiarity: Much less ought the low Phrases and Terms of Art, that are adapted to Husbandry, have any place in such a Work as the *Georgic*, which is not to appear in the natural Simplicity and Nakedness of its Subject, but in the pleasantest Dress that Poetry can bestow on it. . . . And herein consists *Virgil's* Masterpiece, who has not only excell'd all other Poets, but even himself in the Language of his *Georgics*; where we receive more strong and lively Ideas of things from his Words, than we cou'd have done from the Objects themselves: And find our Imaginations more affected by his Descriptions, than they wou'd have been by the very Sight of what he describes.[45]

---

[44] 'On Murder Considered as One of the Fine Arts', *Blackwood's Magazine*, 20 (Feb. 1827), in *Works*, vi. 114.

[45] Addison, 'Essay on the Georgics', in Dryden (trans.), *Works of Virgil*, i. 205.

Addison takes the idea of language as the dress of thought—a central metaphor in neoclassical poetics—to its furthest extreme. Poetry becomes an art of disguise, an exquisite dressing-up game, and the genre of georgic—in the hands of its best practitioners—a tour de force designed to turn the inherently unpoetic into the consummately beautiful.[46] It is the imaginative appeal of this game, and the irresistibility of the artistic challenge it posed, that helps to explain the remarkable persistence of the georgic throughout the eighteenth century.[47]

From a Romantic perspective, however, such an aesthetic rationale betrayed a fundamental misunderstanding of the nature of poetic language, and amounted to a travesty of the art of poetry. The idea that form and content were separable, that poetic language was merely an outer covering, or 'dress', which concealed the naked thought beneath, was, for the Romantics, the most grievous of all errors in the neoclassical system. The genre of georgic, being the ultimate display of linguistic fancy dress, enshrined that error to a maximum degree. So profound are the implications of this mistake that Coleridge devotes the whole of the first chapter of *Biographia Literaria* to exposing it, presenting instead an incarnationist theory of language (words as an embodiment of thought) and making a categorical distinction between 'poetic thoughts' (of which true poetry consists) and 'thoughts translated into the language of poetry' (of which didactic poetry usually consists).[48] Wordsworth makes a similar case in his essays 'On Epitaphs' (1810), as does De Quincey in his essay on Pope, where he cleverly adjusts the incarnationist theory to accommodate the art of rhetoric. Shelley puts the matter most succinctly, stating as his objection to didactic poetry that 'nothing can be equally well expressed in prose that is not tedious and supererogatory in verse'.[49] This turns Addison's argument on its head, and makes vices of the very qualities by which he had defended and canonized the genre.

To equate these various objections and resistances with a generalized desire for 'art for art's sake' would clearly be a gross simplification, though the phrase itself was apparently coined in this period.[50] There are, however, even stronger reasons for rejecting such simplistic identifications, because the hostile reactions thus far encountered tell only part of the story about Romantic attitudes to didactic poetry, and to didacticism in general. What makes the situation so interesting is that a growing distaste for

---

[46] Kevis Goodman, 'Magnifying Small Things: Georgic Modernity and the Noise of History', *European Romantic Review*, 15/2 (2004), 215–27.

[47] Richard Feingold, *Nature and Society: Later Eighteenth-Century Uses of the Georgic and the Pastoral* (New Brunswick, N.J.: Rutgers University Press, 1978); Donald Low, *The Georgic Revolution* (Princeton: Princeton University Press, 1985).

[48] *Biographia Literaria*, i. 19. The implications of this distinction are explored by Emerson R. Marks, *Coleridge on the Language of Verse* (Princeton: Princeton University Press, 1981); and James C. McCusick, *Coleridge's Philosophy of Language* (New Haven: Yale University Press, 1986).

[49] Preface to *Prometheus Unbound*, in *Shelley's Poetry and Prose*, 209.

[50] The first recorded use is during a conversation (in French) between Henry Crabb Robinson and Benjamin Constant in Weimar in 1804 (Burwick, *Mimesis and its Romantic Reflections*, 18–19). For the broader history of this concept, see Albert Guérard, *Art for Art's Sake* (Boston: Lothrop, Lee, and Shepard, 1936); William Wimsatt, Jr, and Cleanth Brooks, *Literary Criticism: A Short History* (London: Routledge and Kegan Paul, 1957), ch. 22; and Angela Leighton, *On Form: Poetry, Aestheticism, and the Legacy of a Word* (Oxford: Oxford University Press, 2007), ch. 2.

didacticism coincided with diametrically opposed tendencies, both in Romantic literature and in the culture at large. It is to these counter-currents that I now turn.

## PALPABLE DESIGNS

As already intimated, the thorny issue of didacticism was part of a wider cultural debate in the Romantic period about the nature and function of literature. The significance of this debate has been obscured by Jerome McGann's 'Romantic ideology' thesis, which attributes to the Romantics a culpable blindness to the ideological implications of their literary theory and practice.[51] This charge may hold true for the theory of organic form, a doctrine whose political overtones its adherents often seem not to have been conscious of. In other respects, though, what is striking about the Romantic period is, on the contrary, its pervasive—even obsessive—awareness of the ideological effects of literature, on the part not only of writers but also of critics, publishers, politicians, and ordinary readers. The same Coleridge who later became the spokesman for literary and social organicism proposed a lecture series in 1795 entitled 'A Comparative View of the English Rebellion under Charles the First, and the French Revolution'. The series (which was advertised but probably not delivered) was to hinge on what the Prospectus calls the 'revolutionary Powers' of literature, Coleridge's argument being that both of these cataclysmic events were caused by the spread of revolutionary ideas—of revolutionary *literature* (the printed word) specifically.[52] A similar premiss informs Isaac D'Israeli's essay 'On the Political Influence of Authors' (1795), which pivots on the ultra-Shelleyan thesis that 'the single thought of a man of genius has sometimes changed the dispositions of a people, and even of an age', a claim D'Israeli couches in germination imagery strikingly similar to that of the 'Ode to the West Wind':

> An eloquent author, who writes in the immutable language of truth, will one day be superior to every power in the state. His influence is active, though hidden; every truth is an acorn which is laid in the earth, and which often the longer it takes to rise, the more vigorous and magnificent will be its maturity. What has long been meditated in the silence of the study, will one day resound in the aweful voice of public opinion.[53]

In arguing for 'the utility of men of letters to national purposes' (p. 178), D'Israeli includes not only political theorists but also poets and other writers: like Coleridge's lectures, the essay is in part an analysis of the intellectual origins of the French Revolution, which he traces to notions of liberty transmitted to France by English writers like Locke, Pope, and Addison. Even those who were appalled by the thought that writers could wield such political power conceded that they probably did, hence

---

[51] Jerome McGann, *The Romantic Ideology: A Critical Investigation* (Chicago: University of Chicago Press, 1983).

[52] *The Collected Works of Samuel Taylor Coleridge*, i: *Lectures 1795: On Politics and Religion*, ed. Lewis Patton and Peter Mann (London: Routledge and Kegan Paul, 1971), 255.

[53] 'On the Political Influence of Authors', in Isaac D'Israeli, *An Essay on the Manners and Genius of the Literary Character* (London, 1795), 175–6, 183–4.

Thomas Mathias's extraordinary claim, in the headnote to his anti-Jacobin satire *The Pursuits of Literature* (1798), that 'LITERATURE, well or ill conducted, is THE GREAT ENGINE, by which all *civilized* states...must ultimately be supported or over-thrown.'[54]

Contemporary fascination with the ideological effects of literature is illustrated, too, by the constant citation of Andrew Fletcher of Saltoun's dictum, 'if a man were permitted to make all the ballads, he need not care who should make the laws of a nation'.[55] The 'very wise man' who communicated this saying to Fletcher in 1703 probably had in mind the Jacobite ballads and songs of the time expressing popular resistance to Hanoverian rule and Union with England. Joanna Baillie, doubtless aware of the significance of citing this iconic Scottish patriot at a time of renewed political instability, recalls the saying in her Introductory Discourse to *Plays on the Passions* (1798), first to signal the dangers of inflaming the passions of 'our potent and formidable ballad-readers' and then to make an analogous claim for the positive influence of drama over the more elevated class of people who go to theatres.[56] Twelve years later, Anna Barbauld applies Fletcher's dictum to yet another genre in her essay 'On the Origin and Progress of Novel Writing', using it in her closing sentence to clinch her argument about the communicative power of the novel.[57] The Irish radical George Ensor makes equally good use of the saying in his tract *On National Education* (1811), a manifesto for a reformed educational system in which he assigns a central role to the teaching of poetry. Like Shelley, who may have drawn on Ensor's tract in *A Defence of Poetry*, he supports his case with many historical examples of poetry's 'irresistible influence'.[58]

Such arguments were not entirely new—the notion of the poet as legislator goes back to Sidney and Puttenham, and recognition (often negative) of writers' influence over public opinion is as old as Plato's *Republic*—but the remarkable currency they acquire in the Romantic period reflects the fact that, as Mathias puts it, 'Government and Literature are now more than ever intimately connected',[59] and the political influence of authors was being demonstrated before people's very eyes. As the radical Irish poet Thomas Dermody observes in his tract *The Rights of Justice* (1793), in the wake of the French Revolution 'every species of literature' had become a 'vehicle of political information':

---

[54] Thomas James Mathias, *The Pursuits of Literature: A Satirical Poem in Four Dialogues. With Notes*, 7th edn (London, 1798), preface to the third dialogue, 161–2.

[55] *An Account of a Conversation Concerning a Right Regulation of Government* (1703), in *The Political Works of Fletcher of Saltoun*, ed. Robert Watson (London, 1798), 164–5. The saying also appears in Fletcher's *Letter to the Marquis of Montrose* (1704).

[56] Joanna Baillie, *Plays on the Passions* (1798 edn), ed. Peter Duthie (Peterborough, Ont.: Broadview, 2001), 103–4. See Ch. 2 above, p. 69.

[57] Anna Letitia Barbauld, *Selected Poetry and Prose*, ed. William McCarthy and Elizabeth Kraft (Peterborough, Ont.: Broadview, 2002), 416–17. Barbauld here reverses the argument of Hugh Blair, who had adapted Fletcher's saying to warn of the dangerous popularity of the novel; *Lectures on Rhetoric and Belles Lettres*, ii. 303.

[58] George Ensor, *On National Education* (London, 1811), 283. For Ensor's possible influence on Shelley, see Ronald Tetreault, *The Poetry of Life: Shelley and Literary Form* (Toronto: University of Toronto Press, 1987), 31–3.

[59] *Pursuits of Literature*, 5.

The Stage is, literally, 'a brief abstract of the Times', our Novels are mere overgrown Pamphlets, our very Ballads are Historical Rhapsodies in embrio, in short, from the venerable Folio; to the diminutive half-sheet, All, (to use a much esteemed metaphor) is redolent of Revolution.[60]

It is this unprecedented situation—a wholesale mobilization in which the entire spectrum of genres had become politicized and pamphletized—that Gillray captures so memorably in his cartoon 'New Morality' (Figure 2.2, discussed in my previous chapter), and that underpins Romanticism's troubled fascination with palpable literary designs.

Political conditions, however, were not the only factor contributing to the instrumentalization of literature. Other factors include the philosophical impact of Utilitarianism, with its call for functional explicitness and its insistence that literature be judged by the same criteria of social or moral utility as any other form of knowledge;[61] developments in education, including the increased use of literature in schools and universities, often for moral as well as aesthetic purposes;[62] the highly polemical culture of reviewing, which ensured immediate and often prejudicial scrutiny of a work's ideological tendencies as well as its literary merit;[63] and the shifting relationship between literature and religion, involving on the one hand a gradual secularization of literary culture, and on the other an expanding role for imaginative literature as some form of substitute religion (Bibles of Hell, Lay Sermons, Political Litanies).[64] These and other cultural pressures translated into a ubiquitous and relentless demand for *usefulness*: for literature to serve some cause, perform some function, or state some purpose—a demand which was at its strongest at just the moment when the idea that art was essentially without purpose, an end in itself, began to crystallize.

Despite Romanticism's quarrel with the more reductive aspects of Utilitarian thinking, the literature of the period was more commonly written in response to than in defiance of this demand. Nowhere is this more visible than in the literature of the 1790s, a decade which witnessed artistic innovations that were to shape the course of British Romanticism, but which also produced some of the most unashamedly tendentious literature ever written—these two principles sometimes combining in brilliantly effective ways. A good example is *Lyrical Ballads*, a collection whose revolutionary quality lies not only in its iconoclastic treatment of poetic language and form but also in its daring experiments with poetic function. As Wordsworth emphasizes in the Preface, the poems are distinguished from popular poetry of the time partly by the fact that each of them has a clearly conceived *purpose*,

---

[60] Thomas Dermody, *The Rights of Justice, or, Rational Liberty: A Letter to an Acquaintance in the Country* (Dublin, 1793), 5.

[61] John Whale, *Imagination under Pressure 1789–1832: Aesthetics, Politics and Utility* (Cambridge: Cambridge University Press, 2000).

[62] Alan Richardson, *Literature, Education and Romanticism: Reading as Social Practice, 1780–1832* (Cambridge: Cambridge University Press, 1994).

[63] Marilyn Butler, 'Culture's Medium: The Role of the Review', in Stuart Curran (ed.), *The Cambridge Companion to British Romanticism* (Cambridge: Cambridge University Press, 1993); Mark Parker, *Literary Magazines and British Romanticism* (Cambridge: Cambridge University Press, 2000).

[64] Robert M. Ryan, *The Romantic Reformation: Religious Politics in English Literature, 1789–1824* (Cambridge: Cambridge University Press, 1997).

whether it be the psychological one of tracing 'the fluxes and refluxes of the mind'[65] or the humanitarian one of effecting a shift in public attitudes towards the poor and disadvantaged. The explicitness with which Wordsworth spells out his objectives (even if he conceals his full political motives) is itself characteristic of the revolutionary decade, as *The Anti-Jacobin* confirms in a mock-critical essay entitled the 'Jacobin Art of Poetry' (1797), which pours scorn on the fashionable policy of prefacing poems 'with a short disquisition on the particular tenet intended to be enforced or insinuated'.[66] Though directed at specific authors, this remark could apply to any number of radical—or indeed anti-radical—works of the 1790s.

Like the formal innovations with which Romanticism is more readily associated, functional transformations affected a huge range of genres, including classical forms like the eclogue and epic, whose ideological coding, as we have seen, was subjected to drastic revision.[67] A more subtle example is the sonnet. A genre which for Charlotte Smith and William Lisle Bowles had been a conduit for lachrymose effusion became, in the 1790s, a vehicle for polemic, a form of news bulletin, and a tool for the analysis of emotion both public and private (the expanded sense of generic purpose is captured in Wordsworth's two well-known sonnets on the sonnet, each in effect a defence of the *utility* of the form). The ode underwent similar redeployment, reversing the trend towards internalization that had begun with Joseph Warton and restoring the public orientation and declamatory manner that had been the genre's original hallmarks (at a later stage, its private and public functions converged, a development I trace in my Conclusion). Even a new and seemingly apolitical genre like the 'conversation poem' was shaped as much by its ideological function as by its formal structure. The conversation poem is 'meditative' in both a personal and a philosophical sense, and the genre's celebration of domesticity, friendship, and the harmonizing power of the imagination carried an unmistakable ideological resonance in the fraught historical circumstances in which the genre evolved, as critics have recognized.[68]

In prose fiction, the instrumentalist trend produces such notable developments as the 'Jacobin novel', the rationale for this openly tendentious brand of fiction being spelt out in Godwin's original, suppressed Preface to *Caleb Williams* (1794), which defends the novel as a form of consciousness-raising directed at 'persons whom books of philosophy and science are never likely to reach'.[69] As his advice to Holcroft, quoted earlier, suggests, Godwin's understanding of the artistic issues involved was more subtle than that of other Jacobin novelists, but the basic methodological premiss was widely

---

[65] *Prose Works*, i. 126, 118.

[66] *Poetry of the Anti-Jacobin*, 6th edn (London, 1813), 3 (no. 1, 20 Nov. 1797).

[67] See Ch. 2 above, pp. 67–8.

[68] Kelvin Everest, *Coleridge's Secret Ministry: The Context of the Conversation Poems 1795–98* (Brighton: Harvester Press, 1979); Paul Magnuson, *Reading Public Romanticism* (Princeton: Princeton University Press, 1998), ch. 3.

[69] William Godwin, *Caleb Williams*, ed. Pamela Clemit (Oxford: Oxford University Press, 2009), app. B, p. 312. The phrase 'Jacobin novel' was coined by Gary Kelly, *The English Jacobin Novel 1780–1805* (Oxford: Clarendon Press, 1976).

accepted, including by his ideological adversaries the 'anti-Jacobin novelists', who rejected his ideas but imitated his techniques.[70] Fanny Burney, an author who fits neither category, was merely voicing a common assumption of the time when, in the Preface to *The Wanderer* (1814), she said of the novel form: 'What is the species of writing that offers fairer opportunities for conveying useful precepts?'[71] Maria Edgeworth carried through the implications of this view by abandoning the generic label of 'novel' for that of 'moral tale' (beginning with *Belinda*, 1801), and contemporary critics drove home the point with exhaustive treatises such as Hugh Murray's *Morality of Fiction, or, An Inquiry into the Tendency of Fictitious Narratives, with Observations on Some of the Most Eminent* (1805) and Edward Mangin's *Essay on Light Reading: As It May be Supposed to Influence Moral Conduct and Literary Taste* (1808). Clearly, the concept of 'light reading' still had some way to go before it signified a purely recreational activity.

Demonstrable didactic intent had, indeed, become a measure of respectability, a means by which uncanonical genres like the novel could gain critical acceptability, and by which female writers could be taken seriously ('instruction', as distinct from 'amusement', being coded as masculine in the gendered critical lexicon of the time[72]). Walter Scott makes just this point in his essay on Jane Austen (1821), noting that the 'new school of fiction'—the novel of domestic realism—had elevated the genre 'into a much higher class' by taking on the function of instruction 'which used to be presented in the shape of formal dissertations, or shorter and more desultory moral essays'.[73] A recent survey has shown that 'in the final third of the century, emphasis upon the need for imaginative literature to be *instructional* increased dramatically', and 'that no preface from the 1790s admitted to entertainment as the single motive for publication'.[74] Even a lightweight magazine like the *Weekly Entertainer* (1773–1819) carried the subtitle 'Agreeable and Instructive Repository', reviving the old Horatian formula for a literary marketplace in which to be 'useful' or 'instructive' was as much a selling point as to be 'entertaining'. An anthology of 1791 entitled *Mental Pleasures* makes the same point, as may be inferred from its unhedonistic subtitle, *Select Essays, Characters, Anecdotes, and Poems. Extracted Chiefly from Fugitive Publications, and Calculated to Improve and Entertain the Mind*.

[70] M. O. Grenby, *The Anti-Jacobin Novel: British Conservatism and the French Revolution* (Cambridge: Cambridge University Press, 2001); Peter H. Marshall, *William Godwin* (New Haven: Yale University Press, 1984), ch. 13.

[71] Frances Burney, *The Wanderer, or, Female Difficulties* (1814), ed. Margaret Anne Doody, Robert L. Mack, and Peter Sabor (Oxford: Oxford University Press, 1991), preface 'To Doctor Burney', 7.

[72] As illustrated by a review of Charlotte Smith's *Desmond* (1792) in the *Monthly Review*, 2nd ser., 9 (Dec. 1792), 406: 'Among the various proofs which the present age affords, that the female character is advancing in cultivation, and rising in dignity, may be justly reckoned the improvements that are making in the kind of writing which is more immediately adapted to the amusement of female readers. Novels, which were formerly little more than simple tales of love, are gradually taking a higher and more masculine tone, and are becoming the vehicles of useful instruction' (quoted by Bartolomeo, *New Species of Criticism*, 123).

[73] 'Miss Austen's Novels', *Quarterly Review* (Jan. 1821), in *The Prose Works of Sir Walter Scott*, 28 vols (Edinburgh, 1835), xviii. 218.

[74] James Raven, *Judging New Wealth: Popular Responses to Commerce in England, 1750–1800* (Oxford: Clarendon Press, 1992), 70, 74.

Drama follows a similar trajectory. The moralizing turn in the late eighteenth century is a familiar chapter in the history of British drama, when even the most trivial forms of theatrical entertainment—forerunners of today's pantomimes—would be shaped by moralistic plot lines and sententious rhetoric, and when popular entertainment of all kinds had to present itself to the public gaze as both entertaining *and* useful. The uses were real enough: as studies have shown, popular or 'illegitimate' theatre was an ideological battleground in which radicals and conservatives fought for the hearts and minds of the British people, and the Revolutionary and Napoleonic wars stimulated the development of many new kinds of political drama and spectacle.[75] Further up the generic hierarchy, the didactic imperative inspired such ambitious projects as Baillie's *Plays on the Passions* (1798), whose attempt 'to delineate the stronger passions of the mind' through a series of juxtaposed tragedies and comedies involved a major rethinking of dramatic form and function.[76] Byron's resuscitation, two decades later, of the medieval genre of the 'mystery' or 'morality' play in *Cain* (1821) and *Heaven and Earth* (1823) is yet another manifestation of the instrumentalist trend, his dramas being no less didactic for the fact he used them to subvert conventional morality.[77] The same can be said of Shelley's *Prometheus Unbound*, which denounces 'didactic poetry' in the Preface but practises its own brand of rhapsodic didacticism through its representation of 'beautiful idealisms of moral excellence'.[78] Shelley himself admits, in a cancelled marginal note to *A Defence of Poetry*, that his own compositions, by promulgating his personal ethical views, may have infringed his anti-didactic rule. Against the statement that a poet 'would do ill to embody his own conceptions of right & wrong' in his poems appears the cross-written remark 'This was Mr. Shelley's error in the Revolt of Islam. He has attempted to cure himself in subsequent publications but, except in the tragedy of the Cenci, with little effect.'[79]

## THE DIDACTIC POEM

The clearest illustration of the didactic trend, however, is the genre of the 'didactic poem' itself, which, far from disappearing in this period, acquired a visibility and prestige it had not experienced since the time of Pope.[80] The key figure in this revival

[75] David Worrall, *Theatric Revolution: Drama, Censorship and Romantic Period Subcultures 1773–1832* (Oxford: Oxford University Press, 2006); Jane Moody, *Illegitimate Theatre in London 1770–1840* (Cambridge: Cambridge University Press, 2000); Julia Swindells, *Glorious Causes: The Grand Theatre of Political Change 1789–1833* (Oxford: Oxford University Press, 2001); Gillian Russell, *Theatres of War: Performance, Politics and Society 1790–1815* (Oxford: Clarendon Press, 1995).

[76] See Ch. 2 above, pp. 68–9.

[77] Martyn Corbett, *Byron and Tragedy* (Basingstoke: Macmillan, 1988), 143–88.

[78] *Shelley's Poetry and Prose*, 209. 'Rhapsodic didacticism' is Wimsatt and Brooks's phrase, in *Literary Criticism: A Short History*, ch. 19.

[79] Bodleian Library, MS Shelley Adds. e. 20, in *The Bodleian Shelley Manuscripts*, vii: *Shelley's Last Notebook*, ed. Donald H. Reiman (New York: Garland, 1990), 189. I am grateful to Michael O'Neill for drawing this to my attention.

[80] I confine myself here to works subtitled, or identified in reviews, as 'didactic poems', a term which increasingly replaced 'georgic' in this period. For georgic itself, see Kurt Heinzelman, 'Roman

is Erasmus Darwin, whose versified scientific treatises *The Loves of the Plants* (1789), *The Economy of Vegetation* (1791), and *The Temple of Nature* (1803) achieved extraordinary popularity, demonstrating that the public appetite for didactic poetry was stronger than ever, despite the growing dominance of lyric genres and the Wartonian theory of poetic 'purity'. Written in rhyming couplets, Darwin's poetry is formally traditional, and his characterization of it as an attempt 'to inlist Imagination under the banner of Science, and to lead her votaries from the looser analogies, which dress out the imagery of poetry, to the stricter ones, which form the ratiocination of philosophy'[81] builds on the standard neoclassical definition of didactic poetry. However, by using traditional poetic methods to present modern scientific arguments, Darwin succeeded both in reinvigorating a dated literary genre and in allaying among his readers the anxiety that the two domains of science and poetry had grown mutually exclusive. Besides awakening a generation of readers to the excitements of botany and zoology, and the logical beauty of the Linnaean classification system, Darwin's poetry provided reassuring confirmation that poetry had a share in the modern intellectual economy.

Like other successes in the lucrative poetry market, Darwin's poetry inspired a host of imitators, and the 1790s and early 1800s saw the composition of didactic poems on everything from the conduct of court cases (*The Pleader's Guide*, 1796) and the *Late Improved Mode of Study, and Examination* at Oxford University (1812) to the activities of *The Shotley Bridge Fox Chace* (1795) and *The Art of Making Breeches* (1800).[82] Some of these are parodies, but it is not always easy to tell which, since an air of implausibility was part of the attraction of didactic poems, and even mock-didactics like *The Pleader's Guide* carried serious footnotes, supplying the hard information that the text of the poem had fun with. There were, in addition, entirely serious productions. Richard Payne Knight helped to popularize the new theories of the picturesque with his didactic poem *The Landscape* (1794), following this up with a more controversial poem called *The Progress of Civil Society* (1796). The Whig sentiments expressed therein attracted the ire of *The Anti-Jacobin*, who objected to Knight's polluting of the Popean didactic poem with 'the coy Muse of *Jacobinism*', and instituted a series of parodies entitled *The Progress of Man: A Didactic Poem, In Forty Cantos, with Notes Critical and Explanatory: Chiefly of a Philosophical Tendency*, this pedantic nomenclature being an allusion to the elaborate subtitles and scholarly

Georgic in the Georgian Age: A Theory of Romantic Genre', *Texas Studies in Literature and Language*, 33 (1991), 182–214; Clifford Siskin, *The Work of Writing: Literature and Social Change in Britain, 1700–1830* (Baltimore: Johns Hopkins University Press, 1998), ch. 5; and Kevis Goodman, *Georgic Modernity and British Romanticism: Poetry and the Mediation of History* (Cambridge: Cambridge University Press, 2004).

    [81] Erasmus Darwin, *The Botanic Garden, Part II. Containing The Loves of the Plants: A Poem. With Philosophical Notes. Volume the Second* (Lichfield, 1789), advertisement.
    [82] [John Anstey,] *The Pleader's Guide: A Didactic Poem, in Two Parts* (London, 1796); Thomas Thorburn, *The Shotley Bridge Fox Chance: A Descriptive Didactic Poem. Interspersed with Allusions and Reflections on the Morals of the Times* (Newcastle, 1795); anon., *Oxoniana: A Didactic Poem, in Several Letters on the Late Improved Mode of Study, and Examination for Degrees in the University of Oxford* (London, 1812); Solomon Irony [Rembrandt Peale?], *Fashion, or, The Art of Making Breeches: An Heroi-Satiri-Didactic Poem* (Philadelphia, 1800).

apparatus of Knight and Darwin's poems.[83] While undoubtedly damaging the reputation of these authors, the *Anti-Jacobin* spoof paradoxically served to give even greater visibility to the genre of the didactic poem (the 'heavy artillery' among genres, as a subsequent *Anti-Jacobin* article mockingly describes it[84]).

The fashion for didactic poems on political themes continued into the new century. George Sanon's *The Causes of the French Revolution; and the Science of Governing an Empire: An Epic and Philosophical Poem* (1806), dedicated to the veteran reformer Capel Lofft, wins the prize for the most hubristic title of the period by conjoining what Shelley called 'the master theme of the epoch—the French Revolution'[85] with the even grander theme of empire, while also integrating the two master genres of epic and 'philosophical poem'. Shelley's own *Queen Mab: A Philosophical Poem; with Notes* (1813) was scarcely less ambitious, a poem whose heady mixture of social criticism and utopian fantasy ensured for it a permanent place in the radical canon, notwithstanding Shelley's retrospective fear that his youthful composition might be 'better fitted to injure than to serve the cause of freedom'.[86] Among the many paratextual devices adorning Shelley's privately printed edition was an epigraph from Lucretius' *De Rerum Natura*, showing that he was fully aware of the genealogy of his chosen genre, just as he was cognizant of the new, political meaning of the word 'philosophy', whose Godwinian connotations he exploits. Like Darwin, an author he much admired, Shelley uses poetry as a way of 'imagining' science, reserving the factual information for the Notes. His aim, though, is not simply to interpret the world but also to change it, as his third epigraph, from the Greek of Archimedes, makes clear: 'Give me a place to stand, and I will move the earth.'[87]

Among other things, the spate of didactic poems provides a missing context for Wordsworth's *The Recluse*, a poetic project which grew out of the 'epomania' of the 1790s, but which also participated in this other, less well-charted generic trend. Indeed, part of the point of Coleridge's description of *The Recluse* as (potentially) 'THE FIRST GENUINE PHILOSOPHIC POEM'[88] may have been to differentiate it from the sub- or mock-philosophical poetry that other writers were producing, in the same way that *Lyrical Ballads* sought to differentiate itself from other kinds of ballad then in vogue. In the Preface to *The Excursion* (1814), the one part of *The Recluse* completed and published, Wordsworth emphasized the novelty of his approach.

---

[83] *The Anti-Jacobin*, 15 (19 Feb. 1798), in Graham Stones and John Strachan (eds), *Parodies of the Romantic Age*, 5 vols (London: Pickering and Chatto, 1999), i. 121–4. Cf. Payne Knight's remarks on didactic poetry in his Preface to *The Progress of Civil Society: A Didactic Poem* (London, 1796).

[84] *The Anti-Jacobin*, 23 (16 Apr. 1798), in Stones and Strachan (eds), *Parodies of the Romantic Age*, i. 164. The run of mock-didactic poems continues in this issue with the first instalment of 'Loves of the Triangles. A Mathematical and Philosophical Poem. Inscribed to Dr Darwin'.

[85] To Lord Byron, 8 Sept. 1816, in *Letters of Percy Bysshe Shelley*, ed. F. L. Jones, 2 vols (Oxford: Clarendon Press, 1964), i. 504.

[86] To Charles Ollier, 11 June 1821, in *Letters*, ii. 305.

[87] For the significance of *Mab*'s epigraphs and the political resonance of the term 'philosophical poem', see my *Romance and Revolution: Shelley and the Politics of a Genre* (Cambridge: Cambridge University Press, 1994), 58–63.

[88] *Biographia Literaria*, ii. 156. Coleridge uses similar phrasing ('the first & finest philosophical Poem') about *The Recluse* in his letter to Richard Sharp, 15 Jan. 1804, in *Collected Letters of Samuel Taylor Coleridge*, ed. E. L. Griggs, 6 vols (Oxford: Clarendon Press, 1956–71), ii. 1034.

The aim of his 'philosophical poem', he explains, is not 'formally to announce a system', but to present 'clear thoughts, lively images, and strong feelings' in such a way that 'the Reader will have no difficulty in extracting the system for himself'.[89] By emphasizing the role of the reader, the poem addresses a recurrent criticism of didactic poetry, and promises a new kind of didacticism attentive to what Wordsworth calls 'the Mind and Man | Contemplating' as well as 'the thing Contemplated'.[90] The use of dialogue, and the interweaving of narrative and didactic passages, are integral to Wordsworth's method: *The Excursion* narrates the life experiences which have shaped the minds of the characters dispensing and receiving philosophical instruction. Only in the fourth book do we find overt moralizing, and even here it is, as Annabel Patterson notes, 'metadidactic' rather than didactic, in the sense that it is '*about* teaching', and offers not dogma per se but a dramatization of the education process.[91]

These distinctions were lost on most, but not all, of Wordsworth's contemporary readers. Francis Jeffrey's brutal review in the *Edinburgh Review* alluded covertly to the poem's interest in reception psychology by declaring that only a lunatic entranced by 'the mystical verbiage of the methodist pulpit' into believing 'that he is the elected organ of divine truth and persuasion' could write such an arrogantly didactic poem.[92] Other readers, though, praised its passionate didacticism. Thomas Noon Talfourd, echoing Milton, called Wordsworth 'a divine philosopher among the poets', his poetry 'not more distinct from the dramatic, or the epic, as from the merely didactic and moral'.[93] The *British Critic* favourably compared the 'noble' and 'elevating' poetic philosophy of *The Excursion* with the meretricious speculation of the 'metaphysical' school of Donne, Cowley, and their followers.[94] Interestingly, some of Wordsworth's most discerning readers thought the poem flawed not by excessive didacticism, but rather by the opposite—insufficient, or inconsistent, didacticism. Coleridge, for instance, questioned whether the poem's central figure, the Wanderer, was 'a character appropriate to a lofty didactick poem',[95] thus imputing a breach of generic decorum. Hazlitt took a similarly neoclassical line by objecting to the admixture of narrative and descriptive elements in what should have been a purely didactic poem.[96] More surprising still is the reaction of Lamb: the same reader who had objected to the obtrusive moral signposting of 'The Old Cumberland Beggar' praised the strongly didactic fourth book of *The Excursion* as 'the most valuable

[89] *Prose Works*, iii. 6.

[90] Prospectus to *The Recluse*, lines 96–7.

[91] Annabel Patterson, 'Wordsworth's Georgic: Genre and Structure in *The Excursion*', *Wordsworth Circle*, 9/2 (1978), 145–54. Cf. Alison Hickey, *Impure Conceits: Rhetoric and Ideology in Wordsworth's 'Excursion'* (Stanford, Calif.: Stanford University Press, 1997).

[92] *Edinburgh Review*, 24 (Nov. 1814), in Reiman (ed.), *Romantics Reviewed*, A ii. 440.

[93] 'On the Genius and Writings of Wordsworth' (second part), *New Monthly Magazine* (1 Dec. 1820), in Robert Woof (ed.), *William Wordsworth: The Critical Heritage*, i: *1793–1820* (London: Routledge, 2001), 866.

[94] *British Critic*, 2nd ser., 3 (May 1815), in Reiman (ed.), *Romantics Reviewed*, A i. 449–50.

[95] *Biographia Literaria*, ii. 118. For Coleridge's shifting attitude to the *Recluse* project, see Paul Hamilton, *Coleridge's Poetics* (Oxford: Blackwell, 1983), 171–6.

[96] 'Character of Mr. Wordsworth's New Poem *The Excursion*', review in 3 pts, *The Examiner* (21 Aug.–2 Oct. 1814), in Reiman (ed.), *Romantics Reviewed*, A ii. 524.

portion of the poem', and judged the poem as a whole as 'without competition among our didactic and descriptive verse'.[97]

## AESTHETIC EDUCATION

The conflicting responses to *The Excursion* epitomize the tensions in Romantic attitudes to didactic poetry. As we have seen, a conception of poetry emerged in this period which was strongly instrumentalist, acutely attuned to the ideological powers and responsibilities of literature, and eager to defend the place of poetry in the modern circle of knowledge. Along with this went a revaluation of the role of the poet: no longer simply a writer of verse, the poet was now a prophet, legislator, physician, teacher—a communicator who could unite, instruct, heal, or change the world (or at least the individual reader). These ideas gave a new impetus to didactic poetry, and to literary didacticism in general. They coexisted, however, with an equally powerful but antithetical argument: that the essence of poetry was imaginative freedom, and that aesthetic experience should not be confused with other kinds of knowledge. Poetry had what Blake called its 'own proper sphere of conception and visionary execution', offering not pre-formulated thoughts, however edifying, but artistic sensations with their own rationale and educative effect.[98]

The latter view gained support from the new theories of aesthetic autonomy emanating from Germany. Yet in Germany, too, the 'didactic' was a contested concept. Kant in his *Critique of Judgment* (1790) brought new philosophical clarity to the notion of 'pure' art by dissociating aesthetic experience from other modes of cognition and developing a theory of art based on the principle of disinterestedness. But he did so amid intense critical debate about artistic 'purpose'.[99] Schiller's observation, in his essay *On Naïve and Sentimental Poetry* (1795–6), that 'The didactic poem in which the thought is itself poetic and remains so has yet to be seen'[100] presupposes Kant's distinction between reasoning and aesthetic judgement, and marks a shift from Schiller's earlier, instrumentalist view of art. But the didactic makes a return in his *Letters on Aesthetic Education* (1795), where he defines the educative function of art in terms that combine the Kantian principle of disinterested pleasure with a utopian programme of political emancipation.[101] Goethe moves in

---

[97] Review of *The Excursion*, *Quarterly Review*, 12 (Oct. 1814–Jan. 1815), in Reiman (ed.), *Romantics Reviewed*, A ii. 829. The review was revised (and ruined, in Lamb's opinion) by William Gifford, so this quotation may not accurately reflect Lamb's views.

[98] *A Descriptive Catalogue* (1809), in *Complete Writings*, 576.

[99] See Timothy J. Chamberlain (ed.), *Eighteenth Century German Criticism* (New York: Continuum, 1992), introd., pp. xxi–xxiii; and Klaus Berghahn, 'From Classicist to Classical Literary Criticism, 1730–1806', in Peter Uwe Hohendahl (ed.), *A History of German Literary Criticism, 1730–1980* (Lincoln: University of Nebraska Press, 1988), 87–98.

[100] H. B. Nesbit (ed.), *German Aesthetic and Literary Criticism: Winckelmann, Lessing, Hamann, Herder, Schiller, Goethe* (Cambridge: Cambridge University Press, 1985), 203.

[101] Martha Woodmansee, '"Art" as a Weapon in Cultural Politics: Reading Schiller's *Aesthetic Letters*', in Paul Mattick, Jr (ed.), *Eighteenth-Century Aesthetics and the Reconstruction of Art* (Cambridge: Cambridge University Press, 1993).

the opposite direction, rejecting didactic poetry in 1827 on the Keatsian grounds that 'All poetry should be instructive, but unobtrusively so', but decisively breaching that principle in his earlier poem 'The Metamorphosis of Plants' (1798), a versified scientific treatise inspired by his reading of a German translation of Darwin's *Loves of the Plants*.[102] Friedrich Schlegel is equally inconsistent. In his *Lectures on the History of Literature* (1812), he maintains that didactic poetry 'contains always something of the frigid and unpoetic', citing Pope as an example of the English predilection for didactic poetry.[103] In his *Dialogue on Poetry* (1800), however, he expresses (through the character of Antonio) a very different view, rejecting the idea of didactic poetry as a separate genre but arguing instead that *every* poem 'should actually be didactic as well as romantic, in that broader sense of the word where it describes the general tendency in its deep and infinite sense'.[104] Thus defined, 'didactic' writing becomes inseparable from the cultural project of *Bildung*—the 'one overriding goal' of early German Romanticism, according to Frederick Beiser[105]—making this yet another expression of Schlegel's ideal of 'progressive universal poetry', the genre of genres that would fuse poetry, philosophy, and rhetoric, and mix 'solid matter for instruction' with irony and inspiration.[106]

The gap between the restrictive definition of 'didactic' and the 'broader sense' invoked by Antonio accounts for some of the confusion surrounding this issue. But the crux is not only linguistic. In Germany as in Britain, there was a genuine conflict of views, and vital artistic and philosophical issues were at stake. The premiss of my argument in this chapter is that these opposing conceptions of the didactic, like the contrasting theories of artistic purpose and purposelessness, were dialectically related, each defining and historically producing the other. The fact that the words 'ideology' and 'aesthetic' entered the English language (one from French, the other from German) at exactly the same moment—the late 1790s[107]—encapsulates that dialectic, demonstrating how

---

[102] 'Didactic Poetry' (1827), in Johann Wolfgang von Goethe, *Essays on Art and Literature*, ed. John Geary, trans. Ellen von Narndroff and Ernest H. von Narndroff (Princeton: Princeton University Press, 1986), 194–5. For the influence of Erasmus Darwin, see Lisbet Koerner, 'Goethe's Botany: Lessons of a Feminine Science', *Isis*, 84/3 (1993), 470–95: 483.

[103] Friedrich Schlegel, *Lectures on the History of Literature, Ancient and Modern*, [trans. J. G. Lockhart], 2 vols (Edinburgh, 1818), ii. 217 (lecture 14).

[104] Friedrich Schlegel, *Dialogue on Poetry and Literary Aphorisms*, trans. Ernst Behler and Roman Struc (University Park: Pennsylvania State University Press, 1968), 89; see also p. 63, where Andrea equates 'didactic' with 'philosophical' poetry, echoing Schlegel's argument in *On the Study of Greek Poetry* (1797), trans. Stuart Barnett (Albany: State University of New York Press, 2001), 31.

[105] Frederick Beiser, *The Romantic Imperative: The Concept of Early German Romanticism* (Cambridge, Mass.: Harvard University Press, 2004), 88. Cf. Marc Redfield, 'Romanticism, *Bildung*, and the Literary Absolute', in Thomas Pfau and Robert F. Gleckner (eds), *Lessons of Romanticism: A Critical Companion* (Durham, N.C.: Duke University Press, 1998).

[106] *Athenaeum Fragments*, no. 116, in Friedrich Schlegel, *Philosophical Fragments*, trans. Peter Firchow (Minneapolis: University of Minnesota Press, 1991), 31–2. See Ch. 5 below, pp. 171–6.

[107] The *OED* credits William Taylor, in articles for the *Monthly Review* (1796) and *Monthly Magazine* (1797), with first English use of 'ideology'; in both cases, he is citing Destutt de Tracy, the French philosopher and politician who coined the word *idéologie*. Taylor, an influential interpreter of German ideas, is also credited with first English use of the adjective 'aesthetic', in a reference to Kant in the *Monthly Review* (1798); the nominal form, denoting a branch of philosophy, enters English the same year. Coleridge helped to give currency to the word 'aesthetic' (see Rosemary Ashton, *The German Idea: Four English Writers and the Reception of German Thought 1800–1860* (Chicago: University of Chicago Press, 1980), 48–9), as did De Quincey in the 'Murder' essays discussed above.

a sharpened awareness of literature's social and political effects could coexist with a deepened sense of the autotelic character of art. Romantic theory wrestles with the contradiction between these positions, but the literature of the period embraces both.

In the British context, it is, moreover, possible to detect an emergent consensus on two fundamental points: first, the idea that poetry does have a higher function of some kind, whether construed in moral, political, spiritual, or psychological terms; and secondly, regarding the manner in which poetry—or imaginative literature in general—can legitimately be said to 'teach'. Art, in this period, is not produced merely for its own sake, even when it does come as naturally as leaves on the tree. On the contrary, it is conscious, sometimes to an extreme degree, of its aims and objectives. In Paul Hamilton's words, 'romantic period writing is often simultaneously a position paper of its own kind of significance'[108]—an aspect of 'metaromanticism' that belies McGann's claim about Romantic writers' blindness to their own ideological purposes. Recent work on the history of the concept of 'literature' underlines this point: what marks the late eighteenth century as a pivotal moment in the emergence of the modern category of the literary is not the idea of autonomy but a new conception of the way in which literature is useful, as a vehicle for self-knowledge and self-cultivation.[109] This new-found sense of purpose does not mean that poetry should, as Barbauld put it, 'follow a system step by step'[110] and present an argument syllogistically, as in a prose exposition. Romantic writers certainly had 'systems' to expound, yet most came to realize (by trial and error, or by studying others' failures) that it was counter-productive to do so directly, without any regard to the artistic medium, or to what happens when an intelligent reader is confronted with undisguised propaganda. 'Designs' there could be and should be, but they must be *im*palpable ones which, as Lamb put it, slide into the reader's mind while he is imagining no such matter.

We have seen that same conclusion drawn by writers as different as Blake and Bowles, Godwin and Scott, Schiller and Shelley. The most cogent formulation, though, is De Quincey's, in the essay on Pope in which he presents, in its fullest form, his distinction between literature of knowledge and power. Having first explained the logical contradiction in the phrase 'didactic poetry', he then goes on to define the kind of teaching which poetry *can* legitimately perform:

Poetry, or any one of the fine arts, (all of which alike speak through the genial nature of man and his excited sensibilities,) can teach only as nature teaches, as forests teach, as the sea

---

[108] Paul Hamilton, *Metaromanticism: Aesthetics, Literature, Theory* (Chicago: University of Chicago Press, 2003), 1.

[109] Richard Terry, *Poetry and the Making of the English Literary Past, 1660–1781* (Oxford: Oxford University Press, 2001), 214. Cf. David Bromwich, 'The Invention of Literature', in his *A Choice of Inheritance: Self and Community from Edmund Burke to Robert Frost* (Cambridge, Mass.: Harvard University Press, 1989); and Trevor Ross, *The English Literary Canon from the Middle Ages to the Late Eighteenth Century* (Montreal: McGill-Queen's University Press, 1998), 'Epilogue: How Poesy Became Literature'.

[110] In her 1795 edition of Akenside's *Pleasures of the Imagination*, quoted by David Simpson, *Romanticism, Nationalism, and the Revolt against Theory* (Chicago: University of Chicago Press, 1993), 150.

teaches, as infancy teaches, viz., by deep impulse, by hieroglyphic suggestion. Their teaching is not direct or explicit, but lurking, implicit, masked in deep incarnations. To teach formally and professedly is to abandon the very differential character and principle of poetry.[111]

In a dazzling sequence of metaphors that itself demonstrates the power of 'implicit' or 'hieroglyphic' expression, De Quincey offers a brilliant summation of the Romantic theory of the aesthetic, building on Kantian arguments but also echoing Wordsworth's great poems on aesthetic education, *The Prelude* and the 'Ode. Intimations of Immortality from Recollections of Early Childhood'. 'Intimation' is, indeed, the term that best encapsulates the Romantic modification of the 'didactic', the indirect mode of cognition and expression that Shelley describes in his *Defence of Poetry* when he writes that poetry 'acts in a divine and unapprehended manner, beyond and above consciousness'.[112] Few works of Romantic literature consistently implement this communicative ideal, and many bear traces of more overt forms of didacticism or position-taking, but the critical touchstone remains a valid one, and the discovery of it is one of Romanticism's most enduring achievements.

111  *Works*, xvi. 359–60.        112  *Shelley's Poetry and Prose*, 516.

# 4

# Archaism and Innovation

It seems to me the problem of our poetry is the synthesis of the essentially modern and the essentially ancient.

(Friedrich Schlegel, letter to A. W. Schlegel, 27 February 1794)

Poetry has advanced beyond the preceding age, simply by going back to one still older; and has put *its* poverty to shame only by unlocking the hoards of a remote ancestor. It has reformed merely by restoring; and innovated by a systematic recurrence to the models of antiquity.

(Francis Jeffrey, *Edinburgh Review*, 48 (September 1828))

In a late interview in 1970, the philosopher–critic Mikhail Bakhtin, then in his seventies, recalled an old school joke: that the ancient Greeks, for all their intellectual brilliance and self-knowledge, did not know the most important thing about themselves—that they were *ancient* Greeks. For Bakhtin, a classical scholar by training, this piece of schoolboy humour concealed an important truth, namely that the temporal distance which transformed the Greeks into *ancient* Greeks also enriched their culture with new meanings, uncovering semantic depths in classical antiquity of which the Greeks themselves were unaware. The attempt to explain a work of art solely in terms of the conditions of its production, within the historical constraints of its own epoch, offers at best a partial view; its fullness of meaning is only revealed in what Bakhtin calls 'great time', across the course of its posthumous life. The task of scholarship is to participate in 'the great cause of liberating antiquity from the captivity of time'.[1]

Bakhtin's eloquent plea for what we might call an open literary history offers an attractive alternative to the more restrictive, and reductive, mode of historicism that currently prevails in Romantic studies, a type of criticism which seeks an ever closer delineation of the contexts of a work's original composition and reception, and insists on a rigorous separation of the observer from the observed, for fear not only of the illusions of hindsight but also (for McGannites, at least) of ideological contamination with Romanticism's misleading self-descriptions. I quote Bakhtin's remarks, though, not to open a debate on methodology—though such issues are never far away when questions of genre are at hand—but to introduce the more specific issue that this chapter will address: the relationship between genre and time. Among other

---

[1] 'Response to a Question from the *Novy Mir* Editorial Staff', in M. M. Bakhtin, *Speech Genres and Other Late Essays*, ed. Caryl Emerson and Michael Holquist (Austin: University of Texas Press, 1986), 4–6. Cf. the discussion of 'great' and 'small' time in 'Toward a Methodology for the Human Sciences' (ibid. 169–70).

things, I hope to show why Bakhtin's joke is, in essence, a *Romantic* joke, and Bakhtin himself a Romantic theorist—in a direct line of philosophical speculation on genre that begins with Friedrich Schlegel and the German Romantics.

Like the Romantics, who wrestled with the relationship between antiquity and modernity, Bakhtin sought to develop a new kind of genre theory that would be built around the problem of time, a dimension absent from classical and neoclassical poetics. Bakhtin turns on its head the static, transcendent model of genre bequeathed by Aristotle and his successors, and argues instead for a dynamic, diachronic model that conceives of genres as evolving entities endowed with a past, present, and future:

A literary genre, by its very nature, reflects the most stable, 'eternal' tendencies in literature's development. Always preserved in a genre are undying elements of the *archaic*. True, these archaic elements are preserved in it only thanks to their constant *renewal*, which is to say, their contemporization. A genre is always the same and yet not the same, always old and new simultaneously. Genre is reborn and renewed at every new stage in the development of literature and in every individual work of a given genre. This constitutes the life of the genre. Therefore even the archaic elements preserved in a genre are not dead but eternally alive; that is, archaic elements are capable of renewing themselves. A genre lives in the present, but always *remembers* its past, its beginning.[2]

For Bakhtin, the literary form which illustrates most forcibly the evolutionary nature of genre, and the dialectic of archaism and innovation that drives that evolution, is the novel, a genre which in English has newness as part of its name. In taking the novel as his paradigm, Bakhtin is following in the footsteps of Friedrich Schlegel, Novalis, and Schelling, who began the 'radical restructuring' of genre theory which, says Bakhtin, the rise of the novel had rendered necessary.[3]

My contention in this chapter is that the dialectic of archaism and innovation is not confined to the novel, but operates across the whole spectrum of genres; and that Romantic literature embodies that dialectic in a peculiarly formative way. Bakhtin categorically distinguishes between poetry and the novel, arguing that the novel not only supersedes the epic and other poetic genres, but also renders them redundant. With the advent of the novel, he claims, other genres came to seem obsolete: 'long since completed', and thus old-fashioned, moribund, stuck in the past. The novel is the opposite: conscious of its novelty, actively developing, and full of possibilities for the future. 'Studying other genres', says Bakhtin, 'is analogous to studying dead languages; studying the novel, on the other hand, is like studying languages that are not only alive, but still young.'[4] The following pages will test that claim by examining how British Romantic poets approached the problem of temporality in genre, and how, in their hands, ancient poetic forms adapted to the challenge of modernity to create the 'synthesis' to which Friedrich Schlegel, in my epigraph, refers. Herder, in a well-known passage that is often seen as heralding Romantic attitudes to the past, speaks of how 'time

---

[2] Mikhail Bakhtin, *Problems of Dostoevsky's Poetics* (1929, rev. 1963), trans. Caryl Emerson (Minneapolis: University of Minnesota Press, 1984), 106.

[3] 'Epic and Novel: Toward a Methodology for the Study of the Novel' (1941), in *The Dialogic Imagination: Four Essays by M. M. Bakhtin*, ed. Michael Holquist, trans. Caryl Emerson and Michael Holquist (Austin: University of Texas Press, 1981), 8.

[4] Ibid. 3.

changes everything': the 'whole human race, indeed even the inanimate world, every nation, and every family', just like 'every art and science', 'are subject to the same law of change'.[5] This chapter will show how that new perception of time, marked by a heightened sense of temporal flux and a new understanding of the historical relativism of cultural forms, entered into Romantic thinking about genre, challenging neoclassical assumptions and ultimately revolutionizing the way literary genres were deployed.

## ANCIENTS AND MODERNS

That the Romantics displayed 'a new awareness of the historicity and even the cultural specificity of literary genres' is now widely accepted.[6] Determining how and when this new awareness developed is not easy, however, and even today the notion of the 'historicity' of genres poses theoretical problems that are far from solved. This is partly because, however much we insist on the variable elements in genre, it is the existence of *in*variant elements—recurrent aspects of subject matter, function, or form—that allows us to speak of 'genre' in the first place. There is thus always, for the genre theorist, both the practical problem of deciding what those invariants are in any given instance, and the philosophical problem of what it means to assert this continuity across time: to posit some transhistorical essence, whether it be called 'tragedy', 'pastoral', or whatever. Even extreme relativists who fully accept Herder's principle that 'time changes *everything*'—i.e. that there is *no* invariance— have to concede that different aspects of genre change, or 'age', at different speeds. Diction, for example, is more time-bound, and ages more rapidly, than metre, so that, other things being equal, a poem written in sixteenth-century English and nineteenth-century metre will probably seem much older to us than a poem in nineteenth-century English and sixteenth-century metre—blank verse, for instance. As we shall see in a moment, such distinctions become crucial when experimentation with genre takes the form of deliberate anachronism or antiquarian forgery.

The adjustment in critical consciousness to accommodate the temporal dimension of literary genres was neither sudden nor straightforward, but its revolutionary quality can be appreciated if we consider the longevity of, and the scale of cultural investment in, the neoclassical code it replaced.[7] Under the old system, as Bernard Weinberg explains, literary genres were regarded 'as Forms, which are always the same, which make no concessions to times or audiences, which impose upon the poet a strict

---

[5] 'On the Ages of a Language', Fragment 2 of Herder's *On Recent German Literature: First Collection of Fragments* (1767), in Timothy J. Chamberlain (ed.), *Eighteenth Century German Criticism* (New York: Continuum, 1992), 105. See Friedrich Meinecke, *Historicism: The Rise of a New Historical Outlook* (1936), trans. J. E. Anderson, rev. H. D. Schmidt, introd. Isaiah Berlin (London: Routledge and Kegan Paul, 1972); Maike Oergel, *Culture and Identity: Historicity in German Literature and Thought 1770–1815* (Berlin: de Gruyter, 2006); and Paul Hamilton, *Historicism* (London: Routledge, 2003).

[6] Tilottama Rajan and Julia M. Wright (eds), *Romanticism, History, and the Possibilities of Genre: Re-forming Literature 1789–1837* (Cambridge: Cambridge University Press, 1998), introd., 1–2; Clifford Siskin, *The Historicity of Romantic Discourse* (Oxford: Oxford University Press, 1988).

[7] See Ch. 1 above, pp. 31–9.

obedience to unalterable rules'.[8] This conception of genre, derived from sixteenth-century Italian commentaries on Aristotle's *Poetics* and elaborated by later theorists from other countries, dominated European criticism for three hundred years. To modern eyes, such beliefs—in the immutability of forms, the total transcendence of context, and prescriptive, universally binding rules—have an almost delusional quality, so manifestly false do they seem, and so contrary to the way literature has been, and should be, written. As we saw in Chapter 1, however, neoclassical genre theory, especially in its rationalist phase associated with critics like Fontenelle in France, Gottsched in Germany, and Rymer and Dennis in England, was in many respects a thoroughly modern intellectual enterprise, motivated not by blind obeisance to received wisdom but by the conviction that poetry, like any other art or science, is susceptible to rational explanation and governed by knowable laws.

In the interpretation of those laws, there were two schools of thought. On one side were the traditionalists (the so-called 'Ancients' in the famous Ancients and Moderns dispute[9]), who believed that the canon of poetic genres was fixed, that classical standards were unsurpassable, and that any deviation from ancient models was a form of sacrilege. This was the view taken by the French philosopher Turgot, who saw a fundamental difference in this respect between the arts and sciences:

Time constantly brings to light new discoveries in the sciences; but poetry, painting and music have a fixed limit which the genius of languages, the imitation of nature, and the limited sensibility of an organ determine, which they obtain by slow steps, and which they cannot surpass. The great men of the Augustan Age reached it, and are still our models.[10]

Similar assumptions inform the comparison between ancient and modern poetry in Sir William Temple's *Of Poetry* (1690), which judges modern compositions in all genres except drama invariably inferior to their classical prototypes, and finds modern writers particularly deficient in the higher echelons such as epic: 'not worthy to sit down at the Feast, they contented themselves with the Scraps, with Songs and Sonnets, with Odes and Elegies, with Satyrs and Panegyricks...wanting either Genius or Application for Nobler or more Laborious Productions'.[11]

On the other side were modernizers (the 'Moderns') like Charles Perrault and Fontenelle, who recognized the need for an updated genre-system and a modification

[8] Bernard Weinberg, *A History of Literary Criticism in the Italian Renaissance*, 2 vols (Chicago: University of Chicago Press, 1961), ii. 1104.

[9] For an overview of this long-running, Europe-wide controversy, see Douglas Lane Patey, 'Ancients and Moderns', in H. B. Nisbet and Claude Rawson (eds), *The Cambridge History of Literary Criticism*, iv: *The Eighteenth Century* (Cambridge: Cambridge University Press, 1997). The most intensive English phase of the quarrel, from 1690 to 1730, is treated by Joseph M. Levine, *The Battle of the Books: History and Literature in the Augustan Age* (Ithaca, NY: Cornell University Press, 1991); R. F. Jones, *Ancients and Moderns: A Study of the Rise of the Scientific Movement in 17th-Century England*, 2nd edn (Berkeley: University of California Press, 1961); and Lawrence Manley, *Convention 1500–1700* (Cambridge, Mass.: Harvard University Press, 1980), 321–47.

[10] Anne-Robert-Jacques Turgot, Baron de l'Aulne, 'Discours sur les progrès successifs de l'esprit humain', in *Œuvres de M. Turgot*, 9 vols (Paris, 1808), ii. 78, quoted by Patey, 'Ancients and Moderns', 40.

[11] William Temple, *Of Poetry* (1690), in J. E. Spingarn (ed.), *Critical Essays of the Seventeenth Century*, 3 vols (Oxford: Clarendon Press, 1908–9), iii. 99.

of generic protocols, and who acknowledged the possibility that, in some genres at least, modern writers could improve on their classical precursors. This was the view of John Dennis, who, citing the newly fashionable theories of Longinus, recommended Christianity as a richer source of the poetic sublime than classical mythology, and championed Milton's *Paradise Lost* as superior even to Homer and Virgil in its rendition of exalted emotion—for Dennis, the mainspring of all great poetry.[12] Thomas Tickell's defence of the modernized, Anglicized pastorals of his contemporary Ambrose Philips (which had breached the convention that pastoral poetry should represent an idealized Arcadian golden age by admitting local, realistic elements) is another example of a Modern's take on genre: his argument, drawn partly from Fontenelle, is not that classical conventions are obsolete but that there are situations where modern writers 'may lawfully deviate from the ancients', loco-descriptive writing being a case in point.[13]

Both Ancient and Modern positions were normative, however, in so far as both posited generic standards and 'rules' against which individual performances could be judged, both conceived of genres as part of a hierarchical canon, and both accepted that the essential character of individual genres had been determined in classical antiquity. Even where generic change *was* acknowledged, in rudimentary literary histories such as Dryden's *Discourse Concerning the Original and Progress of Satire* (1693), this was seen in Aristotelian, teleological terms as movement towards or away from the 'perfect' form of a given genre.[14] It was not until much later that the 'origin and progress' model started to yield more impartial accounts of generic change, and the transformation of genres across time came to be understood as an open-ended, evolutionary process, influenced by both internal and external factors.

It is sometimes said that neoclassical genre theory, for all its prescriptive intent, exerted very little influence on the way literature was actually written; that writers obeyed the rules only if and when it suited them. To some extent, this is palpably true: even in the era of high neoclassicism—in Britain, from the 1670s to roughly 1750—some of the best literature was *not* written in accordance with established precepts, or in critically approved genres. The obvious example is Alexander Pope, a tireless defender of the Ancients' cause, but one who achieved his greatest successes in modern, hybrid genres like the mock-epic, and whose poetry, for all its formal precision, defies in many respects the aesthetics of 'decorum' and 'correctness' that his criticism promotes. The fact remains, however, that much of the writing of the period *was* essentially classical in inspiration, and classical genres, with or without

---

[12] *The Grounds of Criticism in Poetry* (1704), in *The Critical Works of John Dennis*, ed. E. N. Hooker, 2 vols (Baltimore: Johns Hopkins University Press, 1939–43).

[13] *The Guardian*, no. 30 (15 Apr. 1713), in Bryan Loughrey (ed.), *The Pastoral Mode: A Casebook* (Basingstoke: Macmillan, 1984), 54. For the place of pastoral in the Ancients and Moderns dispute, see J. E. Congleton, *Theories of Pastoral Poetry in England 1684–1789* (1952; New York: Haskell House, 1968), ch. 4.

[14] René Wellek, *The Rise of English Literary History* (1941; New York: McGraw-Hill, 1966), 38–9. Aristotle's own position, sufficiently ambiguous to make this a crux for later genre theorists, is examined by Paul Cantor, 'Aristotle and the History of Tragedy', in David Perkins (ed.), *Theoretical Issues in Literary History* (Cambridge, Mass.: Harvard University Press, 1991); and Jean-Marie Schaeffer, *Qu'est-ce qu'un genre littéraire?* (Paris: Seuil, 1989), 10–25.

modern modifications, dominated the poetic field to a degree unparalleled before or since. Despite the fashion for mock-classical forms, the traditional hierarchy of genres still remained largely intact, shaping the œuvre of almost every aspirant poet (Pope himself began conventionally enough, writing pastorals before progressing onto higher genres as Virgil had done).

In this vast literature of classical imitation and adaptation, two motivating factors stand out: the first is what might be called a fantasy of simultaneity with classical antiquity. Integral to neoclassical thought was the belief that the revival of classical genres, the adoption of classical theories of composition, and the imitation of ancient models would, in some sense, put modern Europe on a par with classical antiquity: would dissolve the temporal distance between then and now, and make the Ancients and Moderns contemporaries. The very word 'classical' carried, as it still does, the connotation of transcendence of time; and it is this same impulse that led writers like Dryden and Pope to speak of their own epoch as a new 'Augustan' age, analogous to and equal with the golden age of imperial Rome.[15] Fontenelle, in 1688, brings out the underlying assumption perfectly when, defending his own pastoral poems, he claims the right to speak of his generic precursors Theocritus and Virgil 'as if they had been some living Authors whom I saw every day'.[16]

Alongside this self-empowering fantasy of simultaneity with classical Greece and Rome was an assumption of cultural superiority over earlier periods of native literature, an attitude best revealed in the neoclassical craze for rewriting earlier British authors. Here the watchwords were not 'imitation' and 'emulation' but 'correction', 'improvement', and 'refinement'. The best-known examples are Nahum Tate's scaled-down, tidied-up version of *King Lear* (1681) and Dryden's formalistic reworking of *Antony and Cleopatra* as *All for Love* (1677).[17] But these are just the tip of the iceberg; and it wasn't only the maverick Shakespeare who got the treatment. That 'rough Diamond' Chaucer (as Dryden called him[18]) received similar attention, the results of this 'polishing' work appearing in Dryden's *Fables Ancient and Modern, Translated into Verse* (1700)—a title which begs the question: weren't Chaucer's poems already in verse? Equally revealing is a work like *Spencer Redivivus: Containing the First Book of the 'Faery Queene'. His Essential Design Preserv'd, but his Obsolete Language and Manner of Verse Totally Laid Aside. Deliver'd in Heroick Numbers. By a Person of Quality* (1687), an anonymous exercise in linguistic and

---

[15]  Howard Erskine-Hill, *The Augustan Idea in English Literature* (London: Arnold, 1983).

[16]  Bernard Fontenelle, 'Of Pastorals' (1688), appended to René Le Bossu, *Epick Poetry*, trans. Pierre Motteux (1695), 294–5, quoted by Levine, *Battle of the Books*, 186.

[17]  See Hazelton Spencer, *Shakespeare Improved: The Restoration Versions in Quarto and on the Stage* (Cambridge, Mass.: Harvard University Press, 1927); Emerson R. Marks, *The Poetics of Reason: English Neoclassical Criticism* (New York: Random House, 1968), ch. 6; Michael Dobson, *The Making of the National Poet: Shakespeare, Adaptation and Authorship, 1660–1769* (Oxford: Clarendon Press, 1992); Jean Marsden, *The Re-imagined Text: Shakespeare, Adaptation, and Eighteenth-Century Literary Theory* (Lexington: University Press of Kentucky, 1995); and, for a selection of reworked plays, Sandra Clark (ed.), *Shakespeare Made Fit: Restoration Adaptations of Shakespeare* (London: Dent, 1997).

[18]  Preface to *Fables Ancient and Modern* (1700), in *The Poems of John Dryden*, ed. James Kinsley, 5 vols (Oxford: Clarendon Press, 1958), iv. 1457.

metrical modernization which displays perfectly the artistic assumptions of polite culture, not least in the equation it makes between literary and social status (implying that only a 'person of quality' can write high-quality verse). Even Milton, a byword in later times for verbal craftsmanship, is subjected to 'improvement' (in this case grammatical rather than lexical), in an extraordinary edition by James Buchanan entitled *The First Six Books of Milton's Paradise Lost Rendered into Grammatical Construction; the Words of the Text Being Arranged, at the Bottom of each Page, in the same Natural Order with the Conceptions of the Mind* (1773)—i.e. *Paradise Lost* without the barbarous Miltonic syntax. The same breathtaking confidence in the superiority of current poetic technique is expressed in Francis Atterbury's letter to Pope of 15 June 1722 urging him to do the honours for Milton's *Samson Agonistes*, which 'is capable of being improv'd, with little trouble, into a perfect Model and Standard of Tragic Poetry'.[19] That even *Samson*, one of the most sophisticated transpositions of classical tragedy ever attempted, involving (as is clear from Milton's Preface) a direct engagement with Aristotelian theory, should be deemed wanting by neoclassical standards is a measure of how uncompromising and inflexible those norms could be.[20]

In *The Burden of the Past and the English Poet*, Walter Jackson Bate argued that the neoclassical project of 'improvement'—the poetics of 'correctness'—had ultimately a defensive motive: it was a means for English writers after the Restoration to differentiate their work from the awesome achievements of their Renaissance precursors.[21] One way of doing this was to bring earlier works of literature into conformity with modern—that is neoclassical—ideas about genre. The idea, in essence, was simple: take an old work of literature, brush off the cobwebs, correct the mistakes in versification, make it obey the laws of its chosen genre, and transpose it into that infinitely superior linguistic medium, modern English. Here too, then, is a denial of historical distance, a fantasy of simultaneity: the past is not the past, it is the present in some barbarous old clothes. Solution? The old must be made new: Chaucer, Spenser, Shakespeare, Donne, Milton—the whole ragged bunch of them— must be, in a word, *modernized*; and likewise the literary forms—crude, imperfect, corrupted—in which they had first had the misfortune to appear. In this grand *Advancement and Reformation of Modern Poetry*, as Dennis styled it in his tract of that name (published in 1701), author, text, and genre were to be redeemed simultaneously.

[19] *The Correspondence of Alexander Pope*, ed. George Sherburn, 5 vols (Oxford: Clarendon Press, 1956), ii. 124, quoted by Levine, *Battle of the Books*, 253.

[20] For a reading of Milton's Preface to *Samson Agonistes* (1671) as 'a return to classically regulated formalism' in response to 'the growing tide of Restoration neoclassicism', see Colin Burrow, 'Combative Criticism: Jonson, Milton, and Classical Literary Criticism in England', in Glyn P. Norton (ed.), *The Cambridge History of Literary Criticism*, iii: *The Renaissance* (Cambridge: Cambridge University Press, 1999), 497–9.

[21] W. Jackson Bate, *The Burden of the Past and the English Poet* (London: Chatto and Windus, 1971).

## THE ANTIQUARIAN DILEMMA

Against this somewhat simplified account of neoclassical 'reformation' theory (discussed more fully in Chapter 1), let us set a famous book from the 1760s that was instrumental in shaping Romantic attitudes to genre, and, indeed, helped to inspire a very different kind of reform in English poetry: Thomas Percy's *Reliques of Ancient English Poetry* (1765). Here, on the face of it, is a work saturated in the sense of time, a brilliant feat of the antiquarian imagination whose multifaceted projection of the past extends from the archaic spelling of the word 'relique' in the title, the selective use of black-letter type, and the specially commissioned 'Gothic' illustrations,[22] to the recondite scholarship of the footnotes. Genre, in Percy's hands, is a very different entity from the static template of neoclassical theory. His collection not only showcases a different set of poetic forms— ballads, love songs, and metrical romances, genres normally excluded from the neo-classical canon—it also provides these forms with a history, taking us back to their origins, showing us how they evolved, and constructing, in effect, a *genealogy* for each genre. Percy does this in various ways: first, by printing the 'reliques' themselves, retrieving—sometimes from manuscript, sometimes from printed sources such as chapbooks and broadsides—early examples of each genre that had, in many cases, disappeared from the official literary record. Secondly, by organizing the poems into groups (part thematic, part formal) and ordering them chronologically within each group so as to suggest the evolution of that genre or subgenre (in some cases, Percy demonstrates the continuing development of the tradition by adding a pastiche of his own). Thirdly, by extensive annotation—on contextual as well as textual matters, and always with an eye to the history of the genre as well as of the particular poem. And fourthly, by a series of prefatory essays: 'On the Ancient English Minstrels' and 'On the Origin of the English Stage' in volume i; on alliterative metre in volume ii; and 'On the Ancient Metrical Romances' in volume iii. All of these editorial features serve to reinforce Percy's essential point that a literary genre is a *tradition* not a *template*: an evolving entity that is intimately linked to the history and culture of a nation.

Percy's labours did not take place in a vacuum. An antiquarian trend—in editing, in literary interpretation, and in literary creation itself—was well established by 1765, and Percy was partly building on an earlier anthology called, somewhat prosaically, *A Collection of Old Ballads*, published as long ago as the 1720s.[23] He was responding, too, to the Ossian phenomenon, echoing the title of James Mac-pherson's *Fragments of Ancient Poetry, Collected in the Highlands of Scotland* (1760), while emphasizing the rival claims of the ancient *English* tradition of poetry (though

---

[22] For Percy's meticulous attention to presentational features, see Nick Groom (ed.), *Reliques of Ancient English Poetry*, facs. of 1765 edn, 3 vols (London: Routledge; Thoemmes Press, 1996), introd. Subsequent references to this edition are given parenthetically by volume and page number.

[23] [Ambrose Philips (ed.)?], *A Collection of Old Ballads, Corrected from the Best and Most Ancient Copies Extant, with Introductions Historical, Critical or Humorous*, 3 vols (London, 1723–5). For Percy's debt to and departure from earlier ballad editors, see Nick Groom, *The Making of Percy's 'Reliques'* (Oxford: Clarendon Press, 1999), ch. 2; and Dianne Dugaw, 'The Popular Marketing of "Old Ballads": The Ballad Revival and Eighteenth-Century Antiquarianism Reconsidered', *Eighteenth-Century Studies*, 21 (1987), 71–90.

in fact the *Reliques* contains much Scottish verse—a cultural appropriation typical of this period[24]). Over the coming decades, there were to be many other collections with similar titles, among them Charlotte Brooke's *Reliques of Irish Poetry* (1789), Evan Evans's *Some Specimens of the Poetry of the Antient Welsh Bards* (1764), John Bowle's *Miscellaneous Pieces of Antient English Poesie* (1764), and David Laing's *Select Remains of the Ancient Popular Poetry of Scotland* (1822). As well as catering for an apparently inexhaustible public appetite for 'ancient' literature, such collections expressed a growing fascination with cultural origins and an expanding awareness of the different national traditions within the British archipelago.

Literary genres—certain ones in particular—were a focus for these desires, the construction of national canons within individual genres going hand in hand with the formation of authorial canons through multi-volume editorial projects like Bell's *Poets of Great Britain* (1777–82) and Johnson's *Works of the English Poets* (1779–81).[25] If necessary, generic traditions could be invented when an appropriate genealogy was wanting, a practice in which forger–poets indulged as freely as editors and literary historians. Macpherson, having first published tantalizing fragments of what purported to be poems by the third-century warrior–poet Ossian, translated from Gaelic, went on to produce not one but two 'Ancient Epic Poems', as he labels them on their title page, from the same source: *Fingal* (1762) and *Temora* (1763). These, momentarily, were the answer to everyone's dreams, or almost everyone's—especially in Scotland.[26] They carried, first of all, the immense prestige of epic, still regarded, along with tragedy, as the most elevated form of poetry, 'the highest effort of Poetical Genius', as Hugh Blair, a champion of Macpherson's Ossian, defined it in his *Lectures on Rhetoric and Belles Lettres* (1783).[27] But in addition these were *ancient* epics,

[24] See Philip Connell, 'British Identities and the Politics of Ancient Poetry in Later Eighteenth-Century England', *Historical Journal*, 49/1 (2006), 161–92. Percy's Anglocentrism should not, however, be overstated. A man of the Enlightenment, he was also committed to universalist ideas, and planned a collection of *Specimens of the Ancient Poetry of Different Nations* based on the fashionable hypothesis (advanced by John Brown and others) about the basic identity of all primitive poetry. He envisaged the *Reliques* as part of this project, which he pursued through a range of other publications including translations from Chinese, an edition of Runic poetry (1763), a paraphrase of the *Song of Songs* (1764), and a collection of *Ancient Songs, Chiefly on Moorish Subjects* (1775). See Wellek, *Rise of English Literary History*, 68.

[25] See Julia M. Wright, ' "The Order of Time": Nationalism and Literary Anthologies, 1774–1831', *Papers on Language and Literature*, 33/4 (1997), 339–65, who distinguishes between earlier classifications and the chronological–genealogical method favoured by late eighteenth-century editors. On national canon-formation, see also Trevor Ross, *The English Literary Canon from the Middle Ages to the Late Eighteenth Century* (Montreal: McGill-Queen's University Press, 1998); and Richard Terry, *Poetry and the Making of the English Literary Past 1660–1781* (Oxford: Oxford University Press, 2001).

[26] For the role of genre in the Ossian affair, see David Hall Radcliffe, 'Ossian and the Genres of Culture', *Studies in Romanticism*, 31 (1992), 213–32; Howard D. Weinbrot, *Britannia's Issue: The Rise of British Literature from Dryden to Ossian* (Cambridge: Cambridge University Press, 1993), chs 14–15; and Dafydd Moore, *Enlightenment and Romance in James Macpherson's 'The Poems of Ossian': Myth, Genre and Cultural Change* (Aldershot: Ashgate, 2003). Relevant primary documents are reprinted in Dafydd Moore (ed.), *Ossian and Ossianism*, 4 vols (London: Routledge, 2004).

[27] Hugh Blair, *Lectures on Rhetoric and Belles Lettres*, 2 vols (London, 1783), ii. 406. For Blair's advocacy of Macpherson, see Fiona Stafford, *The Sublime Savage: A Study of James Macpherson and the Poems of Ossian* (Edinburgh: Edinburgh University Press, 1988), 97, 172–5.

antedating by many hundreds of years anything in English that could possibly lay claim to the status of epic (even *Beowulf*, which was not published until 1815, dates back only to the ninth or tenth century). As such, they accorded perfectly with the primitivist theory, first put forward in Thomas Blackwell's *Enquiry into the Life and Writings of Homer* (1735), that true epic could only be produced in the infancy of society, when heroic passions were strong, labour undivided (hence the warrior–poet), and poetry unself-conscious; and when language retained 'a sufficient Quantity of its *Original, amazing, metaphoric* tincture', before it underwent the artificial refinement that obliged later poets to express themselves in a '*Set* of courtly phrases'.[28]

Ballads, too, were the object of such projections, and political agendas lie behind much of the scholarly attention that the genre attracted.[29] This is unsurprising given that the ballad itself was a traditional vehicle for nationalist sentiment; ballad-collecting thus carried unavoidable ideological overtones. Although not part of the neoclassical canon, the ballad, as the quintessentially 'primitive' form, saw its critical fortunes rise in the eighteenth century, its supposed association with epic being a regular theme of discussion among literary historians.[30] The theory, familiar to English ballad editors and later developed by German Homeric scholars like Friedrich Wolf, that the *Iliad* was originally a group of separate heroic ballads[31] was a refinement of this argument, as was Coleridge's boast that he could patch together an epic from Arthurian ballads.[32] These ideas remained controversial, however, like many of the theories of generic origin that circulated in the period.[33] The provenance of the ballad was particularly controversial, not only because it was one of the oldest and most geographically dispersed of forms (making its genealogy particularly hard to trace) but also because, as a folk genre, it had class affiliations which undermined the assumptions of polite culture. One of the many grounds on which Joseph Ritson, for instance, criticized Percy was for presenting a tradition of English minstrelsy which implied that the ballad originated in a courtly milieu rather than among the common people. Ritson's inclusion of the word 'popular' in the title of his own anthology *Pieces of Ancient Popular Poetry* (1791) was thus as much a political as an editorial corrective to Percy's collection (they contain some of the same poems), a

---

[28] Thomas Blackwell, *An Enquiry into the Life and Writings of Homer* (London, 1735), 47, 60.

[29] Steve Newman, *Ballad Collection, Lyric, and the Canon: The Call of the Popular from the Restoration to the New Criticism* (Philadelphia: University of Pennsylvania Press, 2007); Susan Manning, 'Antiquarianism, Balladry and the Rehabilitation of Romance', in James Chandler (ed.), *The Cambridge History of English Romantic Literature* (Cambridge: Cambridge University Press, 2009).

[30] Keith Stewart, 'The Ballad and the Genres in the Eighteenth Century', *English Literary History*, 24 (1957), 120–37.

[31] Jerome McGann, *The Beauty of Inflections: Literary Investigations in Historical Method and Theory* (Oxford: Clarendon Press, 1985), 150–1. McGann notes Percy's influence on Wolf, but the notion that Homer 'was nothing more than a blind Ballad-singer' whose songs were joined together after his death was already commonplace by 1723, when the editor of *A Collection of Old Ballads* described it as a matter of historical record (preface, p. iii).

[32] Cited by Donald M. Foerster, *The Fortunes of Epic Poetry: A Study in English and American Criticism 1750–1950* (Washington: Catholic University of America Press, 1962), 75.

[33] For the analogous case of romance, see Arthur Johnston, *Enchanted Ground: The Study of Medieval Romance in the Eighteenth Century* (London: Athlone Press, 1964), 13–27.

message that Ritson made even more explicit in his provocative anthology of 'ancient poems, songs and ballads' about the folk hero Robin Hood, published at the height of popular radicalism in the 1790s.[34]

In Percy's *Reliques*, the quest for generic origins also extends to pastoral, a genre with multiple cultural roots. Percy includes two early vernacular examples, one English (the anonymous *Harpalus*) and the other Scottish (Henryson's *Robin and Makyne*), both antedating by some fifty years the first canonical English pastoral, Spenser's *Shepheardes Calender* (1579), to which Percy declares them far superior. The labels he attaches to them, 'An ancient English Pastoral' and 'An ancient Scottish Pastoral' respectively, are intended not only to classify and dignify the poems (on the grounds of antiquity, genericity, and ethnicity) but also to modify the category of pastoral itself: first, by insisting on an expansion of the genre to include poems which share some but lack other features that would normally be deemed requisite to pastoral (neither, for instance, draws on the myth of the golden age, central to most neoclassical definitions, and both have balladic elements that purists would consider extraneous to pastoral); secondly, by blurring the boundary between classical and native traditions of rural verse, thus strengthening the claim for a distinctly British contribution to pastoral; and thirdly, by extending the native lineage in the genre further back in time. The result is a naturalized version of pastoral analogous to the currently fashionable 'Oriental eclogues' of William Collins and others, but projected instead onto an ancient British past—a reinvention of generic tradition partly inspired by Macpherson's archaeo-ethnic deployment of pastoral in his *Fragments of Ancient Poetry*.[35] The self-consciously Scottish and English pastorals of Romantic poets like Burns and Wordsworth build on these precedents, the territorialization of genre reinforcing the new sense of generic temporality.[36]

Historical and geographical framing could take many different forms. Brooke's *Reliques of Irish Poetry* includes original Gaelic texts alongside her translations, marking a desire for authenticity often missing from other collections. Yet her retrospective classification of early Gaelic writing into 'heroic poems', 'odes', 'elegies', and 'songs'—the four categories that organize the volume—are part of a patriotic strategy, explicitly declared in the Preface, to 'vindicate' the history of her country and 'prove its claim to scientific [i.e. intellectual, literary] as well as military fame', with neoclassical labels acting, as in Percy and Macpherson, as legitimizing devices.[37]

[34] [Joseph Ritson (ed.)], *Robin Hood: A Collection of all the Ancient Poems, Songs and Ballads Now Extant, Relative to that Celebrated English Outlaw*, 2 vols (London, 1795). For the political resonance of this collection, see Marilyn Butler (ed.), *Burke, Paine, Godwin, and the Revolution Controversy* (Cambridge: Cambridge University Press, 1984), 203–5.

[35] David Hill Radcliffe, 'Ancient Poetry and British Pastoral', in Fiona Stafford and Howard Gaskill (eds), *From Gaelic to Romantic: Ossianic Translations* (Amsterdam: Rodopi, 1998); Stuart Curran, *Poetic Form and British Romanticism* (New York: Oxford University Press, 1986), 95–9.

[36] For other examples of 'territorialized' genres, see Murray Pittock, *Scottish and Irish Romanticism* (Oxford: Oxford University Press, 2008).

[37] Charlotte Brooke, *Reliques of Irish Poetry: Consisting of Heroic Poems, Odes, Elegies, and Songs, Translated into English Verse: With Notes Explanatory and Historical; and the Originals in the Irish Character. To which is Subjoined an Irish Tale* (Dublin, 1789), preface, p. v. For the Irish intellectual context, see Clare O'Halloran, *Golden Ages and Barbarous Nations: Antiquarian Debate and Cultural Politics in Ireland, c.1750–1800* (Cork: Cork University Press, 2004).

The generic nomenclature of Evan Evans's *Specimens of the Poetry of the Antient Welsh Bards* serves a similar function; his Cambrian remapping of the genres of ode and elegy forms a bridge between poems like Thomas Gray's 'The Bard: A Pindaric Ode' (1757), an unashamedly modern, neoclassical treatment of ancient Welsh legend, and the neo-druidic 'Bardism' of Edward Williams (Iolo Morganwg). The latter's portfolio of forgeries, pseudo-translations, and original compositions includes an 'Ode: Imitated from the Gododin of Aneurin, an Ancient British Bard, who Wrote about the Year 550' (1794), which, like Gray's, is a neoclassical Pindaric, but one that purports to be a reworking of a Welsh poem written a thousand years before the ode form actually reached British shores.[38]

Thomas Chatterton takes the invention of generic tradition one stage further in his 'Rowley' poems (composed in the 1760s) by making genre labels like 'eclogue', 'tragedie', 'tragycal enterlude' part of his actual antiquarian forgeries. Not only does the Rowley œuvre—supposedly dating from the fifteenth century or even earlier—include texts that, if authentic, would constitute the earliest English verse tragedy (*Goddwyn*), the earliest English eclogues, and the first native classical-style epic (*Battle of Hastings*, allegedly Rowley's translation of an Anglo-Saxon original), but in several cases Chatterton incorporates these generic labels into the fabricated manuscripts themselves, adding another layer of implausibility. It was not until half a century after the supposed date of Rowley's death that English dramas began to call themselves 'tragedies' and 'tragycal enterludes', and not until the late sixteenth century that 'eclogue' became an active poetic label. It is a measure of the hazy sense of generic chronology at the time of the Chatterton controversy that these palpable anachronisms were not spotted—though many of his others were.[39]

Another perspective on the artificial 'ageing' of genres is afforded by the use of archaic diction, a poetic fashion at its height in the 1750s and 1760s. In the special case of Spenserian imitation, the technique is double-layered, the adoption of archaic spelling and obsolete words like 'I weet' and 'I ween' being an attempt to reproduce Spenser's own deliberate archaisms.[40] But the technique could also be applied to classical genres. Gray avoided lexical archaism, preserving his distance from standard modern English by peppering his poetry instead with Latin syntax and classical allusions. His friend Thomas Warton, however, a Spenserian scholar and an intellectual leader of the antiquarian movement, wrote neoclassical odes and elegies on

---

[38]  Edwards Williams, *Poems, Lyric and Pastoral*, 2 vols (London, 1794), ii. 11–19. For commentary, see Mary-Ann Constantine, *The Truth Against the World: Iolo Morganwg and Romantic Forgery* (Cardiff: University of Wales Press, 2007).

[39]  Genre remains a largely unexplored aspect of the Chatterton forgeries, but his working methods have been scrutinized by, among others, Donald S. Taylor, *Thomas Chatterton's Art: Experiments in Imagined History* (Princeton: Princeton University, 1978); Ian Haywood, *The Making of History: A Study of the Literary Forgeries of James Macpherson and Thomas Chatterton in Relation to Eighteenth-Century Ideas of History and Fiction* (Rutherford, N.J.: Fairleigh Dickinson University Press, 1986); and Margaret Russett, *Fictions and Fakes: Forging Romantic Authenticity, 1760–1845* (Cambridge: Cambridge University Press, 2006). For relevant primary documents, see *Thomas Chatterton: Early Sources and Responses*, facs. repr., 6 vols (London: Routledge; Thoemmes Press, 1993).

[40]  The classic study is B. R. McElderry, Jr, 'Archaism and Innovation in Spenser's Poetic Diction', *Publications of the Modern Language Association of America*, 47/1 (1932), 144–70.

medieval themes which were full of verbal archaisms. This linguistic eclecticism provoked the scorn of Dr Johnson, who ridiculed Warton's efforts in the following piece of doggerel:

> Wheresoe'er I turn my View
> All is strange, yet nothing new;
> Endless Labour all along,
> Endless Labour to be wrong;
> Phrase that Time has flung away,
> Uncouth Words in Disarray:
> Trickt in Antique Ruff and Bonnet,
> Ode and Elegy and Sonnet.[41]

The point here is not that Johnson regarded the ode, elegy, and sonnet as obsolete genres, as some critics have taken these lines to mean. Rather, he is calling attention to Warton's habit (in poems such as 'The Crusade' and 'The Grave of King Arthur', both of which Warton classes as 'odes'[42]) of artificially ageing the genres he employs by dressing them in antique clothes, thus producing fake novelty and fake antiquity simultaneously—a practice somewhat akin to the modern fashion for 'distressed' furniture.[43]

Notice at this point how the connotations of 'ancient' and 'antique' have changed. At the beginning of the eighteenth century, the word 'ancient' was associated, almost exclusively, with classical antiquity, and it signified the *authority* of antiquity rather than the *agedness* of it. Classical civilization belonged, as it were, on a different timescale, or outside time altogether. From this perspective, phrases like 'ancient epic' or 'ancient pastoral' would be tautologies, since these were classical genres that were by definition ancient. By 1760, however, 'ancient', in literary contexts, usually refers to earlier *native* periods—earlier points on the *same* timescale. The word still functions as an honorific, but the prestige it confers derives not from a sense of timeless authority but from an evocation of temporal distance—a newly felt sense of the imaginative appeal of the remote past. Hazlitt's essay 'On Antiquity' (1821), though written half a century later, defines perfectly the logic of this shift:

There is no such thing as Antiquity in the ordinary acceptation we affix to the term. Whatever is or has been, while it is passing, must be modern. The early ages may have been barbarous in themselves; but they have become *ancient* with the slow and silent lapse of successive generations. The 'olden times' are only such in reference to us. The past is rendered strange, mysterious, visionary, awful, from the great gap in time that parts us from it, and the long perspective of waning years.[44]

---

[41] 'Lines Written in Ridicule of Thomas Warton's Poems' (1777–8), quoted by Lawrence Lipking, *The Ordering of the Arts in Eighteenth-Century England* (Princeton: Princeton University Press, 1970), 380–1.

[42] Thomas Warton, *Poems: A New Edition* (London, 1777), 58–72.

[43] Cf. Susan Stewart, 'Notes on Distressed Genres', in her *Crimes of Writing: Problems in the Containment of Representation* (New York: Oxford University Press, 1991).

[44] 'On Antiquity', *London Magazine* (May 1821), in *The Complete Works of William Hazlitt*, ed. P. P. Howe, 21 vols (London: Dent, 1930–4), xii. 252.

Here is Bakhtin's 'ancient Greeks' joke told straight, except that Hazlitt is pondering the further paradox that, from the vantage point of the nineteenth century, *medieval* antiquity seems oddly more 'ancient' even than classical antiquity. Such is the 'involuntary' cultural prejudice of his own epoch, he confesses that the '*dark* or middle ages' seem 'older and farther off, and more inaccessible to the imagination, than the brilliant and well-defined periods of Greece and Rome' (xii. 253). In 1786 Joshua Reynolds made an identical point about gothic architecture, observing that 'though not so ancient as the Grecian', it is 'more so to our imagination'.[45] One result of this shift in historical perception is that by the late eighteenth century the word 'ancient' in British critical discourse usually referred to medieval rather than classical culture.

In Bakhtinian terms, then, we could say that the antiquarians had put the ancientness back into the word 'ancient'; and put it back, too, into the 'ancient' genres—pastoral, ode, and epic among them—whose previous recommendation, in neoclassical theory, was their transcendence of time. But this now was a different 'ancientness', involving a new consciousness of time: a perception of pastness rather than eternal presence. The adjective 'old' underwent a similar semantic shift. Formerly, in literary critical contexts, a pejorative term implying 'obsolete', it was now, for the antiquarians, a valorizing term denoting a temporal distance that was considered an attraction rather than a drawback. The new sense is illustrated by the phrase 'old Romance', much used by Percy and other eighteenth-century writers. This generic label served an obvious logical function: to distinguish old romance (i.e. medieval or Renaissance) from modern romance (i.e. the novel); but, more importantly, it also carried a powerful imaginative charge, as if the oldness and the pastness of 'old Romance' were the guarantor of its authenticity and aesthetic potency. Hence the poignant lament in Keats's *Isabella, or, The Pot of Basil* (1820), 'O for the gentleness of old Romance, | The simple plaining of a minstrel's song!',[46] where 'old Romance' is associated not with crudity and ignorance, as in neoclassical usage, but with gentleness and simplicity. The shifting resonance of the phrase 'old ballad' makes the same point. The condescending humour that the editor of *A Collection of Old Ballads* (1723–5) felt necessary to use disappears entirely from later ballad collections, and by 1750 generic tags like 'old ballad', 'excellent old ballad' and 'rarest old ballad' had become so fashionable as to have become clichés, which may be one reason why Percy abandoned his original, borrowed title 'A Collection of Old Ballads' in favour of the more emphatically old-sounding *Reliques of Ancient English Poetry*.

To regard Percy, or even Macpherson or Chatterton, as an unequivocal promoter of 'oldness' or 'ancientness' would, however, be a mistake. As Macpherson's detractors pointed out, his Ossianic poems are patently anachronistic. Gaelic oral traditions may have supplied their raw material, but their techniques of narration, descriptions

---

[45] Joshua Reynolds, *Discourses on Art*, ed. Robert R. Wark, 2nd edn (New Haven: Yale University Press, 1975), 242 (discourse 13, 11 Dec. 1786).
[46] John Keats, *The Complete Poems*, ed. John Barnard, 2nd edn (Harmondsworth: Penguin, 1977), 251 (lines 387–8).

of landscape, and prevailing sensibility and tone are thoroughly modern.[47] It is a modern, sentimental idea of the ancient bard, and of ancient epic, that is realized in poems like *Fingal* and *Temora*, which are not the 'genuine remains of ancient Scottish poetry' they purport to be,[48] but, in Nick Groom's phrase, a 'chiaroscuro of antiquity and modernity' shaped as much by the aesthetic theories of the Scottish Enlightenment as by Macpherson's literary intuitions of the Celtic past.[49] Chatterton, too, was a product of his own epoch as well as a brilliant imaginer of others, dividing his time between concocting medieval forgeries and writing topical satire in the manner of Pope, Gay, and Swift. The Rowley poems themselves owe their success to Chatterton's acute understanding of the modern hunger for the past: contemporary fascination with medieval literature and history is mimicked by the poems' own inbuilt nostalgia for earlier moments of imaginative plenitude, as in the prefatory verse to *Aella*:

> Straunge dome [doom] ytte ys, that, yn thefe daies of oures,
> Nete [Nought] butte a bare recytalle can hav place;
> Nowe fhapelie poefie haft lofte yttes powers,
> And pynant [insipid] hyftorie ys onlie grace;
> Heie [They] pycke up wolfome [noxious] weedes, ynftedde of flowers,
> And famylies, ynftedde of wytte, theie trace;
> Nowe poefie canne meete wythe ne regrate [esteem],
> Whylfte profe, & herehaughtrie [heraldry], ryfe yn eftate.[50]

Here, the fictitious poet–priest Thomas Rowley expresses to his patron William Canynge a feeling of cultural belatedness which exactly mirrors that of Chatterton's contemporaries. Chatterton projects back onto the fifteenth century the same sense of poetic decline—evinced by the ascendancy of prose over poetry and the displacement of imaginative by historical writing ('pynant hyftorie')—that troubled cultural commentators of his own day, thereby managing at once to displace and to amplify the eighteenth-century 'burden of the past'.

Percy's temporal allegiances are even more transparently divided, the whole enterprise of the *Reliques* being the product of conflicting aesthetic impulses. Percy's texts of medieval ballads are, in many cases, composite versions—regularized, corrected, and modernized, though retaining some of the old spelling. To purists like Ritson, Percy's editorial technique of (often silent) collation and emendation, and his habit of rewriting, cutting, and, on occasion, adding whole passages to the ballads he

---

[47] The degree of fabrication remains a matter of dispute. Macpherson's authentic oral sources (mainly late medieval Gaelic ballads) are analysed by Derick Thomson, *The Gaelic Sources of Macpherson's 'Ossian'* (Edinburgh: Oliver and Boyd, 1951); and Donald Meek, 'The Gaelic Ballads of Scotland: Creativity and Adaptation', in Howard Gaskill (ed.), *Ossian Revisited* (Edinburgh: Edinburgh University Press, 1991). The forged elements are highlighted by, for example, Haywood, *The Making of History*; Stafford, *The Sublime Savage*; Moore, *Enlightenment and Romance*; and K. K. Ruthven, *Faking Literature* (Cambridge: Cambridge University Press, 2001).

[48] *Fragments of Ancient Poetry*, preface [by Hugh Blair], p. iii.

[49] Groom, *Making of Percy's 'Reliques'*, 88.

[50] 'Letter to the Dygne Mastre Canynge', in [Thomas Chatterton], *Poems, Supposed to Have Been Written at Bristol by Thomas Rowley, and Others, in the Fifteenth Century . . . To which are Added, a Preface, an Introductory Account of the Several Pieces, and a Glossary*, [ed. Thomas Tyrwhitt] (London, 1777), 71.

presented, were anathema. Percy understood his readership, however, and correctly assumed that the general reader could take only so much authenticity, when authenticity meant being confronted with the (to modern eyes) crude techniques, unfamiliar language, and bawdy subject matter of medieval ballads. For the same reason, Percy chose to offset the medieval ballads 'with a few modern attempts in the same kind of writing' and 'with little elegant pieces of the lyric kind', in order to 'atone for the rudeness of the more obsolete poems' and to 'take off from the tediousness of the longer narratives'[51] (the word 'atone' typifies the defensive tone of the Preface, implying that a taste for early literature requires justification, even apology). He performs a similar balancing act in his 'Essay on the Ancient English Minstrels', differentiating between the 'aristocratic old balladeers', part of an oral culture, and the 'new race of ballad-writers' who emerged in the age of printing, 'an inferior sort of minor poets, who wrote narrative songs merely for the press'. The 'old Minstrel-ballads', though they 'abound with antique words and phrases, are extremely incorrect, and run into the utmost licence of metre', have nevertheless 'a romantic wildness, and are in the true spirit of chivalry'; whereas 'the other sort', though 'written in exacter measure', have 'a low or subordinate correctness, sometimes bordering on the insipid' (vol. i, pp. xxii–xxiii).

Nowhere are Percy's divided loyalties more forcibly demonstrated than in his treatment of 'Chevy Chase', the poem that opens the first volume (an appropriate choice because this was the ballad that most readers would have known best from Addison's famous essays in *The Spectator*,[52] and also the one that featured Percy's own ancestors—the Northumberland Percys). Whereas with many other ballads he presents a composite text, in this instance he gives *two* versions, one entitled 'The Ancient Ballad of Chevy-Chase' (a fifteenth-century, 'old balladeer' version), the other entitled 'The more modern Ballad of Chevy Chace' (a seventeenth-century, 'press' version). In the headnote to the first, he speaks with his primitivist hat on, calling attention to the 'genuine strokes of nature and artless passion' in 'this fine heroic song'. He claims that he has recovered 'the true original song' Sidney had eulogized in his *Defence of Poesy* (1595), while distancing himself from Sidney's qualifying strictures on its 'evil apparel' and 'rugged garb' (i. 1–2). In the second headnote, by contrast, Percy's neoclassical voice takes over as he introduces 'the more improved edition of that fine Heroic ballad'. Here, he points out the improvements in versification, sentiment, and diction, and suggests that, had Sidney seen this 'improved copy', he would have had no reason to complain of the ballad's 'antiquated phrase' and other 'faults' (i. 231–4). Percy invites the reader to compare the two versions, and, if so inclined, to make a further comparison with Henry Bold's translation of 'Chevy Chace' into Latin rhymes, as published in Dryden's *Miscellanies* (1692). Yet, despite the measured language and the obvious effort at critical impartiality, the impression given is of profound ambivalence rather than scholarly detachment. Percy is evidently pulled in both directions, responsive to the attractions of both medieval and modern versification, and receptive as an

---

[51] *Reliques*, vol. i., preface, p. x.
[52] *The Spectator*, nos 70, 74 (21, 25 May 1711).

editor both to the argument for authenticity and originality, and to the argument for improvement and modernization.

This ambivalence is wholly characteristic of his time. Richard Hurd's influential *Letters on Chivalry and Romance* (1762) ends suspended in doubt between the imaginative enticements of the 'world of fine fabling' of 'old Romance' and the liberating rationality of the Enlightenment, whose cosmopolitan values he was to expound so confidently in his *Dissertation on the Idea of Universal Poetry* (1766).[53] Hurd's wistful comments in the *Letters* on the 'revolution in modern taste' that had dissolved the 'magic' of the old romances and ushered in more sensible, but perhaps less imaginatively compelling, forms of literature are echoed almost verbatim in Thomas Warton's *History of English Poetry* (1774–81), a history that, symptomatically, gets only as far as the sixteenth century.[54] Elsewhere, Warton makes apology for his antiquarian interests, thanking his friend Sir Joshua Reynolds for having 'broke the Gothic chain, | And brought my bosom back to truth again',[55] truth being the classical taste practised and theorized by Reynolds (Warton himself was a classical scholar by profession, as well as a 'truant' romanticist[56]). The Scottish philosopher–poet James Beattie betrays an even sharper ambivalence, beginning his poem *The Minstrel* (directly inspired by Percy's essay) as a celebration of the imaginative power of romance and its influence on the development of a young poet's mind, but then, three years later, in 1774, adding a second book that includes an outright retraction of this premiss, the rallying-cry of the first book ('Perish the lore that deadens young desire!') becoming the reprehensible illusion of the second.[57] On the other hand, even so resolute a rationalist and classicist as Dr Johnson, who condemned the fashionable taste for ballads and black-letter type, denounced Macpherson's Ossian as a 'Scotch conspiracy in national falsehood',[58] and made an enemy of his erstwhile

---

[53] Richard Hurd, *Letters on Chivalry and Romance* (London, 1762), 120. For Hurd's concept of 'universal poetry', see Ch. 5 below, pp. 175–6.

[54] Thomas Warton, *History of English Poetry*, 3 vols (London, 1774–81), ii. 392–3. Lipking, *Ordering of the Arts*, 393, singles out this passage as the emotional climax of Warton's entire *History*.

[55] 'Verses on Sir Joshua Reynolds's Painted Window at New-College Oxford' (1782), lines 63–4, in David Fairer and Christine Gerrard (eds), *Eighteenth-Century Poetry: An Annotated Anthology* (Oxford: Blackwell, 1999). As the editors note (p. 378), Reynolds responded with 'good-humoured scepticism' to Warton's recantation.

[56] Raymond D. Havens, 'Thomas Warton and the Eighteenth-Century Dilemma', *Studies in Philology*, 25 (1928), 36–50. On the paradoxes of the antiquarian poetic, see also David Fairer, 'Thomas Warton, Thomas Gray, and the Recovery of the Past', in W. B. Hutchings and W. Ruddick (eds), *Thomas Gray: Contemporary Essays* (Liverpool: Liverpool University Press, 1993); and Terry, *Poetry and the Making of the English Literary Past*, 316–20.

[57] James Beattie, *The Minstrel, or, The Progress of Genius. A Poem. The Second Book* (London, 1774), 3. The retraction could not be more explicit: Beattie quotes his earlier dictum and rejects it ('"Perish the lore that deadens young desire" | Is the soft tenor of my song no more'). For Beattie's debt to Percy, see Kathryn Sutherland, 'The Native Poet: The Influence of Percy's Minstrel from Beattie to Wordsworth', *Review of English Studies*, 33 (1982), 414–33. For later reworkings of the minstrel motif, see Everard H. King, *James Beattie's 'The Minstrel' and the Origins of Romantic Autobiography* (Lewiston, N.Y.: Edwin Mellen Press, 1992); and Maureen McLane, *Balladeering, Minstrelsy, and the Making of British Romantic Poetry* (Cambridge: Cambridge University Press, 2008).

[58] James Boswell's *Life of Johnson* (1791), quoted in Katie Trumpener, *Bardic Nationalism: The Romantic Novel and the British Empire* (Princeton: Princeton University Press, 1997), 77.

friend Thomas Warton by mocking his medievalist poetry in the satirical lines already quoted, betrayed a sneaking fondness for the 'fictions of romantick chivalry' he publicly disparaged.[59] Vicesimus Knox, another eminent classicist with split loyalties, openly confessed his dilemma, declaring himself a devotee of both the 'old school of English poetry', consisting of ballad enthusiasts and 'lovers and imitators of Spenser and Milton', and the 'modern school', admirers of Dryden, Boileau, and Pope.[60]

Ultimately, however, this was not merely an ambivalence in personal taste but a clash between rival aesthetic systems. The 1760s—the decade of Macpherson and Chatterton, of Percy and Hurd—was a pivotal moment in British cultural history when the claims of antiquity and modernity (in their newly defined senses) were thrown into radical juxtaposition, and British poetry and criticism were confronted by a new and seemingly irreconcilable tension between opposed artistic values and conflicting perceptions of time.[61] To this divided, Janus-faced aesthetic we owe such improbable inventions as the gothic novel, another product of the 1760s, whose prototype, Horace Walpole's *The Castle of Otranto* (1764), is presented as 'an attempt to blend the two kinds of romance, the ancient and the modern', by observing the 'rules of probability' which govern the latter while exercising the imaginative licence associated with the former.[62] That, at least, is the rationale Walpole supplies in the second (1765) edition, whose Preface amalgamates the fashionable romance poetics of Hurd with the novelistic theory of mimetic probability. In the first edition, he provides a different explanation, exploiting yet another cultural fashion by passing the work off as the translation of an old Italian manuscript—a ruse that many readers apparently fell for.[63] Yet even here, in the original Preface, we find a clash of critical discourses, as the aesthetics of forgery is yoked together with a neoclassical theory of tragedy ('the rules of the drama are almost observed throughout', and 'Everything tends directly to the catastrophe'). In private, he changed his story yet again, claiming to friends that he wrote the novel 'in spite of rules, critics, and philosophers'.[64] The one thing missing from all these accounts is an acknowledgement of the ludic quality of the enterprise, palpable not only in the novel itself but also in its infinitely rewritable preface.

---

[59] Eithne Henson, *'The Fictions of Romantick Chivalry': Samuel Johnson and Romance* (Rutherford, N.J.: Fairleigh Dickinson University Press, 1992).

[60] 'On the Prevailing Taste in Poetry', in Vicesimus Knox, *Essays Moral and Literary*, 2nd edn, 2 vols (London, 1782), ii. 186.

[61] Cf. Terry, *Poetry and the Making of the English Literary Past*, 300, who refers to a 'bifurcation' of the English literary tradition in the 1760s, thereafter 'cruelly and enduringly divided between the gothic and the classical'.

[62] Horace Walpole, *The Castle of Otranto: A Gothic Story*, ed. E. J. Clery (Oxford: Oxford University Press, 1998), 10.

[63] For a comparison between Walpole and other literary fabricators such as Chatterton, see Marlon Ross, 'Authority and Authenticity: Scribbling Authors and the Genius of Print in Eighteenth-Century England', in Martha Woodmansee and Peter Jaszi (eds), *The Construction of Authorship: Textual Appropriation in Law and Literature* (Durham, N.C.: Duke University Press, 1994), 250–2.

[64] Letter to Mme du Deffand, 13 Mar. 1767, quoted in Clery (ed.), *The Castle of Otranto*, introd., p. xi.

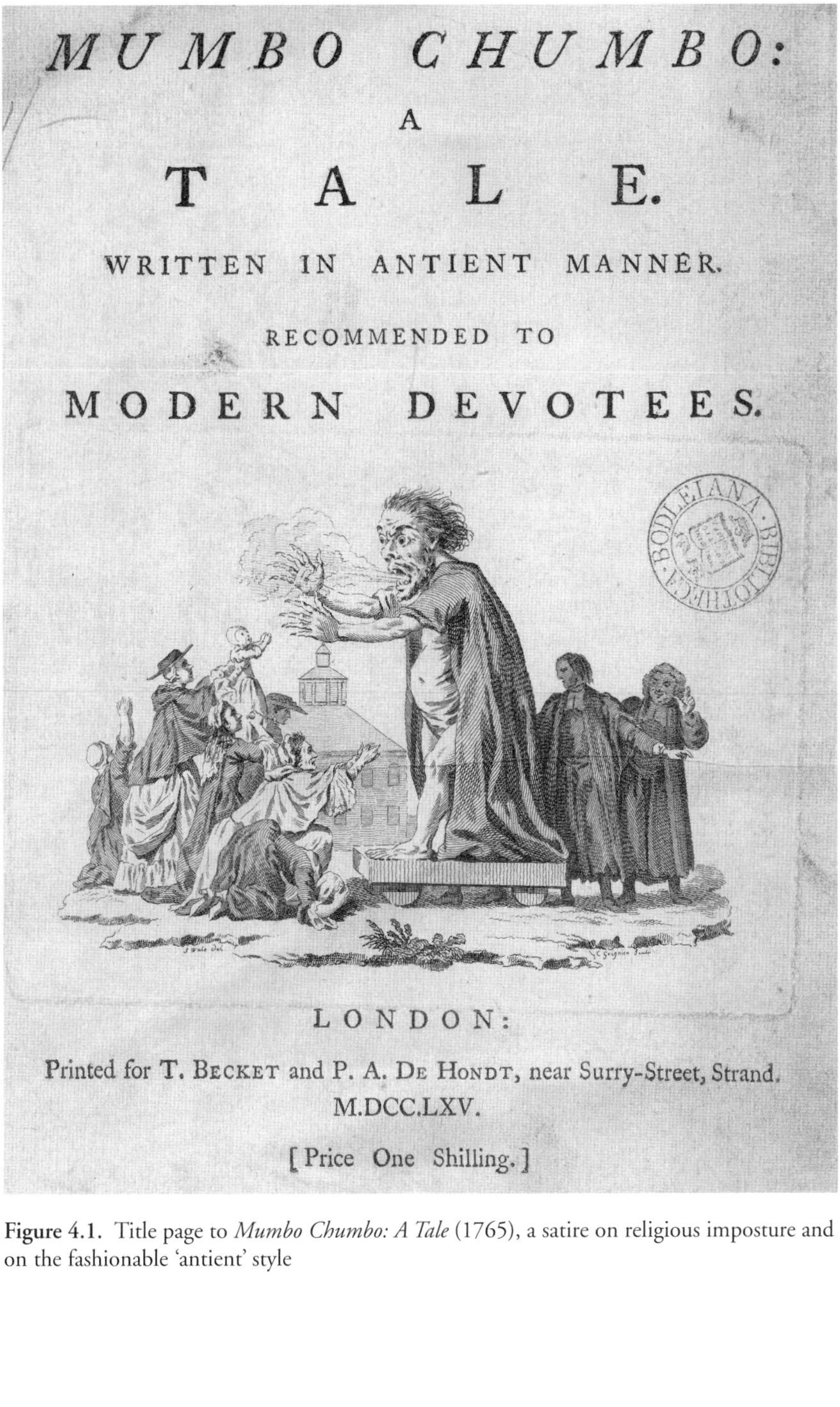

**Figure 4.1.** Title page to *Mumbo Chumbo: A Tale* (1765), a satire on religious imposture and on the fashionable 'antient' style

As the novel's unexpected success proved, Walpole's hybrid formula was a timely one, sufficiently attuned to the contradictory tastes of the mid-eighteenth century to inaugurate a new subgenre of fiction, the gothic novel, whose distinctive idiom and ethos would in turn leave its imprint on many other types of literature. Not coincidentally, the 1760s also saw the birth of gothic's more respectable neighbour, the historical novel, the prototype for which, according to Clara Reeve's *Progress of Romance* (1785), was Thomas Leland's *Longsword: An Historical Romance* (1762).[65] Leland assembles many of the same elements as Walpole—chivalry, love, and religion—but does so in a more historically controlled way, while still displaying no less visibly the 'chiaroscuro of antiquity and modernity' that marks the literature of this decade. So paradoxical a feature of contemporary literary taste could hardly pass unremarked, and alongside 'authentic' forgeries and 'ancient' works of modern literature, we find an anonymous verse satire of 1765 which parodies the whole trend with its irresistibly quirky title *Mumbo Chumbo: A Tale. Written in Antient Manner. Recommended to Modern Devotees.* The main target of the satire is 'Priestcraft', the poem being a Protestant diatribe about the similarities between overbearing Catholic priests and the African tribesmen who, according to a well-known legend, used a factitious idol, the grotesque 'mumbo chumbo' (in reality, a giant puppet), to dupe and scare their wives into submission. The implication of the title, though, is that 'modern devotees' of fashionable literary archaism are the victim of similar duping, since there is nothing 'antient' whatsoever about the tale except the exotic subject matter and the occasional Spenserian word. The illustration on the cover (Figure 4.1) brings the point home, depicting distraught women and children in front of the mumbo chumbo, and grinning men behind it, cynically operating the levers and pulleys. Here, then, is a visual allegory of the age of antiquarian forgery, the mumbo jumbo standing for the spurious 'antientness' to which so many readers of the time had succumbed.

## MAKE IT OLD, MAKE IT NEW

The cultural tensions that crystallize in the 1760s—the ambivalent historicism of Percy, Hurd, and Warton, the contradictory attitudes to the past revealed by the Ossian and Rowley affairs, and the movable metalanguage of the *Otranto* prefaces— carry over into the Romantic movement as a whole. We tacitly acknowledge this in labelling the movement 'romantic', a word whose semantic instability in this period—derisive in one context, approbatory in another—carries with it much of the ambivalence we have been tracing in contemporary perceptions of the past. In the ensuing decades, the antiquarian cult continued unabated, embracing ever wider areas of the linguistic, literary, and cultural past. Anthologies of 'ancient' literature continued to pour off the press, with the result that the adjective became so hackneyed that editors like Ritson had to resort to ever more emphatic ways of signalling genuine antiquity, with titles such as *Pieces of Ancient Popular Poetry: From*

---

[65] Clara Reeve, *The Progress of Romance*, 2 vols (Colchester, 1785), ii. 31–2.

*Authentic Manuscripts and Old Printed Copies* (1791), which buttresses the idea of the 'ancient' with that of the 'authentic' and the 'old' (like the word 'popular', these paratextual signals are an implicit corrective to what Ritson saw as the spurious ancientness of Percy[66]). Just how 'old' was 'ancient' was, however, a moot point. A three-volume set called *The Ancient British Drama* (1810) is not, as the title might suggest, an anthology of medieval texts but a collection of pre-Restoration plays that had dropped out of the repertoire. William Hone's *Ancient Mysteries Described* (1823), on the other hand, *is* an anthology of medieval drama, containing not only 'English miracle plays' but also reports of 'ecclesiastical shows', 'the Festival of Fools and Asses', 'the Lord Mayors Show', and other forms of popular carnival.[67] Hone puns on the phrase 'ancient mysteries', extending the genre of the 'mystery play' to include secular entertainments, while implicitly *de*mystifying the whole tradition of medieval theatre and carnival as an 'ancient' version of the sort of demotic, anti-establishment satire in which he himself specialized.

In many publications, the word 'ancient' gains force from the binary opposition with 'modern', as in David Herd's influential anthology *Ancient and Modern Scots Songs, Heroic Ballads &c. etc.* (1769), in which 'ancient' and 'modern' designate pre- and post-1600. The second edition (1774) carries the subtitle *Collected from Memory, Tradition, and Ancient Authors*, underlining the claim to historical authenticity while simultaneously emphasizing the living tradition of Scots oral poetry. Ritson applies the same approach to English sources in his *Select Collection of English Songs* (1783), juxtaposing ancient and modern examples, and spelling out the relationship between tradition and modernity in a long theoretical introduction entitled 'A Historical Essay on the Origin and Progress of National Song'.[68] Ritson's essay typifies the classificatory techniques, teleological framework, and historical methodology of Enlightenment genre theory, the combined effect being to promote a genealogical perception of genre: an awareness of the ancestry and evolution of poetic forms, or of what Bakhtin would later term genre-memory—the way that a genre 'remembers its past' even as it 'lives in the present'.[69] The rapid development of the theory of song in the decade since John Aiken's pioneering *Essays on Song-Writing* (1772) is a good illustration of how theoretical interest in a genre grew alongside a recovery of its actual history, and of how the development of a viable classification of the genre accompanied the establishment of appropriate national canons.

Genre-memory is invoked by other means in Walter Scott's *Minstrelsy of the Scottish Border* (1802), another famous collection of regional poetry, which organizes itself into three 'Classes of Poems': 'Historical Ballads' in volume i, 'Romantic Ballads' and

---

[66] For Ritson's repeated attacks on Percy and other antiquarians, see Bertrand H. Bronson, *Joseph Ritson, Scholar-at-Arms*, 2 vols (Berkeley: University of California Press, 1938).

[67] For the political resonances of this collection, see Marcus Wood, *Radical Satire and Print Culture 1790–1822* (Oxford: Clarendon Press, 1994), 13; and Marilyn Butler, 'Antiquarianism (Popular)', in Iain McCalman (ed.), *An Oxford Companion to the Romantic Age: British Culture 1776–1832* (Oxford: Oxford University Press, 1999), 335.

[68] [Joseph Ritson (ed.)], *A Select Collection of English Songs*, 3 vols (London, 1783); the essay on national song introduces the first volume.

[69] See above, p. 120.

'Imitations of Ancient Ballads' in volume ii.[70] In this case, the reader is invited to experience originals and imitations simultaneously, and thus to perceive directly the evolutionary relationship later analysed in Scott's 'Essay on Imitations of the Ancient Ballad', appended to the 1830 edition of the *Minstrelsy*. Scott's exploitation of the 'minstrel' motif also extends to his 1810 anthology of *English Minstrelsy*, a collection of 'fugitive poetry' which includes contemporary as well as earlier verse and concludes with Wordsworth's (mistitled) 'On Visiting Tintern Abbey'.[71] Again, the effect of the editorial presentation is to promote a genealogical reading of English poetry as an ancient and continuing tradition of 'minstrelsy' which was still producing powerful examples. The period's interest in genealogies, especially native ones, even extends to the genre of critical theory itself. Joseph Haslewood's *Ancient Critical Essays upon English Poets and Poësy* (1811) is the first ever anthology of exclusively English, and exclusively 'ancient', literary criticism (meaning here Elizabethan: the anthology features works by Puttenham, Webbe, Campion, Daniel, and others), marking the early nineteenth century as truly the moment at which English critical theory comes of age.

As we enter the 'high' Romantic period, however, the archaizing trend is offset by another, equally powerful aesthetic imperative: towards innovation and experiment. Though superficially similar, this is not to be confused with the modernizing trend in neoclassical aesthetics, a project of 'advancement and reformation' predicated on normative assumptions alien to the Herderian age of historical relativity. At the end of the century, Joseph Fawcett could still write a poem called 'The Art of Poetry, According to the Latest Improvements' (1798), but the title is ironic: the 'improvements' in question are no improvement at all, and the purpose of the poem is to satirize recent developments in British poetry, from the perspective not of an unreconstructed neoclassicist (the Preface condemns 'that chilling system of criticism' which values 'correctness' over all else) but of a radical intellectual concerned to differentiate real from spurious 'progress'.[72] Fawcett's satire does, nevertheless, bear witness to a phenomenon which has a crucial bearing on the Romantic movement, and on the larger history of aesthetics: a cult of conspicuous innovation. There is nothing new about novelty, of course, but evidence suggests that the 1790s were the first time in British literary history when 'innovation' became a conscious and fully developed artistic credo, taking one step further the poetics of 'originality' propounded by mid-century critics such as Edward Young, and presenting yet another challenge to the crumbling authority of neoclassical genre theory, based as it was on the opposite principles of imitation and convention.

Wordsworth and Coleridge are often credited with instigating this trend, hence the tongue-in-cheek tribute of *Modern Parnassus, or, The New Art of Poetry* (1814),

---

[70] Walter Scott (ed.), *Minstrelsy of the Scottish Border: Consisting of Historical and Romantic Ballads, Collected in the Southern Counties of Scotland; with a Few of Modern Date, Founded Upon Local Tradition*, 2 vols (Kelso, 1802). A third volume, published in 1803, juxtaposes further examples of the three types.

[71] [Walter Scott (ed.),] *English Minstrelsy: Being a Selection of Fugitive Poetry from the Best English Authors, with some Original Pieces Hitherto Unpublished* (Edinburgh, 1810).

[72] Joseph Fawcett, *Poems: To which is Added Civilised War, before Published under the Title of The Art of War, with Considerable Alterations; and The Art of Poetry, According to the Latest Improvements, with Additions* (London, 1798), preface, p. v.

discussed in Chapter 1.[73] Poetic innovation, however, was already in fashion at the time *Lyrical Ballads* appeared, a fact brought home by another anonymous satire (attributed to Thomas Gisborne) actually entitled *Innovation: A Poem* (1799). The principal targets here are not Wordsworth and Coleridge but Erasmus Darwin and the Della Cruscans, innovators of very different stamp. The lax versification and emotional mannerism of the Robert Merry set and the 'allegoric hyperbolic verse' of Darwin have led, we are told, not to artistic reform but to an impoverishment of the poetic medium, a 'gay confusion' in which 'False, true, old, modern, present, past combine', and in which 'garish ornament' substitutes for genuine poetic expression.[74] These are almost identical to the charges levelled at contemporary poetry by Wordsworth himself, whose 1800 Preface pointedly differentiates his poetic reforms from the 'false refinement' and 'arbitrary innovation' of other modern poets.[75] Fawcett's 'Art of Poetry' is a reaction to the same phenomenon, his satire on 'the Latest Improvements' taking the form of an ironic epistle to young poets eager to learn 'the new way', and its principal targets being, once again, Darwin, 'the SENTIMENTAL tribes', and Germanic horror poetry.[76]

One reason why 'innovation' was such a charged word in these contexts was its association with revolutionary politics: what Burke, in his *Letter to a Noble Lord* (1796), called the 'dreadful innovation' of the French revolutionaries.[77] This connection is implicit in *Innovation: A Poem*, an aesthetically conservative satire whose tone and vocabulary are indelibly coloured by the political rhetoric of anti-Jacobinism. Six years earlier, a barrister called George Lethieullier Schoen had published a verse eulogy to Burke under the exact same title,[78] and the Burkean mantra that 'to innovate is not to reform' is the subtext of numerous other loyalist publications. 'Experiment' was another anti-Jacobin buzzword given currency by Burke, who, in the *Reflections*, figuratively depicts the French Revolution as an 'experiment' in politics that had gone disastrously wrong, and the French republic as a 'theoretic experimental edifice' built on the ruins of solid government.[79] In presenting *Lyrical Ballads* as an 'experiment', rationalized in the theoretic edifice of the 1800 Preface, Wordsworth was seeking to reclaim the compromised discourse of theory and experiment. It is unsurprising, therefore, that contemporary readers saw the project as politically motivated. By 1808 the notion of poems as experiments was sufficiently familiar for the *Eclectic Review* to characterize the whole period as an 'age of poetical

---

[73] See Ch. 1 above, pp. 29–30.

[74] [Thomas Gisborne], *Innovation: A Poem* (London, 1799), 9. For further evidence of the 1790s cult of innovation, see John Jordan, *Why the Lyrical Ballads? The Background, Writing, and Character of Wordsworth's 1798 'Lyrical Ballads'* (Berkeley: University of California Press, 1976), ch. 5.

[75] *The Prose Works of William Wordsworth*, ed. W. J. B. Owen and Jane Worthington Smyser, 3 vols (Oxford: Clarendon Press, 1974), i. 124.

[76] Fawcett, *Poems*, 256, 260.

[77] *The Works of the Right Honorable Edmund Burke*, ed. F. W. Raffety, 6 vols (Oxford: Oxford University Press, 1906–7), 46–7.

[78] George Lethieullier Schoen, *Innovation: A Poem. Addressed to the Right Honourable Edmund Burke* (London, 1793).

[79] Edmund Burke, *Reflections on the Revolution in France, and on the Proceedings in Certain Societies in London Relative to that Event*, ed. Conor Cruise O'Brien (Harmondsworth: Penguin, 1969), 230.

experiment',[80] a claim which reinforced another widely accepted idea, that Britain had witnessed a 'revolution in literature' analogous to the political revolution in France.

There remains, however, a paradox at the heart of the Romantic literary revolution, as was frequently remarked at the time. Francis Jeffrey pinpoints the paradox, noting how the supposed revolution involved, in fact, a reversion. Poetry, he writes in the *Edinburgh Review* in 1828, 'has advanced beyond the preceding age, simply by going back to one still older; and has put *its* poverty to shame only by unlocking the hoards of a remote ancestor. It has reformed merely by restoring; and innovated by a systematic recurrence to the models of antiquity.'[81] By 'antiquity', Jeffrey means here *native* antiquity: the article refers to the influence of Percy's *Reliques*, of medieval romance, and of the Elizabethans and Jacobeans—a genealogy that modifies the polemically Continental one he had given in his *Thalaba* article twenty-five years earlier, where he had traced the origins of the 'new school of poetry' to the 'antisocial principles, and distempered sensibility of Rousseau' and the 'simplicity and energy (*horresco referens*) of Kotzebue and Schiller'.[82] An even dimmer view of these atavistic trends is presented by the aptly named *Imperial Review* in 1804, which sees the 'new school' as a step backwards that had undone the gains of neoclassicism and returned poetry to a state of barbarism: 'Some of our latest poets, from what motive we cannot guess, have laboured, with a sort of retrograde industry, in Tales of Wonder, Lyrical Ballads, &c to barbarize our versification, and, by returning to the lame stanza and prosaic flow of obsolete compositions, to undo the toils of those who have reduced us to correctness.'[83] It is ironic that Wordsworth and Coleridge are lumped together here with M. G. Lewis, whose *Tales of Wonder* (1801) exemplifies the sensationalist trends *Lyrical Ballads* was intended to counteract: Germanic horror ballads, pseudo-tragic drama, and 'idle and extravagant stories in verse'. To defenders of the 'old imperial code', however, such distinctions paled into insignificance in face of a revivalist aesthetic which was in its essence 'retrograde'—a revolution which had turned the clock of literary history backwards.

It was not only traditionalists like Jeffrey who were troubled by these developments. The paradox of 'retrograde progress' is a central theme, too, of Hazlitt's *The Spirit of the Age* (1825). The phrase appears in his chapter on Thomas Moore, where

---

[80] *Eclectic Review*, 4/1 (1808), 35, quoted by A. D. Harvey, *English Poetry in a Changing Society 1780–1825* (London: Alison and Busby, 1980), 13. For another example, in the *Dublin Examiner*, see my second epigraph to Ch. 5 below.

[81] Review of Atherstone's *Fall of Ninevah*, *Edinburgh Review*, 48 (Sept. 1828), in *Jeffrey's Criticism: A Selection*, ed. Peter F. Morgan (Edinburgh: Scottish Academic Press, 1983), 95. As Morgan notes, Christopher North referred to this review as 'Jeffrey's Decline and Fall of Poetry'. For the Scottish Enlightenment background to Jeffrey's view of literary history, see Philip Flynn, 'Francis Jeffrey and the Scottish Critical Tradition', in Massimiliano Demata and Duncan Wu (eds), *British Romanticism and the 'Edinburgh Review': Bicentenary Essays* (Basingstoke: Palgrave Macmillan, 2002).

[82] *Edinburgh Review*, 1 (Oct. 1802), in *Jeffrey's Criticism*, 46. The inset quotation (from Virgil's *Aeneid*, book 2, line 204) translates: 'telling it makes me shudder'.

[83] Review of Thomas Brown's *Poems*, *Imperial Review* (Nov. 1804), quoted by Jordan, *Why the Lyrical Ballads?*, 71–2.

he highlights the compulsive, pathological quality of the cult of innovation, a 'craving of the public mind after novelty and effect' which is symptomatic of 'a false and uneasy appetite'. Poetry 'in its retrograde progress comes at last to be constructed on the principles of the modern OPERA, where an attempt is made to gratify every sense at every instant, and where the understanding alone is insulted and the heart mocked'.[84] Where innovation takes the form of archaism, the results can be even more unsatisfactory. In his chapter on Walter Scott, he writes approvingly of the Waverley novels as successful transformations of the old into the new, but condemns Scott's earlier attempts to do the same thing in poetry: 'The truth is, there is a modern air, in the midst of the antiquarian research of Mr. Scott's poetry. It is history or tradition in masquerade.' Even Hazlitt's great friend Charles Lamb, whose literary tastes were strongly antiquarian, receives at best ambiguous praise:

Mr. Lamb has raked among the dust and cobwebs of a more remote period, has established specimens of curious relics, and pored over moth-eaten, decayed manuscripts, for the benefit of the more inquisitive and discerning part of the public. Antiquity after a time has the grace of novelty, as old fashions revived are mistaken for new ones; and a certain quaintness and singularity of style is an agreeable relief to an insipid monotony of modern composition. Mr. Lamb has succeeded not by conforming to the *Spirit of the Age*, but in opposition to it.[85]

Despite this last comment, the overall impression of Hazlitt's survey of contemporary taste is that the fashion for archaism—antiquity repackaged as novelty—is a defining feature of the period. In previous essays such as 'Why the Arts Are Not Progressive' (1817) and 'On Poetry in General' (1818), Hazlitt had already made the primitivist case that the greatest poets are the earliest ones, and that 'the progress of knowledge and refinement has a tendency to circumscribe the limits of the imagination, and to clip the wings of poetry'.[86] In *The Spirit of the Age*, he analyses the desperate expedients to which modern poets had resorted to counter this cultural atrophy.

The most devastating critique of the revivalist trend, however, is Thomas Love Peacock's satirical essay 'The Four Ages of Poetry' (1820). Peacock picks up the threads of the 'Ancients and Moderns' dispute but changes the terms of reference, combining a quasi-primitivist reverence for classical literary origins with an ultra-Modern faith in the progress of civilization while assuming the philosophical standpoint of Utilitarianism. The whole argument is deeply parodic, the parody extending to his argumentative methods as much as the literary material he surveys, yet Peacock's conclusions about the parlous condition of contemporary poetry are delivered with a conviction that puts the matter beyond a joke. The art of poetry, he insists, has been rendered obsolete by advances in science and technology. Sidelined by the march of progress, poetry is no longer a contributor to knowledge but a hindrance to it, fostering illusions and distracting people from more useful intellectual pursuits. Unwilling to admit this, modern poets have turned back to the past, ransacking the archives for exotic material in a vain attempt to reinvigorate their moribund art form and satisfy those infantile minds that still derive satisfaction from

---

[84] *Complete Works*, xi. 170.
[85] Ibid. xi. 178.    [86] Ibid. v. 9.

it: 'While the historian and the philosopher are advancing in, and accelerating, the progress of knowledge, the poet is wallowing in the rubbish of departed ignorance, and raking up the ashes of dead savages to find gewgaws and rattles for the grown babies of the age.'[87] Each poet specializes in a particular form of 'rubbish', peddling their own brand of infantilism or obscurantism. In Wordsworth's case, it is 'village legends from old women and sextons'; in Coleridge's, 'the dreams of crazy theologians and the mysticisms of German metaphysics':

These disjointed relics of tradition and fragments of second-hand observation, being woven into a tissue of verse, constructed on what Mr. Coleridge calls a new principle (that is, no principle at all), compose a modern–antique compound of frippery and barbarism, in which the puling sentimentality of the present time is grafted on the misrepresented ruggedness of the past into a heterogeneous congeries of unamalgamating manners, sufficient to impose on the common readers of poetry, over whose understanding the poet of this class possesses that commanding advantage, which, in all circumstances and conditions of life, a man who knows something, however little, always possesses over one who knows nothing. (p. 16)

No one, not even the deceived reader, escapes Peacock's indictment. The premise of his argument, however, is that the literary predicament he describes is an inevitable consequence of the historical process. The revivalist aesthetic is not simply a temporary fad but the manifestation of an irresolvable cultural dilemma. The modern poet, born into 'unpoetical times', bereft of material, and torn between the conflicting imperatives to 'make it new' and 'make it old', is condemned to pursue a path which achieves neither.

Such pessimistic conclusions are, however, belied by the sales figures, and by the critical impact of the revivalist poetic. The 'modern–antique compound' which Peacock saw as a fatal flaw in contemporary poetry was regarded by many as the secret of its success—the paradoxical expression of a 'spirit of the age' that was conservative and revolutionary by turns. In an article of 1818, *Blackwood's Magazine* followed Jeffrey in attributing the 'great change in the poetical temper of the country' to the Elizabethan revival, but interpreted this not as a regression but as evidence of a new national literary confidence. Articulating perfectly the cultural assumptions behind what Pascale Casanova has called the 'Herder effect'—a Romantic nationalism in which literary revivalism plays a pivotal role—*Blackwood's* declares: 'A nation must revert to the ancient spirit of its own. The living and creative spirit of literature is its nationality.'[88] Such, too, is the verdict of the *Retrospective Review*, the first ever journal devoted exclusively to literary history, which in its second issue (1820) defends Leigh Hunt against some of the charges levelled at the Cockney School by arguing that, like many modern poets, Hunt is really 'of the old school revived': 'In truth, what has been termed unbounded license, and even vulgarity, in the poems of Leigh Hunt and others, is frequently neither more nor less than a free imitation of

---

[87] *Peacock's 'Four Ages of Poetry'; Shelley's 'Defence of Poetry'; Browning's 'Essay on Poetry'*, ed. H. F. B. Brett-Smith (1921; Oxford: Blackwell, 1971), 15.

[88] *Blackwood's Magazine*, 4 (1818), 264–6, quoted by René Wellek, 'The Concept of Romanticism in Literary History', in his *Concepts of Criticism*, ed. Stephen G. Nichols (New Haven: Yale University Press, 1963), 153. For the 'Herder effect', see Pascale Casanova, *The World Republic of Letters* (1999), trans. M. B. Debevoise (Cambridge, Mass.: Harvard University Press, 2004), 77–81.

the Old English masters of the art, whose spirit they have imbibed, with the addition of the ease and point of modern versification.'[89] This is like neoclassical modernization in reverse: Hunt retains the 'spirit' of his native precursors but loosens the form, engaging not in generic reconstruction of the kind practised by Dryden on Chaucer, but in 'free imitation' of the sort exemplified by *The Story of Rimini* (1816), his long verse narrative based on the Paolo and Francesca episode in Dante's *Inferno*. Hunt's audacious blend of a Renaissance love story, a modern metrical form, and a contemporary poetic idiom represents one solution to the cultural dilemma posed by Peacock.[90] How other writers responded to that challenge and turned the new consciousness of historical time to creative advantage is the subject of the remainder of this chapter.

## THE DIALECTIC OF REVIVALISM

In generic terms, Romanticism can thus be defined, as it often has been, as a revival movement: a revival of romance, of the sonnet, the epic, the ballad, the pastoral, the song, to name just some of its favoured forms. What is important is that in each case an effort of imaginative *retrieval* is involved. Unlike earlier revivalist movements such as neoclassicism, however, Romanticism had to reckon with the temporality of the genres it sought to retrieve and adopt. Genres were now time-bound entities, not transcendent forms. They were defined not by their 'rules', but by their origins, their history, their ethnic associations, their genealogy. 'Literary competence', in Jonathan Culler's sense[91]—the ability to recognize and utilize the codes of a particular genre—now entailed an awareness of that genealogy. This shift had momentous implications, both positive and negative. On the one hand, there were now the pleasures of history, and of time itself: the strangeness and mystery spoken of by Hazlitt, when we are made to experience the 'great gap in time' that separates us from the past. Literary genres could cross that gap, act as time machines to transport us into the imaginative space of the past, but always, for the Romantics, with a sense of the temporal distance travelled, and of the difference between the 'then' and the 'now'. No longer a fantasy of simultaneity, genre was now an exercise in memory. To use a literary genre was to render perceptible the sedimented layers, built up across time, which constitute that genre; to renew, in Bakhtin's words, the 'archaic elements' that lay buried within.

The enriching effect of this new genealogical consciousness can be seen at once in a poem like Keats's 'La Belle Dame sans Merci. A Ballad' (1820), whose multiple layers of balladry and romance include the French troubadour lyric by Alain Chartier that supplied the title; the thirteenth-century ballad of *Thomas the Rymer* reprinted (and

---

[89] *Retrospective Review*, 2 (1820), 167, quoted by Curran, *Poetic Form and British Romanticism*, 26. For the significance of this journal as a landmark of historicism, see Ian Jack, *English Literature 1815–1832* (Oxford: Oxford University Press, 1963), 399–400.

[90] For contemporary reaction to Hunt's generic experiment, see Michael Eberle-Sinatra, *Leigh Hunt and the London Literary Scene: A Reception History of his Major Works* (London: Routledge, 2005), ch. 3.

[91] Jonathan Culler, *Structuralist Poetics: Structuralism, Linguistics and the Study of Literature* (London: Routledge and Kegan Paul, 1975), ch. 6.

reworked) in Scott's *Minstrelsy of the Scottish Border*; Spenser's *Faerie Queene*; the popular ballads of Elizabethan England that Keats had found in Percy's *Reliques*; the fake fifteenth-century ballads of Chatterton (another Keats favourite); and the neo-medieval ballads and romances of contemporaries like Coleridge, Wordsworth, Southey, and M. G. Lewis.[92] The result is a balladic palimpsest whose meaning is constituted by its deep historical layering: in his portrait of pathological eroticism, Keats uncovers the archetype of the femme fatale which underlies so many ballads and romances, tracing the motif to its medieval origins but also making it resonate across time, as if the accumulation of literary allusions were confirmation of the archetype's enduring power.

On the negative side, however, genres now carried the *burden* of their past. Using a genre was no longer (as, in the age of Rymer and Gildon, it had once purported to be) a matter of simply obeying the rules and following best practice. There were precursors to confront, previous claims on the genre to negotiate. In reality, this had always been so, but neoclassical theory had obscured the fact by promoting an angst-free genericity in which a genre was simply a formal structure to be replicated and there was always space for more replicators. For the Romantics, by contrast, a genre was a tradition rather than a template, and in many cases the tradition was already overcrowded. The transformation of simultaneity into chronology brought with it the problem of priority, and a correspondent 'anxiety of influence' for which genre was a primary focus.[93]

A case in point is epic. So powerful and pervasive was the Romantic period's aspiration to this most prestigious of genres that contemporary observers spoke of 'epomania',[94] but the record of the Romantics' endeavours in this department mostly consists of a series of (some would say, losing) battles with their formidable precursor Milton. To write epic in this period was not to worry over 'whether a Catalogue of the Armies sent into the Field is an essential Part of an Epic Poem', the sort of question neoclassical critics asked,[95] but to wonder whether there was anything left to be done with the genre after the masterpiece of *Paradise Lost*. For those most sensitive to the burden of the past (and such sensitivity may be a prerequisite for significant achievement in epic), the only option was to rewrite Milton's poem. The great epics of British Romanticism—*The Prelude*, *Prometheus Unbound*, *Don Juan*, *Jerusalem*—are all footnotes to *Paradise Lost*, and their self-conscious belatedness is

[92] For the literary sources of the poem, see Charles L. Finney, *The Evolution of Keats's Poetry*, 2 vols (Cambridge, Mass.: Harvard University Press, 1936), 593–9; and Earl R. Wasserman, *The Finer Tone: Keats's Major Poems* (Baltimore: Johns Hopkins University Press, 1953), 63–83.

[93] An unstated premiss of Harold Bloom's *The Anxiety of Influence: A Theory of Poetry* (New York: Oxford University Press, 1973) that is made explicit in his essay 'The Internalization of Quest Romance', in Harold Bloom (ed.), *Romanticism and Consciousness: Essays in Criticism* (New York: Norton, 1970).

[94] Southey's term, quoted by Brian Wilkie, *Romantic Poets and Epic Tradition* (Madison: University of Wisconsin Press, 1965), ch. 2.

[95] Edward Gibbon, 'An Enquiry, whether a Catalogue of the Armies sent into the Field is an Essential Part of an Epic Poem' (1763), quoted by H. T. Swedenberg, Jr, *The Theory of the Epic in England 1650–1800* (Berkeley: University of California Press, 1944), 120.

the precondition of their greatness.[96] Only in this period could an author think to write a 4,000-line poem actually entitled *Milton*: Blake's poem is a 'brief epic' rather than the full monty, but the brevity is part of his revisionary strategy, just as unfinishedness is part of Keats's and Byron's.

Even more stark is the case of tragedy. All the major Romantics attempted the genre, yet most of their efforts amount to little more than bad Shakespearean pastiche.[97] Thomas Lovell Beddoes referred to the drama of his time as a 'haunted ruin',[98] and what was haunting it was its own history. With precursors such as Milton and Shakespeare, epic and tragedy were doubtless the most anxiety-inducing of genres, but even humbler genres such as the sonnet, defined by formal rather than by thematic criteria, carried a heavy burden of prior achievement. The generic self-consciousness displayed by Wordsworth's 'Scorn not the sonnet' and 'Nuns fret not' can hardly be said to have induced creative paralysis in his case—he wrote more than five hundred other sonnets, on everything from capital punishment to the coming of the railways—but the very scale of his transactions with the genre could be inter-preted as a defensive manoeuvre: an attempt to outdo his competitors, not only by greater productivity but also by greater diversity of subject matter. Similarly, Mary Robinson's decision to write a sonnet sequence in the persona of the Greek poetess Sappho could be seen as a tactical evasion of the burden of the past. By combining classical content with a non-classical form, Robinson neatly solves the problem of finding something new to do with an overpopulated and cliché-ridden genre.[99]

Having lost their transcendent status, genres were time-bound in another sense too. They now carried a sell-by date—which in many cases had already expired. The ode was, in many people's eyes, a spent force before the Romantics revived it, the genuine sublimity of which the genre was capable having degenerated, in the hands of mediocre eighteenth-century practitioners, into what Coleridge termed 'the madness prepense of Pseudo-poesy', or sheer 'bombast'[100] (as the *European Magazine*

[96] For the Miltonic influence on Romantic epic, see Wilkie, *Romantic Poets and Epic Tradition*; Harold Bloom, *The Visionary Company: A Reading of English Romantic Poetry*, 2nd edn (Ithaca, N.Y.: Cornell University Press, 1971); Leslie Brisman, *Milton's Poetry of Choice and its Romantic Heirs* (Ithaca, N.Y.: Cornell University Press, 1973); Joseph Anthony Wittreich (ed.), *Milton and the Line of Vision* (Madison: University of Wisconsin Press, 1975); Lucy Newlyn, *'Paradise Lost' and the Romantic Reader* (Oxford: Clarendon Press, 1993); and Lisa Low and John Anthony Harding (eds), *Milton, the Metaphysicals, and Romanticism* (Cambridge: Cambridge University Press, 1994).

[97] George Steiner, *The Death of Tragedy* (London: Faber and Faber, 1961), 197–237; Timothy Webb, 'The Romantic Poet and the Stage: A Short, Sad, History', in Richard Allen Cave (ed.), *The Romantic Theatre: An International Symposium* (Gerrards Cross: Colin Smythe, 1986). For a more positive assessment, see Jeffrey N. Cox, *In the Shadows of Romance: Romantic Tragic Drama in Germany, England, and France* (Athens: Ohio University Press, 1987).

[98] Letter of Jan. 1825, quoted by Michael Bradshaw, *Death's Jest-Book: The 1829 Text*, ed. Bradshaw (Manchester: Carcanet, 2003), introd., p. xi. See also Bradshaw's *Resurrection Songs: The Poetry of Thomas Lovell Beddoes* (Aldershot: Ashgate, 2001), ch. 2.

[99] Mary Robinson, *Sappho and Phaon. In a Series of Legitimate Sonnets* (London, 1796); cf. Daniel Robinson, 'Reviving the Sonnet: Women Romantic Poets and the Sonnet Claim', *European Romantic Review*, 6/1 (1995), 98–127.

[100] *The Collected Works of Samuel Taylor Coleridge*, vii: *Biographia Literaria*, ed. James Engell and W. Jackson Bate, 2 vols (London: Routledge and Kegan Paul, 1983), ii. 85.

put it, 'the [ancient] variety is by this time exhausted, and . . . the heroic poem and ode have dwindled to the tale and song'[101]). A modern epic was, according to the same logic, at best improbable and at worst a contradiction in terms: 'Our times are unfavorable, to the last degree, to the writers of that kind of poetry commonly called epic', wrote John Foster[102]—a widely held view which did nothing to stem the flow of new claimants to the genre. Even more implausible, in Francis Jeffrey's eyes, was a modern metrical romance, a genre entirely unsuited to the contemporary world: 'To write a modern romance of chivalry', he wrote in a review of Scott's *Marmion* in 1808, 'seems to be as much such a fantasy as to build a modern abbey, or an English pagoda.'[103] The commercial success of Scott's 'fantasy' form (like that of neo-gothic and pseudo-Chinese architecture, building styles then at the height of fashion[104]) did not make it any less of a paradox. Even graver concerns were raised about the revival of pastoral, a genre whose artistic credibility had been demolished by a century of parody and critique. The fact that there were still some writers willing to write poems about poetic sheep farmers, and to accept what Nathan Drake in 1798 called the 'preposterous conception' that 'one peculiar form, style and manner' of description and narration, invented two thousand years ago by Theocritus and Virgil, was still the proper way to compose them did not amount to proof of the continued existence of the genre in any meaningful sense.[105] The Romantic revival of the sonnet, meanwhile, has been likened in one recent critical study to the opening of a crypt, so moribund was the genre in the preceding century.[106]

Examples could be multiplied, but the message is clear. Many, if not most, of the genres we think of as central to Romantic poetry were considered, prior to and even during their revival, to be outmoded, overworked, or defunct. If, as I have suggested, a genre was now a tradition rather than a template, its users had to contend with the predicament expressed in Ritson's sombre dictum that 'Tradition . . . is a species of alchemy which converts gold to lead.'[107] And, as if breathing new life into moribund literary genres were not enough, the aesthetic imperative to innovate and experiment meant that the Romantics had also to *transform* them: to discover new formal possibilities, new subject matter, new functions and applications; and to do so in the knowledge that, by the inexorable laws of literary evolution and fashion, today's innovation would be tomorrow's cliché. How Romantic writers responded to these

---

[101] *European Magazine*, 23 (1793), 268, quoted by Paul D. Sheats, 'Keats, the Greater Ode, and the Trial of Imagination', in J. Robert Barth SJ and John L. Mahoney (eds), *Coleridge, Keats, and the Imagination: Romanticism and Adam's Dream: Essays in Honor of Walter Jackson Bate* (Columbia: University of Missouri Press, 1990), 175 n. 3.

[102] John Foster, *Biographical, Literary and Philosophical Essays* (New York, 1844), 332–3, quoted by Foerster, *Fortunes of Epic Poetry*, 39.

[103] *Edinburgh Review*, 12 (Aug. 1808), in John O. Hayden (ed.), *Scott: The Critical Heritage* (London: Routledge and Kegan Paul, 1970), 37.

[104] John Morley, *Regency Design 1790–1840* (London: Zwemmer, 1993), ch. 6.

[105] 'On Pastoral Poetry', in Nathan Drake, *Literary Hours, or, Sketches Critical and Narrative* (Sudbury, 1798), 224.

[106] Mark Raymond, 'The Romantic Sonnet Revival: Opening the Sonnet's Crypt', *Literature Compass*, 4/3 (2007), 721–36, available at http://www.blackwell-synergy.com/toc/lico/4/3.

[107] [Joseph Ritson (ed.)], *Scotish Songs*, 2 vols (London, 1794), vol. i, p. lxxxi.

formidable challenges cannot be quickly summarized—much of this book is an attempt to answer this question—but certain strategies, relating especially to the problematic of time, can be singled out.

One strategy involves the fragment, a fashion for which originated with Macpherson's Ossian in the 1760s and was still going strong sixty years later when Keats published his *Poems* (1820). Authentic fragments, fake fragments, newly composed fragments, and completed poems repackaged as fragments filled the anthologies and magazines,[108] and numerous volumes of poetry, prose, and drama were published under this title. All the major Romantics experimented with the fragment, which has been called 'the romantic genre *par excellence*',[109] one which 'matches Romantic ideals and tone as fully and completely as the closed couplet matches the ideals of eighteenth-century neoclassicism'.[110] There is no doubt that, in the late eighteenth and early nineteenth centuries, the fragment flourished as a genre in its own right, with its own name, its own conventions, and, in Germany at least, an impressive body of theory attaching to it.[111] The paradigmatic quality of the fragment, however, rests not only on its importance as a self-contained genre but also on the fact that it functioned as what might be termed a mode of genericity, a way of performing any genre. To be a 'fragment' was a way of belonging and not belonging to a genre simultaneously; and hence of signalling the inaccessibility of a generic condition to which the text nonetheless aspires. It is this that makes the fragment, or fragmentariness, a potential solution to the cultural dilemma of 'making it old' and 'making it new' simultaneously. Fragmentariness provided the Romantic writer with a means of registering their belatedness in their chosen genre while still making an original contribution to it. Alternatively, fragmentariness was a way of invoking or 'sketching' (another key term in Romantic aesthetics[112]) a genre that had not yet come into being, or of which a full performance was not yet possible. In this case, the fragment serves as a foundation stone rather than a ruin, signalling the future possibilities of a

[108] For a list of examples, see Robert Mayo, 'The Contemporaneity of the *Lyrical Ballads*' (1954), in Alan R. Jones and William Tydeman (eds), *Wordsworth: 'Lyrical Ballads': A Casebook* (Basingstoke: Macmillan, 1972), 122.

[109] Philippe Lacoue-Labarthe and Jean-Luc Nancy, *The Literary Absolute: The Theory of Literature in German Romanticism* (1978), trans. Philip Barnard and Cheryl Lester (Albany: State University of New York Press, 1988), 40.

[110] D. F. Rauber, 'The Fragment as Romantic Form', *Modern Language Quarterly*, 30 (1969), 212–21: 214–15. See also Thomas McFarland, *Romanticism and the Forms of Ruin: Wordsworth, Coleridge, and the Modalities of Fragmentation* (Princeton: Princeton University Press, 1981); Balachandra Rajan, *The Form of the Unfinished: English Poetics from Spenser to Pound* (Princeton: Princeton University Press, 1989); Marjorie Levinson, *The Romantic Fragment Poem: A Critique of a Form* (Chapel Hill: University of North Carolina Press, 1986); Anne Janowitz, *England's Ruins: Poetic Purpose and the National Landscape* (Oxford: Blackwell, 1990); Elizabeth Wanning Harries, *The Unfinished Manner: Essays on the Fragment in the Later Eighteenth Century* (Charlottesville: University Press of Virginia, 1994); and Sophie Thomas, *Romanticism and Visuality: Fragments, History, Spectacle* (London: Routledge, 2008).

[111] For German Romantic theories of the fragment, see Rodolphe Gasché, 'Foreword: Ideality in Fragmentation', in Friedrich Schlegel, *Philosophical Fragments*, trans. Peter Firchow (Minneapolis: University of Minnesota Press, 1991).

[112] Richard Sha, *The Visual and Verbal Sketch in British Romanticism* (Philadelphia: University of Pennsylvania Press, 1998).

genre rather than generic depletion or authorial despair over the achievements of the past. This, too, constitutes a solution to the dilemma I have posed, and may be the reason why German theorists foregrounded the fragment in their quest for a genre theory that could embrace the literature of the future as well as that of the past.

Byron's *The Giaour: A Fragment of a Turkish Tale* (1813) is an example of the fragment as sketch, a poem that inaugurates a new genre but does so through a fragmentary version of it, offering the reader an enticing sample of a new literary product of which there is the promise of more to come. There is clearly an element of opportunism here. In 1813, a year after the publication of the first two cantos of *Childe Harold's Pilgrimage*, Byron was at the height of his fame, and author and publisher were both well aware that orientalism, metrical romance, and the fragment were three fashionable literary commodities the combination of which was likely to create another winning formula—as indeed it did.[113] But the strategy of working from fragment to full performance of a genre is artistically as well as commercially significant, and this pattern is repeated elsewhere in Byron's work, not least in *Don Juan* (1819–24), an experimental epic written and published incrementally over five years, and generically modified at each stage in response to public reactions. The strategy, however, was a risky one and its creative implications were complex, as the case of Keats's 'Hyperion', demonstrates. By labelling the first version of his epic (published in his *Poems*, 1820) 'A Fragment', Keats was doubtless exploiting the fashion for fragments, presenting his poem as an artfully constructed classical ruin. At another level, though, the label is an implicit acknowledgement of his failure to sustain the epic vision that the first two and a half books so confidently initiate—a failure which we know from his letters that he felt very keenly. On yet another level, however, the generic subtitle may be an indication of the paradoxical nature of the whole enterprise: a signal to the reader that a 'fragment' is the only form in which an authentically modern epic can exist. Keats's subsequent recasting of the poem as 'The Fall of Hyperion: A Dream' reinforces the point. More fragmentary still, the second poem (published posthumously in 1856) is a 'fallen' version of the first, and a reminder that epic itself, post-Milton, is a 'paradise lost', a genre of which modernity can only dream.[114] The instability of the poem's relation to epic—part sketch, part ruin—is echoed in the opening section of 'The Fall of Hyperion', where Keats ponders the status of his own imaginings, asserting the superiority of poetry to the dreams of fanatics, but conceding that it is ultimately for posterity to decide ('When this warm scribe my hand is in the grave'[115]) into which of the two categories his own work falls.

---

[113] For Byron's astute manipulation of publishing trends, see Jerome McGann, 'The Book of Byron and the Book of the World', in his *Beauty of Inflections*; Jerome Christensen, *Lord Byron's Strength: Romantic Writing and Commercial Society* (Baltimore: Johns Hopkins University Press, 1993); and Alan Rawes, *Byron's Poetic Experimentation: Childe Harold, the Tales, and the Quest for Comedy* (Aldershot: Ashgate, 2000).

[114] For a comparison of the two versions, see Jonathan Bate, 'Keats's Two Hyperions and the Problem of Milton', in Robert Brinkley and Keith Hanley (eds), *Romantic Revisions* (Cambridge: Cambridge University Press, 1992).

[115] John Keats, *The Complete Poems*, ed. John Barnard, 2nd edn (Harmondsworth: Penguin, 1997), 435 (line 16).

The connection between generic fragmentation and belatedness is revealed even more strikingly in Keats's 'Specimen of an Induction to a Poem' (published in *Poems*, 1817), whose strange title draws on yet another literary trend, related to the cult of the fragment, namely the taste for 'specimens' of English poetry, anthologized in collections such as George Ellis's *Specimens of the Early English Poets* (1790), Southey's *Specimens of the Later English Poets* (1807), and Lamb's *Specimens of English Dramatic Poets Who Lived About the Time of Shakespeare* (1808). Keats's poem is about the author's wish to 'tell a tale of chivalry', but the academic connotations of the word 'specimen' immediately establish a distance between Keats and his chosen genre. Indeed, he is doubly distanced, since this is merely a 'specimen' of an 'induction' to such a poem—the fragment of a fragment. Moreover, the poem of which it is intended to be an introductory sample never gets completed. 'Calidore', a Spenserian romance in rhyming couplets, is itself 'A Fragment', scarcely longer than the 'Specimen', and it offers only tantalizing glimpses of romance: a brief character sketch, an inconsequential boating episode, and surface details such as 'plumes', 'palfreys', and 'sweet-lipped ladies'. In both texts, Keats can merely gesture at, aspire to, or look back nostalgically on chivalric romance, not re-create it in any proper sense. 'Lo! I must tell a tale of chivalry,' he writes in the 'Specimen', not once but three times in the space of fifty lines. But the tale is not told, and the 'Specimen' is mainly about his inability to tell it:

> —then how shall I
> Revive the dying tones of minstrelsy,
> Which linger yet about lone gothic arches,
> In dark green ivy, and among wild larches?
> How sing the splendour of the revelries,
> When butts of wine are drunk off to the lees?[116]

Ostensibly, then, the poem is an attempt at a revival of romance but its real message is that revival is impossible, since the genre is expiring even as he tries to resuscitate it, 'dying tones' being all that remains of the once serene melody of 'golden-tongued romance' (as he calls it in his *Lear* sonnet). The cumbersome rubric of the title makes the poem sound like a schoolboy composition exercise, but the task is left unfinished, and Keats's poem, for all its playfulness, turns out to be a specimen not of a modern romance of chivalry but of a more painfully characteristic Romantic genre, a romance about the impossibility of romance, the type of self-reflexive, self-defeating poem that reaches its logical conclusion in Browning's 'Childe Roland to the Dark Tower Came' (1855). More conscious even than Keats's of its belatedness, Browning's poem is a metaromance in which failure is the very object of the quest, and the 'dark tower' of the title, like the 'lonely turret, shattered, and outworn' of 'Calidore', an emblem of a genre that is now only accessible in ruins.

As marginal performances of their chosen genre, both the 'Specimen' and 'Calidore' illustrate the use of the fragment as a mode of genericity, to signal synecdochally a genre yet to be invented or revived, or to represent residually a genre that is now

---

[116] Ibid. 56 (lines 31–6).

extinct. There are many variations on this extremely common technique. In Michael Bruce's 'The Musiad: A Minor Epic Poem. In the manner of Homer. A Fragment' (1770), fragmentation serves a double purpose, exploiting the Ossianic fashion for fragmentary epics while also solving the ticklish problem of how a 'peasant' poet (Bruce's father was a Kinross-shire weaver) could be allowed to write in a 'high' genre like epic. The Homeric reference in the title is intended as a guarantee of authenticity, signalling that what is offered is a primitive epic, albeit a newly composed one; but, as befits a peasant poet, it is a '*Minor* Epic Poem'—and merely a fragment of one. In fact, the whole exercise is a *jeu d'esprit*: 'The Musiad' is a miniature mock-epic about a mouse not a muse, and the title was probably editorial. Bruce had died prematurely, aged 21, in 1767. His posthumous *Poems on Several Occasions* (1770), edited by a student friend, taps into a number of publishing trends, including that of the Chattertonian boy genius. This adds yet another resonance to the idea of fragmentation, that of unfulfilled promise; and the word 'Minor', as well as being a joking allusion to the smallness of mice, may also be a play on the author's juvenile status—a pun that recurs elsewhere in Romantic-era publishing.[117]

Another 'specimen' poem that makes artful use of the poetics of fragmentation is John Thelwall's 'Specimens of The Hope of Albion, or, Edwin of Northumbria. An Epic Poem', published in his *Poems Chiefly Written in Retirement* (1801). In his Preface, Thelwall describes this as a sample of a new genre, the 'National Heroic', which 'was a *desideratum* in English Poetry' at the time his poem was first projected—the early 1790s—but had since been available in abundance.[118] The author's disappointment at being thus overtaken by literary fashion is palpable, and his genuinely frustrated ambition can be gauged by the frequency with which he returned to this poem over the rest of his life, without ever completing it.[119] Yet, as with our previous examples, the non-completion is itself aesthetically significant. As presented in the 1801 collection, Thelwall's 'Specimens' consist of an impressive array of prefatory texts including an Advertisement, an Argument, a Proposition, an Invocation, and an Introduction, but only two completed books of the epic poem proper. The oversupply of paratexts is as marked as the undersupply of the text, an editorial feature that suggests Thelwall is trying to turn misfortune to advantage by making 'specimens' of epic seem more desirable than the epic itself. That there was some such artistic logic behind this self-presentation is confirmed by Thelwall's next attempt at the genre, *The Trident of Albion: An Epic Effusion* (1805), written to celebrate the victory at Trafalgar. On this occasion, the seeming oxymoron of the subtitle is clearly not an acknowledgement of aesthetic failure—inability to complete

---

[117] For other examples, see David Duff, '"The Casket of my Unknown Mind": The 1813 Volume of Minor Poems', in Timothy Webb and Alan Weinberg (eds), *The Unfamiliar Shelley* (Aldershot: Ashgate, 2009), 53–4.

[118] John Thelwall, *Poems Chiefly Written in Retirement: The Fairy of the Lake, A Dramatic Romance; Effusions of Relative and Social Feeling; and Specimens of the Hope of Albion, or, Edwin of Northumbria. An Epic Poem* (Hereford, 1801), prefatory memoir, p. xliii.

[119] For the subsequent history of this poem, further parts of which were published in Thelwall's *The Vestibule of Eloquence* (1810) and elsewhere, see Judith Thompson, 'Overlooking History: The Case of John Thelwall', in Damian Walford Davies (ed.), *Romanticism, History, Historicism: Essays on an Orthodoxy* (London: Routledge, 2008).

a proper epic—but, on the contrary, a deliberate attempt to combine two equally strong but otherwise antithetical trends: the fashion for epics and the fashion for effusions. Besides being a clever marketing ploy, the generic subtitle is thus also an implicit signal that the proper form of 'national epic' for the modern age is the impromptu, lyrical kind, 'poured out, almost spontaneously, on the spur of the moment', in Thelwall's words, rather than the laboured, rule-bound narratives produced by conventional exponents of the genre.[120]

Thus described, Thelwall's poem invites comparison with Wordsworth's *Prelude*, an 'epic effusion' in all but name, and, like Thelwall's, a preliminary specimen of the bigger, better poem that Wordsworth promised would one day ensue. In the event, Wordsworth's *magnum opus*, *The Recluse*, was never completed, and *The Prelude* itself was known to the public in Wordsworth's lifetime only by his tantalizing reference to a 'preparatory poem' in the Preface to *The Excursion* (1814). It has been said that Wordsworth could not write his great philosophical poem, he could only write a prelude to it and an excursion from it. The joke conceals an important artistic fact about Romanticism: the gap between its generic ambitions and its actual perform- ances, and the habit of substituting prospectuses, preludes, and specimens for the thing itself. The pattern of deferral and non-delivery was conspicuous enough to a sceptical contemporary like Peacock for him to be able to satirize it in his *Paper Money Lyrics* (1825). As Kevin Barry has shown, Peacock's collection plays on the contemporary banknote controversy to expose the unreliability of Romantic aesthet- ics, reducing the vaunted ambitions of contemporary poets to a series of worthless promissory notes.[121] Among the poems offered for sale is a 'Proemium of an Epic which will shortly appear' (but of course doesn't). The putative author is Robert Southey, a favourite satirical target of Peacock but a somewhat unfair choice in this particular case since Southey was the one Romantic poet who could and did deliver on his promised epics—in full, and with alarming regularity.

In Barry's analysis of the Romantic 'paper economy', the paradigm of the poem as promissory note is 'Kubla Khan',[122] subtitled (in the 1816 printing) 'A Vision in a Dream. A Fragment'. For present purposes, Coleridge's poem is also the paradigm of generic fragmentariness turned into paradoxical strength. Much of the poem's power lies in its evocation of the narrative patterns and iconography of ancient epic or 'old romance'. In fifty-four lines, Coleridge presents in condensed form all the essential themes and motifs of epic romance, from heroic wars and the building of empires to enchanted landscapes and paradises lost. 'Kubla Khan', in other words, is not simply the fragment of a dream—a 'psychological curiosity', as Coleridge's prefatory note describes it—but the fragment of a genre, a complete imaginative world envisioned in its entirety but then shattered into pieces. Like the 'dying tones of minstrelsy' in Keats's 'Specimen of an Induction', the 'ancestral voices' half-heard in Coleridge's

---

[120] John Thelwall, *The Trident of Albion: An Epic Effusion* (Liverpool, 1805), p. v, quoted by Curran, *Poetic Form and British Romanticism*, 245 n. 6.

[121] Kevin Barry, 'The Aesthetics of Paper Money: National Differences during the Period of Enlightenment and Romanticism', in David Duff and Catherine Jones (eds), *Scotland, Ireland, and the Romantic Aesthetic* (Lewisburg, Pa.: Bucknell University Press, 2007), 72–3.

[122] Ibid. 69–71.

poem epitomize the predicament of the Romantic revivalist confronted with a remembered or imagined antiquity but able to re-create it only in fragments. The art of the Romantic fragment involves turning this predicament to creative advantage, exhuming and reanimating genres by deploying them in fragmentary form through carefully selected and artfully arranged traces. Coleridge does this in a supremely self-conscious way not only by internalizing the theme of generic revival ('Could I revive *within me* | Her symphony and song'[123]) but also by mythologizing the retrieval process itself through his prefatory fiction of dream composition, as if to imply that the archetypes of these ancient genres lie buried in his own unconscious. The fragmentary, unmediated quality of the generic material he resurrects is then highlighted as a proof of its authenticity.

If fragmentation is one way of making it old and making it new simultaneously, a second, equally common Romantic technique is conspicuous anachronism. Where writers of the 1760s, torn between progressive and primitivist impulses, had tried to conceal their anachronisms, to blur the boundaries of the past and present and create (or fabricate) a literature that would be both fashionably archaic and imperceptibly modern, their successors forty years later make a deliberate feature of anachronism, foregrounding the discrepancy between ancient and modern, and making this juxtaposition the essence of their appeal. The strategy is particularly visible in romance, a genre that had been conscious of its belatedness from its inception. Even in the original chivalric romances of Chrétien de Troyes and Marie de France, the genre had presented itself as an attempt imaginatively to retrieve an earlier, more colourful world—the days of King Arthur and of Charlemagne. Remembrance of lost time (real or imagined) is thus, in Bakhtin's term, the fundamental chronotope of romance.[124] By the time of Spenser, the genre had already accumulated multiple layers of memory: the self-conscious archaism of *The Faerie Queene* enacts a nostalgic revival of a medieval mode which was itself predicated on nostalgia, which means that romance had been both 'archaized' and 'internalized' long before the Romantics turned to the genre. It had also been parodied, almost to extinction: Thomas Nashe referred to the old romances as 'worne out absurdities',[125] a view echoed in many late sixteenth- and early seventeenth-century parodies, including Beaumont's *The Knight of the Burning Pestle* (1607) and Cervantes's *Don Quixote* (1605), both of which convert fashionable archaism into comic anachronism. By the mid-eighteenth cen-

---

[123] 'Kubla Khan, or, A Vision in a Dream', lines 42–3 (my italics), in *The Collected Works of Samuel Taylor Coleridge*, xvi: *Poetical Works*, ed. J. C. C. Mays, i: *Poems (Reading Text)*, 2 vols (London: Routledge and Kegan Paul, 2001), i. 514.

[124] 'Forms of Time and Chronotope in the Novel: Notes Toward a Historical Poetics' (1937–8), in Bakhtin, *Dialogic Imagination*. Bakhtin himself makes a different point, identifying the chronotope of the chivalric romance as a miraculous 'adventure-time' in which 'The unexpected, and only the unexpected, is what is expected' (152).

[125] *The Works of Thomas Nashe*, ed. Ronald B. McKerrow, rev. F. P. Wilson, 5 vols (Oxford: Oxford University Press, 1958), i. 26, quoted by Andrew King, 'Sidney and Spenser', in Corinne Saunders (ed.), *A Companion to Romance: From Classical to Contemporary* (Oxford: Blackwell, 2004), 149. For other hostile views of medieval romance in this period, see Vernon Hall, Jr, *Renaissance Literary Criticism: A Study of its Social Context* (New York: Columbia University Press, 1945), 203–7.

tury, the idea that Cervantes has demolished one genre and laid the foundations of another was commonplace: out of the 'ruins' of 'old romance', as Clara Reeve put it in her *Progress of Romance*,[126] had come the 'modern romance', or 'novel'. Ever since, verse romance had been living on borrowed time, leading a precarious existence in the shadow of its prosaic offspring and rival.

Implausibly, the Romantics resurrect 'old romance', turning the clock of literary history backwards by reverting to an earlier stage in the evolution of the genre and making it the basis of a 'new' kind of 'old' romance. But they do so in full knowledge of the anachronistic quality of the enterprise: a knowledge that could take ironic form, as in the burlesque pseudo-medievalism of John Hookham Frere's *Prospectus and Specimen of an Intended National Work, by William and Robert Whistlecraft... Intended to Comprise the Most Interesting Particulars relating to King Arthur and his Round Table* (1817); elegiac form, as in Scott's *The Lay of the Last Minstrel* (1805), whose title foregrounds the sense of temporal displacement and belatedness that inheres, now more acutely than ever, in Scott's chosen genre;[127] allegorical form, as in Keats's 'Poetic Romance' of *Endymion* (1817), a notionally complete romance, but one whose opening affirmation of the permanence of art ('A thing of beauty is a joy for ever') is undermined by its narrative of self-deception and disenchantment; or political form, as in Shelley's *Laon and Cythna, or, The Revolution of the Golden City. A Vision of the Nineteenth Century in the Stanza of Spenser* (1817), which uses the archaic medium of Spenserian romance to write about the quintessentially modern topic of political revolution.[128]

All four forms are embraced in Byron's *Childe Harold's Pilgrimage*. Subtitled 'A Romaunt' when the first two cantos were published to rapturous acclaim in 1812,[129] Byron's poem begins in Quixotic mode, humorously juxtaposing the ideals of chivalry with the realities of the modern world, and recoding the 'belatedness' trope as Harold's world-weary melancholia and sexual ennui. However, in the third and fourth cantos, published in 1816 and 1818, the satiric–elegiac tone of the opening cantos gives way to the more earnest, if no less troubled, voice of a narrator steeped in a quest for ultimate meanings. The genre evolves along with the poem, Byron updating his understanding of romance with each successive canto, in response to developments in modern poetry, to the poem's shifting public reception, and to the events in his own life which the poem enigmatically encodes. The strategy of anachronism (a bone of contention in the early reviews[130]) is sustained throughout,

[126] *Progress of Romance*, i. 8.

[127] For the ideological function and commercial appeal of this nostalgia, see Marlon B. Ross, 'Scott's Chivalric Pose: The Function of Medieval Romance in the Romantic Period', *Genre*, 18 (1986), 267–97; Michael Gamer, 'Marketing a Masculine Romance: Scott, Antiquarianism, and the Gothic', *Studies in Romanticism*, 32/4 (1993), 523–49; and Peter Murphy, *Poetry as an Occupation and an Art in Britain, 1760–1830* (Cambridge: Cambridge University Press, 1993), 142–70.

[128] See my *Romance and Revolution: Shelley and the Politics of a Genre* (Cambridge: Cambridge University Press, 1994), ch. 4.

[129] For the resonance of Byron's subtitle (dropped for Cantos 3 and 4), see Michael Vicario, 'The Implications of Form in *Childe Harold's Pilgrimage* I–II', *Keats–Shelley Journal*, 33 (1984), 103–29.

[130] Ronald A. Schroeder, 'Ellis, Sainte-Palaye, and Byron's "Addition" to the "Preface" of *Childe Harold's Pilgrimage* I–II', *Keats–Shelley Journal*, 32 (1983), 25–30.

but its tenor and purpose shift, so that what began as a Cervantesque parody of Scott and the chivalric revivalists (including Edmund Burke, whose famous lament for the 'age of chivalry' in his *Reflections on the Revolution in France* is ridiculed in the original Preface) ends as a series of trials in which different versions of romance idealism—ancient and modern—are tested and found wanting by the belated Romantic 'pilgrim'. For all its longevity and noble lineage, playfully invoked in the first Preface, romance is shown to be a genre whose centre cannot hold, and Byron's transactions with this, as with other literary genres in whose revival he participates, becomes, in the final analysis, a kind of endgame with genre: at once a revival of romance and a ransacking of it—its apotheosis and its epitaph.

The most spectacular example, however, of a Romantic author playing with time to creative effect is Coleridge's neo-gothic ballad 'The Rime of the Ancyent Marinere'. As Jerome McGann's influential reading made clear,[131] what Coleridge is imitating through the successive versions of the poem is not the 'ancient' ballad per se but the ancient ballad *as transmitted to modern readers* by editors such as Percy. This confirms Albert Friedman's point, in his classic study of the ballad revival, that the most influential poems in Percy were ones with which he took most editorial liberties: 'Sir Cauline', for example, from which Coleridge took the name of Christabel, was a composite ballad–romance, woven from different sources and completed by Percy.[132] Coleridge's addition of a pseudo-seventeenth-century marginal gloss to the 1817 version of 'The Ancient Mariner' adds yet another layer to the complex temporal stratification (all of it entirely fictitious) of the original, 1798 text. McGann interprets Coleridge's deliberate 'evolving' of his own poem as an imaginary implementation of the theories of textual transmission and interpretation in the German 'Higher Criticism' with which he was increasingly absorbed. It could also be seen, though, as self-conscious enactment of an evolutionary theory of genre, the multiplication of textual voices (mariner, narrator, marginal commentator, poet) mimicking both the process of accretion that characterizes the development of a primitive, oral genre like the ballad, and the editorial mediations and interpolations through which such genres were transmitted, in collections like Percy's *Reliques*, to a modern readership. In this sense, the poem is simply an extreme instance of the artificial 'ageing' of genres discussed earlier, the greater complexity of Coleridge's temporal fabrication reflecting his deeper self-consciousness about the paradoxes of generic revivalism, and his uniquely ingenious paratextual imagination. The modernization of the spelling, and the retitling of the poem as 'The Ancient Mariner. A Poet's Reverie', in the 1800 edition of *Lyrical Ballads*, reinforce rather than negate the point, being just one more stage in the poem's complicated textual evolution. By juxtaposing the word 'ancient' with the modern, Rousseauian term 'reverie', the 1800 title brings home even more forcibly the synthesis of ancient and modern

---

[131] 'The Ancient Mariner: The Meaning of the Meanings', in McGann, *Beauty of Inflections*.

[132] Albert B. Friedman, *The Ballad Revival: Studies in the Influence of Popular on Sophisticated Poetry* (Chicago: University of Chicago Press, 1961), 297–8; see also G. Malcolm Laws, Jr, *The British Literary Ballad: A Study in Poetic Imitation* (Carbondale: Southern Illinois University Press, 1972).

poetic modes that is the essence of *Lyrical Ballads* and of the Romantic literary revolution as a whole. The lurking sense of paradox, and parody, in Coleridge's enterprise is confirmed by the 1817 gloss, which, as Steven Jones astutely remarks, 'opens up an ironic countervoice on the main action of the ballad', thereby 'anticipating the inevitable parodies' which the poem did indeed attract.[133] This proleptic ironization, too, is part of the generic ageing process: in the course of his revisions, Coleridge takes the genre of the ballad across its entire life cycle from 'ancient' origins to parodic demise, as if acting out in a single text the theory of literary evolution posited a century later by the Russian Formalists.[134]

In different ways, most of the texts mentioned above also exemplify the evolutionary phenomenon Harold Bloom calls 'internalization', the process whereby literary genres, at a certain stage in their development, cease to represent external subject matter and become instead a vehicle for authorial self-reflection, including reflection on the nature of the genre itself.[135] As Bloom acknowledges, his theory of internalization is a refinement of one of Romanticism's own most suggestive insights, Friedrich Schiller's differentiation of two phases, or tendencies, in the history of poetry that he named 'naive' and 'sentimental', the latter characterized by self-consciousness and artifice, the former by spontaneity and naturalness.[136] Schiller's thesis is both a late reworking of the Ancients–Moderns issue and an intervention in the primitivism debate,[137] but it puts both discussions onto a new footing by incorporating fresh cultural explanations of the mutability of literary forms and an innovative literary psychology that cuts across traditional genre distinctions. Such ideas, although more fully developed in Germany, are not absent from British critical discourse of the period. In 1789 George Richards puzzled over similar questions in his *Essay on the Characteristic Differences between Ancient and Modern Poetry, and the Several Causes from which they Result* (1789). Like Schiller's, the essay is a sustained attempt to address the problem of literary time by showing how 'productions of the same species have been marked at distinct aeras by separate and even opposite characteristics'.[138] While never quite making the shift that Schiller does from a normative to a descriptive, psychological genre theory, Richards rejects the Enlightenment paradigm of overall 'progress' or 'decline', presenting a more nuanced picture of the development of literary forms and probing the cultural factors that account for that development, notably variations in language, national character, and—a particularly suggestive part of his argument—mythology.

---

[133] Steven E. Jones, *Satire and Romanticism* (New York: St Martin's Press, 2000), 52.

[134] Yuri Tynianov, 'On Literary Evolution' (1927), in Ladislav Matejka and Krystyna Pomorska (eds), *Readings in Russian Poetics: Formalist and Structuralist Views* (Cambridge, Mass.: Harvard University Press, 1971).

[135] 'The Internalization of Quest Romance'.

[136] Friedrich Schiller, *On Naïve and Sentimental Poetry* (1795–6), in H. B. Nisbet (ed.), *German Aesthetic and Literary Criticism: Winckelman, Lessing, Hamann, Herder, Schiller, Goethe* (Cambridge: Cambridge University Press, 1985).

[137] See Ernst Behler, *German Romantic Literary Theory* (Cambridge: Cambridge University Press, 1993), 95–110.

[138] George Richards, *An Essay on the Characteristic Differences between Ancient and Modern Poetry, and the Several Causes from which they Result* (Oxford, 1789), 1.

Later British criticism continues to explore the 'characteristic differences' between ancient and modern literature, drawing conclusions that often run remarkably similar to those of Schiller and Bloom. Reviewing Byron's Turkish tales *The Bride of Abydos* and *The Corsair* in 1814, Jeffrey calls attention to the introspective quality of modern literature as compared with the ancient. Observing the tendency of modern writers to dwell on the minutiae of their heroes' thoughts and feelings rather than on their external actions, he remarks: 'It is chiefly by these portraitures of the interior of human nature that the poetry of the present day is distinguished from all that preceded it—and the difference is perhaps most conspicuous when the persons and subjects are borrowed from the poetry of an earlier age.'[139] Coleridge, too, comments in *Biographia Literaria* on the modern '*striving to project* the inward' as distinct from 'the seeming ease with which the poetry of the ancients *reflects* the world without'.[140] John Wilson (Christopher North) writes in similar terms of Canto 4 of *Childe Harold's Pilgrimage*, centring his analysis on a comparison between Byron and Rousseau as two exemplars of a mode of 'empassioned self-delineation' which in each case had a trance-like effect on the reading public.[141] De Quincey, in his 'Lake Reminiscences' (1839), makes the absence of internalization in Southey's romances a specific ground of criticism: they are, he says, 'too intensely *objective*— too much reflect the mind, as spreading itself out upon external things—too little exhibit the mind, as introverting itself upon its own thoughts and feelings'.[142] Coleridge and De Quincey write with a knowledge of recent German theory,[143] but Jeffrey and Wilson operate within native intellectual traditions, in both cases with a robust Scottish scepticism about the phenomenon they describe. Peacock's comment (quoted earlier) on the 'puling sentimentality' of modern poetry and its wilful falsification of the past is even less sympathetic, but the terms of his argument are, again, remarkably similar to Schiller's. All of these accounts focus on the problem of self-consciousness: the inexorable growth of what an American reviewer called 'the habit of self-reflection and introspection, and the increase with time of the mind's disposition to direct its thoughts to the field of contemplation, rather than to that of action', which is so 'strikingly exemplified in the history of poetical literature'.[144]

Genre memory, invented and actual, was part of that self-consciousness, and its paradoxical effects were a defining feature of the spirit of the age. The problem of temporality was now central to critical discussion of genre, and temporal awareness was also a factor in the way literary genres were deployed. Keats, as we have seen, undertakes his 'tale of chivalry' in an almost academically self-conscious way, mimicking the rubric of historical poetry anthologies and analysing (while also sharing)

---

[139] *Edinburgh Review*, 23 (Apr. 1814), in Andrew Rutherford (ed.), *Byron: The Critical Heritage* (London: Routledge and Kegan Paul, 1970), 59.

[140] *Biographia Literaria*, ii. 235 n.

[141] *Edinburgh Review*, 30 (June 1818), in Rutherford (ed.), *Byron: Critical Heritage*, 151.

[142] 'Lake Reminiscences, No. IV: William Wordsworth and Robert Southey', *Tait's Edinburgh Magazine*, new ser., 6 (1839), in *The Works of Thomas De Quincey*, gen. ed. Grevel Lindop (London: Pickering and Chatto, 2000–3), xi. 122.

[143] See Chs 2 and 3 above.

[144] *North American Review*, 73 (n.d.), 130, quoted by Foerster, *Fortunes of Epic Poetry*, 100.

the cultural nostalgia that had produced the romance revival. Byron begins *Childe Harold's Pilgrimage* with an ostentatious display of erudition, not only of precursors in his chosen genre but also of the whole critical debate on the romance revival, including the politicization of that debate by Burke. Scott's *Lay of the Last Minstrel* draws on the same secondary literature, the author being himself a noted collector and theorist of ancient ballads and romances, and the theme of his *Lay*—the fate of medieval minstrelsy—a favourite antiquarian topic since Percy's essay on minstrels. Shelley writes *Laon and Cythna* with a sophisticated understanding of Spenserian allegory and a keen sense of the ideological affinities between chivalric idealism and modern political philosophy. The successive versions of Coleridge's 'Ancient Mariner' enact in a brilliantly ingenious way the textual methodologies and evolutionary theories of recent genre criticism. Such eclectic, ad hoc appropriations of modern literary theory may not be exactly what Friedrich Schlegel had in mind when he called for a 'progressive universal poetry' that would 'mix and fuse . . . inspiration and criticism',[145] nor is their idiosyncratic mix of archaism and innovation perhaps quite what he meant by a 'synthesis of the essentially modern and the essentially ancient'. Yet there are strong reasons for believing that contemporary British poetry, in its 'metaromantic' aspect, was a fuller realization of his aesthetic programme than most critics of his time and ours have acknowledged.

[145] *Athenaeum Fragments*, no. 116, in *Philosophical Fragments*, 31.

# 5

# The Combinatorial Method

The antique art and poetry separate, in a strict manner, things which are dissimilar; the romantic delights in indissoluble mixtures; all contrarieties: nature and art, poetry and prose, seriousness and mirth, recollection and anticipation, spirituality and sensuality, terrestrial and celestial, life and death, are blended together by them in the most intimate manner.... The former is more simple, clear, and like to nature in the self-existent perfection of her separate works; the latter, notwithstanding its fragment-like appearance, approaches more to the secret of the universe.

(August Wilhelm Schlegel, *Lectures on Dramatic Art and Literature*, trans. John Black, 1815)

This is the age of poetical experiment. We sometimes think that the *crania* of most of our modern Poets might not be unaptly considered as so many literary crucibles, in which all the materials furnished by the laboratory of the mind are heated by their fervid imaginations, and then poured out before the public with a full confidence that the heterogeneous mass has been transmuted into the pure gold of fine poetry. Within the limits of our own experience, there is scarcely a species of poetry that the ingenuity of the most fertile fancy could invent, which has not been ventured upon to attract the public favour.

(*Dublin Examiner*, No. 1, June 1816)

The 'modern–antique compounds' discussed in the previous chapter are part of a wider trend in Romanticism towards generically mixed forms of art. In *The Spirit of the Age* (1825), Hazlitt writes of the 'whirling, eccentric motion, the rapid, perhaps extravagant combinations of modern literature'.[1] Signs of that combinatorial impulse are, indeed, everywhere. A revolution in poetry is launched by a book, *Lyrical Ballads*, whose title conflates a high genre with a low, a classical with a modern; its collaborative authorship is another extravagant combination. The period's most successful poet, Lord Byron, while posing as a neoclassical purist, practises a form of writing that, as Walter Scott remarks, is 'didactic, sentimental, romantic, epic, pastoral, according to the taste of the moment'.[2] Scott's own poems and novels are no less eclectic, their felicitous blending of genres being one of the clues to their huge popularity. James Montgomery's *The Wanderer of Switzerland* (1806), another poem closely attuned to contemporary taste which Byron claimed 'was worth a thousand

---

[1] 'Mr. Gifford', *The Spirit of the Age*, in *The Complete Works of William Hazlitt*, ed. P. P. Howe, 21 vols (London: Dent, 1930–4), xi. 117.

[2] Review of *Childe Harold's Pilgrimage Canto IV*, *Quarterly Review*, 19 (1818), in Andrew Rutherford (ed.), *Byron: The Critical Heritage* (London: Routledge and Kegan Paul, 1970), 137.

Lyrical Ballads',[3] is introduced as a 'heroic subject . . . celebrated in a lyric measure, on a dramatic plan',[4] thus uniting all three parts of the modal triad. Dramatic composition itself had become, in Hazlitt's phrase, an entirely *'mixed mode'*,[5] embracing such heterogeneous works as M. G. Lewis's *The Castle Spectre*, 'a drama of a mingled nature, Operatic, Comical, and Tragical' (1797),[6] Shelley's neo-Aeschylean 'lyrical dramas' *Prometheus Unbound* (1820) and *Hellas* (1822), Thomas Lovell Beddoes's *Death's Jest Book: A Dithyrambic in the Florid Gothic Style* (1829),[7] and Charles Lamb's *John Woodvil: A Tragedy* (1802), described by its author as a 'medley . . . of laughter & tears, prose & verse & in some places rhime, songs, wit, pathos, humour, & if possible sublimity'.[8] In fiction the 'medley' principle is equally pervasive, whether it be in Thelwall's 'politico-sentimental' miscellany *The Peripatetic* (1793), the comic novels of Thomas Love Peacock (a 'new species of humorous writing' made out of several old ones[9]), or strangely titled books such as Dennis Lawler's *Vicissitudes in Early Life, or, The History of Frank Neville, a Serio-Comic, Sentimental, and Satirical Tale; Interspersed with Comic Sketches, Anecdotes of Living Characters, and Original Poetry; Elegiac, Amatory, Humourous, Lyrical, and Descriptive* (1808). The latter scarcely lives up to its flamboyant subtitle, but the promise of multiple genre-mixing is clearly intended as a selling point, and Lawler's *Bildungsroman* about a young playwright making his way in the world is thematically and formally typical of its time (at one level, it's an English *Wilhelm Meister*).

The association between Romanticism and genre-mixing does not, however, derive only from works of this kind, ubiquitous though they are. It derives also from Romantic theory—above all, German theory. Genre-mixing is a critical idea as well as a creative fact in this period, an idea that takes shape on the pages of *The Athenaeum* and *The Lyceum*, and in the lectures, conversations, and notebooks of the Jena circle. It is here that we find the conceptual link made between the 'romantic' and the generically mixed: in A. W. Schlegel's definition of 'romantic art' as that which 'delights in indissoluble mixtures';[10] in his brother Friedrich's description of a 'romantic book' as a type of writing 'where all the forms and all the genres

---

[3] *English Bards and Scotch Reviewers*, note to line 424, in Lord Byron, *The Complete Poetical Works*, ed. Jerome J. McGann, 7 vols (Oxford: Clarendon Press, 1980–93), i. 407.

[4] James Montgomery, *The Wanderer of Switzerland, and Other Poems* (London, 1806), preface, p. v.

[5] 'The Drama: No. IV', *London Magazine* (Apr. 1820), in *Complete Works*, xviii. 309.

[6] *St James's Chronicle* (16–19 Dec. 1797), quoted by Gillian Russell, 'Theatrical Culture', in Thomas Keymer and Jon Mee (eds), *The Cambridge Companion to English Literature 1740–1830* (Cambridge: Cambridge University Press, 2004), 102.

[7] Title of the second version (the β text), as transcribed for press in 1833, in H. W. Donner (ed.), *The Works of Thomas Love Beddoes* (London: Oxford University Press, 1935), 322.

[8] Letter to Robert Southey, 28 Nov. 1798, in *The Letters of Charles and Mary Lamb*, ed. Edwin W. Marrs, Jr, 3 vols (Ithaca, N.Y.: Cornell University Press, 1975–8), i. 152.

[9] Jerome de Groot, '"A New Species of Humorous Writing": Thomas Love Peacock and the Renegotiation of Genre', in Sharon Ruston (ed.), *The Influence and Anxiety of the British Romantics: Spectres of Romanticism* (Lewiston, N.Y.: Edwin Mellen Press, 1999).

[10] A. W. Schlegel, *A Course of Lectures on Dramatic Art and Literature*, trans. John Black, 2 vols (London, 1815), ii. 98 (lecture 12).

are mixed and interwoven',[11] or what he elsewhere calls 'a progressive universal poetry';[12] in Friedrich Schelling's claim that 'mixed genres' are the mark of modernity, and 'the *combination of opposites*' the fundamental principle of modern drama;[13] in Jean Paul's distinction between Taste, the neoclassical watchword, which 'can hardly separate the genres, styles, and kinds of poetry enough to satisfy itself', and Genius, 'which makes a whole of wholes, and which vaporizes and blends the genres in its fire';[14] and in many similar statements by Novalis and others. At times a speculative observation ('I can scarcely visualize a novel but as a mixture of story-telling, song, and other forms'[15]), at others an axiomatic command ('The romantic imperative demands the mixing of all genres'[16]), the theoretical connection between the 'romantic' and what Friedrich Schlegel christens the *Mischgedicht*,[17] the generically mixed work of art, becomes as indissoluble as the union of genres that the theory purports to describe. The shift from a classical poetics of generic separation to a Romantic poetics of generic mixture is compared by Friedrich Schlegel to Copernicus' discovery of the motion of the planets,[18] the same analogy Kant had used to describe the philosophical revolution of transcendental idealism (extending the parallel, Peter Szondi speaks of Schlegel's work as a fourth Kantian critique, a 'critique of poetical reason'[19]).

Yet, if Romantic literary historians have in general endorsed Schlegel's claim, scholars of other periods have challenged the idea that Romanticism is unique in this regard, reminding us that earlier periods too had delighted in indissoluble mixtures: that 'the combination or mixtures of forms and parts of forms had come to be taken for granted' by the mid-eighteenth century (Cohen);[20] that 'the heyday of

---

[11] *Kritische Friedrich Schlegel Ausgabe*, ed. Ernst Behler et al., 35 vols (Paderborn: Schöningh, 1958– ), xi. 159–60, quoted by Tzvetan Todorov, *Mikhail Bakhtin: The Dialogical Principle*, trans. Wlad Godzich (Manchester: Manchester Press, 1984), 86.

[12] *Athenaeum Fragments*, no. 116, in Friedrich Schlegel, *Philosophical Fragments*, trans. Peter Firchow (Minneapolis: University of Minnesota Press, 1991), 31–2 (punctuation adjusted).

[13] F. W. J. Schelling, *The Philosophy of Art*, trans. Douglas W. Scott (Minneapolis: University of Minnesota Press, 1989), 207, 267.

[14] MS, quoted in *Horn of Oberon: Jean Paul Richter's School for Aesthetics* (1804), trans. Margaret R. Hale (Detroit: Wayne State University Press, 1973), introd., 58.

[15] Friedrich Schlegel, *Dialogue on Poetry and Literary Aphorisms*, trans. Ernst Behler and Roman Struc (University Park: Pennsylvania State University Press, 1968), 102.

[16] Unpub. fragment of 1797, in Friedrich Schlegel, *Literary Notebooks, 1797–1801*, ed. Hans Eichner (Toronto: University of Toronto Press, 1957), 72 (no. 582).

[17] The term *Mischgedicht* appears in an unpublished fragment of 1797 as part of Schlegel's definition of the *Roman*: *Literary Notebooks*, 19 (no. 4). For the origins of the concept, see Hans Eichner, 'Friedrich Schlegel's Theory of Romantic Poetry', *Publications of the Modern Language Association of America*, 71 (1956), 1018–41 (1023); and id., *Friedrich Schlegel* (New York: Twayne, 1970), 59.

[18] *Athenaeum Fragments*, no. 434, in *Philosophical Fragments*, 90.

[19] Peter Szondi, 'Friedrich Schlegel's Theory of Poetical Genres: A Reconstruction from the Posthumous Fragments', in his *On Textual Understanding and Other Essays*, trans. Harvey Mendelsohn (Manchester: Manchester University Press, 1986), 76.

[20] Ralph Cohen, 'On the Interrelations of Eighteenth-Century Literary Forms', in Phillip Harth (ed.), *New Approaches to Eighteenth-Century Literature* (New York: Columbia University Press, 1974), 47.

sophisticated generic mixture' was the seventeenth century (Fowler);[21] that examples of 'bastard', 'hybrid' genres can be found throughout the Renaissance (Marino).[22] The counter-claims reach back further still. Medievalists point out that writers like Boccaccio and Chaucer used techniques of aggregation and juxtaposition to create their multi-genre masterworks, *The Decameron* and *The Canterbury Tales*.[23] Religious historians make similar claims about the generic construction of the Bible—a 'transcendental synthesis' of the theological kind.[24] And a recent article on classical genre theory argues that Horace's *Ars Poetica*, despite its famous prohibition against genre-mixing, was itself an example of 'generic hybridism', a poetic epistle about critical theory.[25] With so many analogues and anticipations, Schlegel's Copernican revolution begins to look like a reinvention of the wheel.

In some respects, this is a false antithesis. Recognition of the generically mixed character of earlier works of literature was central to the Romantic argument. *The Divine Comedy, The Decameron, Don Quixote*, the plays of Shakespeare, *Tristram Shandy*: these are the iconic, polymorphous texts around which the theory of the 'romantic' took shape. Used of literature, the word 'romantic' implied the same kind of hybridity found in the 'romance' languages. Coleridge, echoing German theorists, called these 'mixed languages' in which 'the decomposed Latin became amalgamated, in different proportions, with the Gothic or Celtic'; 'the word *Romantic* thus meant 'the mixed, as opposed to the *simple* or homogeneous'.[26] 'Romantic poetry', by extension, embraced everything from medieval romance to Shakespearean drama to the contemporary novel[27]—a great tradition of composite art which Romantic theorists frequently contrasted with the generic purity of classical literature. Some versions of Romantic theory dissolved even this distinction, and found generic mixture in the classical world. 'All poems of antiquity join one to the other', writes Friedrich Schlegel in his *Dialogue on Poetry* (1800), and 'Everything interpenetrates everything else.'[28] On this view,

[21] Alastair Fowler, *Kinds of Literature: An Introduction to the Theory of Genres and Modes* (Oxford: Clarendon Press, 1982), 309 n. 52; cf. Rosalie Colie, *The Resources of Kind: Genre-Theory in the Renaissance*, ed. Barbara K. Lewalski (Berkeley: University of California Press, 1973), ch. 3.

[22] Adrian Marino, 'A Definition of Literary Genres', in Joseph P. Strelka (ed.), *Theories of Literary Genre* (University Park: Pennsylvania State University Press, 1978), 52.

[23] Janet Levarie Smarr, 'Symmetry and Balance in the *Decameron*', *Mediaevalia*, 2 (1976), 159–87; Helen Cooper, *The Structure of 'The Canterbury Tales'* (London: Duckworth, 1983).

[24] See e.g. Marvin A. Sweeney, *Form and Intertextuality in Prophetic and Apocalyptic Literature* (Tübingen: Mohr Siebeck, 2005); David Damrosch, *The Narrative Covenant: Transformations of Genre in the Growth of Biblical Literature* (San Francisco: Harper and Row, 1987).

[25] Joseph Farrell, 'Classical Genre in Theory and Practice', *New Literary History*, 34/3 (2003), 383–408: 394.

[26] Prospectus to 1812–13 lecture series, in *The Collected Works of Samuel Taylor Coleridge*, v: *Lectures 1808–1819 On Literature*, ed. R. A. Foakes, 2 vols (London: Routledge and Kegan Paul, 1987), i. 481.

[27] As defined by Friedrich Schlegel, who uses *romantische Poesie, Romanpoesie*, and *Roman* almost interchangeably: see Eichner, 'Friedrich Schlegel's Theory of Romantic Poetry'. Coleridge's definition of 'Romantic Poetry' (e.g. in the Prospectus cited in my previous note) excludes the novel but follows A. W. Schlegel in connecting medieval romance with the 'Romantic Drama' of Shakespeare. For a comprehensive survey of this terminology, see Hans Eichner (ed.), *'Romantic' and its Cognates: The European History of a Word* (Manchester: Manchester University Press, 1972).

[28] *Dialogue on Poetry*, 82.

'romantic' poetry, with its compulsive intermixing of genres, was an attempt to recover the essence of *classical* literature. In yet another version of the theory, 'romantic' and 'classical' ceased to be historical categories at all, designating instead two archetypal, form-creating tendencies present, to varying degrees, in all literary periods: the romantic is the principle of miscegenation, the classical that of separation.[29] Works, authors, eras are characterized by the predominance of one or other principle.

The coexistence in Romantic theory of these conflicting definitions and rival accounts of the history of genre-mixing has left lasting confusions. Modern critics have added to the confusion by selectively appropriating aspects of Romantic theory and adding their own gloss: in Bakhtin's case, by converting the Schlegelian concept of romantic poetry (which explicitly embraces both poetry and prose) into a theory of the novel (defined by Bakhtin in diametric opposition to poetry);[30] in Kristeva's, by broadening Schlegel's notion of the 'interpenetration' of genres into a general theory of 'intertextuality' (the text as a 'mosaic of quotations').[31] Derrida, citing Lacoue-Labarthe and Nancy's influential exposition of German Romanticism, performs a final displacement of transcendental poetics by interpreting Schlegel's call for the universalization of the *Mischgedicht* as a deconstructive argument about the self-contradictoriness of generic categories.[32] The entire dialectic of Romantic theory reduces to the poststructuralist cliché that all works are generically mixed, all genres hybrids of other genres, and every act of belonging to genre simultaneously a subversion of that act.

The aim of this chapter is to disentangle these threads by re-examining Romantic ideas about genre-mixing and setting them against some of the period's own experiments in generic combination. My first section analyses eighteenth-century ideas on which Romanticism builds, and appeals to German theory, with its fuller conceptualization of genre-mixing, to help interpret British developments. In German

---

[29] For examples of this 'archetypal' definition, see Lilian R. Furst, *The Contours of European Romanticism* (London: Macmillan, 1979), ch. 1.

[30] 'Discourse in the Novel' (1934–5), in *The Dialogic Imagination: Four Essays by M. M. Bakhtin*, ed. Michael Holquist, trans. Caryl Emerson and Michael Holquist (Austin: University of Texas Press, 1981). For Bakhtin's extensive borrowing from German Romanticism, see Todorov, *Mikhail Bakhtin*, 85–90; Jennifer Wise, 'Marginalizing Drama: Bakhtin's Theory of Genre', *Essays in Theatre*, 8/1 (1989), 15–22; and Galen Tihanov, 'Bakhtin, Lukács and German Romanticism: The Case of Epic and Irony', in Carol Adlam et al. (eds), *Face to Face: Bakhtin in Russia and the West* (Sheffield: Sheffield Academic Press, 1997).

[31] Kristeva's concept of intertextuality originates in her early work on Bakhtin, e.g. 'Word, Dialogue, and Novel' (1967), in Julia Kristeva, *Desire in Language: A Semiotic Approach to Literature and Art*, ed. Leon S. Roudiez (Oxford: Blackwell, 1981), and is developed in her *Revolution in Poetic Language* (1974), trans. Margaret Waller (New York: Columbia University Press, 1984). For the conceptual gains and losses in her influential recasting of Bakhtinian poetics (and ultimately of Romantic theory), see my 'Intertextuality versus Genre Theory: Bakhtin, Kristeva and the Question of Genre', *Paragraph: A Journal of Modern Critical Theory*, 25/1 (2002), 54–73.

[32] 'The Law of Genre' (1980), trans. Avital Ronell, in Jacques Derrida, *Acts of Literature*, ed. Derek Attridge (London: Routledge, 1992); Philippe Lacoue-Labarthe and Jean-Luc Nancy, *The Literary Absolute: The Theory of Literature in German Romanticism* (1978), trans. Philip Barnard and Cheryl Lester (Albany: State University of New York Press, 1988). Cf. Timothy Clark, 'Modern Transformations of German Romanticism: Blanchot and Derrida on the Fragment, the Aphorism and the Architectural', *Paragraph: A Journal of Modern Critical Theory*, 15/3 (1992), 232–47.

Romanticism, generic experiment is often theory-driven and critical speculation arguably exceeds practical accomplishment. The British situation is different: creative practice remains in advance of theory. It is in Britain, though, that we see most clearly the distinction between what I call 'rough-mixing' and 'smooth-mixing', two different ways of combining genres both of which, I argue, are equally important to Romantic literature. 'Smooth-mixing' is the more familiar kind, the seamless fusion of forms typically associated with biological metaphors of organic unity. 'Rough-mixing', by contrast, involves juxtaposition rather than synthesis, a method of combining genres which the Romantics frequently described in chemical rather than biological terms. My second and third sections explore this distinction, and reveal a political dimension to it by tracing connections with the writing practices of the French Revolution debate. In my final section, I discuss the convergence of theory and practice in the work of Shelley, whose reworking of combinatorial poetics in his theory of the 'great poem' provides a key to his boldest experiment in genre-mixing, *Prometheus Unbound*.

## ORIGINS AND ABSOLUTES

The adoption of genre-mixing as an aesthetic ideal reverses a critical tradition dating back to classical antiquity which had prohibited the mixing of genres and treated hybrid works as indecorous or monstrous (the half-woman, half-fish of Horace's *Ars Poetica*[33]). The shift from a critical dispensation in which genre-mixing was condemned to one in which it was welcomed and even demanded was as great as any in the history of criticism. This remains true even if we acknowledge the partial anticipations of this idea in earlier criticism and the many instances of genre-mixing in earlier literature. With few exceptions, previous critical endorsements of genre-mixing were confined to specific formal combinations and involved a loosening of classificatory boundaries, or a recognition of the connectedness of genres within some overarching system, rather than an abandonment of the principle of generic separation. Joseph Trapp's neoclassical definition of epic, for example, as a genre which 'comprehends within its Sphere all the other Kinds of Poetry whatever'[34] is certainly, as Ralph Cohen notes, an argument for the interrelation of genres and the possibility of combining them in this particular form of writing. Trapp's definition takes its cue from Plato and Aristotle, who had defined epic as a mixed mode

---

[33] 'Imagine a painter who wanted to combine a horse's neck with a human head, and then clothe a miscellaneous collection of limbs with various kinds of feathers, so that what started out at the top as a beautiful woman ended in a hideously ugly fish. If you were invited, as friends, to the private view, could you help laughing? Let me tell you, my Piso friends, a book whose different features are made up at random like a sick man's dreams, with no unified form to have a head or a tail, is exactly like that picture'; Horace, *Ars Poetica*, lines 1–9, in D. A. Russell and M. Winterbottom (eds), *Ancient Literary Criticism: The Principal Texts in New Translations* (Oxford: Oxford University Press, 1972), 279.

[34] Joseph Trapp, *Lectures on Poetry: Read in the Schools of Natural Philosophy at Oxford; Translated from the Latin, with Additional Notes* (London, 1742), 10, cited by Cohen as evidence of eighteenth-century acceptance of genre-mixing ('Interrelations of Literary Forms', 38).

combining narration (diegesis) and direct speech (mimesis); the notion of comprehensiveness was a later extrapolation, dating from the Renaissance, intended to reinforce the epic's claim to pre-eminence in the hierarchy of genres.[35] Inclusiveness, however, did not mean open-endedness. The component parts of epic and the manner in which they were to be combined were carefully prescribed, formal unity being assured by a fixed metre (the heroic couplet) and other kinds of linguistic and structural decorum. In other words, the genre was more rather than less regulated for being mixed, and there was no question of suspending generic distinctions and rules; on the contrary, as Trapp's precursor Scaliger emphasized, the epic, by virtue of its inclusiveness, supplied 'the universal controlling rules for the composition of each other kind'.[36]

The same can be said of verse satire, often defined in neoclassical theory as a mixed genre but of a strictly determinate kind, with narrative, descriptive, and didactic elements integrated in a particular way and for specific effects.[37] In later phases of neoclassicism, the interrelatedness of genres became more generally recognized and the range of acceptable combinations broadened, as we saw in the genre-systems of Enlightenment critics like Hugh Blair, which incorporate numerous modal subdivisions and generic combinations.[38] In part, this more flexible approach proceeded from the realization that, as Kames put it in his *Elements of Criticism* (1762), 'literary compositions run into each other, precisely like colours: in their strong tints they are easily distinguished; but are susceptible of so much variety, and take on so many different forms, that we never can say where one species ends and another begins'.[39] The acknowledgement of generic overlap and interconnection did not, however, alter the basic paradigm: even the most advanced critical treatises of the Enlightenment still conceived of genres as discrete entities susceptible to tabulation and hierarchical ordering, and individual texts were still regarded as belonging to a single genre, however comprehensive. The proliferation of subcategories in works such as Blair's was simply an attempt to refine the classification system by specifying the possible combinations.

Wordsworth's notion of the 'composite species', in his Preface to *Poems* (1815), takes this taxonomic approach one step further.[40] By turning generic combination into the actual name of a genre, and including it in his theoretical genre-system, Wordsworth implies that genre-mixing is as legitimate as any other form of com-

---

[35] For Renaissance accounts of epic as the most 'encyclopedic' of genres, embracing all subjects, forms, and styles, see Barbara Kiefer Lewalski, *'Paradise Lost' and the Rhetoric of Literary Forms* (Princeton: Princeton University Press, 1985), ch. 1. The primitivist theory of epic, discussed below, reformulates the idea of inclusiveness in terms of a primal unity of genres.

[36] Julius Caesar Scaliger, *Select Translations from Scaliger's Poetics*, trans. Frederick Morgan Padelford (New York: Holt, 1905), 54.

[37] Howard D. Weinbrot, *The Formal Strain: Studies in Augustan Imitation and Satire* (Chicago: University of Chicago Press, 1969); P. K. Elkin, *The Augustan Defence of Satire* (Oxford: Clarendon Press, 1973).

[38] See Ch. 1 above, pp. 45–56.

[39] Henry Home, Lord Kames, *Elements of Criticism*, 3 vols (Edinburgh, 1762), iii. 219.

[40] *The Prose Works of William Wordsworth*, ed. W. J. B. Owen and Jane Worthington Smyser, 3 vols (Oxford: Clarendon Press, 1974), iii. 28.

position. His later renaming of the category as 'composite order' reinforces the point, bestowing on this type of writing the legitimacy of a classical architectural style ('composite order' is a term used in Renaissance art theory to designate the mixed style of architectural design added by the Romans to the three original Greek 'orders'—Doric, Ionic, and Corinthian—elements of which it combined). Nevertheless, Wordsworth defines the category very restrictively: 'composite order' refers to one particular poetic combination—of 'the Idyllium', 'the Didactic', and 'philosophical Satire'—and he gives only two examples of it, Young's *Night Thoughts* and Cowper's *The Task*. He makes no attempt to extend the term to other kinds of genre-mixing, or to accommodate his own experiments with composite forms, notably the 'lyrical ballad' (a label which would be tautologous according to his 1815 classification, where 'ballad' is listed as a subset of 'The Lyrical'). In omitting these from his system, Wordsworth stops short of a general endorsement of genre-mixing. There is nothing in the 1815 Preface that approximates to A. W. Schlegel's much broader notion of a 'romantic' poetry which 'delights in indissoluble mixtures', though Wordsworth was probably familiar with this idea since he alludes to Schlegel's doctrine of organic form (which is part of the same argument from the *Lectures on Dramatic Art and Literature*) in his 'Essay, Supplementary to the Preface'.[41] The distance between the two writers is suggested by the fact that Wordsworth uses a metaphor from *classical* architecture for genre-mixing, while reserving the analogy with *romantic* architecture for what was, at this point, a more important idea for him, namely the essential unity of his œuvre (in the 1814 Preface to *The Excursion*, he describes the relationship of his shorter poems to his 'main Work' as like that of the 'little cells, oratories, and sepulchral recesses' to the nave of a 'gothic church'[42]). As we saw in Chapter 2, Wordsworth's critical discourse remains suspended, figuratively and conceptually, between two opposed paradigms.

In German Romanticism, a more radical theoretical shift occurs. Genre-mixing comes to be seen not as a selective, incremental process affecting only certain genres and blurring boundaries, but as a pervasive, transformative phenomenon which dissolves even the firmest of distinctions and puts in question the entire system of generic classifications. The strongest exponent of this view is Friedrich Schlegel, who places genre-mixing, or what he calls his 'theory of the combinatorial method' (*Theorie der combinator[ischen] Methode*)[43] at the centre of his literary philosophy. Schlegel's concept of *Mischgattung*,[44] the mixed genre, and of *Mischgedicht*, the generically mixed artwork, have usually been seen as manifestations of the Romantic idea of unity-in-difference, the relation of parts to whole expressed by the doctrine of organic form. Organic–biological metaphors certainly appear in his work, but an

---

[41] Ibid. iii. 69.

[42] Ibid. iii. 5–6.

[43] *Kritische Friedrich Schlegel Ausgabe*, xviii. 448 (no. 190), quoted by Michel Chaouli, *The Laboratory of Poetry: Chemistry and Poetics in the Work of Friedrich Schlegel* (Baltimore: Johns Hopkins University Press, 2002), 108–9.

[44] Like *Mischgedicht* (see n. 17 above), the term *Mischgattung* appears in Schlegel's unpublished fragments of 1797 as part of his theory of the *Roman*: see *Literary Notebooks*, 24 (no. 55).

analogy he uses much more frequently is with chemistry, a field of knowledge actually known at the time as the 'science of mixing' (*Mischungskunde*).[45] As Michel Chaouli and others have shown, chemical terminology pervades Schlegel's writings, providing figurative descriptions not only of his objects of study—genres, texts, form, the compositional process—but also of his own investigative methods and writing practices.[46] According to Schlegel, literature, like chemistry, is an 'experimental' activity. Chemical experiments mix substances; textual experiments mix genres. Alternatively, textual experimentation involves the *un*mixing of genres: the breaking down of literary compounds into their constituent elements, a process analogous to chemical analysis. Once separated out, the elements can then be recombined in new arrangements. Chemistry, the science of mixing, has a rich vocabulary to describe these various kinds of linkage and separation, making subtle distinctions between 'binding', 'melding', 'permeating', 'mixing', and 'combining' (*verbinden, verschmelzen, durchdringen, mischen, kombinieren*), and between 'separating' and 'dividing' (*scheiden, trennen*).[47] Schlegel makes use of all these terms, and deploys them with sufficient persistence, precision, and originality to justify his claim to have effected a '*revolution* in the field of aesthetics' which 'corresponds very precisely' to the revolution in natural philosophy.[48]

    What is revolutionary is not simply the idea that genre-mixing is more widespread than previously recognized and that more kinds of combination are possible. Schlegel sees the entire literary system as consisting of 'eternally uniting and separating powers',[49] and the *Mischgattung* or *Mischgedicht* as the norm not the exception. Unlike the static, finite forms described in neoclassical genre theory, he pictures genres as 'progressive' structures, shaped and reshaped across time, and 'capable of an infinite transformation'.[50] He also sees them as subject to relations of dominance and subordination, not because of any intrinsic hierarchy of genres, as in neoclassical theory, but because, like chemical elements, genres attract or repel one another, with varying degrees of strength. In any given period, one genre tends to dominate and modify the others, an idea Schlegel captures through the chemical metaphor of permeation or staining: 'Just as the novel colors all modern poetry', he writes in *Athenaeum* fragment 146, 'so satire colors [*tingiert*] and, as it were, sets the tone for all Roman poetry, yes, even the whole of Roman literature.'[51] The combinatorial

---

[45] Peter Kapitza, *Die frühromantische Theorie der Mischung: Über den Zusammenhang von romantischer Dichtungstheorie und zeitgenössischer Chemie* (Munich: Max Hueber Verlag, 1968), 12–13.

[46] Chaouli, *Laboratory of Poetry*; Matthew Tanner, 'Chemistry in Schlegel's *Athenäum* Fragments', *Forum for Modern Language Studies*, 31/2 (1995), 140–53.

[47] Chaouli, *Laboratory of Poetry*, 86.

[48] Notebook entry of 1812, in *Kritische Friedrich Schlegel Ausgabe*, xvii. 371 (no. 258), quoted by Chaouli, *Laboratory of Poetry*, 121.

[49] *Athenaeum Fragments*, no. 412, in *Philosophical Fragments*, 83.

[50] Unpub. fragment of 1798–1801, in *Literary Notebooks*, 186 (no. 1880), quoted by Szondi, 'Schlegel's Theory of Poetical Genres', 87.

[51] *Philosophical Fragments*, 36. A similar idea appears in an unpublished fragment of 1797: 'Three dominant genres [*herrschende Dichtarten*]. 1) Tragedy among the Greeks; 2) Satire among the Romans; 3) The novel among the moderns' (*Literary Notebooks*, 22 (no. 32), quoted by Szondi, 'Schlegel's Theory of Poetical Genres', 87).

theory supplies, too, a rationale for Schlegel's own compositional techniques, notably his use of the fragment, or the *collection* of fragments. As he explains in his study of Lessing (1797), fragmentation is as much part of the combinatorial process as mixing, because the more separations there are, the more combinations will ensue; the juxtaposition of disparate fragments thus has, paradoxically, a unifying effect, for 'only when a plenitude of heterogeneous substances are united can new chemical combinations and their permeations occur'.[52] The 'totality' thereby produced is different, however, from the unity postulated by classicism, since its premiss is contrast rather than consistency or 'decorum'. The discontinuities of subject matter, argument, and tone in the fragment collections of *The Athenaeum* and *The Lyceum* and in other, unpublished collections, illustrate this compositional logic. Each reader must discover his or her own set of affinities among the ideas expressed, assembling the fragments, as it were, in a new way.

The explanatory power of Schlegel's 'theory of the combinatorial method' is attested by its influence both on his contemporaries and on later schools of literary theory. No less impressive are his applications of the theory. His best-known piece of applied criticism is his 1798 review of Goethe's *Wilhelm Meister's Apprenticeship*, a brilliantly insightful essay known punningly to his friends as the 'Übermeister', where he analyses the novel's experimental form while also explaining *Meister's* theorization of itself—Goethe's dissolving of the boundary between literature and criticism being one of the many generic innovations to which Schlegel calls attention. To judge this 'absolutely new and unique book' according to conventional ideas of genre, writes Schlegel, would be 'as if a child tried to clutch the stars and the moon in his hand and pack them in his satchel'.[53] The need for a new theory of genre adequate to Goethe's revolutionary text is part of the stimulus for Schlegel's development of a combinatorial poetics, and for what some critics see as his 'conversion' from the neoclassicism of his *Study of Greek Poetry* (1797). In the earlier study (completed by 1795), Schlegel had condemned the '*anarchy*' of modern literature, rejecting as 'infelicitous' its 'artificial assemblages' and 'chemical experiments in the arbitrary division and mixture of the original arts and the pure types of art'.[54] By 1798 he was claiming precisely the opposite, and his volte-face on this question owes much to the inspiration of Goethe, whose own ambivalence towards genre-mixing (resistant in theory, indulgent in practice) was never resolved[55] but whose recent compositions had helped to convince Schlegel that a generically mixed work could be as artistically satisfying as a generically 'pure' work. Goethe, he now recognized, had

[52] *Kritische Friedrich Schlegel Ausgabe*, iii. 84, quoted by Chaouli, *Laboratory of Poetry*, 128.

[53] Friedrich Schlegel, 'On Goethe's *Meister*' (1798), in J. M. Bernstein (ed.), *Classic and Romantic German Aesthetics* (Cambridge: Cambridge University Press, 2003), 275. For *Meister's* impact on German theory, see Ernst Behler, *German Romantic Literary Theory* (Cambridge: Cambridge University Press, 1993), 165–80; and Marshall Brown, 'Theory of the Novel', in Brown (ed.), *The Cambridge History of Literary Criticism*, v: *Romanticism* (Cambridge: Cambridge University Press, 2000), 263–8.

[54] Friedrich Schlegel, *On the Study of Greek Poetry*, trans. Stuart Barnett (Albany: State University of New York Press, 2001), 19, 30.

[55] For Goethe's divided views on this matter, see René Wellek, *A History of Modern Criticism: 1750–1950*, i: *The Later Eighteenth Century* (New Haven: Yale University Press, 1955), 212–15.

achieved a double synthesis, combining disparate genres while also uniting the strengths of ancient and modern art. As Andrea puts it in the *Dialogue on Poetry*, Goethe had provided a compelling demonstration of how to 'explore the forms of art back to their sources in order to be able to revive or combine them', thereby releasing 'the old power, the sublime spirit' which lies 'dormant' within.[56]

As the supreme contemporary exponent of the *Mischgedicht*, Goethe is part of what Friedrich Schlegel calls 'the great triple chord of modern poetry', along with Dante and Shakespeare.[57] The centrality of these three writers to Romantic theories of genre-mixing is confirmed by other German critics. Like his brother, A. W. Schlegel hails Dante as the 'father of modern poetry', and praises *The Divine Comedy* as a 'unique synthesis of the most heterogeneous elements'.[58] Schelling makes a similar claim in his *Philosophy of Art*, characterizing *The Divine Comedy* as 'neither dramatic, epic, nor lyrical, but rather a completely unique, singular, and incomparable combination of them all', a truly 'universal' poem that represents 'the most indissoluble mixture, the most complete interpenetration of everything' and is thus 'prophetic and prototypical for the entirety of modern poesy'.[59] Where British critics such as Boyd had recognized that Aristotelian categories were rendered redundant by Dante's poem,[60] Schelling goes much further, declaring that it 'requires its own theory, constitutes its own genre, and is a world unto itself' (p. 239). Readers unwilling to rise to this artistic and intellectual challenge, says Schelling, 'should apply the words at the beginning of the first part to themselves: "Leave all hope, ye that enter"' (p. 247). Jean Paul is even more emphatic, his contemplation of Dante's transcendent originality provoking a cascade of dazzling metaphors: 'When Dante's spirit wanted to appear on earth, the epic, lyric, and dramatic eggshells and skulls were too narrow for him; he then dressed himself in vast night and in flame and in heaven's ether all at once, and thus hovered only half-embodied among the strongest, sturdiest critics.'[61]

Combinatorial interpretation of Shakespeare begins with Herder, whose early essay on Shakespeare (1773) highlights the multiplicity of genres and styles that his plays 'combined into a marvellous whole'.[62] Rejecting neo-Aristotelian approaches, Herder insists on the differences between ancient and modern drama, berating the inability of textual editors like Warburton and historical critics like Kames to provide an adequate context for Shakespeare or explain his artistic methods. He reserves particular scorn for one recent German commentator who had 'had the bright idea' of making Polonius into his Aristotle, and taking seriously

---

[56] *Dialogue on Poetry*, 74.

[57] *Athenaeum Fragments*, no. 247, in *Philosophical Fragments*, 52.

[58] A. W. Schlegel, *Geschichte der romantischen Literatur* (1803–4), quoted by Judith Ryan, 'Hybrid Forms in German Romanticism', in Joseph Harris and Karl Reichl (eds), *Prosimetrum: Crosscultural Perspectives on Narrative in Prose and Verse* (Cambridge: D. S. Brewer, 1997), 167. Cf. Friedrich Schlegel, *Dialogue on Poetry*, 67–8.

[59] *Philosophy of Art*, 239, 247.

[60] See Ch. 1 above, p. 44.

[61] *Horn of Oberon: Jean Paul Richter's School for Aesthetics*, 180.

[62] 'Shakespeare', in Herder's *On German Character and Art* (1773), in Timothy J. Chamberlain (ed.), *Eighteenth Century German Criticism* (New York: Continuum, 1992), 151.

the pedantic generic labels that Shakespeare mocked in Act II of *Hamlet*.[63] 'Who would want to build a theory upon that?', asks Herder; Polonius 'is intended to be just a great baby' in this passage. 'And what virtue lies in the distinctions tragedy, comedy, history, pastoral, pastoral–comical or comical–historical–pastoral? And were we to shuffle those-cals a hundred times, what insight would we have in the end? Not one single play would be a Greek tragedy, comedy or pastoral, nor should it be' (p. 160). To make sense of the unique formal properties of Shakespeare's plays, and the theatrical culture out of which they emerged, something more is needed than a static classification system, however subtle its subdivisions and cross-links. Herder's long search for an alternative approach culminates in the argument put forward in his *Letters for the Advancement of the Humanities* (1793–7) that Shakespeare's plays are a reworking of the genre of the *Roman*, whose origins lie in the mixing (*Mischung*) of languages and art forms in the Middle Ages.[64]

Herder's account of the *Roman* as an intrinsically mixed genre, seminal not only for Shakespeare but for the whole of modern (i.e. post-classical) literature, is a major source for Schlegel's theory of 'romantic poetry' (*romantische Poesie*).[65] Extending Herder's evolutionary approach, Schlegel broadens the category of the *Roman* still further, and develops Herder's notion of linguistic and formal *Mischung* into a full-blown combinatorial poetics. At its epicentre, in *Athenaeum* fragment 116, is Schlegel's famous definition of romantic poetry as 'a progressive universal poetry' (*eine progressive Universalpoesie*), an art form so inclusive that it would embrace the entire spectrum of literary forms as well as other modes of thought, expression, and behaviour. The aim of such poetry, he declares,

isn't merely to reunite all the separate species of poetry and put poetry in touch with philosophy and rhetoric. It tries to and should mix and fuse [*bald mischen, bald verschmelzen*] poetry and prose, inspiration and criticism, the poetry of art and the poetry of nature; and make poetry lively and sociable, and life and society poetical; poeticize wit and fill and saturate [*anfüllen und sättigen*] the forms of art with every kind of good, solid matter for instruction, and animate them with the pulsations of humor. It embraces everything that is purely poetic, from the greatest systems of art, containing within themselves still further systems, to the sigh, the kiss that the poetizing child breathes forth in artless song.[66]

What Schlegel means here by the 'purely poetic' is not the ethereal quality described by Joseph Warton in his critique of Pope: a lyrical essence uncontaminated by didactic and satiric intent, or by an admixture of the prosaic.[67] On the contrary, for Schlegel poetry is at its purest—its most 'ideal' and 'transcendental'—when it is at its most composite: when it combines verse and prose, and its forms are 'saturated' with instructional content and animated by wit. The essence of the romantic is its

[63] Heinrich Wilhelm von Gerstenberg, in letter 17 of his periodical *Briefe über Merkwürdigkeiten der Literatur*, 2 (1766), cited by Chamberlain (ed.), *Eighteenth Century German Criticism*, 163 n. 25.

[64] *Letters for the Advancement of the Humanities*, 7th and 8th ser. (1796), cited by Eichner, 'Friedrich Schlegel's Theory of Romantic Poetry', 1020.

[65] Eichner, 'Friedrich Schlegel's Theory of Romantic Poetry', 1019–23; A. Gillies, 'Herder's Preparation of Romantic Theory', *Modern Language Review*, 39/3 (1944), 252–61.

[66] *Athenaeum Fragments*, no. 116, in *Philosophical Fragments*, 31.

[67] See Ch. 3 above, pp. 100–1.

mingling of essences; it 'transcends' genres not by eluding but by combining them.[68] To reinforce the point, Schlegel's definition is itself a *Mischgedicht* which brings together concepts of synthesis and unity from diverse intellectual fields—philosophy, chemistry, biology, linguistics—and blends them into one encyclopedic fragment.

Readers have puzzled over whether the art form Schlegel describes is an actual or merely a potential one. The answer may lie in his distinctive notion of the 'progressive'. Schlegel extends the historicist method of earlier genre theorists by conceptualizing genre in terms not only of its past but also of its future. To understand the characteristic genre of modernity, the *Roman*, it is not enough to narrate its origins and progress, as Clare Reeve had done in her *Progress of Romance* (1785); nor to emphasize its temporal and cultural relativity, as Herder had done. What must enter into the definition is its open-endedness—its infinite potential for future growth. Unlike previous genres which have completed their evolution, says Schlegel, 'the romantic kind of poetry is still in the state of becoming; that, in fact, is its real essence: that it should forever be becoming and never be perfected' (p. 32). The term 'progressive', which Schlegel borrows from Condorcet's *Sketch for a Historical Picture of the Progress of the Human Mind* (1794), encapsulates this idea of limitless improvement.[69] A new, future-orientated art requires, in turn, a new form of criticism. Whereas other, 'finished' genres 'are now capable of being fully analyzed', romantic poetry, as an emergent and limitless genre, 'can be exhausted by no theory and only a divinatory criticism would dare to characterize its ideal' (p. 32). Even Schlegel's 'chemical' poetics is inadequate to the task: compositional analysis must be complemented by a direct apprehension of its polymorphous essence. Thus, to adapt another of Schlegel's aphorisms, just as the historian must be a prophet facing backwards,[70] the 'divinatory' critic must be a literary historian facing forwards.

What this might mean becomes clearer once we recognize that 'progressive universal poetry' postulates both an endpoint of the literary and a point of origin. In projecting a future synthesis which will be a 'reuniting' of genres originally unified and then separated, Schlegel is developing a strand in eighteenth-century genre theory which can be traced, via Herder and others, to a seminal British text, John Brown's *Dissertation on the Rise, Union, and Power, the Progressions, Separations, and Corruptions of Poetry and Music* (1763). Though little read now, Brown's is a classic statement of Enlightenment primitivism, a critical trend that originated in the 1730s in discussion of Homeric epic by critics like Thomas Blackwell, and by the 1760s had become a full-blown theory of literary history analogous to the 'universal histories' then fashionable among Enlightenment historians.[71] For Brown, as for other primitivists, the progress of civilization

---

[68] See Szondi, 'Friedrich Schlegel's Theory of Poetical Genres', 93–4; and Lori Wagner, 'Chaos and Logos in Friedrich Schlegel's Concept of Romantic Poetry and the *Roman* Form', *European Romantic Review*, 5/1 (1994), 15–31, who explores the connection between *romantische Poesie, transzcendentale Poesie*, and *ideale Poesie*, a 'trinitarian concept [that] permeates Schlegel's writings' (16).

[69] Behler, *German Romantic Literary Theory*, 65–71.

[70] *Athenaeum Fragments*, no. 80, in *Philosophical Fragments*, 27.

[71] For the intellectual context of Brown's treatise, see René Wellek, *The Rise of English Literary History* (1941; New York: McGraw-Hill, 1966), 61–94; Judith A. Plotz, *Ideas of the Decline of Poetry: A Study in English Criticism from 1700 to 1830* (1965; New York: Garland, 1987), 105–7; Lois Whitney,

marked a kind of Fall, since poetry, in its original state, had possessed more breadth, more potency, and more freshness than in later periods. Blackwell had made this case in terms of language; Brown makes it in terms of genre, arguing that 'Till a certain Period of Civilization, Letters and Art, the several kinds would of course lie confused, in a Sort of undistinguished Mass, and be mingled in the same Composition, as Inclination, Enthusiasm, or other Incidents might impel.'[72] Only later, with 'the Progress of Polity and Arts', did 'a Separation of the Several Parts or Branches' arise and the roles of poet, prophet, and legislator become gradually separated. Music and poetry then became separate art forms, acquiring, through 'repeated Trial and Experiment', a 'more artificial Manner'; and 'the several Kinds of Poem', once promiscuously mixed, assumed 'their legitimate Forms' (p. 40). To illustrate his argument, Brown traces the evolution of poetry not only among the ancient Greeks and Romans, but also in the early history of other European countries, among the Hebrews, and in China, Peru, and India, making this a genuinely 'universal' literary history. In a final chapter, Brown speculates about 'the possible Re-Union of Music and Poetry', rejecting various abortive combinations but expressing cautious confidence that the 'narrative or Epic Odes' of Dryden and Pope, together with their musical settings, represented an authentic reintegration of the two art forms.[73]

Eloquent and original, Brown's *Dissertation* was widely admired and cited, both in Britain and abroad.[74] One of the admirers was Hugh Blair, who incorporates parts of it almost verbatim in his *Lectures on Rhetoric and Belles Lettres* (1783), supplementing Brown's primitivist hypothesis with further speculations about the primeval mingling of genres and the cultural processes that led to their eventual separation.[75] Parodied, Brown's grand narrative also supplies the mock-serious history of poetry in Peacock's *Four Ages of Poetry* (1820), with its pessimistic conclusion that poetry is doomed to an irreversible decline as civilization advances. Jeffrey, too, draws on Brown in his various accounts of the decline and fall of poetry, the primitivist theory of origins having become a standard topos in Scottish Enlightenment criticism.[76] It is in Germany, though, that Brown's ideas undergo their most striking development.[77] One line of development involves what Tilottama Rajan calls the 'stemmatic' method

---

*Primitivism and the Idea of Progress in English Popular Literature of the Eighteenth Century* (1934; New York: Octagon, 1965); and Murray Krieger, 'The Arts and the Idea of Progress', in Gabriel A. Almond et al. (eds), *Progress and its Discontents* (Berkeley: University of California Press, 1982).

[72] John Brown, *A Dissertation on the Rise, Union, and Power, the Progressions, Separations, and Corruptions, of Poetry and Music: To which is Prefixed, The Cure of Saul, A Sacred Ode* (London, 1763), 40. The title of the abridged version, *The History of the Rise and Progress of Poetry through it's Several Species* (Newcastle, 1764), highlights the centrality of genre to Brown's thesis.

[73] *Dissertation on the Rise, Union, and Power*, 221–38.

[74] For its British reception, see Wellek, *Rise of English Literary History*, 81; and Walter Jackson Bate, *The Burden of the Past and the English Poet* (London: Chatto and Windus, 1971), 51.

[75] Hugh Blair, *Lectures on Rhetoric and Belles Lettres*, 2 vols (London, 1783), ii. 322–3.

[76] For Peacock and Jeffrey, see Ch. 4 above, pp. 142–5.

[77] Lawrence Marsden Price, *English Literature in Germany* (Berkeley: University of California Press, 1953), 245. A translation by Johann Joachim Eschenburg, *Dr. Browns Betrachtungen über die Poesie und Musik, nach ihrem Ursprunge, ihrer Vereinigung, Gewalt, Wachsthum, Trennung und Verderbniss*, was published in Leipzig in 1769.

of tracing the various species of composition to a single ur-genre.[78] For Herder, a pioneer of this approach, 'the fountain-head of poetic art' was the ode, which he describes as the 'germ cell' from which 'the entire great original array of poetic forms, their manifold and often paradoxical progression, will grow'.[79] For Goethe the ur-genre was the ballad, though he also makes a parallel case for Greek tragedy as a primal combination of the three *Naturformen*: lyric, epic, and drama.[80] Other triadic theorists—Hölderlin and Schelling, for example—reverse the order, assigning priority to lyric and treating epic as a later development, with drama as a synthesis of the two.[81] For Schiller, arguably the most profound investigator of cultural origins, the key evolutionary development was the fall into self-consciousness, a shift from a 'naive' mode of poetic expression into a 'sentimental' one.[82] Generic distinctions are a symptom of the latter: sentimental poetry, preoccupied with the gulf between the ideal and the real, splits into satire, elegy, and idyll, whereas naive poetry 'resists all generic determination' and is 'primal and undifferentiated, both in the mind and in the poem'.[83]

There are, then, many versions of Brown's argument, each of which seeks to explain the evolution of literature in terms of the 'progressions, separations, and corruptions' of some originary source, a fecund chaos or *genus universum* opposite in character to the regimented, segregated, rule-bound 'species of composition' that make up the modern genre-spectrum. Friedrich Schlegel's decisive contribution is to transpose this theoretical topos from the beginning of literary history to the end of it, converting primitivist nostalgia for a prelapsarian ur-poetry into messianic longing for a 'universal poetry' of the future. His claim is that the synthesis of genres that other literary historians had located in remote antiquity can happen again in the here and now. 'All poems of antiquity', he writes in the *Dialogue on Poetry*, 'join one to the other, till from the ever increasing masses and members the whole is formed. Everything interpenetrates everything else, and everywhere there is one and the same spirit, only expressed differently. And thus it is truly no empty image to say: Ancient poetry is a single, indivisible, and perfect poem. Why should what has once

---

[78] Tilottama Rajan, 'Theories of Genre', in Brown (ed.), *Cambridge History of Literary Criticism*, v: *Romanticism*, 231.

[79] 'Fragments of a Treatise on the Ode' (1766–8), in Johann Gottfried Herder, *Selected Early Works 1764–1767: Addresses, Essays, and Drafts; Fragments on Recent German Literature*, ed. Ernest A. Menze and Karl Menges, trans. Ernest A. Menze with Michael Palma (University Park: Pennsylvania State University Press, 1992), 36. Originally drafted as preparatory material for a general aesthetic theory, Herder's fragments on the ode influenced many later theorists, including Friedrich Schlegel: see John David Pizer, *The Historical Perspective in German Genre Theory: Its Development from Gottsched to Hegel* (Stuttgart: Hans-Dieter Heinz Akademischer Verlag, 1985), 135–6.

[80] Goethe, *West–East Divan* (1819), cited by Gérard Genette, *The Architext: An Introduction* (1979), trans. Jane E. Lewin (Berkeley: University of California Press, 1992), 39.

[81] For these and other permutations of the triad, see Genette, *Architext*, 42–3.

[82] Friedrich Schiller, *On Naïve and Sentimental Poetry*, in H. B. Nisbet (ed.), *German Aesthetic and Literary Criticism: Winckelmann, Lessing, Hamann, Herder, Schiller, Goethe* (Cambridge: Cambridge University Press, 1985).

[83] Cyrus Hamlin, 'The Origins of a Philosophical Genre Theory in German Romanticism', *European Romantic Review*, 5/1 (1994), 3–14: 11.

been not come alive again?'[84] *Athenaeum* fragment 116 fleshes out this daring suggestion, envisioning a 'progressive universal poetry' which will combine the spontaneous 'organic' unity of classical poetry with the self-reflexive 'chemical' unity of the romantic *Mischgedicht*.

Schlegel's radical restructuring of genre theory can be brought out further by a final comparison, with the British text which first gave currency to the phrase 'universal poetry': Richard Hurd's *Dissertation on the Idea of Universal Poetry* (1766). Schlegel almost certainly read this essay,[85] and he acknowledges Hurd in his *Lectures on the History of Literature* (1812) as one of the English critics who had provided a vital stimulus to German criticism.[86] In this case, however, the stimulus was largely antithetical. Hurd, like other critics of the 1760s, was both a traditionalist and a progressive, and the *Dissertation* is a mixture of neoclassical and Romantic tendencies. In neoclassical vein, he speaks approvingly of the 'rules' governing different 'species of composition', and calls for another Aristotle to complete the work that the *Poetics* left unfinished by legislating for other genres.[87] His own essay is offered as a modest preliminary to such a task, in that it attempts to define the genus, 'universal poetry', of which individual poetic forms are the species. Starting from Francis Bacon's premiss that pleasure and not instruction is the 'ultimate and appropriate end of poetry' (p. 4), Hurd attempts to specify the linguistic, thematic, and formal means by which such pleasure is generated. The first section concentrates on imagery, the 'sort of figurative expression [that] is universally pleasing to us' (p. 6). The second summarizes the innovative ideas on 'fine fabling' and imaginative invention that he had advanced in his *Letters on Chivalry and Romance* (1762). The third and final part is devoted to form and hinges on the question of whether the novel should be treated as a type of poetry, as Fielding and others had proposed.

On this last matter, Hurd abandons the progressive stance of earlier sections and adopts an ultra-conservative position, insisting that metre 'is essential to every work of poetic art' (p. 18), and that modern prose fiction should in no way be admitted into even the most 'universal' definition of poetry. Novels are 'hasty, imperfect, and abortive poems', the prevailing taste for which is attributable to 'a vitiated, palled, and sickly imagination—that last disease of learned minds, and sure prognostic of expiring Letters' (pp. 21–2). Whatever the 'temporary success' of such 'novelties', he continues,

good sense will acknowledge no work of art but such as is composed according to the laws of its *kind*. These KINDS, as arbitrary things as we account them (for I neither forget nor dispute what our best philosophy teaches concerning *kinds* and *sorts*), have yet so far their foundation in

---

[84] *Dialogue on Poetry*, 82. Schlegel repeats this claim in his *Ideas* (1800), no. 95, in *Philosophical Fragments*, 102–3.

[85] James Engell, 'Romantische Poesie: Richard Hurd and Friedrich Schlegel', in Gregory Maertz (ed.), *Cultural Interactions in the Romantic Age: Critical Essays in Comparative Literature* (Albany: State University of New York Press, 1998).

[86] Friedrich Schlegel, *Lectures on the History of Literature, Ancient and Modern* [trans. J. G. Lockhart], 2 vols (Edinburgh, 1818), ii. 220 (lecture 14).

[87] Richard Hurd, *A Dissertation on the Idea of Universal Poetry* (London, 1766), 4–5.

nature and the reason of things, that it will not be allowed us to multiply, or vary them, at pleasure. We may, indeed, mix and confound them if we will (for there is a sort of literary luxury, which would engross all pleasures at once, even such as are contradictory to each other), or, in our rage for incessant gratification, we may take up with half-formed pleasures, such as come first to hand, and may be administered by any body: But true taste requires chaste, severe, and simple pleasures; and true genius will only be concerned in administering such. (pp. 22–3)

What is striking here is that Hurd fully recognizes the composite quality of the novel form—its mixing of genres and of the various pleasures associated with them—but does only negatively. The blurring of boundaries and mingling of 'half-formed pleasures' are precisely what he objects to in the novel, not merely as a breach of literary decorum (the Horatian precept to which he makes repeated appeal) but as a 'luxury' that is both morally and aesthetically corrupting. Faced with the novel, the proto-Romanticism of the *Letters on Chivalry and Romance* vanishes, and the neo-classicist and Christian moralist in Hurd combine to defend the law of genre in its strongest form.

The gap between Hurd's account of 'universal poetry' and Schlegel's gives some indication of the revolution in taste that had intervened. Everything that Hurd condemns, Schlegel approves; the distinctions that Hurd upholds, Schlegel dissolves; and the 'literary luxury' that Hurd declares illicit and degrading—the 'engrossing' of different textual pleasures simultaneously—is commended by Schlegel as the purest of aesthetic sensations. Literary history was clearly on Schlegel's side. Far from being the temporary fad described by Hurd, novels continued their inexorable rise, and by the 1820s, as Hazlitt's survey shows, these and other 'extravagant combinations' were visible across the genre-spectrum and in every cultural sphere from the unlicensed theatres to the elite publishing houses. Rather than laying claim to neoclassical purity, literary works now flaunted their generic promiscuity in titles, subtitles, and prefaces. Such hybrid compositions still attracted disapproval from a certain class of critics, but the fact that they now existed in abundance, throughout all areas of the literary system, is confirmation that genre-mixing had become integral to the poetics of British Romanticism, and the *Mischgedicht* part of the staple diet of the British reading public. Having traced its origins, let us now look more closely at what that regime involved.


ROUGH-MIXING AND SMOOTH-MIXING

One advantage that Schlegel's 'chemical' poetics has over the more familiar organicist model is that it recognizes different *degrees* of unity and different *kinds* of combination. In general, such distinctions are missing from British critical discourse of this period, but there is evidence (thus far overlooked by scholars) that the science of mixing contributed, independently of Friedrich Schlegel but in ways that parallel his, to one of the central achievements of British Romanticism, Coleridge's theory of imagination. A fragmentary note by Coleridge written on the backs of three admission tickets to his London lecture series of May–June 1812 shows him explaining the difference between fancy and imagination through an analogy with chemical mixing. Coleridge begins by describing two chemical experiments:

Difference between synthesis and juxta-position/ illustrated by chemistry. I can put oil and water in juxta-position by adding an alcali I produce a synthesis or combination/ or divide a vessel by glass so thin & clear as to be invisible & I place Nitric Acid and Alcohol in juxta-position I blend them & have *Ether*—[88]

In each case, two substances are first placed next to one another, in 'juxta-position', and then chemically united, to produce a 'synthesis or combination'. With oil and water, chemical synthesis requires the addition of an alkaline catalyst; whereas nitric acid and alcohol spontaneously combine when the glass screen separating them is removed. For his knowledge of these experiments, Coleridge was indebted to his close friend the virtuoso chemist Humphry Davy, whose *Elements of Chemical Philosophy* (1812) includes a section 'On chemical Attraction, and the Laws of Combination and Decomposition' which includes, among others, the example of oil and water. These two substances, writes Davy, 'will not mix intimately; they will not *combine*; and they are said to have no chemical *attraction* or *affinity* for each other', whereas if an alkali is added, '*chemical combination*' will occur—an illustration of the difference between what he calls 'mechanical mixtures' and 'true chemical compounds'.[89] Davy, an accomplished poet as well as a chemist, frequently used artistic analogies in his scientific work; Coleridge, in turn, says he attended Davy's lectures 'to increase my stock of metaphors'.[90] Just how fertile a metaphorical resource chemistry proved to be is demonstrated by the second part of Coleridge's note, which uses the juxtaposition–synthesis distinction to characterize two contrasting methods of literary composition associated with two distinct mental faculties, fancy and imagination. The former produces 'harmonious Combination' through 'the resemblances of different objects' or 'by the Law of Contrast', whereas 'Imagination is the synthetic Power' which 'must modify each by each, and as it were fuse—it is truly the analogue of creation'.[91]

Ideas and phrasing from the 1812 note find their way directly into Coleridge's famous descriptions of the creative process in *Biographia Literaria* (1817). The comparison in chapter 13 between imagination and fancy, and between the primary and secondary imagination, draws on many sources and uses a variety of metaphors, the most prominent of which is the organic–mechanical binary he employs when contrasting the 'essentially *vital*' imagination with the 'fixities and definites' of the fancy.[92] More

[88] 'Distinction between Imagination and Fancy' (editorial heading), in *The Collected Works of Samuel Taylor Coleridge*, xi: *Shorter Works and Fragments*, ed. H. J. and J. R. de J. Jackson, 2 vols (London: Routledge and Kegan Paul, 1995), i. 289.

[89] Humphry Davy, *Elements of Chemical Philosophy* (London, 1812), 98–9, 108.

[90] Quoted by John Ayrton Paris, *The Life of Sir Humphry Davy*, 2 vols (London, 1831), i. 138. See also Molly Lefebure, 'Humphry Davy: Philosophic Alchemist', in Richard Gravil and Molly Lefebure (eds), *The Coleridge Connection: Essays for Thomas McFarland* (Basingstoke: Macmillan, 1990); and, for the broader context, Jan Golinski, *Science as Public Culture: Chemistry and Enlightenment in Britain, 1760–1820* (Cambridge: Cambridge University Press, 1992).

[91] *Shorter Works and Fragments*, i. 289.

[92] *The Collected Works of Samuel Taylor Coleridge*, vii: *Biographia Literaria*, ed. James Engell and W. Jackson Bate, 2 vols (London: Routledge and Kegan Paul, 1983), i. 304–5.

unusual and striking, however, is his use of chemical terminology. What distinguishes the secondary from the primary imagination is how it 'dissolves, diffuses, dissipates, in order to re-create', exactly in the manner of a chemical synthesis or combination. In chapter 14, Coleridge expands the phrase 'synthetic Power' into a sequence of chemical metaphors, producing one of his most eloquent definitions: 'He [the poet, described in *ideal* perfection] diffuses a tone, and spirit of unity, that blends, and (as it were) *fuses*, each into each, by that synthetic and magical power, to which we have exclusively appropriated the name of imagination.'[93] The inclusion of the qualifier 'as it were' confirms the link with the 1812 note. The ability of chemical substances to 'fuse', 'blend', and form new substances remains his key metaphor for poetic creation, but he now adds another figurative layer that suggests the essential strangeness and mystery of this process: the imagination, he says, is a power at once synthetic and *magical*. Davy, in his semi-autobiographical *Consolations in Travel* (1830), portrays himself as 'the chemical philosopher';[94] Coleridge, in *Biographia Literaria*, presents himself as the chemical poet—that is, as both theorist and practitioner of what could be called not the science but the art of mixing.

Mixing of *what*, however? Coleridge refers to the raw materials of poetry as 'the images, thoughts, and emotions of the poet's own mind',[95] a statement consistent with his psychological account of the creative process. But the artistic medium of poetry is language and form, and an obvious extension of Coleridge's argument is to the mixing of genres. Friedrich Schlegel's version of chemical poetics makes the application to genre explicit; Coleridge's does not, but his discussions of genre and form presuppose and imply this analogy. Moreover, Coleridge's juxtaposition–synthesis distinction, not found in Schlegel, suggests a binary classification of genre-mixing which, I will argue, proves remarkably illuminating when applied to the 'extravagant combinations' of modern literature. For the sake of clarity, I propose to adjust Coleridge's metaphor and rename the two types *rough-mixing* and *smooth-mixing*, defined as follows. Rough-mixing is a type of generic combination in which the formal surfaces of the constituent genres are left intact: heterogeneous elements are juxtaposed rather than integrated, thus creating the aesthetic effect of discontinuity, or 'roughening'. Smooth-mixing is a type of generic combination in which the formal boundaries are dissolved: a synthesis occurs in which heterogeneous elements are transformed and assimilated, creating the aesthetic effect of 'organic unity'. Two different types of artwork result: each is generically mixed but in the former the joins are visible while in the latter there is the impression of seamless unity. Both types are equally 'finished', however fragmentary the results; the meaning which the term 'rough-mix' carries in recording technology—'a preliminary blend of separately recorded parts of a piece of music' (*OED*)—is not relevant here, except for its implication that, in rough-mixing, the constituent parts of the composition are still discernible. In smooth-mixing they are not.

---

[93] *Biographia Literaria*, ii. 16.

[94] 'Dialogue the Fifth: The Chemical Philosopher', in Humphry Davy, *Consolations in Travel* (London, 1830).

[95] *Biographia Literaria*, i. 15.

Smooth-mixing is the more familiar kind: familiar because the dominant formal paradigm of Romanticism, organicism, has always envisaged genre-mixing in this way, emphasizing balance, integration, and the interdependence of parts. According to this view of Romantic art, the classic expression of which is Coleridge's definition of imagination in *Biographia*, creative success is measured by a writer's ability to balance and unify 'discordant qualities' and thereby produce a harmonious artwork.[96] Coleridge's own 'conversation poems' illustrate this method of composition. A product of his experiments with poetic form in the 1790s, this new type of poetry combined structural and stylistic features from many existing genres, including the sonnet, epigram, verse epistle, pastoral eclogue, loco-descriptive poem, irregular Pindaric ode, Miltonic epic, blank-verse inscription, and the amorphous lyric form known as 'effusion'—a label Coleridge borrowed for his first exercise in the new genre, the poem later entitled 'The Eolian Harp' ('conversation poem' was a term he applied only to 'The Nightingale'; the extension of this label to the whole group of poems is a modern extrapolation). Critics have investigated the literary origins of the genre in impressive detail.[97] Knowledge of its provenance, and of the multiple genres that contributed to it, does not, however, reveal the essential fact about the new genre, which is that the aesthetic experience it offers is one of seamless 'organic' unity. Unity, indeed, is the explicit theme of the conversation poems, which depict the 'self-watching subtilizing mind'[98] in the process of unifying seemingly disparate experiences, and which mirror that organizational process in their formal structure. Traces of the source genres can be exposed by critical analysis (the recursive structure, for example, can be shown to derive from sonnet form, while the switches of tempo and register derive from the Pindaric ode), but these components are not perceptible in an actual reading experience. The artistic appeal of the genre lies in its subtle modulations and its harmonious synthesis of heterogeneous formal and linguistic elements. The catalyst for this synthesis is blank verse: the diverse metres and sound patterns of the source genres are transposed into unrhymed iambic pentameter, a verse form flexible enough to register the rhythmic shifts which accompany the motion of consciousness, but regular enough to smooth out the formal disjunctions which would otherwise result from the mixing of widely different genres. These two unifying features—lyrical self-reflection and the verse form—are foregrounded in the name Coleridge eventually settled on for his new genre when grouping the poems together for the first time in *Sibylline Leaves*: 'Meditative Poems in Blank Verse'.

These techniques can be seen on a much larger scale in *The Prelude*, which, like Coleridge's conversation poems (on which it is partly modelled), both thematizes

---

[96] Ibid., i. 17.

[97] See e.g. George McLean Harper, 'Coleridge's Conversation Poems' (1928), in M. H. Abrams (ed.), *English Romantic Poets: Modern Essays in Criticism* (New York: Oxford University Press, 1975); Reeve Parker, *Coleridge's Meditative Art* (Ithaca, N.Y.: Cornell University Press, 1975); George Dekker, *Coleridge and the Literature of Sensibility* (London: Vision, 1978); and Kelvin Everest, *Coleridge's Secret Ministry: The Context of the Conversation Poems, 1795–1798* (Brighton: Harvester, 1979).

[98] A phrase from the first printed version of 'Frost at Midnight', in Coleridge's pamphlet *Fears in Solitude: Written in 1798, during the Alarm of an Invasion. To which are added, France, an Ode; and Frost at Midnight* (London, 1798), 20.

and enacts a process of 'organic' integration. In Wordsworth's psychic mythology, the 'dark | Invisible workmanship that reconciles | Discordant elements'[99] is the restorative power which converts experiential trauma into imaginative strength and bestows unity on an otherwise fractured self. The artistic correlative for this is the poem's own genesis, a remarkable sequence of formal expansions and syntheses that turned the 'glad preamble' of 1798 and other scattered fragments into the 13,000-line epic of 1805. The result is a 'composite order' of fascinating complexity, incorporating a series of genres which are deployed not in their full formal distinctness but in their modal extension, as linguistic fields and image clusters associated with particular ways of seeing the world. The narrative moves through these various modes, the transitions between them symbolically mirroring different stages in Wordsworth's imaginative growth. Readers have registered the effect of this in various ways. Coleridge emphasizes the astonishing coherence of the poem, describing it as an 'orphic song' which 'Makes audible a linked lay of Truth, | Of Truth profound a sweet continuous lay'[100]—an impression that was doubtless enhanced by hearing the poem read aloud, in its entirety, in the author's own voice (the allusion to the Orpheus myth underlines Coleridge's recognition of the poem's power to harmonize 'discordant elements'). Abbie Findlay Potts, in a book-length study of the poem's literary form, analyses the various generic components (epic, romance, satire, pastoral, philosophical poem) but, like Coleridge, emphasizes its artistic unity, introducing his reading with a cancelled passage from 1798–1800 where Wordsworth describes the act of composition in explicitly organic terms as a 'slow creation' that

> doth impart to speech
> Outline and substance even, till it has given
> A function kindred to organic power,
> The vital spirit of a perfect form.[101]

New historicist studies such as Alan Liu's, however, question this appearance of unity and highlight instead the generic discontinuities, arguing that some of the literary modes through which the narrative moves are intended to signal imaginative aberration (romance, for example, stands for youthful idealism but also for illusion and error, notably in the French Revolution books).[102] In a sense, though, this reading simply confirms the power of Wordsworth's 'invisible workmanship': it is because the genres, and the experiences they encode, are so discordant that they require synthesis. Stuart Curran makes just this point, acknowledging the various generic 'intrusions'

---

[99] 1805 version, book 1, lines 351–3, in Wordsworth, *The Prelude 1799, 1805, 1850: Authoritative Texts, Context and Reception, Recent Critical Essays*, ed. Jonathan Wordsworth, M. H. Abrams, and Stephen Gill (New York: Norton, 1979), 46.

[100] 'To William Wordsworth, Composed on the Night after his Recitation of a Poem on the Growth of an Individual Mind' (1807), lines 58–9, in *The Collected Works of Samuel Taylor Coleridge*, xvi: *Poetical Works*, ed. J. C. C. Mays, i: *Poems (Reading Text)*, 2 vols (London: Routledge and Kegan Paul, 2001), ii. 818.

[101] Abbie Findlay Potts, *Wordsworth's 'Prelude': A Study of its Literary Form* (1953; New York: Octagon, 1972), 29.

[102] Alan Liu, *Wordsworth: The Sense of History* (Stanford, Calif.: Stanford University Press, 1989), ch. 8 (especially the section 'The Contest of Genres', 362–87).

that punctuate the narrative but claiming that they are ultimately subsumed and integrated: the poem's mixture of genres enacts 'a dialectical progression toward a oneness of personality', and the 'intricate balance' of pastoral, romance, and epic reflects 'the process leading to psychic equilibrium'.[103] Again, blank verse is a key unifying factor.

Though texts like these are the locus classicus, smooth-mixing techniques are not confined to Romantic poetry, the genre most obviously associated with the organic paradigm. The way in which Jane Austen, for example, combines the novel of manners, romantic comedy, epistolary fiction, and non-realistic modes such as gothic could be described as a novelistic exercise in smooth-mixing, a unifying agent in this case being her ubiquitous sense of irony (a dominant stylistic as well as tonal principle, modifying her disparate materials). The difference in this respect between her early novel *Northanger Abbey* (drafted in 1798), where the transition from the Bath scenes to the gothic parody of the Northanger section involves an abrupt switch of mimetic register, and the more complex but seamless combination of genres in *Emma* (1816) underlines the essential direction of her talent. An analogous point could be made about the development of the historical novel, a genre whose evolution from the medieval pastiche of Thomas Leland's *Longsword, Earl of Salisbury: An Historical Romance* (1762), via the topical allegory of the Irish 'National Tale', to the brilliantly imagined reconstructions of the past in Scott's Waverley novels represents a gradual overcoming of the technical problem of combining the two narrative discourses of history and fiction. Scott's prior success in blending ballad and verse romance shows his mastery of the art of generic synthesis, and the many popular adaptations of his romances and novels for the stage (theatrical and operatic) suggest how strong his basic formula was: a generic hybrid both distinctive enough to establish a new type of fiction and durable enough to withstand transposition into different media.

So smooth is the generic blending in such cases that works of this kind are not necessarily experienced as hybrids at all: the fully 'organic' Romantic text is one that effaces its generic diversity and presents itself to the reader as a wholly unified artwork produced (as Coleridgean theory has it) in accordance with formal laws of its own origination. There is, however, another type of Romantic text whose method of combining genres involves juxtaposition rather than synthesis, friction rather than fusion; and in which formal heterogeneity is foregrounded rather than concealed. A spectacular example is Blake's *The Marriage of Heaven and Hell* (1790–3). Blake is the composite artist par excellence, and the *Marriage* displays that artistry to an extreme degree, combining in its twenty-seven plates an extraordinary range of forms, styles, registers, and discourses.[104] As well as utilizing all three presentational

---

[103] Stuart Curran, *Poetic Form and British Romanticism* (New York: Oxford University Press, 1986), 184, 190. Cf. Stuart Peterfreund, '*The Prelude*: Wordsworth's Metamorphic Epic', *Genre*, 14/4 (1981), 441–72.

[104] Summarized in Morris Eaves, Robert N. Essick, and Joseph Viscomi (eds), *Blake's Illuminated Books*, iii: *The Early Illuminated Books* (London: William Blake Trust, 1993), introd., 116–18. For the compositional history of the *Marriage*, crucial to an understanding of its form, see Joseph Viscomi, 'The Evolution of William Blake's *The Marriage of Heaven and Hell*', *Huntington Library Quarterly*, 58 (1997), 281–344.

modes (narrative, dramatic, and lyrical), it mixes poetry and prose; moves through virtually the entire spectrum of literary genres, from epithalamion (marriage poem) to epic (the Miltonic 'Argument') to satire (the Swiftian dialogues) to song (the closing 'Song of Liberty'); employs a range of non-literary or sub-literary forms, such as the pamphlet, the manifesto, the treatise, the philosophical symposium, and the travelogue; and imitates a series of biblical genres, including Old Testament proph- ecy, the book of Proverbs, and the Apocalypse. Sacred and secular discourses, high and low genres, comic and serious registers, symbolic and literal modes of signifi- cation are freely intermixed, as are at least five distinct speech genres: proclamation, expostulation, table talk (the after-dinner conversation with Isaiah and Ezekiel), confession, joke. As if this generic abundance were not enough, there is also the mixing of verbal and visual media, a continuous dialectic between word and image involving not only pictorial illustration and counter-illustration, but also illuminated lettering and many kinds of visual marginalia, and drawing on multiple artistic traditions.[105]

No genre enters the *Marriage* unaltered. Most undergo a drastic transformation of scale (typically, compression) or tone (ironization), and many submit to ideological recoding, as in the brilliantly iconoclastic 'Proverbs of Hell' and the anti- Swedenborgian 'Memorable Fancies', which deconstruct and parody the visionary narratives Swedenborg called 'Memorable Relations'. Equally striking is the manner in which these diverse elements combine. Genres are juxtaposed rather than inte- grated; they collide rather than merge, in accordance with Blake's own principle 'Without Contraries is no progression.'[106] The juxtaposed genres remain sharply distinct from one another, preserving their formal and linguistic differences. The epic 'Argument' retains in grandiose register, the manifesto its declamatory style, the philosophical treatise its numbered propositions, the literary commentary its foot- note. Moreover, between the different sections of the *Marriage* there is no modula- tion, in the musical sense, but, instead, abrupt transition: of tempo, tone, idiom, subject matter. The primeval allegorical world of 'The Argument', of Rintrah roaring and shaking his fires in the burdened air, is utterly different from the modern, urbane 'Voice of the Devil'; and the concentrated symbolism and paradoxical logic of the 'Proverbs of Hell' stand in stark contrast to the expansive narrative and humorous dialogue of the 'Memorable Fancies', or to the apocalyptic lyricism of the 'Song of Liberty'. Blake foregrounds the separateness of the various parts by the use of generic subtitles. There are no fewer than ten of these, in a work of under 500 lines ('The Argument', 'The Voice of the Devil', five 'Memorable Fancies', 'Proverbs of Hell', 'A Song of Liberty', 'Chorus'), each spread across the page in large decorative lettering

---

[105] For the text–image relationship, see Jean H. Hagstrum, *William Blake, Poet and Painter: An Introduction to the Illuminated Verse* (Chicago: University of Chicago Press, 1964); W. J. T. Mitchell, *Blake's Composite Art: A Study of the Illuminated Poetry* (Princeton: Princeton University Press, 1978); and Joseph Viscomi, *Blake and the Idea of the Book* (Princeton: Princeton University Press, 1993).

[106] *The Marriage of Heaven and Hell*, pl. 3, in William Blake, *Complete Writings*, ed. Geoffrey Keynes (London: Oxford University Press, 1966), 149. Subsequent page references in the text are to this edition.

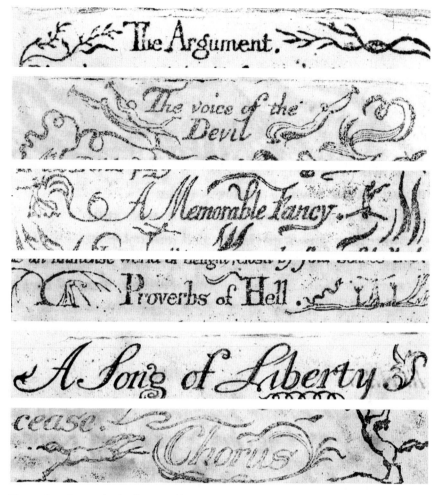

**Figure 5.1.** Sectional subtitles to William Blake's *The Marriage of Heaven and Hell* (1790–3)

(Figure 5.1). Even the footnote is clearly labelled 'Note'—a noun that becomes an imperative verb in Blake's insistently deictic text.

The artistic logic here can be explained in terms of defamiliarization, a technique named by the Russian Formalists but already widely practised by the Romantics.[107]

---

[107] Viktor Shklovsky, 'Art as Technique' (1917), in Lee T. Lemon and Marion J. Reiss (eds and trans.), *Russian Formalist Criticism: Four Essays* (Lincoln: University of Nebraska Press, 1965). Anticipations of this concept in Romantic theory (e.g. by Coleridge, Shelley, and Novalis) are noted by Victor Erlich, *Russian Formalism: History—Doctrine*, 3rd edn (New Haven: Yale University Press, 1981), 179; and R. H. Stacy, *Defamiliarization in Language and Literature* (Syracuse, N.Y.: University of Syracuse Press, 1977), ch. 5.

The rough surfaces and abrupt transitions of the *Marriage* have precisely the intensifying effect postulated in Shklovsky's theory of defamiliarization: a heightened state of artistic awareness achieved through a sharpened perception of form. The difference is that for Blake artistic perception is not an end in itself; it is a means to what, in the second 'Memorable Fancy', he calls 'a perception of the infinite' (p. 154). The generic discontinuities and (in Shklovsky's term) 'roughened form' of the *Marriage*, like the tactical 'obscurity' Blake defends in his letter to Dr Trusler of 1799, are an artistic device which 'rouzes the faculties to act'—in particular the faculty of imagination, the organ of 'Vision'.[108] In the *Marriage*, the defamiliarizing process is captured in the chemical metaphor of 'corrosives . . . melting apparent surfaces away, and displaying the infinite which was hid' (p. 154), an allusion to Blake's 'infernal method' of printing, copperplate etching. In ideological terms, defamiliarization means the stripping away of false consciousness: a laying bare of the errors, confusions, and blind spots associated with obsolete modes of thought. '*The semblance of the finite should be overthrown*,' writes Friedrich Schlegel in his 'Introduction to the Transcendental Philosophy' (1800), 'and in order to do this, *all knowledge should be brought into a revolutionary condition*.'[109] Blake's *Marriage*—a manifesto for his own brand of transcendental philosophy—does just this, and in the way that Schlegel decrees: by bringing the *forms* of knowledge into a revolutionary condition. Blake dislodges all preconceptions and deconstructs all dogmas by breaking open the verbal and formal structures in which outworn ideas are enshrined and transmitted. Blake's yoking together of disparate genres and highlighting of the contrasts between them are means of cleansing 'the doors of perception' (p. 154), a perceptual clarification which is both artistic and intellectual. The *Marriage*, in short, is a *Mischgedicht* with a purpose: a deployment of the 'combinatorial method' to effect a revolution in consciousness.

In the violence of its techniques, the *Marriage* is an extreme example of rough-mixing. The basic method, however, was extremely common in the period, and contemporary readers often drew attention to it. Peacock's comment, quoted in my last chapter (p. 144), on the 'heterogeneous congeries' of contemporary poetry refers primarily to its clumsy mixture of archaic and modern subject matter, but is directed too at its hybrid formal construction, which involved, as Peacock saw it, a continuous violation of the laws of genre. Peacock's own novels, however, are as heterogeneous as the poetry he condemns, not only in their comic exploitation of anachronism, but also in their use of Menippean satire, a type of composition which thrives on parodic juxtapositions.[110] *Melincourt* (1817), for example, is predicated on generic contrast: chivalric romance is set against political satire, the pastoral ideal against the comedy of manners; and the wildly speculative discourse of linguistic anthropology is

---

[108]  Letter to Dr Trusler, 23 Aug. 1799, in *Complete Writings*, 793.

[109]  Friedrich Schlegel, 'Introduction to the Transcendental Philosophy' (1800), in Jochen Schulte-Sasse et al., *Theory as Practice: A Critical Anthology of Early German Romantic Writings* (Minneapolis: University of Minnesota Press, 1997), 249.

[110]  Linda M. Brooks, 'Lucian and Peacock: Peacock's Menippean Romanticism', *Revue belge de philologie et d'histoire*, 66 (1988), 590–601. For the classical prototype, see Joel C. Relihan, *Ancient Menippean Satire* (Baltimore: Johns Hopkins University Press, 1993).

reduced to the absurd through the figure of Sir Oran Haut-ton, an orang-utang transposed into a Regency dandy. Passages of sentimental verse are interspersed with racy, ironic prose, always to the detriment of the former, and the narrative repeatedly halts to allow mock-debates on sundry topics such as transcendental idealism, rotten boroughs, and 'The Philosophy of Ballads'.

Another, exactly contemporaneous novel which mixes genres to similarly disruptive effect is Mary Shelley's *Frankenstein* (1818). Often credited with inaugurating the genre of science fiction through its original blend of scientific and literary discourse, the novel also draws on a huge range of other genres, including the letter form, the gothic novel, the philosophical fable, the 'parallel life' (Plutarch), the novel of education, Jacobin and anti-Jacobin writing, Rousseauian confession, and travel literature, while maintaining too a continuous intertextual dialogue with contemporary poetry. Again, though, it is the jarring way in which these diverse components are brought together that reveals Mary Shelley's artistic purpose. The construction of Frankenstein's creature from disparate body parts becomes an emblem of the construction of the novel itself, a gruesome parody of organic unity which takes its place alongside the novel's other exploded myths of Romantic creativity. Whether or not some of the narrative roughness is due to authorial inexperience, it serves the novel perfectly, reinforcing the theme of psychic disintegration while enacting the artistic defamiliarization which is part of Mary Shelley's assault on Romantic aesthetics (that she should invoke, at a particularly bleak moment, the paradigm of lyric organicism and of the egotistical sublime, 'Tintern Abbey', is confirmation of this contrastive artistic logic).

Though he sometimes posed as a neoclassical traditionalist, another master of the Romantic rough-mix is Byron. His use of mixed modes in *Childe Harold's Pilgrimage* has already been mentioned, but it is *Don Juan* that reveals the full extent and tendency of his combinatorial powers. Shelley called *Don Juan* 'a poem totally of its own species',[111] but its uniqueness lies partly in its irreverent commingling of other, more familiar species. The poem plays throughout with the conventions of epic, explicitly invoking the Aristotelian rules it so effectively subverts, while taking further liberties with the neoclassical conception of epic as a genre which 'comprehends within its Sphere all the other Kinds'.[112] The orderly integration of subordinate forms that Trapp had in mind when he so defined the genre is the opposite of Byron's epic *bricolage*, which, in Leigh Hunt's words, produces a 'heterogeneous mixture' containing 'specimens of all the author's modes of writing, which are mingled together and push one another about in a strange way'.[113] The poem refers to itself at one point as an 'Epic Satire',[114] a description that underlines Byron's allegiances to the mock-heroic tradition of Pope's *The Dunciad* (1728–43), the only poem in English that can rival Byron's encyclopedic exposé of social folly and literary 'cant'. Pope's poem, though, is very different in its artistic methods and ideological targets,

---

[111] Shelley, letter to Byron, 21 Oct. 1821, in Rutherford (ed.), *Byron: Critical Heritage*, 197.

[112] See p. 165 above.

[113] Review of Cantos 1 and 2, *The Examiner* (31 Oct. 1819), in Rutherford (ed.), *Byron: Critical Heritage*, 176, 174.

[114] *Don Juan*, Canto 14 (1823), stanza 99, line 6, in *Complete Poetical Works*, v. 587.

and Byron gave a better clue to the literary character of *Don Juan* when he described it as 'a poetical T[ristram] Shandy'.[115] It is not only the ironic self-consciousness that Byron shares with Sterne (an author also revered by the German Romantics, and by Shklovsky), but also the mastery of comic juxtaposition, digression, ellipsis, and other defamiliarizing techniques, a comprehensive 'laying bare' that extends to his own compositional thought processes. The result is a novelized poem whose novelism is deliberately self-subverting, and whose main unifying feature—the author's all-pervasive personality—is gleefully promiscuous, in matters of genre as in all else. The use of *ottava rima*, while lending metrical consistency to the poem, provides yet another opportunity for juxtaposition, the incongruous couplings that generate many of the rhymes being one of Byron's primary mechanisms for demystification and satire.

In each of these examples, the rough-mixing of genres serves a purpose which is palpably ideological as well as aesthetic, a dual motivation which can also be found in much political fiction of the period. Joep Leerssen speaks of the 'mongrel heterogeneity' and 'unblended accumulation of superimposed discursive sediments' in Lady Morgan's *The Wild Irish Girl* (1806),[116] and Ina Ferris has detected similar 'generic jostlings and heteroglossic textures' in Morgan's later novel *The O'Briens and the O'Flahertys* (1827).[117] Eliza Fenwick's *Secresy* (1795) is another political novel in which, as Julia Wright notes, 'genres do not mingle, but collide', the effect being to 'mark separations in cultural perspectives and the principles of order with which they are commensurate'.[118] That this abrasive type of genre-mixing should play a part in the evolution of the Irish 'National Tale' is unsurprising given the ferocious political and cultural conflicts out of which the genre arises; nor should we be surprised to find similar tactics being employed in a novel such as Fenwick's, which uses artistic abrasion to probe the disharmonious class structure of English society and the distortions of personal relationship that result. The same is true when Scotland is the subject and the social analysis is projected backwards in time, as in James Hogg's *The Three Perils of Man: War, Women and Witchcraft* (1822), whose haphazard assemblage of border legend, pseudo-medievalism, actual history, and folk-tale diablerie is a reminder both of the formal incoherence to which the historical novel can tend[119] and of the disparate kinds of source material synthesized by a 'smooth' (at his best) practitioner of the genre like Walter Scott. Hogg's intentions in this proto-'magical realist' novel[120] are ultimately comic, but here again generic

---

[115] Letter to Douglas Kinnaird, 14 Apr. 1823, in Lord Byron, *Letters and Journals*, ed. Leslie A. Marchand, 12 vols (London: Murray, 1973–82), x. 150.

[116] Joep Leerssen, 'How *The Wild Irish Girl* Made Ireland Romantic', *Dutch Quarterly of Anglo-American Letters*, 18 (1988), 209–27: 211.

[117] Ina Ferris, 'Writing on the Border: The National Tale, Female Writing, and the Public Sphere', in Tilottama Rajan and Julia M. Wright (eds), *Romanticism, History, and the Possibilities of Genre: Re-forming Literature 1789–1837* (Cambridge: Cambridge University Press, 1998), 95.

[118] Julia M. Wright, ' "I Am Ill Fitted": Conflicts of Genre in Eliza Fenwick's *Secresy*', in Rajan and Wright (eds), *Romanticism, History, and the Possibilities of Genre*, 153.

[119] Douglas Gifford, *James Hogg* (Edinburgh: Ramsay Head Press, 1976), 93.

[120] Ian Duncan, *Scott's Shadow: The Novel in Romantic Edinburgh* (Princeton: Princeton University Press, 2007), 194.

discontinuity serves a mimetic purpose, mirroring the social tensions and clashing belief systems of the late medieval world, while also foregrounding the different forms of cultural memory, necessarily fragmentary, out of which a society reconstructs or invents its past.

## THE POLITICS OF MISCELLANY

The ideological resonances of the smooth-mix–rough-mix distinction are part of a broader politics of genre-mixing whose origins lie in the French Revolution debate, where notions of literary combination acquire an explicitly political colouring. Friedrich Schlegel hints at the analogy between combinatorial poetics and revolutionary politics in *Athenaeum* fragment 426, where he describes the French as a 'chemical nation' who 'always conduct their experiments—not least in moral chemistry—on a grand scale'. Political revolutions are 'chemical not organic movements', characteristic of a 'chemical' age; and it is therefore natural that the 'chemical' French 'should more or less dominate the age'. It is in Britain, however, that the political implications of organic and anti-organic analogies are developed most fully, and that the problem of genre-mixing—once a specialized topic in literary criticism—is brought directly to bear on the discussion of events in France. When William Windham, a leading Whig politician, referred in a House of Commons speech on 4 March 1790 to 'the strange mixture of metaphysics with politics, which we are witnessing in the neighbouring country', he was drawing attention to two features of French revolutionary discourse which he saw as symptomatic of 'the dangerous and progressive spirit of innovation' in France: its highly abstract character ('it would seem as if the ideal world were about to overrun the real') and its conflation of speculative and practical reasoning.[121] This hostile characterization of 'French theory', as it came to be known, draws not only on the instinctive mistrust of abstract reasoning fostered by British empiricism, but also on the resistance to genre-mixing—or blurred intellectual boundaries in general—that, as we have seen, was part of the 'old imperial code' of neoclassicism.

It was Windham's parliamentary colleague Edmund Burke, though, who pushed to centre stage the issue of genre-mixing in political discourse, drawing on both neoclassical and Romantic literary codes. The polemical onslaught of *Reflections on the Revolution in France* (1790) begins with his denunciation of the 'very extraordinary miscellaneous sermon' of Richard Price, in which 'moral and political sentiments' are 'mixed up in a sort of porridge of various political opinions and reflections', 'the grand ingredient in the cauldron' being 'the revolution in France'.[122] The 'political sermon' (p. 96) to which Burke refers is Price's *Discourse on the Love of*

---

[121] William Windham, Speech on Mr. Flood's Motion, House of Commons, 4 Mar. 1790, in Alfred Cobban (ed.), *The Debate on the French Revolution*, 2nd edn (London: Adam and Charles Black, 1960), 106.

[122] Edmund Burke, *Reflections on the Revolution in France, and on the Proceedings in Certain Societies in London Relative to that Event*, ed. Conor Cruise O'Brien (Harmondsworth: Penguin, 1969), 93.

*our Country* (1789), originally delivered as an address to the Revolution Society at the Old Jewry in London and then published as a pamphlet. Burke condemns both the address itself and its subsequent pamphletization as massive transgressions of generic decorum, a confusion of theology and politics dangerously reminiscent of the Civil War of the 1640s. He crystallizes his fears in the metaphor of the 'cauldron', linking the confusion of discursive domains to the indigestibility of Scotch 'porridge' (since Dr Johnson's famous dictionary entry, a byword for culinary barbarism) and, by a subliminal extension of the Scottish theme, to the more lethal concoction in Shakespeare's *Macbeth*, the political witch's brew from which only toil and trouble can be expected. Burke has further recourse to the neoclassical principle of generic purity when, in another passage, he denounces the 'monstrous tragi-comic scene of the French Revolution' as a 'strange chaos of levity and ferocity' in which 'the most opposite passions necessarily succeed and sometimes mix with each other in the mind' (pp. 92–3). The French Revolution, from this perspective, is a grotesque and sinister *Mischgedicht* whose discursive impurity symbolizes the political chaos of which Burke warns.

The irony is that the *Reflections*—Burke's 'revolutionary book against the Revolution', as Novalis shrewdly called it[123]—is itself a *Mischgedicht*, one whose mesmerizing rhetorical power is attributable in part to its combination of expressive modes, which include Old Testament prophecy, the Miltonic sublime, Scriblerian satire, chivalric romance, elegy, georgic, aphorism, tragic theatre, and street spectacle. The generic diversity of Burke's writing, highlighted in recent scholarship,[124] was fully apparent to his contemporaries. Many of the published responses to Burke's pamphlets comment directly on his aestheticization of politics and tendentious commingling of different genres, and turn against him his own rhetorical use of critical terminology, making the whole Revolution debate read at times like a protracted exercise in literary criticism. Mary Wollstonecraft's reply to the *Reflections*, *A Vindication of the Rights of Men* (1790), accuses Burke of 'slavish paradoxes' and of reproducing in his 'turgid bombast' the worst features of 'modern poetry'—a 'romantic spirit' marked not by genius and originality but by 'stale tropes and cold rodomontade', 'artificial flowers', and 'a mixture of verse and prose producing the strangest incongruities'.[125] James Mackintosh, in his *Vindiciae Gallicae* (1791), while conceding that Burke's use of the 'epistolary effusion' (notionally the *Reflections* takes the form of a *Letter Intended to have been Sent to a Gentleman in Paris*) had granted him a certain 'latitude and laxity', complained that he had taken that liberty to an unwarranted extreme and used his writing as a form of 'miscellaneous and desultory

---

[123] *Miscellaneous Observations* (1797), no. 115, in Novalis [Friedrich von Hardenberg], *Philosophical Writings*, trans. and ed. Margaret Mahony Stoljar (Albany: State University of New York Press, 1997), 43.

[124] See e.g. Gerald W. Chapman, *Edmund Burke: The Practical Imagination* (Cambridge, Mass.: Harvard University Press, 1967), ch. 5; Ronald Paulson, *Representations of Revolution (1789–1820)* (New Haven: Yale University Press, 1983), 57–72; and Frans de Bruyn, *The Literary Genres of Edmund Burke: The Political Uses of Literary Form* (Oxford: Clarendon Press, 1996).

[125] *A Vindication of the Rights of Men* (1790), in Mary Wollstonecraft, *Political Writings*, ed. Janet Todd (Oxford: Oxford University Press, 1994), 28.

warfare' whose aim was to provoke rather than to persuade.[126] Paine was even more scornful about Burke's lack of method, introducing the 'Miscellaneous Chapter' of his *Rights of Man*, Part I (1791), with the damning remark that 'Mr Burke's book is *all* Miscellany. His intention was to make an attack on the French Revolution; but instead of proceeding with an orderly arrangement, he has stormed it with a mob of ideas tumbling over and destroying one another.'[127] Like Novalis, Paine sees Burke's work as deeply self-contradictory: its politics are reactionary but its intellectual and stylistic tactics are those of the revolutionary mob.

A more impartial analysis, however, reveals that Burke's 'miscellaneous and desultory' manner, far from evincing a lack of control, is entirely deliberate; and, moreover, that the *Reflections* embodies in its formal construction precisely the kind of organic unity that Burke defended in the political sphere. Conceptually, Burke's book is a classic exposition of the theory of the organic state; stylistically, it is a perfect exemplification of the organic text. What makes the *Reflections* so rhetorically effective is the sustained, unbroken quality of its performance: although the stylistic and emotional range is infinitely varied, the reader is taken through the turns and counter-turns of the argument in one breathless sweep, an effect facilitated by the lack of chapter breaks or other subdivisions (in this, as in other respects, stretching to the extreme the conventions of the letter form to which the text nominally subscribes[128]). Burke's 'manifesto of a counter revolution', as Mackintosh called it,[129] is thus also the paradigm for a type of miscellaneous writing which implements the aesthetic ideal of organic unity with a full sense of its political ramifications.

Such is the mirroring effect of the Revolution debate, though, that Burke's opponents, while condemning his compositional methods, often employ a type of genre-mixing that is fully equivalent to Burke's but opposite in its structure and tendency: mechanical rather than organic, elucidatory rather than mystificatory, rough rather than smooth. The best example of this is Paine, who explicitly rejects Burke's organic theory and lays claim to a discursive purity lacking from his opponent, but does so in a text that is as generically mixed as the one he attacks. The difference is in the genres he selects and the way he combines them. Where Burke buttresses his arguments with literary allusions and citations, Paine supports his with facts and figures. Instead of Greek and Latin phrases, he gives us numbered propositions and tables of statistics, using data from economic reports and government papers. In each case, Paine retains the formats of his documentary sources, allowing his inset tables, figures, and subheadings to break up his own prose and roughen the texture of his writing. Instead of the unbroken 360-page outpouring of the *Reflections*, *Rights of Man* is divided into titled chapters. One consists of the

---

[126] James Mackintosh, *Vindiciae Gallicae: Defence of the French Revolution and its English Admirers, Against the Accusations of the Right Hon. Edmund Burke* (London, 1791), introd., pp. vi–vii.

[127] Thomas Paine, *Rights of Man*, ed. Henry Collins (Harmondsworth: Penguin, 1969), 138.

[128] Angela Keane, 'Reflections and Correspondences: The Unfamiliarity of Burke's Familiar Letter', in John Whale (ed.), *Edmund Burke's 'Reflections on the Revolution in France'* (Manchester: Manchester University Press, 2000).

[129] *Vindiciae Gallicae*, p. xi.

French *Declaration of the Rights of Man and of Citizens*, reproduced entire (in translation) and labelled as such. This is followed by a chapter of 'Observations on the Declaration of Rights' and by the 'Miscellaneous Chapter' already mentioned, which disarms any suggestion of its desultoriness by acknowledging its own miscellaneity. The sectional divisions and formal interruptions become even more frequent in the second part of *Rights of Man* (1792), where Paine incorporates large amounts of statistical and other data.

Paine's foregrounding of documentary and statistical sources, and his retention of their original forms and formats, has a double effect: it underlines the authenticity of his raw materials and it bolsters his own authority, reinforcing the impression (conveyed also by his plain style) that he is an honest and ordinary man, confident enough of the veracity of his cause to let the facts speak for themselves—unlike Burke, who absorbs all external reference into his unashamedly subjective eloquence. The one source Paine does not let speak for itself is Burke's *Reflections*: when citing his enemy text, Paine employs an aggressively intrusive critical method which involves long passages of quotation broken up with ironic asides and counter-statements. The rough handling of Burke's prose is an analytic device intended not only to dismantle his arguments but also to dissolve its appearance of organic unity, a feature which Paine correctly identified as crucial to its ideological effects.

As well as serving Paine's polemic, the analytic method and modular structure of *Rights of Man* made it very easy to excerpt and reproduce. The many radical miscellanies of the 1790s which incorporate selections from Paine are another manifestation of the anti-organic, rough-mix aesthetic. Juxtaposing ad hoc editorial comment with quotations, parodies, aphorisms, allegorical fables, and other popular genres, collections such as Daniel Isaac Eaton's *Hog's Wash* (1793–5) and Thomas Spence's *Pig's Meat* (1793–5) played a key role in disseminating radical ideas and in transmitting a radical aesthetic that was itself a political force. Through their forms and publishing formats as much as their arguments, they promoted a way of writing and reading that was sceptical, ironic, and resistant to literary convention, and that relished generic and stylistic incongruity as part of the 'collision of mind with mind' Godwin saw as the only road to truth.[130] As recent criticism has recognized, such collections provide a crucial context for Blake's *Marriage of Heaven and Hell* and Thelwall's *Peripatetic*, and the anti-organic aesthetic they establish carries through to the next generation, to the work of William Hone and other radical satirists, and the radical newspaper press of the 1810s.[131] The 'combinatoric form', as Steven Jones calls it,[132] of graphic caricaturists like Gillray and Cruikshank—where the relationship of word and image again relies more often on ironic contrast than on organic

---

[130] William Godwin, *An Enquiry Concerning Political Justice, and its Influence on General Virtue and Happiness*, 2 vols (London, 1793), i. 21.

[131] Graham Pechey, '*The Marriage of Heaven and Hell*: A Text and its Conjuncture', *Oxford Literary Review*, 3 (1979), 52–76; Jon Mee, *Dangerous Enthusiasm: William Blake and the Culture of Radicalism in the 1790s* (Oxford: Clarendon Press, 1992), 5; Kevin Gilmartin, *Print Politics: The Press and Radical Opposition in Early Nineteenth-Century England* (Cambridge: Cambridge University Press, 1996), 88–9.

[132] Steven E. Jones, 'Combinatoric Form in Nineteenth-Century Satiric Prints', in Alan Rawes (ed.), *Romanticism and Form* (Basingstoke: Palgrave Macmillan, 2007).

assimilation—are a further example of a rough-mixing technique, in this case with more ambivalent political tendencies. Whatever the political colouring, the distinguishing feature of this abrasive kind of *Mischgedicht* is that it foregrounds rather than conceals heterogeneity, refuses to cohere into an illusion of organic unity, and revels instead in its formal irregularity and illegitimacy. Traditionally, the Romantic has been equated with the organic, but the evidence from Britain suggests that the anti-organic, rough-mix method of combination is as common in this period as the organic, constituting a vital if previously neglected strand in the aesthetics of Romanticism.

## SHELLEY AND THE 'GREAT POEM'

Of the British Romantics, none goes further in the art of genre-mixing, and in the theorization of that art, than Percy Bysshe Shelley. His 'lyrical drama' *Prometheus Unbound* (1820) is not only the most formally complex of all mixed-genre works of the period, but also the most startling combination of, in Friedrich Schlegel's phrase, 'the essentially modern and the essentially ancient'.[133] Inspired by the French Revolution and the millenarian dreams it unleashed, *Prometheus Unbound* demonstrates in its very conception the link between revolutionary politics, idealist philosophy (in Shelley's case, Godwin rather than Fichte), and the aesthetics of the *Mischgedicht* which Friedrich Schlegel posited as the three seminal 'tendencies' of the age.[134] It does so, however, through the medium of ancient Greek mythology, modifying and supplementing the Prometheus legend to make it a universal allegory of man's struggle for freedom and desire for a better world. More fully even than Goethe's *Wilhelm Meister* or—a text it more closely resembles—*Faust*, *Prometheus Unbound* exemplifies Schlegel's ideal of 'progressive universal poetry', though Shelley had probably never read *The Athenaeum*, and Schlegel was certainly never to read *Prometheus Unbound*.[135] That few of Shelley's British contemporaries recognized its significance is unsurprising given the general hostility to his work, though the critical record in this instance was particularly dismal. The only distinction granted to *Prometheus Unbound* was that of being the supremely baffling text of its time: 'absolutely and intrinsically unintelligible', in the words of the *Quarterly Review*; 'a melange of nonsense, cockneyism, poverty, and pedantry', according to the *Literary Gazette*; a 'pestiferous mixture of blasphemy, sedition, and sensuality', according to *Blackwood's* (interestingly, its composite and 'absolute' quality is acknowledged even as its motivations are condemned).[136]

---

[133] Friedrich Schlegel letter to A. W. Schlegel, 27 Feb. 1794, quoted by Oskar Walzel, *German Romanticism*, trans. Alma Elise Lussky (1932; New York: Capricorn, 1966), 40.

[134] *Athenaeum Fragments*, no. 216, in *Philosophical Fragments*, 46.

[135] Susanne Schmid, *Shelley's German Afterlives 1814–2000* (Basingstoke: Palgrave Macmillan, 2007). See also M. Roxana Klapper, *The German Literary Influence on Shelley* (Salzburg: Institut für Englische Sprache und Literatur, University of Salzburg, 1975); and Timothy Webb, *The Violet in the Crucible: Shelley and Translation* (Oxford: Clarendon Press, 1976), chs 4–5.

[136] [W. S. Walker], *Quarterly Review*, 26 (Oct. 1821); *Literary Gazette, and Journal of Belles Lettres*, 190 (9 Sept. 1820); [John Gibson Lockhart?], *Blackwood's Edinburgh Magazine*, 7 (Sept. 1820), in James E. Barcus (ed.), *Shelley: The Critical Heritage* (London: Routledge and Kegan Paul, 1975), 254, 226, 238.

There is, however, no need to turn to Germany to find a theory of poetry appropriate to the revolutionary aims and methods of *Prometheus Unbound*, because the author provided one, a year later, in his *Defence of Poetry*. In fact, the *Defence* itself bears traces of German influence: Shelley's remarks on Shakespearean drama clearly owe something to A. W. Schlegel's *Lectures on Dramatic Art and Literature*, which Shelley read in Black's translation in 1818,[137] and he adopts, albeit fleetingly, the triadic lyric–epic–dramatic classification then in vogue among German critics. The immediate stimulus for the *Defence*, however, was Peacock's attack on poetry in *The Four Ages of Poetry* (1820). Shelley's reply (unpublished until 1840) continues the playful rivalry that had marked the relationship between the two writers since they first met in 1812, adopting in its title the idiom of chivalric combat in which they had sparred in their recent correspondence. In this 'defence' of the wounded 'honour' of poetry, more was at stake than personal pride. The quarrel between Peacock and Shelley was, in many ways, a paradigmatic confrontation between the competing accounts of modernity and antiquity traced in this book. In dismissing poetry as an obsolete and useless art form, Peacock makes no mention of his own literary calling, satirical novelist, but the novel is the unspoken Bakhtinian subtext of his essay, being the one literary genre that is attuned to modernity, that has no illusions, and that is able, in Peacock's hands, to perform the supposedly useful intellectual task of exposing the inadequacies of other literary forms. Indeed, the *Four Ages* itself, in its heteroglossic eloquence, sweeping iconoclasm, and mordant irony is just such a novelistic performance—one that demonstrates by both argument and example what Peacock deems so lamentably absent from modern poetry.

Shelley's riposte is, likewise, both discursive and performative, its logical turns and counter-turns, leaps of imagination, and metaphoric inventiveness making it as much a prose poem as a work of literary theory (a generic distinction of the sort it expressly rejects). Though written in an oracular first person singular, the *Defence* is a richly dialogic text which, along with Peacock, engages with a huge range of other writers and critics. Shelley's basic premiss is the cooperative and cumulative nature of artistic endeavour, and, like Friedrich Schlegel and Coleridge, he describes poetry as a combinatory art, using chemical (and alchemical) metaphors to describe its operations. The *Defence* opens with a distinction between 'two classes of mental action': reason, 'the principle of analysis', which involves the contemplation of 'the relations borne by one thought to another'; and imagination, 'the principle of synthesis', which involves the mind acting upon thoughts 'so as to colour them with its own light, and composing from them, as from other elements, other thoughts, each containing within itself the principle of its own integrity'.[138] Poetry, as 'the

---

[137] Ronald Tetreault, *The Poetry of Life: Shelley and Literary Form* (Toronto: University of Toronto Press, 1987), 124–5 and 272 n. 5. In his unfinished pamphlet *A Philosophical View of Reform* (1819), Shelley cites as evidence of the 'rapidly maturing revolution' in Germany 'their severe, bold, and liberal spirit of criticism' and 'their subtle and deep philosophy'; *Shelley's Prose, or, The Trumpet of a Prophecy*, ed. David Lee Clark (1954; London: Fourth Estate, 1988), 237. Shelley recycled parts of the *Philosophical View* in his *Defence of Poetry* but omitted this passage.

[138] *Shelley's Poetry and Prose*, 2nd edn, ed. Donald H. Reiman and Neil Fraistat (New York: Norton, 2002), 510. All subsequent references are to this edition.

expression of the Imagination' (p. 511), is thus not only expressive but also combinatorial: poetry creates new thoughts through the 'synthesis' of existing ones, exactly as Davy describes chemical compounds being formed in his section 'On Analysis and Synthesis' in *Elements of Chemical Philosophy*, a text Shelley knew well.[139] This is true of all art forms—and Shelley initially uses 'poetry' (*poesis*) in a 'general' sense to cover all of them—but it is particularly true of 'poetry in a more restricted sense', whose medium is language, which 'has relation to thoughts alone' and 'is susceptible of more various and delicate combinations, than colour, form, or motion' (p. 513). The extreme plasticity of language is the precondition of poetry's most powerful combinatorial tool, metaphor, which in turn is the basis of its psychological and ethical power. Through metaphor, poetry 'awakens and enlarges the mind itself by rendering it the receptacle of a thousand unapprehended combinations of thought', which (in a continuation of the chemical metaphor) 'have the power of attracting and assimilating to their own nature all other thoughts', a perpetual replenishment which is also a perpetual synthesis. By this process, it 'strengthens that faculty which is the organ of the moral nature of man', the imagination, 'in the same manner as exercise strengthens a limb' (p. 517). In another passage Shelley echoes Coleridge's theory of imagination in *Biographia*, attributing to poetry the power to combine opposites: 'it subdues to union under its light yoke all irreconcilable things' (p. 533).

Combination also takes place at the level of form, a term which has multiple meanings in the *Defence*. Its broadest sense is illustrated by Shelley's claim that imagination 'has for its objects those forms which are common to universal nature and to existence itself' (p. 510), which include poetry and 'the kindred expressions of the poetical faculty; architecture, painting, music, the dance, sculpture, philosophy, and we may add the forms of civil life' (p. 518)—a notable extension to the normal list of art forms. Shelley also applies the term, more restrictively, to particular modes or genres—'the epic, dramatic, and lyrical forms' (p. 514)—or subcategories thereof, such as tragedy, comedy, or 'bucolic poetry'. Sometimes Shelley uses the term more restrictively still, to designate a technical structure such as metre or rhyme, 'traditional forms of harmony and language' which may not be essential to the genre or art form in question. Thus, 'Plato was essentially a poet' by virtue of the 'truth and splendour of his imagery and the melody of his language', even though 'he forbore to invent any regular plan of rhythm which would include, under determinate forms, the varied pauses of his style' (p. 514). In the same paragraph, Shelley implies a distinction between form itself and the 'spirit' of the form, a distinction analogous to the one Goethe (following Shaftesbury) makes between 'outer' and 'inner' form, or that Coleridge (following Schelling) makes between 'Shape as superinduced' and 'Form as proceeding'.[140] Shelley, though, never quite allows form to become the

---

[139] *Elements of Chemical Philosophy*, 180–94. For Shelley's knowledge of this and other works by Davy, see Carl Grabo, *A Newton Among Poets: Shelley's Use of Science in Prometheus Unbound* (New York: Gordian Press, 1968), ch. 7; Mark Kipperman, 'Coleridge, Shelley, Davy, and Science's Millennium', *Criticism: A Quarterly for Literature and the Arts*, 40/3 (1998), 409–36; and Sharon Ruston, *Shelley and Vitality* (Basingstoke: Palgrave Macmillan, 2005), 95–101.

[140] See Ch. 2 above, pp. 80, 83.

antithesis of some more essential quality, because form itself carries for him a Platonic resonance, implying an ideal against which the actual instance is measured. The potential confusions can be seen in the passage where he contrasts the 'accidental vesture' of a poet's conceptions—the 'temporary dress in which his creations must be arrayed'—with their 'internal nature': the latter cannot be so far concealed by the former 'that the spirit of its form shall communicate it to the very disguise, and indicate the shape it hides from the manner in which it is worn' (p. 516). 'Spirit' here is not the opposite of 'form' but the essence of it; and 'shape' is not superinduced but inherent and 'internal'. Thus defined, Shelley's language of forms is also a language of essences, and the combining of forms a means, as for Coleridge, of apprehending some ultimate multeity-in-unity. Edgar Allan Poe's reformulation of this key Romantic motif brings out the Platonic logic perfectly: 'Inspired by an ecstatic prescience of the glories beyond the grave, we struggle, by multiform combinations among the things and thoughts of Time, to attain a portion of that Loveliness whose very elements, perhaps, appertain to eternity alone.'[141]

Platonic (and Aristotelian) assumptions are also operative in Shelley's argument that each genre has an ideal form to which individual instances can and should approximate. His chief example is drama, 'that form under which a greater number of modes of expression of poetry are susceptible of being combined than any other' (p. 521). It is indisputable, says Shelley, that drama 'never was understood or practised according to the true philosophy of it, as at Athens'. Athenian drama 'co-existed with the moral and intellectual greatness of the age' (pp. 519–20) and 'the Athenians employed language, action, music, painting, the dance, and religious institutions, to produce a common effect', each element being 'disciplined into a beautiful proportion and unity one towards the other' (p. 518). Modern drama employs only a few of these elements, although in one respect it has advanced beyond the Greeks, since the 'modern practise of blending comedy and tragedy, though liable to great abuse in point of practise, is undoubtedly an extension of the dramatic circle' (p. 519). By this Shelley means not ordinary 'tragicomedy', but works like *King Lear*, in which the 'comedy' is 'universal, ideal and sublime'. *Lear*, indeed, 'may be judged to be the most perfect specimen of the dramatic art existing in the world', despite Shakespeare's 'ignorance of the philosophy of the Drama which has prevailed in modern Europe' (p. 519). At the opposite extreme is Restoration drama, 'a cold imitation of the form of the great masterpieces of antiquity, divested of all harmonious accompaniment of the kindred arts; and often the very form misunderstood'. Distorted by a corrupt and cynical society, comedy in this period lost 'its ideal universality' and became an expression not of 'sympathetic merriment', but of 'malignity, sarcasm and contempt' (pp. 520–1).

As these remarks suggest, Shelley's own 'philosophy' of genre involves a mixture of artistic, ethical, and social factors, and the *Defence* offers a unique synthesis of critical discourses. Shelley's essentialist theory of form rescues Plato and Aristotle from

---

[141] 'The Poetic Principle' (1850), in Edgar Allan Poe, *Complete Poems and Selected Essays*, ed. Richard Gray (London: Dent, 1993), 159.

neoclassical formalism and rethinks their philosophy of form in terms of modern conceptions of organic unity and multiplicity. At the same time, though, his approach to genre is irreducibly historical and political. Peacock, in linking the rise and fall of poetry to changing intellectual conditions and the division of labour, had drawn on the stadial theories of the Scottish Enlightenment, but his recasting of their arguments served the purposes of parody. Shelley also draws on those arguments, but develops them into a full-blooded sociology of genre which brings together history, literary criticism, and ideological critique in an unprecedented way. Where contemporaries like Leigh Hunt were still engaging in polemics against the rule-bound theories of the 'French school' and their damaging effects on English poetry, Shelley exposes the far deeper corruption of poetry that took place after the Restoration for historical and political reasons. Not only drama but 'all forms of poetry in which poetry had been accustomed to be expressed became hymns to the triumph of kingly power over liberty and virtue', with Milton as the solitary exception, 'illuminating an age unworthy of him' (p. 520).

Underpinning his political history of literature is Shelley's thesis about poetry's ultimately redemptive nature. Such is 'the connexion of poetry and social good', he says, that 'in periods of the decay of social life', poetry (drama especially, as the most social of forms) necessarily 'sympathizes with that decay' (pp. 520–1). Even in its corrupted state, though, poetry 'contains within itself the seeds at once of its own and of social renovation' (p. 522). To make his point, he takes a second historical example, 'the bucolic and erotic poetry' of ancient Sicily and Egypt—the works of Theocritus, Callimachus, Moschus, Bion, and others. Judged by the standards of Homer and Sophocles, this poetry was imperfect, vitiated by an 'excess of sweetness' and an imbalance of feeling to thought. But it was valuable nonetheless, because it counteracted the political decadence of the societies in which it was produced, and kept alive the idea of a true community:

corruption must have utterly destroyed the fabric of human society before Poetry can ever cease. The sacred links of that chain have never been entirely disjoined, which descending through the minds of many men is attached to those great minds, whence as from a magnet the invisible effluence is sent forth, which at once connects, animates and sustains the life of all . . . And let us not circumscribe the effects of the bucolic and erotic poetry within the limits of those to whom it was addressed. They may have perceived the beauty of those immortal compositions, simply as fragments and isolated portions: those who are more finely organized, or born in a happier age, may recognize them as episodes to that great poem, which all poets, like the co-operating thoughts of one great mind, have built up since the beginning of the world. (p. 522)

The last part of this remarkable passage can be read as an answer to Peacock's charge about the competitive nature of poetic endeavour: his claim that the origins of poetry, like other 'trades', lies in 'the natural desire of every man to engross to himself as much power and property as he can acquire by any of the means which might makes right'.[142] Against this Hobbesian view, Shelley asserts the collective and

---

[142] *Peacock's 'Four Ages of Poetry'; Shelley's 'Defence of Poetry'; Browning's 'Essay on Poetry'* (1921; Oxford: Blackwell, 1971), 3.

collaborative nature of poetry, appealing to Plato's notion of the 'one great mind' of which we are all portions (a cornerstone of Shelley's metaphysical system) to make an analogous point about the 'great poem' to which all poets contribute. This, in turn, serves to reinforce the argument Shelley had already made in the Preface to *Prometheus Unbound* in response to a charge laid by the *Quarterly Review* that he was 'an unsparing imitator' of Wordsworth.[143] In the Preface, he had countered this with the statement that 'As to imitation; Poetry is a mimetic art. It creates, but it creates by combination and representation': new literary creation occurs not *ex nihilo*, but through a fresh combination of existing elements, and there is necessarily a 'generic resemblance' between contemporaries arising from the spirit of the age (p. 208). The *Defence* expands this counter-argument: the 'great poem' is literary combination writ large, an endlessly self-renewing artwork produced by the 'co-operating thoughts' of writers across time. As if to demonstrate his point, Shelley echoes a statement from the Preface to *Lyrical Ballads* about how 'the Poet binds together by passion and knowledge the vast empire of human society, as it is spread over the whole earth, and over all time'.[144] Developing Wordsworth's idea, Shelley extends his 'binding' metaphor into a sequence of physical, chemical, and biological images: poetry as a 'chain' whose 'sacred links' attach 'the minds of many men' with 'great minds'; 'a magnet'; and an 'invisible effluence' which 'connects, animates, and sustains the life of all' (an allusion to contemporary speculation about the principle of vitality). By imitating and amplifying Wordsworth, Shelley performs the mimetic, combinatorial process even as he defines it.

There is, however, yet another dimension to the 'great poem' passage. Indirectly, it offers a solution to the Ancients and Moderns crux, an issue still very much alive in contemporary criticism. In Shelley's theory of the 'great poem', this hoary distinction—mischievously reworked by Peacock—simply disappears. Ancient and modern, classical and romantic, constitute, for Shelley, a continuum: the 'great poem' subsumes all types of poetry, all literary periods, all national traditions. More inclusive even that Friedrich Schlegel's *progressive Universalpoesie*, Shelley's conception of poetry 'in the most universal sense of the word' (p. 512) embraces the work not just of poets but also of philosophers and historians, legislators, prophets, 'authors of revolutions in opinion', the 'child at play', the 'savage', and, in 'the infancy of society' (when the metaphors are still fresh), 'language itself' (pp. 511–12, 515).

Intriguingly, Shelley's inspiration for this strand of his argument may lie in classical literature. Elsewhere in the *Defence*, Shelley introduces yet another metaphor for his vision of interconnection and unity: the 'cyclic poem'. The 'cyclic poets' (p. 518) were the post-Homeric 'rhapsodists' of ancient Greece who performed and reworked the stories of the *Iliad* and *Odyssey*, making their own poems and Homer's part of one continuous cycle—as described in Plato's *Ion*, parts of which Shelley translated while writing the *Defence*.[145] The *OED* cites the *Defence* (misdating it to

---

[143] [John Taylor Coleridge], review of *Laon and Cythna*, 21 (Apr. 1819), in Barcus (ed.), *Shelley: Critical Heritage*, 125.

[144] Preface to *Lyrical Ballads* (1805), in *Prose Works*, i. 141.

[145] James A. Notopoulos, *The Platonism of Shelley: A Study of Platonism and the Poetic Mind* (Durham: Duke University Press, 1949), 462.

1822) for first use of 'cyclic' in this sense of 'belonging to a cycle of mythic and heroic story'. In fact, though, Shelley had already used the word in his Preface to *Peter Bell the Third* (1819), referring playfully to his and other parodies as a 'series of cyclic poems' inspired by Wordsworth's original *Peter Bell*.[146] In the *Defence*, moreover, he uses 'cyclic poem' in both a literal and an extended, metaphorical sense, applying it to the origins of natural languages, each of which 'near to its source is in itself the chaos of a cyclic poem' (p. 512), and then, in an even more daring move, to the 'revolutions of ancient Rome', whose artistic creations and institutional structures 'are the episodes of the cyclic poem written by Time upon the memories of men. The Past, like an inspired rhapsodist, fills the theatre of everlasting generations with their harmony' (p. 523). Here, the 'cyclic poem' becomes a comprehensive metaphor for literary tradition and cultural memory: the capacity of great works of the past— artistic and otherwise—to live beyond their own historical moment, acquire new meanings across time, and inspire later acts of creativity. Shelley's theory of the 'great poem' completes this sequence of ideas. The notion of art as 'imitation and com-bination'—as a collective and cumulative endeavour which reveals itself across what Bakhtin (in a strikingly similar phrase) calls 'great time'—finds its ultimate expres-sion in Shelley's vision of a progressive, universal poem, the 'episodes' of which are like 'the co-operating thoughts of one great mind'.

Such theories cannot be proved or disproved. The ideas of the *Defence* do, however, have a demonstrable application to Shelley's own poetry, and one poem in particular illuminates the full force of his combinatorial poetics: *Prometheus Unbound*. Not only is Shelley's 'lyrical drama' a supreme example of Romantic genre-mixing, it is also a brilliant enactment of the idea of the 'great poem', an idea that the writing of the play undoubtedly helped him to crystallize. Of the vast range of texts, forms, voices, and discourses embedded in *Prometheus Unbound*, many critics have spoken—mostly with horror in contemporary reviews; mostly with admiration in recent scholarship.[147] Far from concealing its affiliations with other works of literature, the poem ostentatiously displays them. Shelley signals his intertextual methods and revisionary motives from the start with his epigraph, a coded address to Aeschylus in which he calls upon his great precursor to pay attention to his audacious reworking of Greek tragedy; and with his Preface, where he justifies his revision of the Prometheus legend and explains his view of poetry as a combinatorial art. In effect, Shelley becomes a self-styled rhapsodist, and *Prometheus Unbound* part of a 'cyclic poem' which supplements and modifies the many poems that precede it. So comprehensive is the range of reference, and so intricate the combination, that the effect of Shelley's compositional strategy is to reveal the essential connectedness of the entire European literary tradition, from classical antiquity through to the present day. Aeschylean tragedy, Virgilian pastoral, Dantean dream vision, Spenserian quest romance, Miltonic epic, Jonsonian masque, Mozartian

---

[146] *Shelley's Poetry and Prose*, 340.
[147] Earlier attempts to describe the form of the poem are summarized in Percy Bysshe Shelley, *Prometheus Unbound: A Variorum Edition*, ed. Lawrence J. Zillman (Seattle: University of Washing-ton Press, 1959), 46–53. Some recent descriptions are cited below.

opera, Wordsworthian lyric: *Prometheus Unbound* takes us through a universal history of genres, inhabiting one by one all the major forms of expression that have constituted the history of European literature.

While deploying these genres, Shelley also transforms and combines them, show-ing one genre metamorphosing into another and new forms being created out of the fusion of old ones. Ideologically, too, Shelley transforms his chosen genres, purging them, where necessary, of their reactionary associations and bringing them into the revolutionary condition which shows the latently 'progressive' tendency of all true art. Tragedy loses its defeatism by ending not in death but in release and regeneration; pastoral is recoded as utopian rather than nostalgic; quest romance is secularized and internalized; and masque ceases to be aristocratic masquerade and becomes instead a dance of *un*masking, in which disguises are stripped away and things assume their true form. Thus adapted, the voices and forms of literary tradition become harbingers of change, contributing incrementally to the promised revolution that is the play's 'far goal of Time' (III. iii. 174). In Act II we get a figurative expression of this idea when Asia, visiting a 'Pinnacle of Rock among Mountains', witnesses a 'sun-awakened avalanche'. She interprets this as an emblem of how revolutionary change occurs: first the slow build-up of knowledge, as 'Flake after flake, in Heaven-defying minds | ... thought by thought is piled'; then the avalanche, the sudden loosening of 'some great truth', to which 'the nations echo round | Shaken to their roots: as do the mountains now' (II. iii. 36–42). Manuscript evidence suggests this passage is another response to the accusations of plagiarism in the *Quarterly Review*.[148] As such, it is also an anticipation of the 'great poem' idea in the *Defence*, but with one crucial difference: the process has an endpoint. When the build-up of 'co-operating thoughts' by 'Heaven-defying minds' has reached a critical point, the next thought will prove decisive, and revolutionary change will occur. *Prometheus Unbound* aspires to be that decisive contribution: not just a continuation of the 'great poem' but its pivotal, apocalyptic episode—the final snowflake that causes the avalanche.

Is the genre-mixing rough or smooth? At one level, undoubtedly the former. What differentiates *Prometheus Unbound* from a work of comparable scope like *The Prelude* is its extreme formal discontinuity. Quite apart from the overarching tension be-tween lyric and dramatic modes signalled by the title—a crux in many modern readings of the play[149]—the movement between genres is marked not only by abrupt linguistic and tonal transitions but also by startling metrical shifts. The juxtaposition of passages of blank verse with other verse forms is a continuous feature of the play, but the balance between them shifts markedly from scene to scene and act to act. The interspersal of iambic pentameter and lyrical metres which in Act I mimics the interplay of character dialogue and choral odes in classical tragedy has by Act IV given way to a quasi-operatic structure in which aria-like lyrics are maximized and

---

[148] Timothy Webb, ' "The Avalanche of Ages": Shelley's Defence of Atheism and *Prometheus Unbound*', *Keats–Shelley Memorial Bulletin*, 35 (1984), 1–39: 13.

[149] Angela Leighton, *Shelley and the Sublime: An Interpretation of the Major Poems* (Cambridge: Cambridge University Press, 1984), 76; Tilottama Rajan, 'Deconstruction or Reconstruction: Reading Shelley's *Prometheus Unbound*', *Studies in Romanticism*, 23/3 (1984), 317–38.

blank-verse recitative minimized. The sudden changes of speed, in the turnover of genres as much as in the action of the play, have the same roughening effect: the static torture scene in Act I, a pure example of lyrical tragedy in which everything is felt and nothing happens, contrasts utterly with Act II, an accelerated quest romance in which elements of ode, dream vision, pastoral, and epic follow one another in rapid succession. The principle of juxtaposition is presented even more starkly in Act III, which opens with the toppling of Jupiter, an ironic reversal of the situation in Act I, and also a reminder that the tragic, or pseudo-tragic, plot in the Prometheus myth is that of Jupiter, not Prometheus: it is the former's, not the latter's, pride that leads to downfall, but Jupiter's is a *peripeteia* without the saving grace of self-knowledge, and the focus of the play immediately shifts elsewhere. It is the formal discontinuities as much as the intellectual complexities of *Prometheus Unbound* which led contemporary reviewers to describe it as 'unintelligible', a charge usually accompanied, as we have seen, by references to its hybrid quality ('melange', 'pestiferous mixture'). In so far as such readings register Shelley's aesthetic shock tactics, they could be taken as a measure of the play's effectiveness as a rough-mix *Mischgedicht*.

At another level, though, the aesthetic effect is strangely harmonious. For all the formal discontinuity, the different parts of *Prometheus Unbound* are held together by patterns of imagery which have an almost systematic unity. A striking feature is the way Shelley penetrates to the archetypal substratum of the genres he deploys—the 'icy rocks' and barren landscape of tragedy, the 'green world' and spring awakening of romance. Genres, pared to their figurative essence and welded together in seasonal sequence, become part of an overarching allegory of regeneration that is another kind of 'cyclic poem'—a universal genre-system of the sort Frye describes in *Anatomy of Criticism* (a theory of genre mainly inspired by another Romantic visionary, Blake).[150] Geographical, psychological, and historical symbolism work together, the mythological idiom of the play fusing its different frames of reference. Verbal details reinforce the impression of unity, connecting otherwise disparate elements. Jupiter's downfall in Act III, scene 1, arguably the moment of maximum generic discord in the play since it conflicts so sharply with surrounding scenes, is captured in language which echoes, in grim parody, earlier parts of the play. Jupiter's opening address to the 'congregated Powers of heaven' mirrors Prometheus' opening speech in Act I, but only to expose by contrast Jupiter's unheroic and tyrannical self-delusion. Jupiter's speech contains, too, an ironic inversion of the avalanche passage in Act II, Asia's snowfall of revolutionary thoughts being metamorphosed into Jupiter's blizzard of 'curses', which,

> through the pendulous air
> Like snow on herbless peaks, fall flake by flake
> And cling to it,                                   (III. i. 11–13)

precipitating another kind of avalanche: his own downfall. Throughout the play, as well as allegorizing a political trajectory, the progression of genres—from tragedy to

---

[150] Northrop Frye, *Anatomy of Criticism: Four Essays* (Princeton: Princeton University Press, 1957). For a reading of *Prometheus Unbound* in terms of generic *mythoi*, see Frye's *A Study of English Romanticism* (1968; Brighton: Harvester Press, 1983), 87–124.

romance to comedy to masque—has also a psychological correlative. The transitions between genres are abrupt, but there is a clear development in the logic of emotion: tragic pain and fear gives way to a poetry of desire (quest romance), which then transforms into a poetry of joy expressed through the 'transcendental' form of masque and opera.[151] As Curran observes, 'in no other work of literature do genres serve so fully and self-consciously as modes of apprehension', the mixing of genres implying 'an uncompromising multiperspectivism' whereby 'the mind reorders the elements that constitute its universe'.[152]

Ultimately, there is no single way of reading *Prometheus Unbound*, and the smoothness or roughness of the poem's formal texture lies partly in the eye of the beholder. That is, how we perceive the artistic construction depends partly on the formal presuppositions that we bring to bear. According to McGann's influential critique,[153] readings of Romantic texts have been unduly shaped by Romanticism's own critical doctrines: notions of organic unity, in particular, have tended to promote what I have called 'smooth' readings. It is noticeable that some of the 'rough' readings have come from contemporaries who were historically closer to those critical doctrines, recognized their ideological load, and were in many cases resistant to them. A more recent tradition of rough reading has developed in light of the new historicist critique, by dispensing with Romantic theory and applying, instead, a modern hermeneutics of suspicion—'reading against the grain'. In this chapter, I have suggested a third way of proceeding, which involves recovering the anti-organic, 'rough' strand in Romantic theory, and reading Romantic texts in light of it. This makes possible another kind of historically sensitive reading, which can do justice both to the intimate connection of theory and practice (the 'metaromantic' dimension) that is an undeniable fact of much Romantic writing, and to the actual artistic properties of the work in question, whether rough or smooth. Since Shelley espoused both rough and smooth principles—an organic and an anti-organic poet-ics[154]—this might allow us to conclude that *Prometheus Unbound* is both a 'pestifer-ous mixture' and a work of transcendental synthesis. At one level it is designed to shake readers out of their assumptions, at another to evoke the fecund chaos that primitivists like Brown had imagined to be literature's primal origins and that visionaries like Schlegel imagined to be its absolute goal.

---

[151] Angus Fletcher, *The Transcendental Masque: An Essay on Milton's 'Comus'* (Ithaca, N.Y.: Cornell University Press, 1971). For masque elements in *Prometheus Unbound*, see Earl Wasserman, *Shelley: A Critical Reading* (Baltimore: Johns Hopkins University Press, 1971), 360–73. For its operatic features, see Tetreault, *Poetry of Life*, ch. 8; and Peter Conrad, *Romantic Opera and Literary Form* (Berkeley: University of California Press, 1977), 72.

[152] Curran, *Poetic Form and British Romanticism*, 203; see also Curran's more extended reading of the play in *Shelley's Annus Mirabilis: The Maturing of an Epic Vision* (San Marino, Calif.: Hunting-don Library, 1975).

[153] Jerome McGann, *The Romantic Ideology: A Critical Investigation* (Chicago: University of Chicago Press, 1983).

[154] For the anti-organic strand, see Hugh Roberts, *Shelley and the Chaos of History: A New Politics of Poetry* (University Park: Pennsylvania State University Press, 1997), 238–43.

# Conclusion

> I am sorry that Coleridge has christened his Ancient Marinere 'a poet's Reverie'—it is as bad as Bottom the Weaver's declaration that he is not a Lion but only the scenical representation of a Lion.
>
> (Charles Lamb, letter to William Wordsworth, 30 January 1801)

In face of the evidence presented in this book, the claim that Romanticism represents a movement 'beyond genre' is unsustainable, and indeed largely meaningless. The decline of traditional theories of genre resulted not in an erosion of genre-consciousness but in an enhancement of it. Attempts to reform, or jettison, the 'old imperial code' of neoclassicism made it paradoxically all the more visible, and the new critical codes were as preoccupied with genre as the old one; more so, in the sense that the concept itself was under theoretical scrutiny for the first time, as was the related, and no less problematic, concept of form. Generic classifications and rankings, the origin and evolution of genres, national and international canons, the relationship between internal and external structure, organic and anti-organic form: these and other topics were the subject of relentless critical debate. In the creative sphere, too, generic concerns were ever present. Even the most radical literary practice of the period involved, typically, not the transcendence of genres but the transformation of them: literary genres were revived, fabricated, internalized, ironized, subverted, fragmented, brought together in new combinations, adapted to new ideological purposes, made to reflect on themselves (and on one another)—but not, with rare exceptions, abandoned altogether. The idea that a literary text can be a 'genre in itself' acquired some currency, and there are many Romantic compositions which foreground their generic idiosyncrasies through subtitles, footnotes, and in other ways. But, such was the size of the market and the sophistication of the publication industry that this was also a period in which experiments were replicated, innovations standardized, and new genres established, in some cases with extraordinary speed and commercial success.

No single example can illustrate all of these trends and counter-trends, but it might be helpful, by way of conclusion, to consider how some of these factors impacted on a particular genre which has some claim to be representative of Romanticism: the ode. To attempt a description of the ode's development in this period is to be confronted immediately with the methodological problems I indentified at the outset: where to begin and end, how to separate the history of this genre from that of others, which works to consider as belonging to the genre. Now that the broader context has been established, however, a tentative account can be ventured. The flourishing of the ode in this period is a matter of indisputable record. No other period of English poetry can rival the concentration of achievement in this form of lyric represented by the finest odes of Coleridge, Wordsworth, Shelley, and Keats; and at no other point in its long history does the ode occupy so central a place in British literary consciousness. Ralph Waldo Emerson's claim that Wordsworth's 'Immortality Ode' represents 'the high-water-mark which the intellect has reached in this age'[1] might be regarded by some as hyperbole, but it gives an accurate indication of the scale of intellectual ambition that underpins such masterworks as the 'Immortality Ode', Coleridge's 'Dejection: An Ode', Shelley's 'Ode to the West Wind', and Keats's great odes of 1819. Nor were these isolated performances: with the exception of Blake, all the major Romantic poets experimented repeatedly with the genre, and their endeavours constitute only a small fraction of the total number of odes written in this period.[2] In Britain, as in Germany, the ode is as integral to the development of Romanticism as Romanticism is to the modern development of the ode.[3]

So familiar are the accomplishments of the Romantic ode, indeed, that their paradoxical quality is often overlooked. For in many ways the poetics of the ode can be said to run directly counter to the general literary norms of the period, especially to those stylistic tenets by which the first-generation Romantic poets sought to distinguish themselves from their neoclassical precursors. If Jonathan Culler is right in identifying apostrophe, the quintessentially 'literary' figure of speech, as the defining technique of the ode,[4] the condition of language to which all odes aspire, nothing could be more at odds with an aesthetic programme which sought to revolutionize British poetry by excluding all rhetorical contrivance and replacing poetic diction with the language of ordinary speech. No genre of poetry, with the possible exception of the sonnet, had traditionally depended more heavily on the kind of ostentatious linguistic artifice Wordsworth had in mind when he spoke of 'poetic diction', and none had made more habitual use of the device of personification, which he deemed admissible (that is, emotionally 'natural') in only the rarest of circumstances.[5] Nowhere, in fact, was one more likely to find displayed

---

[1] *English Traits* (1856), in *The Collected Works of Ralph Waldo Emerson*, v, ed. Douglas Emory Wilson et al. (Cambridge, Mass.: Harvard University Press, 1994), 168.

[2] There is still no comprehensive study of the English ode in this period; partial surveys include George N. Shuster, *The English Ode from Milton to Keats* (New York: Columbia University Press, 1940), chs 8–9; John Heath-Stubbs, *The Ode* (Oxford: Oxford University Press, 1969), ch. 6; John D. Jump, *The Ode* (London: Methuen, 1974), ch. 4; Paul H. Fry, *The Poet's Calling in the English Ode* (New Haven: Yale University Press, 1980), chs 6–10; and Stuart Curran, *Poetic Form and British Romanticism* (New York: Oxford University Press, 1986), ch. 4.

[3] For German developments, see John Hamilton, 'The Revival of the Ode', in Michael Ferber (ed.), *A Companion to European Romanticism* (Oxford: Blackwell, 2005); Cyrus Hamlin, 'Reading the Ode' (1979), in his *Hermeneutics of Form: Romantic Poetics in Theory and Practice* (New Haven: Henry R. Schwab, 1998); and the classic study by Karl Viëtor, *Geschichte der deutschen Ode* (1923; Hildesheim: Olms, 1961).

[4] 'Apostrophe', in Jonathan Culler, *The Pursuit of Signs: Semiotics, Literature, Deconstruction* (London: Routledge and Kegan Paul, 1981), ch. 7.

[5] Preface to *Lyrical Ballads* (1800) and Appendix (1802), in *The Prose Works of William Wordsworth*, ed. W. J. B. Owen and Jane Worthington Smyser, 3 vols (Oxford: Clarendon Press, 1974), i. 130, 160–5.

the whole panoply of rhetorical devices—exclamation, periphrasis, hyperbole, parallelism, and a hundred other amplifying techniques—by which poets had traditionally been taught, in their *Arts of Poetry* and their rhetorical handbooks, to 'build the lofty rhyme'.[6]

This proclivity of the ode towards manufactured emotion—the fake 'poetic fervor' that Coleridge called 'the madness prepense of Pseudo-poesy, or the startling *hysteric* of weakness over-exerting itself, which bursts on the unprepared reader in sundry odes and apostrophes to abstract terms'[7]—would seem to make this genre, if not incompatible with, at least highly uncongenial to, a poetical system that defined the 'spontaneous' expression of powerful emotion as a touchstone of authentic creativity. Whether this tendency was intrinsic to the ode, or (as Coleridge argued) symptomatic only of its misuse, eighteenth-century poetry collections were choked with bombastic ode-writing of this sort, and the decades prior to Romanticism are notable chiefly for their many parodies of the ode—a sure sign, according to Russian Formalist theory, of a genre's decline.[8] How, then, do we explain the fascination of the Romantics, self-styled reformers of poetry, with this outmoded, exhausted genre, once held by neoclassical critics to be the noblest form of lyric, inferior only to the epic and tragedy in the hierarchy of literary genres, but now treated by many writers and readers with contempt and derision?[9]

Without fully registering this paradox, literary historians have generally followed the lead of the Romantics themselves in arguing that poets of the period were interested in the ode, as in other traditional genres, only to transcend or transform it. Hazlitt's remark, in his essay on Wordsworth in *The Spirit of the Age* (1825), that 'The Ode and Epode, the Strophe and the Antistrophe, he laughs to scorn', epitomizes this view, implying as it does a direct correspondence between Wordsworth's revolutionary politics and his 'levelling' attitude to traditional genres and generic hierarchies.[10] Modern scholars have refined Hazlitt's thesis, one influential reformulation being M. H. Abrams's celebrated account of the 'greater Romantic lyric'. This is the label Abrams assigns to a new type of poem, 'the earliest Romantic formal invention', which 'displaced what neoclassical critics had called "the greater ode"—the elevated Pindaric, in distinction to "the

---

[6] Milton's phrase from 'Lycidas' (line 11), whose own odic properties are discussed by Clay Hunt, *'Lycidas' and the Italian Critics* (New Haven: Yale University Press, 1979), ch. 4.

[7] *The Collected Works of Samuel Taylor Coleridge*, vii: *Biographia Literaria*, ed. James Engell and W. Jackson Bate, 2 vols (London: Routledge and Kegan Paul, 1983), ii. 84–5.

[8] Yuri Tynianov, 'Dostoevsky and Gogol: Towards a Theory of Parody' (1921), partially trans. in Victor Erlich (ed.), *Twentieth-Century Russian Literary Criticism* (New Haven: Yale University Press, 1975). For his more general theory, see id., 'On Literary Evolution' (1927), in Ladislav Matejka and Krystyna Pomorska (eds), *Readings in Russian Poetics: Formalist and Structuralist Views* (Cambridge, Mass.: Harvard University Press, 1971).

[9] For the ode's shifting status, see Norman Maclean, 'From Action to Image: Theories of the Lyric in the Eighteenth Century', in R. S. Crane (ed.), *Critics and Criticism: Ancient and Modern* (Chicago: University of Chicago Press, 1952); Howard D. Weinbrot, *Britannia's Issue: The Rise of British Literature from Dryden to Ossian* (Cambridge: Cambridge University Press, 1995), chs 9–10; and Ralph Cohen, 'The Return to the Ode', in John Sitter (ed.), *The Cambridge Companion to Eighteenth Century Poetry* (Cambridge: Cambridge University Press, 2001).

[10] 'Mr. Wordsworth', *The Spirit of the Age* (1825), in *The Complete Works of William Hazlitt*, ed. P. P. Howe, 21 vols (London: Dent, 1930–4), xi. 87.

lesser ode" modeled chiefly on Horace—as the favored form for the long lyric poem',[11] and which includes all the bona fide 'odes' I have mentioned as well as many others which normally carry a different generic designation or none at all, including most of Coleridge's conversation poems, Wordsworth's 'Tintern Abbey', Shelley's 'Stanzas Written in Dejection', and Keats's 'To Autumn'. The new genre, according to Abrams, differs from the poetic forms it subsumed or replaced (not only the ode, but also the sonnet, the inscription, and the loco-descriptive poem) in its looser formal structure, its more conversational idiom, and its structural subordination of description to meditation, technical changes which permitted a more faithful registration of the flow of consciousness and thus a fuller realization of the Romantic impulse to self-expression.

For all its sensitivity to the history of poetic form, Abrams's argument gives a somewhat misleading impression of the trajectory of the ode in this period. That a generic transformation, or series of transformations, of the kind described—involving the modification and mixing of existing genres—did occur is undeniable, and the formal characteristics Abrams attributes to the resultant hybrid are demonstrable in the examples he cites. But the idea that this new type of lyric 'displaced' the ode, or— the larger assumption implicit in this claim—that the tendency of Romantic lyricism was to dissolve traditional poetic categories, needs careful qualification. Not only are there countless examples in Romanticism of the retention of traditional poetic forms and generic nomenclature, but in many cases the salient development was not *away from* but *towards* established forms. Against Coleridge's conversation poems, which are rightly held to exemplify the shift from fixed to more open-ended poetic forms, can be set the 'Dejection' ode, which began life as an informal verse letter to Sara Hutchinson but which Coleridge then progressively remodelled into the poem he saw fit to describe by the formal designation 'Dejection: An Ode'. Despite the meticulous critical attention that has been paid to the successive versions of this poem, most commentators have failed to remark on this transparent reversal of the Romantic urge to 'transcend' genre, or to explain the continued appeal of the ode form to a poet whose conversation poems (all of which pre-date 'Dejection') had supposedly already rendered that form obsolete.[12] In fact, Coleridge wrote regular Pindarics, irregular Pindarics, odes that called themselves odes, odes that did not, odes that originated as prose works (the most bizarre example is his 'Prospectus and Specimen of a Translation of Euclid in a Series of Pindaric Odes', 1792[13]), and ironical quasi-odes with nonce labels such as 'The Nose: An Odaic Rhapsody' (1789).[14] There is no clear pattern except one of relentless experimentation, not only with the form of the ode but also with its nomenclature. Part of his fascination

---

[11] M. H. Abrams, 'Structure and Style in the Greater Romantic Lyric' (1965), in Harold Bloom (ed.), *Romanticism and Consciousness: Essays in Criticism* (New York: Norton, 1970), 202–3.

[12] An exception is A. Harris Fairbanks, who describes 'Dejection' as 'a synthesis of the magnitude and dynamics of the ode with the personal style and immediacy of the conversation poem' ('The Form of Coleridge's Dejection Ode', *Publications of the Modern Language Association of America*, 90 (1975), 874–84: 875).

[13] *The Collected Works of Samuel Taylor Coleridge*, xvi: *Poetical Works*, ed. J. C. C. Mays, i: *Poems (Reading Text)*, 2 vols (London: Routledge and Kegan Paul, 2001), i. 33 n.

[14] Ibid. i. 15.

with the genre seems to be the sheer multiplicity of possible variants, as is suggested by his decision in 1798 to publish a quarto pamphlet which juxtaposes three odes in varying stages of transformation or displacement: 'France: An Ode', a semi-regular Pindaric in a high oratorical style about the French Revolution; 'Fears in Solitude', a partially conversationalized poem in blank verse which still retains strong odic features such as apostrophes to God, Britain, and his endangered countrymen; and 'Frost at Midnight', an introspective poem in blank verse which is now regarded as the paradigmatic 'conversation poem' (though it does not carry that label).[15]

Wordsworth's transactions with the ode are similarly complex. The Cornell edition speaks of Wordsworth's belated 'love affair with the ode' in 1816–17,[16] which produced, among other poems, his violently patriotic 'Thanksgiving Ode', written to celebrate the victory at Waterloo. His initial infatuation with the genre, however, dates back to 1798–1804, his most consciously experimental phase, when, we are often told, his resistance to traditional poetic forms was at its maximum. The fact that the 'Immortality Ode' (written 1802–4), one of his most characteristic and technically audacious poems, was originally entitled simply 'Ode' (the full title was only added in 1815) emphasizes the importance of this genre in Wordsworth's thinking,[17] and exposes the falsity of the opposition sometimes posited between genericity and experimentalism. Not only are the poem's intellectual breakthroughs inseparable from its exploitation of the formal conventions of the ode, but the ability to write odes—to achieve the 'timely utterance' of odic expression itself—is implicitly the yardstick by which Wordsworth measures his creative recovery, making this another example of 'metageneric' poetry: poetry which reflects on its own generic status. Even 'Tintern Abbey', apparently an example par excellence of Abrams's thesis about the 'greater Romantic lyric', is less straightforward than it seems. The poem can certainly be seen as an evolutionary step beyond the 'greater ode' in its relaxation of Pindaric structure and style, its shift from an oratorical to a conversational register, and its incorporation of formal features derived from other genres. In the 1800 edition of *Lyrical Ballads*, however, Wordsworth adds a footnote which draws attention to the very odic properties which his formal innovations had concealed: 'I have not ventured to call this Poem an Ode; but it was written in the hope that in the transitions, and the impassioned music of the versification would be found the principal requisites of that species of composition.'[18] Wordsworth lays claim to the genre even as he nominally abandons it.[19]

[15] Samuel Taylor Coleridge, *Fears in Solitude: Written in 1798, during the Alarm of an Invasion. To which are added, France, an Ode; and Frost at Midnight* (London, 1798).

[16] William Wordsworth, *Shorter Poems, 1807–1820*, ed. Carl H. Ketcham (Ithaca, N.Y.: Cornell University Press, 1989), introd., 12.

[17] Joseph Sitterson, 'The Genre and Place of the Intimations Ode', *Publications of the Modern Language Association of America*, 101 (1986), 24–35.

[18] William Wordsworth, *'Lyrical Ballads', and Other Poems, 1797–1800*, ed. James Butler and Karen Green (Ithaca, N.Y.: Cornell University Press, 1992), 357.

[19] For a reading which emphasizes the odic properties, see Alan Rawes, 'Romantic Form and New Historicism: Wordsworth's "Lines Written a Few Miles above Tintern Abbey"', in Rawes (ed.), *Romanticism and Form* (Basingstoke: Palgrave Macmillan, 2007).

Among the 'second-generation' Romantics, the persistence of the ode as a form of poetic utterance to which to aspire, rather than to leave behind, is still more apparent, and the remarkable formal experiments of Keats and Shelley are better understood as attempts to extend the possibilities of the genre rather than to dissolve or transcend it. Keats's odes of 1819 are the culmination of years of practice with the genre,[20] and his search for a new stanza form for the ode begins at least as early as his 'Ode to Apollo' (1815), a progress poem heavily influenced by but already structurally very different from Gray's regular Pindaric 'The Progress of Poesy' (1757). Shelley's contribution to the genre lies as much in his rediscovery of its primal energies (the 'Ode to the West Wind' is, in metaphoric daring and apostrophic power, arguably the most purely Pindaric poem in English) as in his brilliant structural innovations; and, as with Keats, his interest in the genre spans his career, from the ode-like verses of the Esdaile Notebook to the 'Ode to Liberty', 'Ode to Naples', and 'To a Skylark' of 1820.[21] The *Prometheus Unbound* volume (1820) gathers some of his recent experiments together, and presents, like Coleridge's 1798 pamphlet, a genealogy of the ode in various stages of transformation and hybridization.

In part, the impulse to refashion the ode may be attributable to a sense of constraint at its formal conventions, and on occasion the Romantics do display the kind of impatience with the genre that has given credence to the notion of Romantic anti-formalism. A case in point is Southey, a poet who cut his teeth on the ode and co-authored a volume with the eminently neoclassical title *Poems: Containing The Retrospect, Odes, Elegies, Sonnets, Etc.* (1795), but then went on to denounce the genre in his *Poems* (1797) as 'the most worthless species of composition as well as the most difficult'[22] (this did not prevent him from resuming the composition of odes in 1813 when required to do so as Poet Laureate). Such statements are comparatively rare, however, and most descriptions of the ode by Romantic practitioners suggest its continuing prestige, despite the huge quantities of mediocre verse, or 'Pseudo-poesy', that had been and were still being produced in its name.

So conspicuous, indeed, is the presence of the ode in the Romantic period, and so powerful the aspiration to the aesthetic values it embodied (magniloquence, sublimity, complexity, audacity), that it could more plausibly be viewed not as a genre in the process of being displaced but as one exercising increasing dominance within the hierarchy of poetic genres. To speak of the ode as the 'royal genre', in Ireneusz Opacki's sense,[23] of British Romanticism is to risk oversimplifying a complex literary

---

[20] Paul D. Sheats, 'Keats, the Greater Ode, and the Trial of Imagination', in J. Robert Barth SJ and John L. Mahoney (eds), *Coleridge, Keats, and the Imagination: Romanticism and Adam's Dream. Essays in Honor of Walter Jackson Bate* (Columbia: University of Missouri Press, 1990).

[21] For the odes of 1820, see Michael Erkelenz, 'Unacknowledged Legislation: The Genre and Function of Shelley's "Ode to Naples"', in Betty T. Bennett and Stuart Curran (eds), *Shelley: Poet and Legislator of the World* (Baltimore: Johns Hopkins University Press, 1996); and id., 'Shelley's First *Pythian*', *Modern Philology*, 97/3 (2000), 393–416.

[22] Robert Southey, *Poems* (Bristol, 1797), untitled prefatory note.

[23] Ireneusz Opacki, 'Royal Genres' (1963), trans. David Malcolm, in David Duff (ed.), *Modern Genre Theory* (London: Longman, 2000), an essay which extends Tynianov's work on literary evolution (see n. 8 above). 'Royal' here is metaphorical, denoting dominance in a hierarchy of genres.

situation in which many genres, old and new, competed for aesthetic or commercial pre-eminence. In many respects, though, the behaviour of the ode in this period follows very closely the pattern analysed by Opacki and others in their theorization of the phenomenon of generic dominance. The genre-mixing that Abrams interprets as a dispersal and displacement of the 'greater ode' could instead be interpreted as an example of the process of cross-fertilization that Opacki defines as symptomatic of a genre moving towards a position of dominance. The same evolutionary principle, according to Opacki, would explain the proliferation of genre variants, a sign not of the ode's loss of a distinct identity but of its capacity to transform neighbouring genres—the sonnet, the elegy, the loco-descriptive poem—into a semblance of itself (Abrams's decision to subsume all the Romantic variants and offshoots of the ode into the single synoptic category of the 'greater Romantic lyric' obscures this hybridization process). The shaping influence of the ode can thus be felt even when the genre itself is not present, or when the generic label has been dispensed with, as in 'Tintern Abbey'.

Properly to chart the progress of the Romantic ode in terms of modern theories of literary evolution would require a more detailed literary history of the period than is possible here. The colonizing power of the ode at this pivotal moment in its development is discernible not only in the way it colours, modifies, and absorbs other forms of lyric, but also in its transformative effect on less closely related forms. Among the many things that contemporary reviewers objected to in Southey's 'metrical romance' *Thalaba the Destroyer* (1801) were its 'abrupt and lyrical' form of narration, its 'extravagant' imagery, and its 'disorderly' versification (which involved a continuously shifting metre and line length).[24] These features of 'the Thalaba style' derive directly from Southey's early experiments with the ode, making this a perfect illustration of Tynianov's argument about how the 'constructive principle' of a genre can survive when the genre itself has been discarded.[25] A similar colonizing tendency may account for the inclusion of the ode-like 'Hymn to Pan' in Keats's *Endymion: A Poetic Romance* (1816) and for the lyrical interludes in Shelley's romantic epic *Laon and Cythna, or, The Revolution of the Golden City* (1817). The latter offer yet another perspective on the evolution of the ode: Cythna's ode to Equality in Canto 6 is modelled on the ceremonial odes performed at the *fêtes de fédération* during the French Revolution, whereas Laon's post-revolutionary 'blasts of Autumn' speech in Canto 9 is an allegorical meditation on the revolving political seasons which closely anticipates the 'Ode to the West Wind'. The odic passages in Shelley's 'lyrical drama' *Prometheus Unbound* are an even bolder example of generic cross-fertilization, the whole poem being, at one level, a re-enactment of the primordial union of lyricism and drama in classical Greek drama (Asia's 'My soul is an enchanted Boat' song in Act II, scene v, has also correctly been read as an 'Immortality

---

[24] [William Taylor], *Critical Review* (1803); and [Francis Jeffrey], *Edinburgh Review* (1802), in Lionel Madden (ed.), *Robert Southey: The Critical Heritage* (London: Routledge and Kegan Paul, 1972), 92, 78–81.

[25] Yuri Tynianov, 'The Ode as an Oratorical Genre' (1927), trans. Ann Shukman, *New Literary History*, 34/3 (2003), 565–96: 591. See also Tynianov, *The Problem of Verse Language*, trans. Michael Sosa and Brent (Ann Arbor: Ardis, 1981), 42–7; and my commentary, 'Maximal Tensions and Minimal Conditions: Tynianov as Genre Theorist', *New Literary History*, 34/3 (2003), 553–63.

Ode' in reverse). Wordsworth's *Prelude*, a poem whose generic models are similarly multifarious, also bears the unmistakable imprint of the ode, not least in its abrupt temporal leaps and frequent recourse to the device of apostrophe.[26] So deeply, in fact, had the structural principles of the ode been absorbed into the poetics of the period—notwithstanding the stylistic paradox I began with—that Coleridge could seek to defend the unity of the *Lyrical Ballads* collection on the grounds that, for all their differences, the poems 'are in a certain degree *one work* . . . as an Ode is one work'.[27]

Behind Coleridge's remark lies a sophisticated understanding of the structural properties of the ode and an interest in emergent theories of organic unity. As we saw in Chapter 2, Coleridge's early discovery of what Edward Young had once called the 'logic' of the ode, whereby lyric poetry was able to appear imaginatively chaotic while retaining an underlying order and control, played a crucial part in his development as a practitioner and theorist of poetry.[28] It is this poetic logic that is so strikingly manifest in the greatest odes of the period. The principle of rapid transition, a structural feature derived from the ode's original association with dance, became for the Romantics a means of exploring the complex emotional states that increasingly comprised the subject matter of poetry. The ode form, whose elevated linguistic register and formal discontinuities had once made it a byword for artistic licentiousness and bombast, now commended itself to the Romantics as an accurate vehicle for the representation of what Wordsworth called 'the fluxes and refluxes of the mind'[29] (a phrase that Coleridge echoed when describing the 'Immortality Ode' in *Biographia Literaria*[30]). The enduring power of poems like 'Dejection' and 'Immortality' partly rests on the skill with which they move between the great Romantic contraries of hope and despair, joy and sorrow, an emotional modulation that is made possible by the technical structure of the ode form. The convention of apostrophe, seemingly so alien to a poetics of 'spontaneous overflow', becomes a natural and appropriate figure of speech when the feelings to be expressed have the intensity, urgency, and complexity of poems such as these. By the same token, it is the ability of the ode to articulate these intensities and complexities that explains the seminal role of the genre in the Romantic period.

The application of the logic of the ode to what Coleridge brilliantly terms the 'self-watching subtilizing mind'[31] completes a process of internalization of the genre that began in the mid-eighteenth century with Gray and Collins; and Curran may be right in saying that these introspective tendencies had been implicit in the English ode from the start.[32] In this respect, the difference between the pre-Romantic and Romantic ode is mainly one of degree: the level of intensity with which this

---

[26] Mary Jacobus, 'Apostrophe and Lyric Voice in *The Prelude*', in Chaviva Hošek and Patricia Parker (eds), *Lyric Poetry: Beyond New Criticism* (Ithaca, N.Y.: Cornell University Press, 1985).

[27] To Joseph Cottle, 28 May 1798, in *Collected Letters of Samuel Taylor Coleridge*, ed. Earl Leslie Griggs, 6 vols (Oxford: Clarendon Press, 1956–71), i. 412.

[28] See Ch. 2 above, pp. 87–9.

[29] Preface to *Lyrical Ballads* (1800), in *Prose Works*, i. 126.

[30] *Biographia Literaria*, ii. 147.

[31] 'Frost at Midnight' (1798 version), in *Fears in Solitude*, 20.

[32] Curran, *Poetic Form and British Romanticism*, 66.

psychological function is pursued, and the sophistication with which it is realized. The same is true of the ode's self-reflexive character. The centrality of the ode to Romantic literary consciousness is suggested by the way it not only utilizes but also *analyses* the new poetics, taking as its central theme the 'shaping spirit of imagination', of which successful ode-writing—the ability to sustain heightened lyricism, and to confer aesthetic unity on a seemingly disparate poetic structure—is itself a display. This self-reflexive element in the genre arguably goes right back to Pindar, whose victory odes assert the power of the poet even as they celebrate the achievements of athletes and heroes. In the English ode of the eighteenth century, the same tendency expresses itself in an almost obsessive preoccupation with the theme of the 'poetical character'. The Romantics inherit this obsession, and carry the investigation of the nature and sources of poetic power to new depths.

The internalization manifest in such profoundly self-questioning poems as 'Dejection' and 'Immortality', 'Hymn to Intellectual Beauty', and 'Ode to a Nightingale' does not mean, however, that the Romantics ignored the public dimension of the ode, just as the stylistic shift to a more conversational register does not mean that the Romantics failed to exploit the oratorical possibilities of the genre. On the contrary, two key factors in the Romantic revaluation of the ode were the heightened awareness of literature's public voice and the explosion of demand in newspapers, journals, and magazines for grandiloquent poetry on political themes. In this sense, history itself can be said to have contributed to the revaluation of the genre, since the ode emerged as one of the literary forms best able to capture the emotional and linguistic energies awakened by the cataclysmic events of the period. The very features of the genre that made it suspicious to the neoclassical mind—'wildness', 'lawlessness', 'swiftness of transition'—made it suitable for representing the startling transformations of the revolutionary age: Coleridge's 'France: An Ode', Byron's 'Ode to Napoleon Buonaparte', Wordsworth's 'Thanksgiving Ode', Shelley's 'Ode to Naples' are just some of the many poems which demonstrate this felicitous union of theme and form. The public recital of odes, a practice which dates back to Pindar but which had degenerated by the late eighteenth century into an eccentric academic ritual, became in the wake of the French Revolution a meaningful political tradition again, unleashing the full declamatory power of the ode at just the point in its history when it was being used to explore the internal world of private emotion.[33] The greatest odes of the Romantic period reflect this double orientation, and it is no coincidence that a recurrent theme of the Romantic ode is the public power of the individual voice and the politics of the poetic imagination.

There are, then, both internal and external reasons why the ode proved so attractive to the Romantics, and why it assumed a position of prominence, even dominance, in the hierarchy of Romantic genres. Though one of the oldest and most conventionalized of genres, the ode contributed to some of the strongest literary innovations of the period, and the rediscovery of the poetic logic of the form

---

[33] For the public dimension, see Angela Esterhammer, 'The Romantic Ode: History, Language, Performance', in Esterhammer (ed.), *Romantic Poetry* (Amsterdam: Benjamins, 2002); and James von Geldern, 'The Ode as a Performative Genre', *Slavic Review*, 50/4 (1991), 927–39.

constitutes one of Romanticism's major achievements. If Bakhtin is right in claiming that all genres have their own 'chronotope', their particular relation to time and space,[34] the chronotope of the Romantic ode is an especially interesting case because the genre was so conscious of its origins, its ability to transport the reader from the here and now to the mental world of ancient Greece and Rome (as in Keats's use of the ode as a vehicle for the exploration of Greek mythology and art, or the rhapsodic classicism of certain of Shelley's odes). And yet, at the same time, this seemingly archaic, backward-looking genre was also being used to comment on the political events and ideological issues of the contemporary world. Both soaked in antiquity and bound up with modernity, toying with ideas of immortality at one moment and operating as a vehicle for polemic at another, the ode embodied the contradictory impulses of Romanticism, and served as the medium for some of its most powerful and complex utterances.

One final issue can be raised. Wordsworth's hesitation over whether or not to call 'Tintern Abbey' an ode alerts us to a more general problem which could be seen as an inevitable consequence of the developments I have charted in this book.[35] 'Tintern Abbey' is a composite work, however smooth its joins, and the question of what to label it exposed the inadequacy of a monogeneric classification system in the age of the *Mischgedicht*. No single label could hope to capture the generic complexity of the poem, just as no single term could capture the polymorphous essence of *The Prelude* (another poem he left unlabelled—and indeed untitled). But there may be a further reason for Wordsworth's dilemma. Aesthetically, 'Tintern Abbey' is a revolutionary poem, and knows itself to be such: whatever the debt to Coleridge, to earlier poets, and to Wordsworth's previous work, it marks a decisive break with the past and the beginning of a new kind of poetry. To inscribe the poem within an existing genre would, at some level, be to compromise its originality and draw attention away from one of its most striking innovations, namely a new kind of self-awareness in which the poet talks about how both *he*, the poet, and *it*, the poem, came into being. In German terms, this is the transcendental turn: here, for the first time, Wordsworth starts to write the kind of 'romantic' poetry described by Friedrich Schlegel in *Athenaeum* fragment 238, a 'poetry of poetry' which represents 'the producer along with the product', unites the 'raw materials and preliminaries of a theory of poetic creativity', and 'by analogy to philosophical jargon, should be called transcendental poetry'.[36] British Romanticism had no such philosophical jargon, nor had the word 'romantic' acquired the transcendental resonance it now carried in Germany. Even if Wordsworth had used a philosophical label of this kind, no one except Coleridge would have known what it meant, so it would have presented its own kind of distraction, instead of directing the reader to his revolutionary purposes.

---

[34] 'Forms of Time and Chronotope in the Novel: Notes Toward a Historical Poetics' (1937–8), in *The Dialogic Imagination: Four Essays by M. M. Bakhtin*, ed. Michael Holquist, trans. Caryl Emerson and Michael Holquist (Austin: University of Texas Press, 1981).

[35] For a fuller discussion of this issue, see my 'Paratextual Dilemmas: Wordsworth's "The Brothers" and the Problem of Generic Labelling', *Romanticism*, 6/2 (2000), 234–61.

[36] Friedrich Schlegel, *Philosophical Fragments*, trans. Peter Firchow (Minneapolis: University of Minnesota Press, 1991), 50–1.

This is confirmed by Coleridge's attempt at transcendental labelling in *Lyrical Ballads*: his decision, in the second edition, to retitle 'The Rime of the Ancyent Marinere' as 'The Ancient Mariner. A Poet's Reverie'. The new subtitle, like the altered spelling, is a strategic modernization: the self-reflexive phrase 'poet's reverie' and the Rousseauian term 'reverie' associate the poem with new, Continental modes of literary cognition. The problem with this strategy, however, is pointed out in a typically astute and witty remark by Charles Lamb: 'I am sorry', he tells Wordsworth in a letter, 'that Coleridge has christened his Ancient Marinere "a poet's Reverie"'—it is as bad as Bottom the Weaver's declaration that he is not a Lion but only the scenical representation of a Lion.'[37] The new title, Lamb is saying, is tautologous and therefore redundant: what else is poetry but reverie, and who else's but a poet's? Coleridge apparently took the point: in *Sibylline Leaves* (1817), the original title is reinstated (though the modernized spelling is retained—and other paratexts are added). Once again, then, we are presented with contradictory impulses. In Romanticism, genres exist in multiple states; so do individual poems; and so do the paratextual labels by which poems identify and interpret themselves. Coleridge gives us both the 'Rime' and the 'Reverie', an 'ancient' and a modern version (and many permutations thereof[38]). Wordsworth gives us a nine-line lyric called 'The Rainbow'; a 200-line expansion of that lyric called, simply, 'Ode'; and a retitled version of the latter called, magnificently, 'Ode. Intimations of Immortality from Recollections of Early Childhood'. The continual reworking of titles and subtitles, like the endless revision of texts, is symptomatic of a paradigm shift in British poetry, a literary revolution at the heart of which lies Romanticism's tangled relationship with genre.

[37] *The Letters of Charles and Mary Lamb*, ed. Edwin W. Marrs, Jr, 3 vols (Ithaca, N.Y.: Cornell University Press, 1975–8), i. 266.

[38] Jack Stillinger, *Coleridge and Textual Instability: The Multiple Versions of the Major Poems* (New York: Oxford University Press, 1994), 60–73.

# Select Bibliography

For reasons of space, secondary works on individual authors have been omitted; references can be found in the notes. Pre-1900 criticism is listed among the primary sources. Anonymously published works are listed alphabetically by title where authorship is unknown; otherwise, by author or editor with the name in square brackets.

## PRIMARY SOURCES

Adams, John (ed.), *The English Parnassus: Being a New Selection of Didactic, Descriptive, Pathetic, Plaintive, and Pastoral Poetry, Extracted from the Works of the Latest and Most Celebrated Poets* (London, 1789).

[Addison, Joseph], 'An Essay on the Georgics', in *The Works of Virgil: Containing his Pastorals, Georgics and Aeneis, Translated into English Verse by Mr Dryden*, 5th edn, 3 vols (London, 1721).

[Aiken, John], *Essays on Song-Writing: With a Collection of such English Songs as are Most Eminent for Poetical Merit. To which are Added some Original Pieces* (London, 1772).

Alexander, Gavin (ed.), *Sidney's 'The Defence of Poesy' and Selected Renaissance Literary Criticism* (Harmondsworth: Penguin, 2004).

Allott, Miriam (ed.), *Novelists on the Novel* (London: Routledge and Kegan Paul, 1965).

*The Ancient British Drama*, 3 vols (London, 1810).

Anderson, Robert (ed.), *A Complete Edition of the Poets of Great Britain*, 14 vols (London, 1792–5).

[Anstey, John], *The Pleader's Guide: A Didactic Poem, in Two Parts* (London, 1796).

Ashfield, Andrew, and Peter de Bolla (eds), *The Sublime: A Reader in British Eighteenth-Century Aesthetic Theory* (Cambridge: Cambridge University Press, 1996).

[Axtell, J. (ed.)], *The British Apollo, or, Songster's Magazine, Containing a Choice Selection of English, Irish, and Scotch Songs, Cantatas, Duets, Trios, Catches, Glees, &c.... Interspersed with Many Originals, viz. Bacchanalian, Love, Hunting, Martial, Nautical, Pastoral, Political, Satirical, Humourous, &c. To which are Added, a Variety of Toasts and Sentiments* (London, 1792).

Baillie, Joanna, *Plays on the Passions (1798 Edition)*, ed. Peter Duthie (Peterborough, Ont.: Broadview, 2001).

Baillie, John, *An Essay on the Sublime* (London, 1747).

Barbauld, Anna Letitia, *Selected Poetry and Prose*, ed. William McCarthy and Elizabeth Kraft (Peterborough, Ont.: Broadview, 2002).

—— (ed.), *The Poetical Works of William Collins, with a Prefatory Essay* (London, 1797).

Batteux, Charles, *A Course of the Belles Lettres, or, The Principles of Literature*, trans. John Miller, 4 vols (London, 1761).

*The Beauties of Ancient Poetry: Intended as a Companion to the Beauties of English Poetry* (London, 1794).

Beddoes, Thomas Lovell, *Death's Jest-Book: The 1829 Text*, ed. Michael Bradshaw (Manchester: Carcanet, 2003).

—— *The Works of Thomas Love Beddoes*, ed. H. W. Donner (London: Oxford University Press, 1935).

*Bell's Classical Arrangement of Fugitive Poetry*, 18 vols [of projected 25] (London, 1789–97).

*Bell's Edition: The Poets of Great Britain Complete from Chaucer to Churchill*, 109 vols (London, 1777–83).

Bentham, Jeremy, 'Essay on Nomenclature and Classification', in his *Chrestomathia*, ed. M. J. Smith and W. H. Burston (Oxford: Clarendon Press, 1983).

Bernstein, J. M. (ed.), *Classic and Romantic German Aesthetics* (Cambridge: Cambridge University Press, 2003).

Bindman, David, *The Shadow of the Guillotine: Britain and the French Revolution*, exhibition catalogue (London: British Museum, 1989).

Blackwell, Thomas, *An Enquiry into the Life and Writings of Homer* (London, 1735).

Blair, David [Richard Phillips], *The Universal Preceptor: Being an Easy Grammar of Arts, Sciences, and General Knowledge*, 2nd edn (London, 1811).

Blair, Hugh, *Lectures on Rhetoric and Belles Lettres*, 2 vols (London, 1783).

Blake, William, *Blake's Illuminated Books*, iii: *The Early Illuminated Books*, ed. Morris Eaves et al. (London: William Blake Trust, 1993).

—— *Complete Writings*, ed. Geoffrey Keynes (London: Oxford University Press, 1966).

Bond, Donald F. (ed.), *The Spectator*, 5 vols (Oxford: Clarendon Press, 1965).

—— (ed.), *The Tatler*, 3 vols (Oxford: Clarendon Press, 1987).

Bowles, William Lisle, *The Invariable Principles of Poetry: In a Letter Addressed to Thomas Campbell Esq; Occasioned by some Critical Observations in his Specimens of British Poets, particularly relating to the Poetical Character of Pope* (London, 1819).

Boyd, Henry, *A Translation of the Inferno of Dante Aligheri, in English Verse: With Historical Notes, and the Life of Dante*, 2 vols (London, 1785).

Brooke, Charlotte (ed.), *Reliques of Irish Poetry: Consisting of Heroic Poems, Odes, Elegies, and Songs, Translated into English Verse: With Notes Explanatory and Historical; and the Originals in the Irish Character. To which is Subjoined an Irish Tale* (Dublin, 1789).

Brown, John, *A Dissertation on the Rise, Union, and Power, the Progressions, Separations, and Corruptions, of Poetry and Music: To which is Prefixed, The Cure of Saul, A Sacred Ode* (London, 1763).

—— *The History of the Rise and Progress of Poetry through it's Several Species* (Newcastle, 1764). [Abbreviated edn of the *Dissertation*]

Bruce, Michael, *Poems on Several Occasions* (Edinburgh, 1770).

Buchanan, James (ed.), *The First Six Books of Milton's Paradise Lost Rendered into Grammatical Construction; the Words of the Text Being Arranged, at the Bottom of each Page, in the same Natural Order with the Conceptions of the Mind; and the Ellipsis Properly Supplied, without any Alteration in the Diction of the Poem* (Edinburgh, 1773).

Burke, Edmund, *Reflections on the Revolution in France, and on the Proceedings in Certain Societies in London Relative to that Event*, ed. Conor Cruise O'Brien (Harmondsworth: Penguin, 1969).

Burney, Frances, *The Wanderer, or, Female Difficulties*, ed. Margaret Anne Doody et al. (Oxford: Oxford University Press, 1991).

Butler, Marilyn (ed.), *Burke, Paine, Godwin, and the Revolution Controversy* (Cambridge: Cambridge University Press, 1984).

Byron, Lord, *The Complete Poetical Works*, ed. Jerome J. McGann, 7 vols (Oxford: Clarendon Press, 1980–93).

—— *Letters and Journals*, ed. Leslie A. Marchand, 12 vols (London: Murray, 1973–82).

Bysshe, Edward, *The Art of English Poetry*, 3rd edn (London, 1708).

Campbell, George, *The Philosophy of Rhetoric*, 2 vols (London, 1776).

Campbell, Thomas (ed.), *Specimens of the British Poets: With Biographical and Critical Notices, and an Essay on English Poetry*, 7 vols (London, 1819).

Chamberlain, Timothy J. (ed.), *Eighteenth Century German Criticism* (New York: Continuum, 1992).

[Chatterton, Thomas], *Poems, Supposed to Have Been Written at Bristol by Thomas Rowley, and Others, in the Fifteenth Century... To which are Added, a Preface, an Introductory Account of the Several Pieces, and a Glossary*, [ed. Thomas Tyrwhitt] (London, 1777).

*Choice Fragments, or, Blossoms of Literature, for Juvenile Minds; Containing Upwards of Forty-five Pieces, Culled with the Greatest Care, and Each Embellished with an Appropriate Engraving on Wood* (London, *c.*1808).

Clare, John, *Major Works*, ed. Eric Robinson and David Powell (Oxford: Oxford University Press, 2004).

Cobban, Alfred (ed.), *The Debate on the French Revolution 1789–1800*, 2nd edn (London: A. and C. Black, 1960).

Coleridge, Samuel Taylor, *Collected Letters*, ed. Earl Leslie Griggs, 6 vols (Oxford: Clarendon Press, 1956–71).

—— *The Collected Works*, gen. ed. Kathleen Coburn (London: Routledge and Kegan Paul, 1969– ).

—— *Fears in Solitude: Written in 1798, during the Alarm of an Invasion. To which are Added, France, an Ode; and Frost at Midnight* (London, 1798).

—— *The Notebooks*, ed. Kathleen Coburn (London: Routledge and Kegan Paul, 1957– ).

—— *Poems, by S. T. Coleridge, Second Edition: To which are now Added Poems by Charles Lamb, and Charles Lloyd* (Bristol, 1797).

—— *Sibylline Leaves: A Collection of Poems* (London, 1817).

Congreve, William, *A Pindarique Ode, Humbly Offer'd to the Queen... To which is Prefix'd, A Discourse on the Pindarique Ode* (London, 1706).

Cornwall, Barry [Bryan Waller Procter], *Essays and Tales in Prose*, 2 vols (Boston, 1853).

Cox, Jeffrey N., and Michael Gamer (eds), *The Broadview Anthology of Romantic Drama* (Peterborough, Ont.: Broadview, 2003).

Cross, John C., *Parnassian Bagatelles: Being a Miscellaneous Collection of Poetical Attempts* (London, 1796).

—— *Parnassian Trifles: Being a Collection of Elegiac, Pastoral, Nautic, and Lyric Poetry* (London, 1792).

Darwin, Erasmus, *The Botanic Garden, Part II. Containing The Loves of the Plants: A Poem. With Philosophical Notes. Volume the Second* (Lichfield, 1789).

Davy, Humphry, *Elements of Chemical Philosophy* (London, 1812).

Dennis, John, *The Critical Works*, ed. Edward Niles Hooker, 2 vols (Baltimore: Johns Hopkins University Press, 1939–43).

De Quincey, Thomas, *The Works*, gen. ed. Grevel Lindop, 21 vols (London: Pickering and Chatto, 2000–3).

Dermody, Thomas, *The Rights of Justice, or, Rational Liberty: A Letter to an Acquaintance in the Country* (Dublin, 1793).

De Staël, Germaine, *Major Writings*, trans. Vivian Folkenflik (New York: Columbia University Press, 1987).

—— *A Treatise on Ancient and Modern Literature: Illustrated by Striking References to the Principal Events and Characters that have Distinguished the French Revolution. Translated from the French*, 2 vols (London, 1803).

D'Israeli, Isaac, *Curiosities of Literature: Consisting of Anecdotes, Characters, Sketches, and Observations, Literary, Critical, and Historical* (London, 1791).

—— *An Essay on the Manners and Genius of the Literary Character* (London, 1795).

—— *The Literary Character, Illustrated by the History of Men of Genius, Drawn from their Own Feelings and Confessions* (London, 1818).

—— *The Literary Character, Illustrated by the History of Men of Genius*, 3rd edn, 2 vols (London, 1822).

—— *A Second Series of Curiosities of Literature: Consisting of Researches in Literary, Biographical, and Political History; of Critical and Philosophical Inquiries; and of Secret History*, 3 vols (London, 1823).

—— *Specimens of a New Version of Telemachus: To which is Prefixed, A Defence of Poetry* (London, 1791).

Drake, Nathan, *Literary Hours, or, Sketches Critical and Narrative* (Sudbury, 1798).

Dryden, John, *The Poems*, ed. James Kinsley, 5 vols (Oxford: Clarendon Press, 1958).

Duff, William, *An Essay on Original Genius: And its Various Modes of Exertion in Philosophy and the Fine Arts, particularly in Poetry* (London, 1767).

Dunlop, John, *The History of Fiction: Being A Critical Account of the Most Celebrated Prose Works of Fiction, from the Earliest Greek Romances to the Novels of the Present Age*, 3 vols (London, 1814).

Dyer, George, *Poems* (London, 1800).

—— *Poetics, or, A Series of Poems and Disquisitions on Poetry*, 2 vols (London, 1812).

Ellis, George (ed.), *Specimens of the Early English Poets: To which is Prefixed an Historical Sketch of the Rise and Progress of the English Poetry and Language*, 3 vols (London, 1801).

*Encyclopaedia Britannica, or, A Dictionary of Arts, Sciences, and Miscellaneous Literature, on a Plan Entirely New*, 3rd edn, 18 vols (Edinburgh, 1788–97).

Enfield, William, *A Familiar Treatise on Rhetoric and Belles Lettres* (London, 1809).

Ensor, George, *On National Education* (London, 1811).

Fawcett, Joseph, *Poems: To which is Added Civilised War, before Published under the Title of The Art of War, with Considerable Alterations; and The Art of Poetry, According to the Latest Improvements, with Additions* (London, 1798).

Feldman, Paula R., and Daniel Robinson (eds), *A Century of Sonnets: The Romantic-Era Revival, 1750–1850* (New York: Oxford University Press, 1999).

Fletcher, Andrew, of Saltoun, *The Political Works: With Notes, &c. To which is Prefixed a Sketch of his Life, with Observations, Moral, Philosophical and Political*, ed. Robert Watson (London, 1798).

*Flowers of British Poetry: Consisting of Fugitive and Classical Pieces of the Best Poets of Great Britain* (Newcastle upon Tyne, 1802).

Foster, John, 'On the Application of the Epithet Romantic', in his *Essays in a Series of Letters to a Friend*, 2 vols (London, 1806).

Frere, J. Hookham, *Prospectus and Specimen of an Intended National Work, by William and Robert Whistlecraft . . . Intended to Comprise the Most Interesting Particulars relating to King Arthur and his Round Table* (London, 1817).

Furst, Lilian (ed.), *European Romanticism: Self-Definition: An Anthology* (London: Methuen, 1980).

Fuseli, Henry, *The Life and Writings*, ed. John Knowles, 3 vols (London, 1831).

Gildon, Charles, *The Complete Art of Poetry*, 2 vols (London, 1718).

—— (ed.), *The Laws of Poetry, as Laid Down by the Duke of Buckinghamshire in his Essay on Poetry, by the Earl of Roscommon in his Essay on Translated Verse, and by the Lord Lansdowne on Unnatural Flights in Poetry, Explain'd and Illustrated* (London, 1721).

[Gisborne, Thomas], *Innovation: A Poem* (London, 1799).

Godwin, William, *Caleb Willliams*, ed. Pamela Clemit (Oxford: Oxford University Press, 2009).

Godwin, William, *The Enquirer: Reflections on Education, Manners, and Literature. In a Series of Essays* (London, 1797).

—— *An Enquiry Concerning Political Justice, and its Influence on General Virtue and Happiness*, 2 vols (London, 1793).

Goethe, Johann Wolfgang von, *Essays on Art and Literature*, ed. John Geary, trans. Ellen von Narndroff and Ernest H. von Narndroff (Princeton: Princeton University Press, 1986).

—— *Wilhelm Meister's Apprenticeship*, trans. Eric A. Blackhall with Victor Lange (Princeton: Princeton University Press, 1989).

Goldsmith, Oliver (ed.), *The Beauties of English Poesy*, 2 vols (London, 1767).

Grant, David, *The Beauties of Modern British Poetry, Systematically Arranged* (Aberdeen, 1831).

—— (ed.), *Elegant Selections in Verse: From the Works of Scott, Byron, Southey, and Other Popular Poets, chiefly of the Present Age. By David Grant, Teacher of English, Writing &c. in Aberdeen* (Edinburgh, 1818).

[Richard Graves (ed.)], *The Festoon: A Collection of Epigrams Ancient and Modern: Panegyrical, Satyrical, Amorous, Moral, Humorous, Monumental; with an Essay on that Species of Composition* (London, 1766).

Guy, J. (ed.), *Songs, Consisting of Political, Convivial, Sentimental, Pastoral, Satirical, and Masonic* (London, 1797).

[Harris, James], *Upon the Rise and Progress of Criticism* ([London?], 1752).

Haslewood, Joseph (ed.), *Ancient Critical Essays upon English Poets and Poësy*, 2 vols (London, 1811–15).

Hayley, William, *An Essay on Epic Poetry: In Five Epistles to the Revd Mr Mason. With Notes* (London, 1782).

Hazlitt, William, *The Complete Works*, ed. P. P. Howe, 21 vols (London: Dent, 1930–4).

—— (ed.), *Select British Poets, or, New Elegant Extracts from Chaucer to the Present Time, with Critical Remarks* (London, 1824).

Headley, Henry (ed.), *Select Beauties of Ancient English Poetry*, 2 vols (London, 1787).

Hegel, Georg Wilhelm Friedrich, *Aesthetics: Lectures on Fine Art*, trans. T. M. Knox, 2 vols (Oxford: Clarendon Press, 1975).

Herd, David (ed.), *Ancient and Modern Scottish Songs, Heroic Ballads, etc. Collected from Memory, Tradition, and Ancient Authors*, 2nd edn, 2 vols (Edinburgh, 1774).

Herder, Johann Gottfried, *Philosophical Writings*, ed. Michael N. Forster (Cambridge: Cambridge University Press, 2002).

—— *Selected Early Works 1764–1767: Addresses, Essays, and Drafts; Fragments on Recent German Literature*, ed. Ernest A. Menze and Karl Menges, trans. Ernest A. Menze with Michael Palma (University Park: Pennsylvania State University Press, 1992).

Hölderlin, Friedrich, *Essays and Letters on Theory*, trans. Thomas Pfau (Albany: State University of New York Press, 1998).

Home, Henry, Lord Kames, *Elements of Criticism*, 3 vols (Edinburgh, 1762).

Hone, William, *Ancient Mysteries Described, Especially the English Miracle Plays, Founded on Apocryphal New Testament Story, Extant Among the Unpublished Manuscripts in the British Museum: Including Notices of Ecclesiastical Shows, the Festivals of Fools and Asses—the English Boy Bishop—the Descent into Hell—the Lord Mayors Show—the Guildhall Giants—Christmas Carols &c* (London, 1823).

[Hunt, Leigh], *The Descent of Liberty: A Mask* (London, 1815).

—— *Selected Writings*, 6 vols (London: Pickering and Chatto, 2003).

—— and S. Adams Lee (eds), *The Book of the Sonnet*, 2 vols (London, 1867).

Hurd, Richard, *A Dissertation on the Idea of Universal Poetry* (London, 1766).

—— *Horazens Episteln an die Pisonen und an den Augustus. Mit Kommentar... von R. Hurd*, trans. Johann Joachim Eschenburg, 2 vols (Leipzig, 1772).

—— *Letters on Chivalry and Romance* (London, 1762).

Irony, Solomon [Rembrandt Peale?], *Fashion, or, The Art of Making Breeches: An Heroi-Satiri-Didactic Poem* (Philadelphia, 1800).

Jeffrey, Francis, *Jeffrey's Criticism: A Selection*, ed. Peter F. Morgan (Edinburgh: Scottish Academic Press, 1983).

Johnson, Samuel, *The Critical Opinions of Samuel Johnson*, ed. Joseph Epes Brown (1926; New York: Russell and Russell, 1961).

Jones, Edmund D. (ed.), *English Critical Essays: Nineteenth Century* (1916; Oxford: Oxford University Press, 1971).

Kames, Henry Home, Lord, *Elements of Criticism*, 3 vols (Edinburgh, 1762).

Kant, Immanuel, *Critique of the Power of Judgment*, ed. Paul Guyer, trans. Paul Guyer and Eric Matthews (Cambridge: Cambridge University Press, 2000).

Keats, John, *The Complete Poems*, ed. John Barnard, 2nd edn (Harmondsworth: Penguin, 1977).

—— *Letters, 1814–1821*, ed. H. E. Rollins, 2 vols (Cambridge, Mass.: Harvard University Press, 1958).

Kent, David A., and D. R. Ewen (eds), *Romantic Parodies, 1797–1831* (Rutherford, N.J.: Fairleigh Dickinson University Press, 1992).

Knight, Richard Payne, *The Landscape: A Didactic Poem, in Three Books* (London, 1794).

—— *The Progress of Civil Society: A Didactic Poem, in Six Books* (London, 1796).

Knox, Vicesimus, *Essays Moral and Literary*, new edn, 2 vols (London, 1782).

—— (ed.), *Elegant Extracts, or, Useful and Entertaining Pieces of Poetry, Selected for the Improvement of Youth, in Speaking, Reading, Thinking, Composing; and in the Conduct of Life. Being Similar in Design to Elegant Extracts in Prose* (London, 1789).

Lamb, Charles, *The Complete Works and Letters* (New York: Modern Library, 1935).

—— and Mary Lamb, *The Letters*, ed. Edwin W. Marrs, Jr, 3 vols (Ithaca, N.Y.: Cornell University Press, 1975–8).

—— and Charles Lloyd, *Blank Verse* (London, 1798).

Lawler, Dennis, *Vicissitudes in Early Life, or, The History of Frank Neville, a Serio-Comic, Sentimental, and Satirical Tale; Interspersed with Comic Sketches, Anecdotes of Living Characters, and Original Poetry; Elegiac, Amatory, Humourous, Lyrical, and Descriptive. With a Caricature Frontispiece*, 2 vols (London, [1808]).

Lowth, Robert, *Lectures on the Sacred Poetry of the Hebrews*, trans. G. Gregory, 3 vols (London, 1787).

Mackintosh, James, *Vindiciae Gallicae: Defence of the French Revolution and its English Admirers, Against the Accusations of the Right Hon. Edmund Burke* (London, 1791).

Macpherson, James, *Fingal: An Ancient Epic Poem in Six Books. Together with Several Other Poems, Composed by Ossian, the Son of Fingal. Translated from the Galic Language* (London, 1762).

—— *Fragments of Ancient Poetry, Collected in the Highlands of Scotland, and Translated from the Gaelic or Erse Language* (Edinburgh, 1760).

—— *Temora: An Ancient Epic Poem, in Eight Books. Together with Several other Poems, Composed by Ossian, the Son of Fingal. Translated from the Galic Language* (London, 1763).

[Malcolm, Robert (ed.)], *Lyrical Gems: A Selection of Moral, Sentimental and Descriptive Poetry from the Works of the Most Popular Modern Writers. Interspersed with Originals* (Glasgow, 1825).

Mangin, Edward, *An Essay on Light Reading, as it May be Supposed to Influence Moral Conduct and Literary Taste* (London, 1808).

Mathias, Thomas James, *The Pursuits of Literature: A Satirical Poem in Four Dialogues. With Notes*, 7th edn (London, 1798).

Mavor, William, and Samuel Pratt (eds), *Classical English Poetry, for the Use of Schools, and of Young Persons in General. Selected from the Works of the Most Favourite of our National Poets, with Some Original Pieces* (London, 1801).

*Mental Pleasures, or, Select Essays, Characters, Anecdotes, and Poems. Extracted Chiefly from Fugitive Publications, and Calculated to Improve and Entertain the Mind*, 2 vols (London, 1791).

Milton, John, *The Poems*, ed. John Carey and Alastair Fowler (London: Longman, 1968).

*Modern Parnassus, or, The New Art of Poetry, A Poem. Designed to Supersede the Rules of Aristotle, Horace, Longinus, Vida, Boileau, and Pope* (London, 1814).

Montgomery, James, 'Lecture on the British Poets, Delivered at the Royal Institution, April 11, 1837', 2 instalments, *Metropolitan*, 19 (May 1837), 1–7; 19 (June 1837), 113–19.

—— *Lectures on Poetry and General Literature, Delivered at the Royal Institution in 1830 and 1831* (London, 1833).

*Mumbo Chumbo: A Tale. Written in Antient Manner. Recommended to Modern Devotees* (London, 1765).

[Murray, Hugh], *Morality of Fiction, or, An Inquiry into the Tendency of Fictitious Narratives, with Observations on Some of the Most Eminent* (Edinburgh, 1805).

*The Muse's Banquet: Consisting of a Select Collection of Pieces in the Different Species of Poetical Composition. By the Most Celebrated Authors*, 5th edn (Dublin, 1779).

[Newbery, John (ed.)], *Poetry Made Familiar and Easy to Young Gentlemen and Ladies, and Embellished with a Great Variety of the most Shining Epigrams, Epitaphs, Songs, Odes, Pastorals &c. from the Best Authors. Being the Fourth Volume of the Circle of the Sciences*, 3rd edn (London, 1769); first pub. as *The Art of Poetry Made Easy* (1746).

Nisbet, H. B. (ed.), *German Aesthetic and Literary Criticism: Winckelmann, Lessing, Hamann, Herder, Schiller, Goethe* (Cambridge: Cambridge University Press, 1985).

Novalis [Friedrich von Hardenberg], *Philosophical Writings*, trans. and ed. Margaret Mahony Stoljar (Albany: State University of New York Press, 1997).

Ogilvie, John, *Britannia: A National Epic Poem, in Twenty Books. To which is Prefixed, a Critical Dissertation on Epic Machinery* (Aberdeen, 1801).

—— *Philosophical and Critical Observations on the Nature, Characters, and Various Species of Composition*, 2 vols (London, 1774).

*Oxoniana: A Didactic Poem, in Several Letters on the Late Improved Mode of Study, and Examination for Degrees in the University of Oxford* (London, 1812).

Paine, Thomas, *Rights of Man*, ed. Henry Collins (Harmondsworth: Penguin, 1969).

Peacock, Thomas Love, *Peacock's 'Four Ages of Poetry'; Shelley's 'Defence of Poetry'; Browning's 'Essay on Poetry'*, ed. H. F. B. Brett-Smith (1921; Oxford: Blackwell, 1971).

Pennie, John (ed.), *The Harp of Parnassus: A New Selection of Classical English Poetry, including Several Original Pieces never before Published. Designed for Schools and Young Readers in General* (London, 1822).

Percy, Thomas, *Reliques of Ancient English Poetry*, facs. of 1st edn (1765), ed. Nick Groom, 3 vols (London: Routledge; Thoemmes Press, 1996).

[Pinkerton, John], *Letters of Literature. By Robert Heron* (London, 1785).

Poe, Edgar Allan, *Complete Poems and Selected Essays*, ed. Richard Gray (London: Dent, 1993).

*Poetical Pastimes, or, Gambols Round the Base of Parnassus* (Edinburgh, 1814).

*Poetry of the Anti-Jacobin*, 6th edn (London, 1813).

Poole, Joshua, *The English Parnassus, or, A Help to English Poesie, Containing a Short Institution of that Art, a Collection of All Rhyming Monosyllables, the Choicest Epithets, and Phrases; with some General Forms upon All Occasions, Subjects, and Theams, Alphabetically Arranged* (London, 1657).

Pope, Alexander, *The Poems*, ed. John Butt (London: Methuen, 1965).

Price, Uvedale, *Essay on the Picturesque, as Compared with the Sublime and the Beautiful: And on the Use of Studying Pictures for the Purpose of Improving Real Landscape* (London, 1794).

Pye, Henry James, *A Commentary Illustrating the Poetic of Aristotle, by Examples Chiefly Taken from the Modern Poets. To which is Prefixed a New and Corrected Edition of the Translation of the Poetic* (London, 1792).

Redpath, Theodore (ed.), *The Young Romantics and Critical Opinion 1807–1824* (London: Harrap, 1973).

Reeve, Clara, *The Progress of Romance, through Times, Countries and Manners . . . in a Course of Evening Conversations*, 2 vols (Colchester, 1765).

Reiman, Donald H. (ed.), *The Romantics Reviewed: Contemporary Reviews of British Romantic Writers*, facs. repr., 9 vols (New York: Garland, 1972).

Reynolds, Joshua, *Discourses on Art*, ed. Robert R. Wark, 2nd edn (New Haven: Yale University Press, 1975).

Richards, George, *An Essay on the Characteristic Differences between Ancient and Modern Poetry, and the Several Causes from which they Result* (Oxford, 1789).

Richter, Jean Paul, *Horn of Oberon: Jean Paul Richter's School for Aesthetics*, trans. Margaret R. Hale (Detroit: Wayne State University Press, 1973).

[Ritson, Joseph (ed.)], *Pieces of Ancient Popular Poetry: From Authentic Manuscripts and Old Printed Copies* (London, 1791).

—— *Robin Hood: A Collection of all the Ancient Poems, Songs and Ballads Now Extant, Relative to that Celebrated English Outlaw*, 2 vols (London, 1795).

—— *Scotish Songs*, 2 vols (London, 1794).

—— *A Select Collection of English Songs*, 3 vols (London, 1783).

*Roach's Beauties of the Modern Poets of Great Britain, Carefully Selected and Arranged*, 3 vols (London, 1793).

Robinson, Henry Crabb, *Crabb Robinson in Germany 1800–1805: Extracts from his Correspondence*, ed. Edith J. Morley (Oxford: Oxford University Press, 1929).

—— *Henry Crabb Robinson on Books and their Writers*, ed. Edith J. Morley, 3 vols (London: Dent, 1938).

Russell, D. A., and M. Winterbottom (eds), *Ancient Literary Criticism: The Principal Texts in New Translations* (Oxford: Oxford University Press, 1972).

Sanon, George, *The Causes of the French Revolution, and the Science of Governing an Empire: An Epic and Philosophical Poem* (London, 1806).

Scaliger, Julius Caesar, *Select Translations from Scaliger's Poetics*, trans. Frederick Morgan Padelford (New York: Holt, 1905).

Schelling, Friedrich Wilhelm Joseph, *The Philosophy of Art*, trans. Douglas W. Scott, with foreword by David Simpson (Minneapolis: University of Minnesota Press, 1989).

Schiller, Friedrich, *On Naïve and Sentimental Poetry*, trans. Julius A. Elias, in H. B. Nisbet (ed.), *German Aesthetic and Literary Criticism: Winckelmann, Lessing, Hamann, Herder, Schiller, Goethe* (Cambridge: Cambridge University Press, 1985).

—— *On the Aesthetic Education of Man, in a Series of Letters*, trans. Elizabeth M. Wilkinson and L. A. Willoughby (Oxford: Clarendon Press, 1967).

Schlegel, August Wilhelm, *A Course of Lectures on Dramatic Art and Literature*, trans. John Black, 2 vols (London, 1815).

Schlegel, Friedrich, *Dialogue on Poetry and Literary Aphorisms*, trans. Ernst Behler and Roman Struc (University Park: Pennsylvania State University Press, 1968).

Schlegel, Friedrich, *Lectures on the History of Literature, Ancient and Modern*, [trans. J. G. Lockhart], 2 vols (Edinburgh, 1818).

—— *Literary Notebooks, 1797–1801*, ed. Hans Eichner (Toronto: University of Toronto Press, 1957).

—— *On the Study of Greek Poetry*, trans. Stuart Barnett (Albany: State University of New York Press, 2001).

—— *Philosophical Fragments*, trans. Peter Firchow, with foreword by Rodolphe Gasché (Minneapolis: University of Minnesota Press, 1991).

Schoen, George Lethieullier, *Innovation: A Poem. Addressed to the Right Honourable Edmund Burke* (London, 1793).

Schulte-Sasse, Jochen, et al. (eds), *Theory as Practice: A Critical Anthology of Early German Romantic Writings* (Minneapolis: University of Minnesota Press, 1997).

Scott, Walter, *The Miscellaneous Prose Works*, 28 vols (Edinburgh, 1852).

—— *The Poetical Works*, ed. J. Logie Robertson (1904; Oxford: Oxford University Press, 1960).

[—— (ed.)], *English Minstrelsy: Being a Selection of Fugitive Poetry from the Best English Authors, with some Original Pieces Hitherto Unpublished* (Edinburgh, 1810).

—— (ed.), *Minstrelsy of the Scottish Border: Consisting of Historical and Romantic Ballads, Collected in the Southern Counties of Scotland; with a Few of Modern Date, Founded upon Local Tradition*, 2 vols (Kelso, 1802).

Shaftesbury, Anthony Ashley Cooper, Earl of, *Characteristicks of Men, Manners, Opinions, Times*, 3 vols (London, 1711).

—— *Second Characters, or, The Language of Forms*, ed. Benjamin Rand (Cambridge: Cambridge University Press, 1914).

Shelley, Percy Bysshe, *Letters*, ed. F. L. Jones, 2 vols (Oxford: Clarendon Press, 1964).

—— *Shelley's Poetry and Prose: Authoritative Texts, Criticism*, 2nd edn, ed. Donald H. Reiman and Neil Fraistat (New York: Norton, 2002).

—— *Shelley's Prose, or, The Trumpet of a Prophecy*, ed. David Lee Clark (1954; London: Fourth Estate, 1988).

Sidnell, Michael J. (ed.), *Sources of Dramatic Theory*, ii: *Voltaire to Hegel* (Cambridge: Cambridge University Press, 1994).

Simon, Irène (ed.), *Neo-Classical Criticism 1660–1800* (London: Arnold, 1971).

Simpson, David (ed.), *German Aesthetic and Literary Criticism: Kant, Fichte, Schelling, Schopenhauer, Hegel* (Cambridge: Cambridge University Press, 1984).

—— *The Origins of Modern Critical Thought: German Aesthetic and Literary Criticism from Lessing to Hegel* (Cambridge: Cambridge University Press, 1988).

Smith, Charlotte, *The Poems*, ed. Stuart Curran (New York: Oxford University Press, 1993).

Southey, Robert, 'Introductory Essay on the Lives and Works of Our Uneducated Poets', prefixed to John Jones, *Attempts in Verse* (London, 1831).

—— *Joan of Arc: An Epic Poem* (Bristol, 1796).

—— *The Minor Poems*, 3 vols (London, 1815).

—— *Poems* (Bristol, 1797).

—— *Poems*, 2nd edn (London, 1800).

—— *Poetical Works, 1793–1810*, ed. Lynda Pratt, Tim Fulford, and Daniel S. Roberts, 5 vols (London: Pickering and Chatto, 2004).

—— (ed.), *Select Works of the British Poets from Chaucer to Jonson, with Biographical Sketches* (London, 1831).

—— (ed.), *Specimens of the Later English Poets, with Preliminary Notices*, 3 vols (London, 1807).

—— and Samuel Taylor Coleridge, *Omniana, or, Horae Otiosiores*, ed. Robert Gittings (Fontwell: Centaur Press, 1969).

*Spencer Redivivus: Containing the First Book of the 'Faery Queene'. His Essential Design Preserv'd, but his Obsolete Language and Manner of Verse Totally Laid Aside. Deliver'd in Heroick Numbers. By a Person of Quality* (London, 1687).

Spingarn, J. E. (ed.), *Critical Essays of the Seventeenth Century*, 3 vols (Oxford: Clarendon Press, 1908–9).

Staniford, Daniel, *The Art of Reading: Containing a Number of Useful Rules, Exemplified by a Variety of Selected and Original Pieces, Narrative, Didactic, Argumentative, Poetical, Descriptive, Humorous, and Entertaining … Designed for the Use of Schools and Families* (Boston, 1800).

Stockdale, Percival, *An Inquiry into the Nature and Genuine Laws of Poetry, including a Particular Defence of the Writings and Genius of Pope* (London, 1778).

Stones, Graeme, and John Strachan (eds), *Parodies of the Romantic Age*, 5 vols (London: Pickering and Chatto, 1999).

Strachan, John (ed.), *British Satire, 1785–1840*, 5 vols (London: Pickering and Chatto, 2003).

Thelwall, John, *The Peripatetic*, ed. Judith Thompson (Detroit: Wayne State University Press, 2001).

—— *Poems Chiefly Written in Retirement: The Fairy of the Lake, a Dramatic Romance; Effusions of Relative and Social Feeling; and Specimens of the Hope of Albion, or, Edwin of Northumbria: An Epic Poem* (Hereford, 1801).

Thomson, Alexander, *The British Parnassus, at the Close of the Eighteenth Century: A Poem, in Four Cantos* (Edinburgh, 1801).

Thorburn, Thomas, *The Shotley Bridge Fox Chance: A Descriptive Didactic Poem. Interspersed with Allusions and Reflections on the Morals of the Times* (Newcastle, 1795).

Trapp, Joseph, *Lectures on Poetry: Read in the Schools of Natural Philosophy at Oxford; translated from the Latin, with Additional Notes* (London, 1742).

Twining, Thomas, *Aristotle's Treatise on Poetry: Translated, with Notes on the Translation and Original; and Two Dissertations, on Poetical and Musical Imitation* (London, 1815).

Walpole, Horace, *The Castle of Otranto: A Gothic Story*, ed. E. J. Clery (Oxford: Oxford University Press, 1998).

Warner, Eric, and Graham Hough (eds), *Strangeness and Beauty: An Anthology of Aesthetic Criticism 1840–1910*, 2 vols (Cambridge: Cambridge University Press, 1983).

Warton, Joseph, *An Essay on the Genius and Writings of Pope* (London, 1756).

—— *Odes on Various Subjects* (London, 1746).

—— (ed.), *The Works of Virgil in Latin and English … With … Three Essays on Pastoral, Didactic and Epic Poetry by the Editor*, 4 vols (London, 1753).

Warton, Thomas, *The History of English Poetry, from the Close of the Eleventh to the Commencement of the Eighteenth Century*, 4 vols (London, 1774–81).

—— *Poems: A New Edition* (London, 1777).

Wheeler, Kathleen (ed.), *German Aesthetic and Literary Criticism: The Romantic Ironists and Goethe* (Cambridge: Cambridge University Press, 1984).

Williams, Edward (*pseud*. Iolo Morganwg), *Poems, Lyric and Pastoral*, 2 vols (London, 1794).

Williams, Helen Maria, *Poems*, 2 vols (London, 1786).

Williams, Ioan (ed.), *Novel and Romance 1700–1800: A Documentary Record* (London: Routledge and Kegan Paul, 1970).

Willson, A. Leslie (ed.), *German Romantic Criticism* (New York: Continuum, 1982).

[Wolcot, John], *Ode upon Ode, or, A Peep at St. James's; or New-Year's Day; or What You Will. By Peter Pindar, Esq.* (London, 1787).

[Wolcot, John], *Pindariana, or, Peter's Portfolio, Containing Tale, Fable, Translation, Ode, Elegy, Epigram, Song, Pastoral, Letters; with Extracts from Tragedy, Comedy, Opera, &c. By Peter Pindar* (London, 1794).

Wollstonecraft, Mary, *Political Writings*, ed. Janet Todd (Oxford: Oxford University Press, 1994).

Womersley, David (ed.), *Augustan Critical Writing* (Harmondsworth: Penguin, 1997).

Wordsworth, William, *'Lyrical Ballads', and Other Poems, 1797–1800*, ed. James Butler and Karen Green (Ithaca, N.Y.: Cornell University Press, 1992).

—— *Poems: Including Lyrical Ballads, and the Miscellaneous Pieces of the Author. With Additional Poems, A New Preface, and a Supplementary Essay*, 2 vols (London, 1815).

—— *The Prelude 1799, 1805, 1850: Authoritative Texts, Context and Reception, Recent Critical Essays*, ed. Jonathan Wordsworth, M. H. Abrams and Stephen Gill (New York: Norton, 1979).

—— *The Prose Works*, ed. W. J. B. Owen and Jane Worthington Smyser, 3 vols (Oxford: Clarendon Press, 1974).

—— *Shorter Poems, 1807–1820*, ed. Carl H. Ketcham (Ithaca, N.Y.: Cornell University Press, 1989).

—— and Dorothy Wordsworth, *The Letters*, ed. Ernest de Selincourt, 2nd edn, rev. Alan G. Hill, 8 vols (Oxford: Clarendon Press, 1967–93).

[—— and Samuel Taylor Coleridge], *Lyrical Ballads, with a Few Other Poems* (London, 1798).

Wu, Duncan (ed.), *Romantic Women Poets: An Anthology* (Oxford: Blackwell, 1997).

Young, Edward, *Conjectures on Original Composition* (London, 1759).

—— 'On Lyric Poetry', in *Ocean: An Ode . . . To which is Prefaced, An Ode to the King; and a Discourse on Ode* (London, 1728).

## SECONDARY SOURCES

Abrams, M. H., 'English Romanticism: The Spirit of the Age' (1963), in Harold Bloom (ed.), *Romanticism and Consciousness: Essays in Criticism* (New York: Norton, 1970).

—— *The Mirror and the Lamp: Romantic Theory and the Critical Tradition* (New York: Oxford University Press, 1953).

—— 'Structure and Style in the Greater Romantic Lyric' (1965), in Harold Bloom (ed.), *Romanticism and Consciousness: Essays in Criticism* (New York: Norton, 1970).

Altick, Richard D., *The English Common Reader: A Social History of the Mass Reading Public 1800–1900* (Chicago: University of Chicago Press, 1957).

Armstrong, Charles, *Romantic Organicism: From Idealist Origins to Ambivalent Afterlife* (New York: Palgrave Macmillan, 2003).

Ashton, Rosemary, *The German Idea: Four English Writers and the Reception of German Thought, 1800–1860* (Chicago: University of Chicago Press, 1980).

Atkins, J. W. H., *English Literary Criticism: 17th and 18th Centuries* (1951; London: Methuen, 1966).

Babbitt, Irving, *The New Laokoon: An Essay on the Confusion of the Arts* (Boston: Houghton Mifflin, 1910).

Backscheider, Paula R., *Eighteenth-Century Women Poets and their Poetry: Inventing Agency, Inventing Genre* (Baltimore: Johns Hopkins University Press, 2005).

Bakhtin, Mikhail, *The Dialogic Imagination: Four Essays*, ed. Michael Holquist, trans. Caryl Emerson and Michael Holquist (Austin: University of Texas Press, 1981).

—— *Problems of Dostoevsky's Poetics* (1929, rev. 1963), trans. Caryl Emerson (Minneapolis: University of Minnesota Press, 1984).

—— *Speech Genres and Other Late Essays*, ed. Caryl Emerson and Michael Holquist, trans. Vern W. McGee (Austin: University of Texas Press, 1986).

Barrell, John, *The Birth of Pandora and the Division of Knowledge* (Basingstoke: Macmillan, 1992).

Bartolomeo, Joseph F., *A New Species of Criticism: Eighteenth-Century Discourse on the Novel* (Newark: University of Delaware Press, 1994).

Bate, Walter Jackson, *The Burden of the Past and the English Poet* (London: Chatto and Windus, 1971).

—— *From Classic to Romantic: Premises of Taste in Eighteenth-Century England* (New York: Harper, 1946).

Beebee, Thomas O., *The Ideology of Genre: A Comparative Study of Generic Instability* (University Park: Pennsylvania State University Press, 1994).

Behler, Ernst, *German Romantic Literary Theory* (Cambridge: Cambridge University Press, 1993).

—— 'The Origins of the Romantic Literary Theory', *Colloquia Germanica*, 2 (1968), 109–26.

Behrens, Irene, *Die Lehre von der Einteilung der Dichtkunst, vornehmlich vom 16. bis 19. Jahrhundert: Studien zur Geschichte der Poetischen Gattungen* (Halle: Niemeyer, 1940).

Beiser, Frederick C., *The Romantic Imperative: The Concept of Early German Romanticism* (Cambridge, Mass.: Harvard University Press, 2004).

Benjamin, Walter, 'The Concept of Criticism in German Romanticism' (1920), in his *Selected Writings*, i: *1913–1926*, ed. Marcus Bullock and Michael W. Jennings (Cambridge, Mass.: Belknap Press, 1996).

Blanchot, Maurice, '*The Athenaeum*' (1969), trans. Deborah Esch and Ian Balfour, *Studies in Romanticism*, 22 (1983), 163–72.

Bloom, Harold, *The Anxiety of Influence: A Theory of Poetry* (New York: Oxford University Press, 1973).

—— 'The Internalization of Quest Romance', in Harold Bloom (ed.), *Romanticism and Consciousness: Essays in Criticism* (New York: Norton, 1970).

—— *The Visionary Company: A Reading of English Romantic Poetry*, 2nd edn (Ithaca, N.Y.: Cornell University Press, 1971).

—— (ed.), *Romanticism and Consciousness: Essays in Criticism* (New York: Norton, 1970).

Bonnell, Thomas F., *The Most Disreputable Trade: Publishing the Classics of English Poetry 1765–1810* (Oxford: Oxford University Press, 2008).

Boulton, James T., *The Language of Politics in the Age of Wilkes and Burke* (London: Routledge and Kegan Paul, 1963).

Bradley, Arthur, and Alan Rawes (eds), *Romantic Biography* (Aldershot: Ashgate, 2003).

Brewer, John, *The Pleasures of the Imagination: English Culture in the Eighteenth Century* (New York: Farrar Strauss Giroux, 1997).

Bromwich, David, 'The Invention of Literature', in his *A Choice of Inheritance: Self and Community from Edmund Burke to Robert Frost* (Cambridge, Mass.: Harvard University Press, 1989).

Brown, Homer Obed, *The Institutions of the English Novel* (Philadelphia: University of Pennsylvania Press, 1997).

Brown, Marshall (ed.), *The Cambridge History of Literary Criticism*, v: *Romanticism* (Cambridge: Cambridge University Press, 2000).

Burwick, Frederick (ed.), *Approaches to Organic Form: Permutations in Science and Culture* (Dordrecht: Reidel, 1987).

Butler, Marilyn, 'Culture's Medium: The Role of the Review', in Stuart Curran (ed.), *The Cambridge Companion to British Romanticism* (Cambridge: Cambridge University Press, 1993).

—— *Romantics, Rebels and Reactionaries: English Literature and its Background 1760–1830* (Oxford: Oxford University Press, 1981).

Cafarelli, Annette Wheeler, *Prose in the Age of Poets: Romanticism and Biographical Narrative from Johnson to De Quincey* (Philadelphia: University of Pennsylvania Press, 1990).

Carruthers, Gerard, and Alan Rawes (eds), *English Romanticism and the Celtic World* (Cambridge: Cambridge University Press, 2003).

Casanova, Pascale, *The World Republic of Letters* (1999), trans. M. B. Debevoise (Cambridge, Mass.: Harvard University Press, 2004).

Cassirer, Ernst, *The Philosophy of the Enlightenment* (1932), trans. Fritz C. A. Koelln and James P. Pettegrove (Princeton: Princeton University Press, 1951).

Cave, Richard Allen (ed.), *The Romantic Theatre: An International Symposium* (Gerrards Cross: Colin Smythe, 1986).

Chai, Leon, *Romantic Theory: Forms of Reflexivity in the Revolutionary Era* (Baltimore: Johns Hopkins University Press, 2006).

Chandler, James, *England in 1819: The Politics of Literary Culture and the Case of Romantic Historicism* (Chicago: University of Chicago Press, 1998).

—— (ed.), *The Cambridge History of English Romantic Literature* (Cambridge: Cambridge University Press, 2009).

Chartier, Roger, *The Order of Books: Readers, Authors and Libraries in Europe between the Fourteenth and Eighteenth Centuries* (1992), trans. Lydia G. Cochrane (Cambridge: Polity Press, 1993).

Christmas, William J., *The Lab'ring Muses: Work, Writing, and the Social Order in English Plebeian Poetry, 1730–1830* (Newark: University of Delaware Press, 2001).

Clery, E. J., *The Rise of Supernatural Fiction, 1762–1800* (Cambridge: Cambridge University Press, 1995).

Cohen, Ralph, 'History and Genre', *Neohelicon*, 13/2 (1986), 87–105.

—— 'On the Interrelations of Eighteenth-Century Literary Forms', in Phillip Harth (ed.), *New Approaches to Eighteenth-Century Literature* (New York: Columbia University Press, 1974).

—— 'The Return to the Ode', in John Sitter (ed.), *The Cambridge Companion to Eighteenth Century Poetry* (Cambridge: Cambridge University Press, 2001).

—— and Hayden White (eds), *Theorizing Genres I* and *II*, *New Literary History*, special issues, 34/2 and 34/3 (2003).

Coleman, Francis Xavier Jerome, *The Aesthetic Thought of the French Enlightenment* (Pittsburgh: University of Pittsburgh Press, 1971).

Colie, Rosalie L., *The Resources of Kind: Genre-Theory in the Renaissance*, ed. Barbara K. Lewalski (Berkeley: University of California Press, 1973).

Congleton, J. E., *Theories of Pastoral Poetry in England 1684–1789* (1952; New York: Haskell House, 1968).

Connell, Philip, 'British Identities and the Politics of Ancient Poetry in Later Eighteenth-Century England', *Historical Journal*, 49/1 (2006), 161–92.

Cox, Jeffrey N., *In the Shadows of Romance: Romantic Tragic Drama in Germany, England, and France* (Athens: Ohio University Press, 1987).

—— *Poetry and Politics in the Cockney School: Keats, Shelley, Hunt and their Circle* (Cambridge: Cambridge University Press, 1998).

Cox, Philip, *Gender, Genre and the Romantic Poets* (Manchester: Manchester University Press, 1996).

Crawford, Robert, *Devolving English Literature*, 2nd edn (Edinburgh: Edinburgh University Press, 2000).

Crisafulli, Lilla, and Cecilia Pietropoli (eds), *Romantic Women Poets: Genre and Gender* (Amsterdam: Rodopi, 2007).

Cronin, Richard, *The Politics of Romantic Poetry: In Search of the Pure Commonwealth* (Basingstoke: Macmillan, 2000).

Culler, Jonathan, *The Pursuit of Signs: Semiotics, Literature, Deconstruction* (London: Routledge and Kegan Paul, 1981).

—— *Structuralist Poetics: Structuralism, Linguistics and the Study of Literature* (London: Routledge and Kegan Paul, 1975).

Curran, Stuart, *Poetic Form and British Romanticism* (New York: Oxford University Press, 1986).

Davies, Damian Walford (ed.), *Romanticism, History, Historicism: Essays on an Orthodoxy* (London: Routledge, 2008).

Davis, Leith, Ian Duncan, and Janet Sorensen (eds), *Scotland and the Borders of Romanticism* (Cambridge: Cambridge University Press, 2004).

De Bolla, Peter, *The Discourse of the Sublime: Readings in History, Aesthetics, and the Subject* (Oxford: Blackwell, 1989).

De Man, Paul, *Blindness and Insight: Essays in the Rhetoric of Contemporary Criticism*, 2nd edn (London: Routledge, 1983).

Derrida, Jacques, 'The "Law of Genre"' (1980), trans. Avital Ronell, in David Duff (ed.), *Modern Genre Theory* (Harlow: Longman, 2000).

Doležel, Lubomír, *Occidental Poetics: Tradition and Progress* (Lincoln: University of Nebraska Press, 1990).

Donohue, James J., *The Theory of Literary Kinds: The Ancient Classes of Poetry* (Dubuque: Loras College Press, 1949).

—— *The Theory of Literary Kinds: Ancient Classifications of Literature* (Dubuque: Loras College Press, 1943).

Draper, John W., *The Funeral Elegy and the Rise of English Romanticism* (1929; London: Frank Cass, 1967).

Dubrow, Heather, *Genre* (London: Methuen, 1982).

Duff, David (ed.), *Modern Genre Theory* (Harlow: Longman, 2000).

—— and Catherine Jones (eds), *Scotland, Ireland, and the Romantic Aesthetic* (Lewisburg, Pa.: Bucknell University Press, 2007).

Duncan, Ian, *Modern Romance and Transformations of the Novel: The Gothic, Scott, Dickens* (Cambridge: Cambridge University Press, 1992).

Dyer, Gary, *British Satire and the Politics of Style, 1789–1832* (Cambridge: Cambridge University Press, 1997).

Eagleton, Terry, *The Ideology of the Aesthetic* (Oxford: Blackwell, 1990).

Egan, Rose Frances, *The Genesis of the Theory of 'Art for Art's Sake' in Germany and in England*, Smith College Studies in Modern Languages, 2/4 (1921).

Eichner, Hans (ed.), *'Romantic' and its Cognates: The European History of a Word* (Manchester: Manchester University Press, 1972).

Empson, William, *Some Versions of Pastoral* (1935; London: Hogarth Press, 1986).

Engell, James, *The Creative Imagination: Enlightenment to Romanticism* (Cambridge, Mass.: Harvard University Press, 1981).

Engell, James, *Forming the Critical Mind: Dryden to Coleridge* (Cambridge, Mass.: Harvard University Press, 1989).

Erickson, Lee, *The Economy of Literary Form: English Literature and the Industrialization of Publishing, 1800–1850* (Baltimore: Johns Hopkins University Press, 1996).

Erskine-Hill, Howard, *The Augustan Idea in English Literature* (London: Arnold, 1983).

Esterhammer, Angela, 'The Romantic Ode: History, Language, Performance', in Esterhammer (ed.), *Romantic Poetry* (Amsterdam: Benjamins, 2002).

Farrell, Joseph, 'Classical Genre in Theory and Practice', *New Literary History*, 34/3 (2003), 383–408.

Feingold, Richard, *Nature and Society: Later Eighteenth-Century Uses of the Georgic and the Pastoral* (New Brunswick: Rutgers University Press, 1978).

Felluga, Dino Francis, *The Perversity of Poetry: Romantic Ideology and the Popular Male Poet of Genius* (Albany: State University of New York Press, 2004).

Ferber, Michael (ed.), 'The Romantic System of the Arts', in Ferber (ed.), *A Companion to European Romanticism* (Oxford: Blackwell, 2005).

Ferris, Ina, *The Romantic National Tale and the Question of Ireland* (Cambridge: Cambridge University Press, 2002).

Ferry, Anne, *The Title to the Poem* (Stanford: Stanford University Press, 1996).

Fischer, Hermann, *Romantic Verse Narrative: The History of a Genre* (1964), trans. Sue Bollans (Cambridge: Cambridge University Press, 1991).

Fishelov, David, *Metaphors of Genre: The Role of Analogies in Genre Theory* (University Park: Pennsylvania State University Press, 1993).

Fitzgerald, William, *Agonistic Poetry: The Pindaric Mode in Pindar, Horace, Hölderlin, and the English Ode* (Berkeley: University of California Press, 1987).

Foerster, Donald M., *The Fortunes of Epic Poetry: A Study in English and American Criticism 1750–1950* (Washington: Catholic University of America Press, 1962).

Foucault, Michel, *The Order of Things: An Archaeology of the Human Sciences* (1966; New York: Vintage, 1973).

Fowler, Alastair, *Kinds of Literature: An Introduction to the Theory of Genres and Modes* (Oxford: Clarendon Press, 1982).

Fraistat, Neil, *The Poem and the Book: Interpreting Collections of Romantic Poetry* (Chapel Hill: University of North Carolina Press, 1985).

—— (ed.), *Poems in their Place: The Intertextuality and Order of Poetic Collections* (Chapel Hill: University of North Carolina Press, 1986).

Franta, Andrew, *Romanticism and the Rise of the Mass Public* (Cambridge: Cambridge University Press, 2007).

Friedman, Albert B., *The Ballad Revival: Studies in the Influence of Popular on Sophisticated Poetry* (Chicago: University of Chicago Press, 1961).

Frow, John, *Genre* (London: Routledge, 2006).

Fry, Paul H., *The Poet's Calling in the English Ode* (New Haven: Yale University Press, 1980).

Frye, Northrop, *Anatomy of Criticism: Four Essays* (Princeton: Princeton University Press, 1957).

Gamer, Michael, *Romanticism and the Gothic: Genre, Reception, and Canon Formation* (Cambridge: Cambridge University Press, 2000).

Genette, Gérard, *The Architext: An Introduction* (1979), trans. Jane E. Lewin (Berkeley: University of California Press, 1992).

—— *Palimpsests: Literature in the Second Degree* (1982), trans. Channa Newman (Lincoln: University of Nebraska Press, 1998).

—— *Paratexts: Thresholds of Interpretation* (1987), trans. Jane E. Lewin (Cambridge: Cambridge University Press, 1997).

—— et al., *Théorie des genres* (Paris: Éditions du Seuil, 1986).

Gilmartin, Kevin, *Print Politics: The Press and Radical Opposition in Early Nineteenth-Century England* (Cambridge: Cambridge University Press, 1996).

—— *Writing against Revolution: Literary Conservatism in Britain, 1790–1832* (Cambridge: Cambridge University Press, 2007).

Golinski, Jan, *Science as Public Culture: Chemistry and Enlightenment in Britain, 1760–1820* (Cambridge: Cambridge University Press, 1992).

Goodman, Dena, *The Republic of Letters: A Cultural History of the French Enlightenment* (Ithaca, N.Y.: Cornell University Press, 1994).

Goodman, Kevis, *Georgic Modernity and British Romanticism: Poetry and the Mediation of History* (Cambridge: Cambridge University Press, 2004).

—— 'Magnifying Small Things: Georgic Modernity and the Noise of History', *European Romantic Review*, 15/2 (2004), 215–27.

Gorman, David, 'A Bibliography of German Romantic Literary Criticism and Theory in English', *Style*, 28/4 (1994), 500–24.

Grafton, Anthony, *The Footnote: A Curious History* (London: Faber, 1997).

Grenby, M. O., *The Anti-Jacobin Novel: British Conservatism and the French Revolution* (Cambridge: Cambridge University Press, 2001).

Guérard, Albert, *Art for Art's Sake* (Boston: Lothrop, Lee, and Shepard, 1936).

Guillén, Claudio, *Literature as System: Essays Toward the Theory of Literary History* (Princeton: Princeton University Press, 1971).

Guillory, John, *Cultural Capital: The Problem of Literary Canon Formation* (Chicago: University of Chicago Press, 1993).

Hamilton, Paul, *Historicism* (London: Routledge, 2003).

—— *Metaromanticism: Aesthetics, Literature, Theory* (Chicago: University of Chicago Press, 2003).

Hamlin, Cyrus, *Hermeneutics of Form: Romantic Poetics in Theory and Practice* (New Haven: Henry R. Schwab, 1998).

—— 'The Origins of a Philosophical Genre Theory in German Romanticism', *European Romantic Review*, 5/1 (1994), 3–14.

Harries, Elizabeth Wanning, *The Unfinished Manner: Essays on the Fragment in the Later Eighteenth Century* (Charlottesville: University Press of Virginia, 1994).

Harth, Phillip (ed.), *New Approaches to Eighteenth-Century Literature* (New York: Columbia University Press, 1974).

Harvey, A. D., *English Poetry in a Changing Society 1780–1825* (London: Allison and Busby, 1980).

Hayden, John O., *Polestar of the Ancients: The Aristotelian Tradition in Classical and English Literary Criticism* (Newark: University of Delaware Press, 1979).

Hays, Michael, and Anastasia Nikolopoulos (eds), *Melodrama: The Cultural Emergence of a Genre* (Basingstoke: Macmillan, 1999).

Heath-Stubbs, John, *The Ode* (Oxford: Oxford University Press, 1969).

Heinzelman, Kurt, 'Roman Georgic in the Georgian Age: A Theory of Romantic Genre', *Texas Studies in Literature and Language*, 33 (1991), 182–214.

Hernadi, Paul, *Beyond Genre: New Directions in Literary Classification* (Ithaca, N.Y.: Cornell University Press, 1972).

Hipple, Walter John, *The Beautiful, the Sublime and the Picturesque in Eighteenth-Century British Aesthetic Theory* (Carbondale: Southern Illinois University Press, 1957).

Hohendahl, Peter Uwe (ed.), *A History of German Literary Criticism, 1730–1980* (Lincoln: University of Nebraska Press, 1988).

Hollander, John, 'Romantic Verse Form and the Metrical Contract', in Harold Bloom (ed.), *Romanticism and Consciousness: Essays in Criticism* (New York: Norton, 1970).

Hošek, Chaviva, and Patricia Parker (eds), *Lyric Poetry: Beyond New Criticism* (Ithaca, N.Y.: Cornell University Press, 1985).

Hutcheon, Linda, *A Theory of Parody* (New York: Methuen, 1985).

Jack, Ian, *English Literature, 1815–1832* (Oxford: Clarendon Press, 1963).

Jackson, H. J., *Romantic Readers: The Evidence of Marginalia* (New Haven: Yale University Press, 2005).

Jackson, J. R. de J., *Annals of English Verse 1770–1835: A Preliminary Survey of the Volumes Published* (New York: Garland, 1985).

—— *Romantic Poetry by Women: A Bibliography 1770–1835* (Oxford: Oxford University Press, 1993).

Jackson, Kevin, *Invisible Forms: A Guide to Literary Curiosities* (London: Picador, 1999).

Jakobson, Roman, *Language in Literature*, ed. Krystyna Pomorska and Roman Jakobson (Cambridge, Mass.: Harvard University Press, 1987).

Janowitz, Anne, *England's Ruins: Poetic Purpose and the National Landscape* (Oxford: Blackwell, 1990).

—— *Lyric and Labour in the Romantic Tradition* (Cambridge: Cambridge University Press, 1998).

Jauss, Hans Robert, *Toward an Aesthetic of Reception*, trans. Timothy Bahti, introd. Paul de Man (Minneapolis: University of Minnesota Press, 1982).

Javitch, Daniel, 'The Emergence of Poetic Genre Theory in the Sixteenth Century', *Modern Language Quarterly*, 59/2 (1998), 139–69.

Johns-Putra, Adeline, *Heroes and Housewives: Women's Epic Poetry and Domestic Ideology in the Romantic Age (1770–1835)* (New York: Peter Lang, 2001).

—— *The History of the Epic* (Basingstoke: Palgrave, 2006).

Johnson, James William, *The Formation of English Neo-Classical Thought* (Princeton: Princeton University Press, 1967).

Johnston, Arthur, *Enchanted Ground: The Study of Medieval Romance in the Eighteenth Century* (London: Athlone Press, 1964).

Johnston, Kenneth R., et al. (eds), *Romantic Revolutions: Criticism and Theory* (Bloomington: Indiana University Press, 1990).

Jones, R. F., *Ancients and Moderns: A Study of the Rise of the Scientific Movement in 17th-Century England*, 2nd edn (Berkeley: University of California Press, 1961).

Jones, Steven E., *Satire and Romanticism* (New York: St Martin's Press, 2000).

—— (ed.), *The Satiric Eye: Forms of Satire in the Romantic Period* (New York: Palgrave Macmillan, 2003).

Jump, John D., *The Ode* (London: Methuen, 1974).

Keach, William, *Arbitrary Power: Romanticism, Language, Politics* (Princeton: Princeton University Press, 2004).

Keegan, Bridget, *British Labouring-Class Nature Poetry, 1730–1837* (New York: Palgrave Macmillan, 2008).

Keen, Paul, *The Crisis of Literature in the 1790s: Print Culture and the Public Sphere* (Cambridge: Cambridge University Press, 1999).

Kelly, Gary, *English Fiction of the Romantic Period, 1789–1830* (London: Longman, 1989).

—— *The English Jacobin Novel 1780–1805* (Oxford: Clarendon Press, 1976).

—— 'The Limits of Genre and the Institution of Literature: Romanticism between Fact and Fiction', in Kenneth R. Johnston et al. (eds), *Romantic Revolutions: Criticism and Theory* (Bloomington: Indiana University Press, 1990).

Klancher, Jon P., *The Making of English Reading Audiences, 1790–1832* (Madison: University of Wisconsin Press, 1987).

Kramnick, Jonathan Brody, *Making the English Canon: Print-Capitalism and the Cultural Past 1700–1770* (Cambridge: Cambridge University Press, 1998).

Krieger, Murray, 'The Arts and the Idea of Progress', in Gabriel A. Almond et al. (eds), *Progress and its Discontents* (Berkeley: University of California Press, 1982).

Kristeller, Paul Oskar, 'The Modern System of the Arts' (1951), in his *Renaissance Thought and the Arts: Collected Essays* (Princeton: Princeton University Press, 1980).

Kroeber, Karl, *Romantic Narrative Art* (Madison: University of Wisconsin Press, 1966).

Labbe, Jacqueline M., *The Romantic Paradox: Love, Violence and the Uses of Romance, 1760–1830* (Basingstoke: Macmillan, 2000).

Lacoue-Labarthe, Philippe, and Jean-Luc Nancy, *The Literary Absolute: The Theory of Literature in German Romanticism*, trans. Philip Barnard and Cheryl Lester (New York: State University of New York, 1988).

Laird, Andrew (ed.), *Ancient Literary Criticism* (Oxford: Oxford University Press, 2006).

Langbaum, Robert, *The Poetry of Experience: The Dramatic Monologue in Modern Literary Tradition* (New York: Norton, 1957).

Laws, G. Malcolm, *The British Literary Ballad: A Study in Poetic Imitation* (Carbondale: Southern Illinois University Press, 1972).

Leask, Nigel, *Curiosity and the Aesthetics of Travel Writing, 1770–1840: 'From an Antique Land'* (Oxford: Oxford University Press, 2004).

Leighton, Angela, *On Form: Poetry, Aestheticism, and the Legacy of a Word* (Oxford: Oxford University Press, 2007).

Lemon, Lee T., and Marion J. Reiss (eds and trans.), *Russian Formalist Criticism: Four Essays* (Lincoln: University of Nebraska Press, 1965).

Levine, Joseph M., *The Battle of the Books: History and Literature in the Augustan Age* (Ithaca, N.Y.: Cornell University Press, 1991).

Levinson, Marjorie, *The Romantic Fragment Poem: A Critique of a Form* (Chapel Hill: University of North Carolina Press, 1986).

Lindenberger, Herbert, 'Theories of Romanticism: From a Theory of Genre to a Genre of Theory', in his *The History in Literature: On Value, Genre, Institutions* (New York: Columbia University Press, 1990).

Lipking, Lawrence, *The Ordering of the Arts in Eighteenth-Century England* (Princeton: Princeton University Press, 1970).

Loughrey, Bryan (ed.), *The Pastoral Mode: A Casebook* (London: Macmillan, 1984).

Low, Anthony, *The Georgic Revolution* (Princeton: Princeton University Press, 1985).

Lukács, Georg, *The Theory of the Novel: A Historico-Philosophical Essay on the Forms of Great Epic Literature* (1916), trans. Anna Bostock (London: Merlin Press, 1978).

McCalman, Iain (ed.), *An Oxford Companion to the Romantic Age: British Culture, 1776–1832* (Oxford: Oxford University Press, 1999).

McFarland, Thomas, *Romantic Cruxes: The English Essayists and the Spirit of the Age* (Oxford: Clarendon Press, 1987).

—— *Romanticism and the Forms of Ruin: Wordsworth, Coleridge, and the Modalities of Fragmentation* (Princeton: Princeton University Press, 1981).

McGann, Jerome, *The Beauty of Inflections: Literary Investigations in Historical Method and Theory* (Oxford: Clarendon Press, 1985).

McGann, Jerome, *The Romantic Ideology: A Critical Investigation* (Chicago: University of Chicago Press, 1983).

Machlup, Fritz, *Knowledge: Its Creation, Distribution, and Economic Significance*, ii: *The Branches of Learning* (Princeton: Princeton University Press, 1982).

McLane, Maureen, *Balladeering, Minstrelsy, and the Making of British Romantic Poetry* (Cambridge: Cambridge University Press, 2008).

Maclean, Norman, 'From Action to Image: Theories of the Lyric in the Eighteenth Century', in R. S. Crane (ed.), *Critics and Criticism: Ancient and Modern* (Chicago: University of Chicago Press, 1952).

Maddison, Carol, *Apollo and the Nine: A History of the Ode* (London: Routledge and Kegan Paul, 1960).

Madsen, Deborah L., *Rereading Allegory: A Narrative Approach to Genre* (New York: St Martin's Press, 1994).

Magnuson, Paul, *Reading Public Romanticism* (Princeton: Princeton University Press, 1998).

Mahoney, John L., *The Whole Internal Universe: Imitation and the New Defense of Poetry in British Criticism, 1660–1830* (New York: Fordham University Press, 1995).

Mandelbrote, Giles, and K. A. Manley (eds), *The Cambridge History of Libraries in Britain and Ireland*, ii: *1640–1850* (Cambridge: Cambridge University Press, 2006).

Manley, Lawrence, *Convention 1500–1700* (Cambridge, Mass.: Harvard University Press, 1980).

Manning, Susan, 'Antiquarianism, Balladry and the Rehabilitation of Romance', in James Chandler (ed.), *The Cambridge History of English Romantic Literature* (Cambridge: Cambridge University Press, 2009).

—— 'Antiquarianism, the Scottish Science of Man, and the Emergence of Modern Disciplinarity', in Leith Davis, Ian Duncan, and Janet Sorensen (eds), *Scotland and the Borders of Romanticism* (Cambridge: Cambridge University Press, 2004).

Marks, Emerson R., *The Poetics of Reason: English Neoclassical Criticism* (New York: Random House, 1968).

Matejka, Ladislav, and Krystyna Pomorska (eds), *Readings in Russian Poetics: Formalist and Structuralist Views* (Cambridge, Mass.: Harvard University Press, 1971).

Mattick, Paul (ed.), *Eighteenth-Century Aesthetics and the Reconstruction of Art* (Cambridge: Cambridge University Press, 1993).

Mayer, David, *Harlequin in his Element: The English Pantomime, 1806–1836* (Cambridge, Mass.: Harvard University Press, 1969).

Mee, Jon, *Romanticism, Enthusiasm and Regulation: Poetics and the Policing of Culture in the Romantic Period* (Oxford: Oxford University Press, 2003).

Michael, Ian, *Literature in Schools: A Guide to the Early Sources 1700–1830* (Swansea: Textbook Colloquium, 1999).

Monk, Samuel Holt, *The Sublime: A Study of Critical Theories in Eighteenth-Century England* (1935; Ann Arbor: University of Michigan Press, 1960).

Moody, Jane, *Illegitimate Theatre in London, 1770–1840* (Cambridge: Cambridge University Press, 2000).

Mortensen, Peter, *British Romanticism and Continental Influences: Writing in an Age of Europhobia* (New York: Palgrave Macmillan, 2004).

Murphy, Peter T., *Poetry as an Occupation and an Art in Britain, 1760–1830* (Cambridge: Cambridge University Press, 1993).

Newlyn, Lucy, *Reading, Writing and Romanticism: The Anxiety of Reception* (Oxford: Oxford University Press, 2000).

Newman, Steve, *Ballad Collection, Lyric, and the Canon: The Call of the Popular from the Restoration to the New Criticism* (Philadelphia: University of Pennsylvania Press, 2007).

Nisbet, H. B., and Claude Rawson (eds), *The Cambridge History of Literary Criticism*, iv: *The Eighteenth Century* (Cambridge: Cambridge University Press, 1997).

Norton, Glyn P. (ed.), *The Cambridge History of Literary Criticism*, iii: *The Renaissance* (Cambridge: Cambridge University Press, 1999).

O'Halloran, Clare, *Golden Ages and Barbarous Nations: Antiquarian Debate and Cultural Politics in Ireland, c.1750–1800* (Cork: Cork University Press, 2004).

Olson, Elder (ed.), *Aristotle's 'Poetics' and English Literature: A Collection of Critical Essays* (Chicago: University of Chicago Press, 1965).

O'Neill, Michael, *Romanticism and the Self-Conscious Poem* (Oxford: Clarendon Press, 1997).

Ong, Walter J., *Rhetoric, Romance, and Technology: Studies in the Interaction of Expression and Culture* (Ithaca, N.Y.: Cornell University Press, 1971).

Opacki, Ireneusz, 'Royal Genres' (1963), trans. David Malcolm, in David Duff (ed.), *Modern Genre Theory* (Harlow: Longman, 2000).

O'Quinn, Daniel, and Jane Moody (eds), *The Cambridge Companion to British Theatre, 1730–1830* (Cambridge: Cambridge University Press, 2007).

Orsini, G. N. G., 'The Organic Concepts in Aesthetics', *Comparative Literature*, 21 (1969), 1–30.

O'Toole, L. M., and A. Shukman (eds), *Russian Poetics in Translation*, v: *Formalism: History, Comparison, Genre* (Oxford: Holdan, 1978).

Overton, Bill, *The Eighteenth-Century British Verse Epistle* (Basingstoke: Palgrave Macmillan, 2007).

Parker, Blanford, *The Triumph of Augustan Poetics: English Literary Culture from Butler to Johnson* (Cambridge: Cambridge University Press, 1998).

Parker, Mark, *Literary Magazines and British Romanticism* (Cambridge: Cambridge University Press, 2000).

Parrinder, Patrick, *Authors and Authority: English and American Criticism 1750–1900*, 2nd edn (New York: Columbia University Press, 1990).

Patey, Douglas Lane, ' "Aesthetics" and the Rise of Lyric in the Eighteenth Century', *Studies in English Literature*, 33 (1993), 587–608.

—— *Probability and Literary Form: Philosophic Theory and Literary Practice in the Augustan Age* (Cambridge: Cambridge University Press, 1984).

Paulson, Ronald, *Representations of Revolution (1789–1820)* (New Haven: Yale University Press, 1983).

Perkins, David, 'Literary Classifications: How Have They Been Made?' in Perkins (ed.), *Theoretical Issues in Literary History* (Cambridge, Mass.: Harvard University Press, 1991).

Pfau, Thomas, and Robert F. Gleckner (eds), *Lessons of Romanticism: A Critical Companion* (Durham, N.C.: Duke University Press, 1998).

Phelan, Joseph, *The Nineteenth-Century Sonnet* (Basingstoke: Palgrave Macmillan, 2005).

Pizer, John David, *The Historical Perspective in German Genre Theory: Its Development from Gottsched to Hegel* (Stuttgart: Hans-Dieter Heinz Akademischer Verlag, 1985).

Plotz, Judith A., *Ideas of the Decline of Poetry: A Study in English Criticism from 1700 to 1830* (1965; New York: Garland, 1987).

Porter, Roy, and Mikuláš Teich (eds), *Romanticism in National Context* (Cambridge: Cambridge University Press, 1988).

Preminger, Alex, and T. V. F. Brogan (eds), *The New Princeton Encyclopedia of Poetry and Poetics* (Princeton: Princeton University Press, 1993).

Price, Lawrence Marsden, *English Literature in Germany* (Berkeley: University of California Press, 1953).

Price, Leah, *The Anthology and the Rise of the Novel: From Richardson to George Eliot* (Cambridge: Cambridge University Press, 2000).

Prince, Michael, *Philosophical Dialogue in the British Enlightenment: Theology, Aesthetics, and the Novel* (Cambridge: Cambridge University Press, 1996).

Radcliffe, David Hall, 'Ancient Poetry and British Pastoral', in Fiona J. Stafford and Howard Gaskill (eds), *From Gaelic to Romantic: Ossianic Translations* (Amsterdam: Rodopi, 1998).

Rader, Ralph W., 'The Concept of Genre and Eighteenth-Century Studies', in Phillip Harth (ed.), *New Approaches to Eighteenth-Century Literature* (New York: Columbia University Press, 1974).

Rajan, Balachandra, *The Form of the Unfinished: English Poetics from Spenser to Pound* (Princeton: Princeton University Press, 1989).

Rajan, Tilottama, 'Romanticism and the Death of Lyric Consciousness', in Chaviva Hošek and Patricia Parker (eds), *Lyric Poetry: Beyond New Criticism* (Ithaca, N.Y.: Cornell University Press, 1985).

—— 'Theories of Genre', in Marshall Brown (ed.), *The Cambridge History of Literary Criticism*, v: *Romanticism* (Cambridge: Cambridge University Press, 2000).

—— and Julia M. Wright (eds), *Romanticism, History, and the Possibilities of Genre: Re-forming Literature 1789–1837* (Cambridge: Cambridge University Press, 1998).

Rauber, D. F., 'The Fragment as Romantic Form', *Modern Language Quarterly*, 30 (1969), 212–21.

Raven, James, *Judging New Wealth: Popular Responses to Commerce in England, 1750–1800* (Oxford: Clarendon Press, 1992).

Rawes, Alan (ed.), *Romanticism and Form* (Basingstoke: Palgrave Macmillan, 2007).

Reiman, Donald H. (ed.), *The Romantics Reviewed: Contemporary Reviews of British Romantic Writers*, facs. repr., 9 vols (New York: Garland, 1972).

Richardson, Alan, *Literature, Education, and Romanticism: Reading as Social Practice 1780–1832* (Cambridge: Cambridge University Press, 1994).

Richetti, John (ed.), *The Cambridge History of English Literature, 1660–1780* (Cambridge: Cambridge University Press, 2005).

Richter, David H., *The Progress of Romance: Literary Historiography and the Gothic Novel* (Columbus: Ohio State University Press, 1996).

Rivers, Isabel (ed.), *Books and their Readers in Eighteenth-Century England: New Essays* (London: Leicester University Press, 2001).

Robinson, Daniel, 'Reviving the Sonnet: Women Romantic Poets and the Sonnet Claim', *European Romantic Review*, 6 (1995), 98–127.

Rose, Margaret A., *Parody: Ancient, Modern and Post-modern* (Cambridge: Cambridge University Press, 1993).

Rosmarin, Adena, *The Power of Genre* (Minneapolis: University of Minnesota Press, 1985).

Ross, Marlon, *The Contours of Masculine Desire: Romanticism and the Rise of Women's Poetry* (New York: Oxford University Press, 1989).

Ross, Trevor, *The English Literary Canon from the Middle Ages to the Late Eighteenth Century* (Montreal: McGill-Queen's University Press, 1998).

Rousseau, G. S. (ed.), *Organic Form: The Life of an Idea* (London: Routledge and Kegan Paul, 1972).

Rowland, William G., Jr, *Literature and the Marketplace: Romantic Writers and their Audiences in Great Britain and the United States* (Lincoln: University of Nebraska Press, 1996).

Runge, Laura L., *Gender and Language in British Literary Criticism 1660–1790* (Cambridge: Cambridge University Press, 1987).

Russell, Gillian, *Theatres of War: Performance, Politics and Society 1790–1815* (Oxford: Clarendon Press, 1995).

Russett, Margaret, *Fictions and Fakes: Forging Romantic Authenticity, 1760–1845* (Cambridge: Cambridge University Press, 2006).

Ryan, Judith, 'Hybrid Forms in German Romanticism', in Joseph Harris and Karl Reichl (eds), *Prosimetrum: Crosscultural Perspectives in Narrative in Prose and Verse* (Cambridge: Brewer, 1997).

St Clair, William, *The Reading Nation in the Romantic Period* (Cambridge: Cambridge University Press, 2004).

Saunders, Corinne (ed.), *A Companion to Romance: Classical to Contemporary* (Oxford: Blackwell, 2004).

Schaeffer, Jean-Marie, 'Literary Genres and Textual Genericity', trans. Alice Otis, in Ralph Cohen (ed.), *The Future of Literary Theory Today* (New York: Routledge, 1989).

—— *Qu'est-ce qu'un genre littéraire?* (Paris: Seuil, 1989).

Sha, Richard, *The Visual and Verbal Sketch in British Romanticism* (Philadelphia: University of Pennsylvania Press, 1998).

Shankman, Steven, 'The Pindaric Tradition and the Quest for Pure Poetry', *Comparative Literature*, 40 (1988), 219–44.

Shepard, Leslie, *The History of Street Literature: The Story of Broadside Ballads, Chapbooks, Proclamations, News-Sheets, Election Bills, Tracts, Pamphlets, Cocks, Catchpennies, and Other Ephemera* (Newton Abbott: David and Charles, 1973).

Shuster, George N., *The English Ode from Milton to Keats* (New York: Columbia University Press, 1940).

Simpson, David, *Romanticism, Nationalism, and the Revolt against Theory* (Chicago: University of Chicago Press, 1993).

Siskin, Clifford, *The Work of Writing: Literature and Social Change in Britain, 1700–1830* (Baltimore: Johns Hopkins University Press, 1998).

Smith, Nigel, *Literature and Revolution in England 1640–1660* (New Haven: Yale University Press, 1994).

Smith, Olivia, *The Politics of Language, 1791–1819* (Oxford: Clarendon Press, 1984).

Stabler, Jane, *Burke to Byron, Barbauld to Baillie, 1790–1830* (Basingstoke: Palgrave, 2002).

Steiner, George, *The Death of Tragedy* (London: Faber and Faber, 1961).

Stewart, Keith, 'The Ballad and the Genres in the Eighteenth Century', *English Literary History*, 24 (1957), 120–37.

Stewart, Susan, *Crimes of Writing: Problems in the Containment of Representation* (New York: Oxford University Press, 1991).

Stokoe, F. W., *German Influence in the English Romantic Period, 1788–1818: With Special Reference to Scott, Coleridge, Shelley and Byron* (Cambridge: Cambridge University Press, 1926).

Stone, P. W. K., *The Art of Poetry 1750–1820: Theories of Poetic Composition and Style in the Late Neo-Classic and Early Romantic Periods* (London: Routledge and Kegan Paul, 1967).

Strachan, John, *Advertising and Satirical Culture in the Romantic Period* (Cambridge: Cambridge University Press, 2007).

Strelka, Joseph P. (ed.), *Theories of Literary Genre* (University Park: Pennsylvania State University Press, 1978).

Swedenberg, H. T., Jr, *The Theory of the Epic in England 1650–1800* (Berkeley: University of California Press, 1944).

Tayler, Irene, and Gina Luria, 'Gender and Genre: Women in British Romantic Poetry', in Marlene Springer (ed.), *What Manner of Woman: Essays on English and American Life and Literature* (Oxford: Blackwell, 1977).

Terry, Richard, *Mock-Heroic from Butler to Cowper: An English Genre and Discourse* (Aldershot: Ashgate, 2005).

—— *Poetry and the Making of the English Literary Past, 1660–1781* (Oxford: Oxford University Press, 2001).

Thomas, Sophie, *Romanticism and Visuality: Fragments, History, Spectacle* (London: Routledge, 2008).

Todorov, Tzvetan, *Genres in Discourse*, trans. Catherine Porter (Cambridge: Cambridge University Press, 1990).

Treadwell, James, *Autobiographical Writing and British Literature, 1783–1834* (Oxford: Oxford University Press, 2005).

Trumpener, Katie, *Bardic Nationalism: The Romantic Novel and the British Empire* (Princeton: Princeton University Press, 1997).

Tucker, Herbert F., *Epic: Britain's Heroic Muse 1790–1910* (Oxford: Oxford University Press, 2008).

Tynianov, Yuri, 'Dostoevsky and Gogol: Towards a Theory of Parody', in Victor Erlich (ed.), *Twentieth-Century Russian Literary Criticism* (New Haven: Yale University Press, 1975).

—— 'The Literary Fact' (1924), trans. Ann Shukman, in David Duff (ed.), *Modern Genre Theory* (Harlow: Longman, 2000).

—— 'The Ode as an Oratorical Genre' (1927), trans. Ann Shukman, *New Literary History*, 34/3 (2003), 565–96.

—— *The Problem of Verse Language* (1924), trans. Michael Sosa and Brent Harvey (Ann Arbor: Ardis, 1981).

Vogler, Thomas A., *Preludes to Vision: The Epic Venture in Blake, Wordsworth, Keats and Hart Crane* (Berkeley: University of California Press, 1971).

Wagner, Jennifer Ann, *A Moment's Monument: Revisionary Poetics and the Nineteenth-Century English Sonnet* (Madison: Fairleigh Dickinson University Press, 1996).

Walzel, Oskar, *German Romanticism*, trans. Alma Elise Lussky (1932; New York: Capricorn, 1966).

Watt, James, *Contesting the Gothic: Fiction, Genre, and Cultural Conflict, 1764–1832* (Cambridge: Cambridge University Press, 1999).

Weinberg, Bernard, *A History of Literary Criticism in the Italian Renaissance*, 2 vols (Chicago: University of Chicago Press, 1961).

Weinbrot, Howard D., *Britannia's Issue: The Rise of British Literature from Dryden to Ossian* (Cambridge: Cambridge University Press, 1993).

—— *The Formal Strain: Studies in Augustan Imitation and Satire* (Chicago: University of Chicago Press, 1969).

Wellek, René, 'The Concept of Romanticism in Literary History' (1949), in his *Concepts of Criticism*, ed. Stephen G. Nichols (New Haven: Yale University Press, 1963).

—— 'Genre Theory, the Lyric and *Erlebnis*' (1967), in his *Discriminations: Further Concepts of Criticism* (New Haven: Yale University Press, 1970).

—— *A History of Modern Criticism: 1750–1950*, 8 vols (New Haven: Yale University Press, 1955–95).

—— *The Rise of English Literary History* (1941; New York: McGraw-Hill, 1966).

Wesling, Donald, *The New Poetries: Poetic Form since Coleridge and Wordsworth* (Lewisburg, Pa.: Bucknell University Press, 1985).

Whale, John, *Imagination under Pressure 1789–1832: Aesthetics, Politics and Utility* (Cambridge: Cambridge University Press, 2000).

Wheatley, Kim (ed.), *Romantic Periodicals and Print Culture* (London: Frank Cass, 2003).

Whitney, Lois, *Primitivism and the Idea of Progress in English Popular Literature of the Eighteenth Century* (1934; New York: Octagon, 1965).

Wilkie, Brian, *Romantic Poets and Epic Tradition* (Madison: University of Wisconsin Press, 1965).

Wimsatt, William K., Jr, and Cleanth Brooks, *Literary Criticism: A Short History* (London: Routledge and Kegan Paul, 1957).

Wolfson, Susan J., *Formal Charges: The Shaping of Poetry in British Romanticism* (Stanford, Calif.: Stanford University Press, 1997).

Wood, Marcus, *Radical Satire and Print Culture 1790–1822* (Oxford: Clarendon Press, 1994).

Woodmansee, Martha, *The Author, Art, and the Market: Rereading the History of Aesthetics* (New York: Columbia University Press, 1994).

Worrall, David, *The Politics of Romantic Theatricality, 1787–1832: The Road to the Stage* (Basingstoke: Palgrave Macmillan, 2007).

—— *Theatric Revolution: Drama, Censorship and Romantic Period Subcultures 1773–1832* (Oxford: Oxford University Press, 2006).

Wright, Julia M., '"The Order of Time": Nationalism and Literary Anthologies, 1774–1831', *Papers on Language and Literature*, 33/4 (1997), 339–65.

Zimmerman, Sarah M., *Romanticism, Lyricism, and History* (Albany: State University of New York Press, 1999).

# Index